Legal Executions in Georgia

Also by Daniel Allen Hearn
and from McFarland

Legal Executions in Illinois, Indiana, Iowa, Kentucky and Missouri: A Comprehensive Registry, 1866–1965 (2016)

Legal Executions in North Carolina and South Carolina: A Comprehensive Registry, 1866–1962 (2015)

Legal Executions in Delaware, the District of Columbia, Maryland, Virginia and West Virginia: A Comprehensive Registry, 1866–1962 (2015)

Legal Executions in New England: A Comprehensive Reference, 1623–1960 (2008 [1999 hardback])

Legal Executions in Georgia

A Comprehensive Registry, 1866–1964

DANIEL ALLEN HEARN

McFarland & Company, Inc., Publishers
Jefferson, North Carolina

Library of Congress Cataloguing-in-Publication Data [new form]

Names: Hearn, Daniel Allen, 1958– author.
Title: Legal executions in Georgia : a comprehensive registry, 1866–1964 / Daniel Allen Hearn.
Description: Jefferson, North Carolina : McFarland & Company, Inc., 2016 | Includes index.
Identifiers: LCCN 2015044991 | ISBN 9780786498697 (softcover : acid free paper)
Subjects: LCSH: Executions and executioners—Georgia—History—Chronology. | Executions and executioners—Georgia—Registers.
Classification: LCC HV8699.U6 G444 2016 | DDC 364.6609758/0904—dc23
LC record available at http://lccn.loc.gov/2015044991

British Library cataloguing data are available

ISBN (print) 978-0-7864-9869-7
ISBN (ebook) 978-1-4766-2000-8

On the cover: *Hanging of the Scuffletonians*, Lucian Manuel, Hiram Jackson, Hyre Brewington, Weldon Gordon, and Purse Strickland (not necessarily in that order) standing on the gallows just prior to being hanged in Mount Vernon, Georgia, on September 29, 1893. © A. H. Prince (Robertson Register Historical Photographs)

Printed in the United States of America

McFarland & Company, Inc., Publishers
Box 611, Jefferson, North Carolina 28640
www.mcfarlandpub.com

The truth is on the march
and nothing will stop it!

—Emile Zola

Table of Contents

Introduction

Legal Executions in Georgia: A Comprehensive Registry, 1866–1964 is the latest volume in an ongoing series that makes available to the public a chronicle of the United States of America's historical experience with capital punishment. This effort began with the pilot *Legal Executions in New York State, 1639–1963* (Hearn, 1997), which was followed by identically modeled compendiums for the six New England states (Hearn, 1999), New Jersey (Hearn, 2005), and the Middle Atlantic region of North Carolina and South Carolina (Hearn, 2015) plus Delaware, Washington, D.C., Maryland, Virginia, and West Virginia (Hearn, 2015). California (Berry, O'Hare and Silva, 2006), Tennessee (Laska, 2009), and other Western and Midwestern states (Wilson, 2010, 2011 and 2012). Future volumes are planned until all areas of the country have been similarly researched. Their purpose is to present the historical record of American executions in an unbiased manner and provide a handy reference for further studies.

The intent of my books is strictly to convey facts. It is not my purpose to comment on the political issue of capital punishment; it is my belief that the states are individually capable of deciding such matters for themselves. My own motive for writing books in this series is simply to set the historical record straight and/or bring it as close thereto as reasonably possible. A growing number of reputable scholars (Blackman and McLaughlin,[1] Ellefson,[2] and Laska,[3] among others) have expressed concern about the quality of prior attempts to compile a comprehensive database of American executions. I concur in their criticisms. To be specific, the endeavors of this kind by the late George P. Upton (1834–1919), Raymond T. Bye (1892–1976), Negley K. Teeters (1896–1971) and M. Watt Espy, Jr. (1933–2009), all fell short of their goals. Their findings are outdated, error-ridden and incomplete. Even worse, perhaps, has been a tendency on the part of unwary scholars to accept these obsolescent sources at face value, which in turn shows in the quality of their own research. To better illustrate this point, I offer the following comparison for the number of legal executions in Georgia:

Date Range	Upton & Bye[4]	Espy[5]	Hearn
1866–1869	N/A	10	22
1870–1879	N/A	54	75
1880–1889	N/A	65	79
1890–1895	75	59	84
1896–1900	60	46	72
1901–1905	37	55	68
1906–1910	32	56	68
1911–1915	48	61	73
1916–1917	12	7	16
1918–1919	N/A	2	12
1920–1924	N/A	12	33
Totals:	Incomplete	427	602

The disparities in these figures should give pause to any serious observer. They also provide grounds for a thorough re-evaluation of the empirical data that has up until now been used in numerous studies and dissertations on the topic of capital punishment. The same holds true for many states besides Georgia.

The greater part of my 25-year quest to hunt down Georgia's post–Civil War record of legal executions took place before the coming of the Internet and digital imaging. I went about the task by scouring archival materials such as court records, appellate reports, gubernatorial correspondence and old newspapers on microfilm or original hard copy. Most of the historical newspapers were located at Yale University and especially the University of Georgia at Athens. There were also courthouse visits and written requests to Superior Court clerks throughout Georgia, nearly all of whom were assiduous in answering my queries. I initially had no idea that this fact-finding mission would take more than two decades to complete.

For assistance in ferreting out some of the more esoteric facts, I owe a special debt of gratitude to two remarkable men: Gregory Jarrell of the Georgia Department of Archives and History (since retired) and Steven Engerrand (since promoted to deputy director of that institution) for their professional expertise and willingness to give generously of their time. Both recognized the merit of what I was doing, even though death penalty research was until very recently a taboo topic in many parts of the South. My Georgia efforts in that regard would have been checkmated were it not for Greg and Steve. Both of them retain a place of honor in my personal esteem.

The reason why the year 1866 was chosen for the starting point of this volume is the same as for every other Southern state on which I have published: there are too many lost and missing records from the earlier decades. Courthouse fires, neglect and—above all—wartime vandalism (1861–1865) combined to take a terrible toll on the documentary history of Georgia. What does survive from the years prior to 1866 is fragmented. Conversely, Georgia's post–Civil War records of this category are largely intact and coalesce into a database that is very close to complete. It is too risky to base historical conclusions on fragmentary evidence. So I have deferred the prewar era to a future volume. A great deal of research toward that goal still remains to be done.

Unmitigated homicide was the most common felony for which Georgia courts imposed the death penalty. The same holds true for every other state. Forcible rape was the runner-up offense to be so punished, but in much lower numbers than may be popularly imagined. I have identified many long-dead rape victims by name. The decision to do so was not easily taken, so I opted for a compromise measure. The names of such persons are noted only in cases where they had been previously divulged in a published source such as a newspaper or appellate report. Similarly, the name is also given if the sexual assault victim came forward voluntarily in an interview or news conference. Otherwise anonymity is maintained. A considerable number of hitherto censored rape-victim names did become known to me during the course of my research. I correlated them with census records, marriage records and death records to ascertain the ages of such persons, but I decline to reveal their names (even when dead) out of common courtesy to their living relatives and also because I could find no precedent for publicizing them.

One of the revelations I encountered during research for this volume was the high number of legal executions that had taken place on Georgia soil for black-on-black crimes. Indeed, the frequency of such cases was so substantial that it calls into question whether Georgia applied the death penalty in a racially discriminatory manner as has been alleged. I make no pretense of being an expert on such matters, but I do believe that a basis for reconsidering claims of that sort can be found in the contents of this book. I leave it to other interested parties to explore this question more fully.

Notes

1. Paul H. Blackman and Vance McLaughlin, "The Espy File on American Executions: User Beware," *Homicide Studies* 15, no. 3 (August 2011).
2. C. Ashley Ellefson, *Seven Hangmen of Colonial Maryland* (*Maryland Archives*, vol. 819, 2009). Appendix A, 143–159, contains a scathing critique of *The Espy File.*
3. Lewis L. Laska, "Fact Based Death Penalty Research," *Tennessee Journal of Law and Policy*, 2007.
4. Raymond T. Bye, *Capital Punishment in the United States* (Menasha, WI: Collegiate Press/Geo. Banta, 1919), 56–58.
5. *Executions in the United States, 1608–1987: The Espy File* (Inter University Consortium for Political and Social Research, University of Michigan, 1987).

Georgia

1866

Negro Isaac (black, age not recorded). *Murder.* The crime was committed on 7/4/1865 in Hancock County. Rifle slaying of 52-year-old Henry Amos (white, his former owner), who was murdered in his bed. Motive: apparent vindictiveness. Isaac had run away during the war and joined the Yanks. His master said that he would shoot him on sight if he ever dared to return. Isaac did return. He poked a rifle barrel through Mr. Amos' bedroom window and shot the man as he slept. Isaac was tried before a military tribunal because the civilian courts had not yet been reorganized in the aftermath of the war. He was hanged at the garrison town of Augusta on January 12, 1866. Source: *Macon Daily Telegraph,* 7/12/65 (2:3). *Western Democrat* (Charlotte, NC), 1/9/66 (2:1). *Augusta (GA) Constitutionalist,* 1/13/66 (3:1). See also: 1850 and 1860 U.S. Census (Hancock Co., GA), which note Mr. Amos.

Private Murray (white, age and first name uncertain). *Murder.* The crime was committed on 7/1/1865 in Bibb County. Handgun slaying of 27-year-old James Samuel Clock (white), a captain in L Company of the 3rd Ohio Cavalry. Motive: fracas in a whorehouse. The killer was a bugler in A Company, 4th U.S. Cavalry, and an Irishman by birth. He and some of his similarly minded comrades in arms had become so loud and obnoxious while in the aforesaid resort that its proprietress complained to the officer of the day, the town then being under martial law. This was Capt. J. S. Clock. He went with a small detachment of troops to the scene of the disturbance for the purpose of restoring order. Resenting this, Murray started shooting. Three bullets ended the life of Capt. Clock. A noose did the same for the rowdy bugler pursuant to the sentence of a general court-martial at Macon on January 12, 1866. Source: *Macon Daily Telegraph,* 7/4/65 (3:1) & 1/13/66 (3:2).

Thomas J. Musgrove (white, age 23). *Murder.* The crime was committed on 8/28/1865 in Randolph County. Executed for the killing of 21-year-old Isaac Newton Armstrong (white), a solder in C Company of the 145th Indiana Infantry. Armstrong had been decoyed into a wooded area near Cuthbert, shot dead, and his person picked clean of valuables. The killer took a moral stand to the effect that he was incensed by the way Yankee occupation forces had been behaving toward Southern women. The fact that the homicide victim had been robbed, however, indicated a baser motive. Martial law then being in effect, Musgrove was brought to the garrison town of Macon and tried before a military tribunal. The verdict went against him. He was hanged on March 16, 1866. Source: *Savannah Daily Herald,* 3/21/66 (1:1). See also Armstrong's gravestone in

Springville Baptist Cemetery, Perry, IN.

Essex Walker (black, age not recorded). *Murder.* The crime was committed on 7/18/1865 in Burke County. Executed for the gunshot slaying of 44-year-old Thomas A. Byne (white), his former owner. Motive: misguided beliefs. Byne had been a noteworthy landowner, slave owner and physician. His home was in the upper part of Burke County. Six or seven of his newly freed slaves formed a conspiracy to do away with him in a deluded belief that his land would then be parceled out among them. It is uncertain whether Essex Walker was the ringleader, the actual triggerman or both. He was legally hanged at the garrison town of Augusta on March 23, 1866. Source: *Macon Daily Telegraph,* 7/22/65 (2:3). *Augusta Constitutionalist,* 3/24/66 (3:1). See also 1850 and 1860 U.S. Census (Burke Co., GA), which note Dr. Byne.

Annie Middlebrooks (black female, age not recorded). *Murder.* The crime was committed on 6/29/1864 in Jones County. Child killer. Legally hanged for the fatal and deliberate poisoning of 3-year-old Francis Morgan Finney (white), the son of Mr. Oliver Perry Finney and Mrs. Ora Ann Morgan Finney of Clinton. Motive: innate malevolence. The murderess had tried to wipe out the entire Finney family by serving them a lethal breakfast. At least one member thereof was dead by noon that same day. The child's parents died in 1881 and 1927 respectively. Annie had been their maid servant. She was awaiting trial in the Jones County jail when Northern vandals broke that place open and let her escape. Then in April of 1866 somebody spotted her on the streets of Macon. She had a narrow escape from lynching when a Jones County vengeance squad rode into town and seized her. Local blacks saved her from the would-be lynchers so that she lived to face a court of law. She was executed at Gray on June 1, 1866. Source: *Macon (GA) Telegraph,* 7/11/64 (2:6) & 6/26/85 (2:7) in retro. *Columbus (GA) Daily Examiner,* 4/19/66 (2:2). *Daily Constitutionalist* (Augusta, GA), 4/20/66 (2:3). *Evening Union* (Wash., DC), 6/5/66 (2:3). See also the Finney family gravestones in Clinton U.M.C. Cemetery, Clinton.

William Burns (white, age not recorded) and **John Jackson** (black, age not recorded). *Murder.* Their crime was committed on 10/9/1865 in Cobb County. Both executed for the murder of Charles H. Tew (white, age uncertain), who had his head chopped off with a broadax. Motive: highway robbery and mendacity. The culprits were freelance wagoners hired by the victim to transport his possessions from Athens to Marietta. They all camped in a field six or seven miles from their destination. Tew was apparently sleeping when the sinister fate befell him. He had been recently wed to the eldest daughter of Col. Arnoldus Van der Horst Brumby, founder of the highly prestigious Georgia Military Institute at Marietta. The killers were tried by a military tribunal at the garrison town of Augusta. They were legally hanged there on June 22, 1866. Source: *Macon Daily Telegraph,* 10/18/65 (3:3). *Augusta (GA) Constitutionalist,* 6/23/66 (3:1).

David Howell (white, age not recorded). *Murder.* The crime was committed on 8/23/1866 in Cobb County. This is a little-known case of a white man who was apparently hanged at Marietta on October 26, 1866, for the malicious killing of a black man named Henry Gamble. Surviving details are sparse. The trial papers are inaccessible. We know of it from three alternate sources. The first of these is a Freedmen's Bureau report called "Persons Murdered in Marietta GA," dated 10/11/66. The second and third are somewhat garbled retrospective mentions published in the *Atlanta Constitution*, 3/5/81 (1:8) & 8/30/00 (2:4), concerning previous executions in Cobb County in which the name of the hanged man is given as "Dan Howard" and "Dave Long," with the added note that the events took place "shortly after the War."

Dennis Harris, alias "Negro William," alias "Negro Bill" (black, age abt. 40). *Murder.* The crime was committed on 6/27/1866 in Wilkinson County. Executed for the murder of Mrs. Louisa Rollins (white, age uncertain), who was battered to death with a club. Motive: robbery and home invasion. Two drifters, Harris and another freedman named Pompey O'Bannon, had heard that there was cash stashed in the house of John Rollins. They waited until Mr. Rollins was away on business. Then they went to his residence in the guise of supplicants seeking food. Also beaten and left for dead were an 8-month-old baby and a 3-year-old toddler. A 12-year-old black girl escaped to tell all. Irate neighbors caught up with O'Bannon two days later. They bound him to a tree, tortured him by cutting off his ears and other protuberances, and then roasted him alive. His accomplice (Harris) evaded capture for a month. He was held at an impregnable location pending trial. He was legally hanged at Irwinton on November 2, 1866. Source: *Macon Daily Telegraph*, 6/29/66 (2:2), 7/1/66 (2:8) & 11/7/66 (2:1). *Georgia Weekly Telegraph* (Macon), 7/23/66 (5:2). *Atlanta Daily Intelligencer*, 10/14/66 (3:1).

Elias Mims, alias "Bronson" (black, age not recorded). *Habitual Criminal.* Serial burglar and thief. The crime for which he was executed was committed on 10/19/1866 in Bibb County. Condemned for effecting a forced nocturnal entry into the house of 49-year-old Benjamin F. Ross (white) and stealing "two fine gold watches and a pocketbook containing 20 or 22 dollars" along with some negotiable notes worth upwards of $250. Recidivist Offender. On 4/20/1865 this same felon (while under sentence of death for a similar crime) got loose when Northern invaders (under the command of Gen. James H. Wilson) wrecked the Bibb County jail. Mims reportedly "put on a gay uniform and joined the Federal army." Then he went on a crime spree that lasted until his so-called "liberators" realized that they had been duped. Mims was said to have belonged to a larcenous brood since birth. His own mother was reported to have taken an active part in his crimes. He was legally hanged at Macon on December 14, 1866. Source: *Daily Telegraph* (Macon, GA), 10/25/66 (3:3), 12/12/66 (3:2) & 12/15/66 (2:1). Also: *Atlanta Constitution*, 11/2/87 (2:1) in retrospect.

1867

Moses Bayfield (black, age not recorded) and **Jack Dortch**, alias "Jewett" (black, age not recorded). *Murder.* Their crime was committed on 8/11/1866 in Chatham County. Shotgun slaying of 39-year-old Henry Seckinger (white). Motive: highway robbery. Both were hanged at Savannah on April 19, 1867. Source: *Georgia Weekly Telegraph* (Macon), 8/20/66 (2:6). *Daily News & Herald* (Savannah), 4/20/67 (2:2). See also: 1850 and 1860 U.S. Census (Effingham Co., GA), which note the murdered man.

James Sumter (black, age not recorded). *Murder.* The crime was committed on 5/24/1867 in Bartow County. Executed for the musket slaying of another black man named Samuel Yancey, age not recorded. Motive: rivalry for a female. He was hanged at Cartersville on November 1, 1867. Source: 1867 Freedmen's Bureau report of freed people assaulted with intent to kill in the sub-district of Rome. Also: *Daily Constitutionalist* (Augusta, GA), 11/12/67 (3:4).

William Smart Bass (black, age 35). *Murder.* The crime was committed on 9/2/1867 in Taylor County. Handgun slaying of 26-year-old Jacob Cozatt (white), a passenger train conductor. Motive: resisting arrest. Bass was aboard a railroad car en route from Columbus to Macon. Other passengers observed him engaged in a furtive conversation with a Jew. The latter paid Bass for a gold watch of superior quality—so valuable in fact that it was obviously beyond the vendor's means. Conductor Cozatt (with the assistance of several other men) arrested Bass on suspicion of selling stolen goods. Bass was taken off the train at the next station. He broke free and made a run for it with Cozatt in pursuit. Then he spun around with a loaded revolver that he had pulled from his waistband and opened fire. This killer had formerly been a slave belonging to Mr. Nathan Bass of Macon. He was taken along as body servant to his "young master" when the latter fought in the War for Southern Independence. Both were captured at Gettysburg but the future killer returned to his "old master" voluntarily. He did not turn to crime until after the war. He was hanged at Butler on November 22, 1867. Source: *Georgia Weekly Telegraph* (Macon), 9/6/67 (2:2). *Weekly Atlanta Intelligencer*, 12/4/67 (1:7). See also: 1860 U.S. Census (Taylor Co., GA), which notes Cozatt. Also: 1860 U.S. Census (Slave Schedule for Bibb Co., GA), which notes a 28-year-old black male owned by Nathan Bass of Macon.

Alfred Brannon, alias "Alfred Bell" (black, age not recorded). *Murder.* The crime was committed on 8/17/1867 in Wilkinson County. Uxoricide. Legally hanged for the fatal flogging of Jennie Brannon (black, age not recorded), whom he had attacked with a horse whip. Motive: a so-called "family quarrel." This brutal wife killer was executed at Irwinton on November 22, 1867. Source: 1867 Freedmen's Bureau report of persons murdered in the sub-district of Macon. See also: *Federal Union* (Milledgeville), 8/27/67 (2:6) and Wilkinson Co. Superior Court Minutes (October 1867 session), 43.

1868

Amos Gorman (black, age not recorded), **Levi Jenkins** (black, age not recorded) and **Robert Whittus** (black, age not recorded). *Murder.* Their crime was committed on 8/25/1868 in Bibb County. All three executed for the handgun slaying of Jonathan Sheffield (white, age not recorded), a storekeeper. Motive: armed robbery. The killers had gone to Sheffield's place of business after closing time. They rapped on a window and said that they wanted to buy ten cents' worth of tobacco. Sheffield opened the window and accepted a proffered dime. Then he handed a pack of chew to his callers through the same window. One of the trio grabbed hold of Sheffield's arm and pulled him out the window. Another one pressed the muzzle of a pistol to his rib area and fired. Then the culprits fled with Sheffield's wallet and whatever other valuables they found on his person. All three were described as drifters from Americus. They were all hanged at Macon on October 9, 1868. Source: *Georgia Weekly Telegraph* (Macon), 8/28/68 (8:3), 9/18/68 (8:2) & 10/16/68 (6:6). *New Hampshire Patriot*, 9/9/68 (2:3).

Sebron Simmons (black, age not recorded). *Murder.* The crime was committed on an unknown date in Early County. Child killer. Legally hanged for the malicious killing of an unnamed victim described only as "a little colored boy." Surviving details of this case are sparse. They must have been particularly heinous, however, given the fact that Simmons was not spared by the clemency-prone governor of Georgia at that time, Rufus Bullock. Execution of the death sentence took place at the town of Blakeley on November 25, 1868. Source: *Early County Superior Court Minutes Book* (1857–1876), 510. *Louisville (KY) Courier Journal*, 12/4/68 (2:1).

Alfred Butler (black, age not recorded). *Murder.* The crime was committed on 8/19/1868 in Spalding County. Uxoricide. Executed for the killing of Sallie Butler (black, age not recorded), she having been found floating in a swamp with her throat cut. Motive: adultery on his part. This wife-killer was hanged at Griffin on December 11, 1868. Source: *Georgia Weekly Telegraph* (Macon), 8/28/68 (3:3). *Savannah Morning News*, 12/17/68 (2:1). See also: Freedmen's Bureau report of murders committed in the sub-district of Macon during the year 1868.

1869

Thomas Tate (black, age not recorded). *Murder.* The crime was committed on or about 10/1/1868 in Lincoln County. Executed for the deliberate killing of a black woman named Julia Ann Walton (age not recorded), whose skeletal remains had been found near her home on 1/30/1869. The decedent's skull had been stove in by a heavy wooden water bucket. Motive: personal vendetta. Tate had vowed to kill both the woman and her husband because they had informed on him for stealing a hog. He pounced on Julia Ann as she was going to draw water from a spring on the property of her former owner, a cotton grower named William Walton. There was no appeal. Thomas Tate was hanged at Lincolnton on May 28, 1869. Source: *Lincoln County Superior Court Evidence Records (1869–1884)*, 1–7. Microfilm drawer no. 88, reel no. 8, GA State Archives. The actual trial minutes are lost, but confirmation that Tate was legally executed for his crime came about through a remarkable coincidence. The *Lincoln (GA) Journal*, 6/15/11 (4:3), in reporting on another execution there, said that exactly 42 years had then gone by since the previous one. Even more specifically, the *Atlanta Journal*, 6/12/11 (6:3), said that the sheriff who presided at the 1911 Lincoln County execution (Gustavus T. Wright) had been born on the very day of the earlier legal hanging there. Wright's burial record at New Hope Baptist Church Cemetery (Lincolnton, GA) notes 5/28/1869 as his date of birth.

Bob Arnold (black, age not recorded). *Murder.* The crime was committed on 3/30/1869 in Wilkes County. Rifle slaying of 42-year-old Thomas Thaxton (white), who was shot by a sniper as he drove his buggy along a public road. Motive: uncertain. Thaxton was homeward bound after having attended a court session. Whether a litigant was behind his assassination or whether the killer mistook him for someone else is speculative. Whatever the reason, Bob Arnold was identified as the shooter. He was legally hanged at Washington on July 30, 1869. Source: *Georgia Weekly Telegraph* (Macon), 4/9/69 (8:2) & 8/13/69 (8:1). See also: 1860 U.S. Census (Wilkes Co., GA), which notes the murdered man.

Jesse Watkins (black, age abt. 18). *Murder.* The crime was committed on 8/31/1868 in Chatham County. Child killer. Shotgun slaying of 14-year-old Charles Wilson (white). Motive: he wanted to steal the white boy's fishing pole. The puppet governor of Georgia at that time (Rufus Bullock) studied this case intensely in the hope of finding something that would furnish him with a reason for commuting the death sentence. Damning proof of malice aforethought was the only thing he found. The law was then allowed to take its course at Savannah on September 10, 1869. Source: *Savannah Morning News*, 9/7/69 (2:2) & 9/11/69 (3:2). *Southern Banner* (Athens, GA), 9/17/69 (1:6). *Daily News & Herald* (Savannah, GA), 9/2/68 (3:2).

1870

Ben Godby (black, age 39). *Murder.* The crime was committed on 6/16/1869 in Richmond County. Fatal stabbing of 35-year-old Adkins D. Lewis (white, his employer), who was knifed multiple times. Motive: big attitudes. Godby worked on the Lewis family farm. His wife held the position of cook in the Lewis family home and his daughter was nursemaid to the white couple's baby. Trouble began when Mrs. Lewis scolded the nursemaid for some infraction of the household rules. The girl sassed Mrs. Lewis and got a slap for it. She then ran to the kitchen and riled up her mother. The latter in turn confronted Mrs. Lewis in a highly insolent manner, demanding to know how dare she hit her child. Mr. Lewis heard the commotion. He got between the two women only to receive the same verbal barrage as his wife. Incensed by this insubordination on the part of domestic employees, Adkins Lewis in his own turn slapped Mammy Godby a couple of good ones and said that she was fired out of his house. The former then ran to her husband (Ben Godby) and told him a one-sided account of what had happened. He proved no better by his reaction. He went on the warpath and murdered his boss. He was legally hanged for this at Augusta on March 11, 1870. Source: *Atlanta Constitution*, 6/26/69 (1:3) & 3/12/70 (2:4). *Georgia Weekly Telegraph* (Macon), 6/25/69 (6:4). *Savannah Morning News*, 6/19/69 (1:3). See also: 1860 U.S. Census (Burke Co., GA), which notes "Atkins" Lewis.

Bythe Barlow (black, age 29). *Murder.* The crime was committed on 2/26/1870 in Butts County. Executed for the killing of 70-year-old John McCluskey (white), a farmer who was looking for his missing cows. The exact details of what Barlow did to the aging white man (in addition to murdering him) were said to have been so heinous that no newspaper would print them.

Venue changed from Butts County to Spalding County. Soft on crime Governor Rufus Bullock allowed the resultant death sentence to be carried out in this case because of its atrocious circumstances and the killer's long criminal record. Barlow was hanged at Griffin on July 29, 1870. Source: *Weekly Columbus (GA) Enquirer*, 3/8/70 (2:2) & 8/9/70 (1:4). See also: 1860 U.S. Census (Butts Co., GA), which notes McCluskey, and 1870 U.S. Census (Butts Co., GA), which notes Barlow.

1871

Prince Albert (black, age 23). *Murder.* The crime was committed on 12/8/1870 in Lee County. Fatal stabbing of 20-year-old William Miller (white). Motive: political violence. An unruly crowd of former slaves had descended on the town of Starkville on the above date. They were led by two incendiary members of the state legislature named George Page (white) and Philip Joiner (black), whose party affiliation was "Radical Republican." Their purpose was to disrupt a campaign appearance by the congressional candidate of the opposition party. First came catcalls. Next came fist fights. Then both sides started shooting at each other in what became known as "the Phil Joiner Riot." There was at least one fatality: that of young William Miller. He lay wounded in the street with a bullet in the belly. Albert finished him off with a knife, knowing that Miller was unable to defend himself. There were plenty of witnesses. Governor Bullock dared not intervene lest such an action further empower his political adversaries. Prince Albert was then left to his fate following his conviction in a court of law. He was hanged at Leesville on May 26, 1871. Source: *Weekly Sumter Republican* (Americus, GA), 12/16/70 (3:2). *Atlanta Constitution*, 5/31/71 (1:1). *Georgia Weekly Telegraph* (Macon), 5/30/71 (6:6). See also: 1870 U.S. Census (Lee Co., GA), which notes Albert.

Diego Valliant (black, age not recorded). *Murder.* The crime was committed at some point during the year 1867 in McIntosh County. Executed for the killing of another black man named Campbell Lewis (age not recorded) by undisclosed means. Motive: the homicide victim had bullied the killer's father, or so the story went. This case is historically certain but short on details. The trial record was lost to fire in 1873. Diego Valliant was hanged at Darien on June 9, 1871. Source: *Daily Constitutionalist* (Augusta, GA), 7/1/71 (1:3). *Savannah Morning News*, 6/14/71 (1:1). *Atlanta Constitution*, 6/30/83 (1:2) in retro. See also: *Executive Minutes of the Governor of Georgia*, entry dated 12/22/70.

James Toombs (black, age abt. 28). *Murder*. The crime was committed on 5/9/1871 in Houston County. Handgun slaying of 37-year-old Reuben Hunter (black). Motive: flare-up while working the fields. Some newspapers were still advertising a $1,000 reward for the capture of this killer two and three weeks after he was executed. Georgia's mercy-prone governor at that time (Rufus Bullock) probably would have commuted the death sentence (as he had so many others) had Toombs not broken jail and cost the state treasury a substantial amount of gold payable to bounty hunters. Toombs was hanged at Perry on July 28, 1871. Source: *Savannah Morning News*, 8/4/71 (1:1). *Georgia Weekly Telegraph* (Macon), 6/13/71 (3:4) & 8/8/71 (1:7). *Southern Banner* (Athens, GA), 8/11/71

(4:3) & 8/18/71 (4:3). See also: 1870 U.S. Census (Houston Co., GA), which notes Hunter.

1872

Sam Hicks, alias "Blount" (black, age not recorded). *Murder.* The crime was committed on 2/25/1872 in Wilkinson County. Executed for the malicious killing of 30-year-old Joel Burke (white, a one-armed CSA veteran) who was battered about the head with a heavy stick and then finished off by having his throat cut. Motive: highway robbery. Hicks was hanged at Irwinton on April 26, 1872. Source: *Georgia Weekly Telegraph* (Macon), 3/12/72 (1:2) & 5/14/72 (4:4). *Weekly Enquirer-Sun* (Columbus, GA), 4/16/72 (2:2). See also: 1870 U.S. Census (Wilkinson Co., GA), which notes the murdered man.

John Watkins (black, age 27). *Murder.* The crime was committed on 4/4/1872 in Oglethorpe County. Gunshot slaying of 27-year-old Gabriel Johnson (black). Motive: rivalry for a female. This killer was legally hanged at Lexington on May 31, 1872. Source: *Atlanta Daily Sun*, 4/10/72 (3:1) & 6/4/72 (3:3). See also: 1870 U.S. Census (Oglethorpe Co., GA), which notes both parties.

Wesley Walker (black, age not recorded). *Murder.* The crime was committed on or about 12/19/1871 in Miller County. Gunshot slaying of another black man named Jacob Cowart (age not recorded). Motive: speculative. The homicide took place on the John Randolph Whitehead plantation. The killer's last words (spoken while actually standing on the gallows) included a dire warning to his mother that she would "go to hell howling if she did not turn from her evil ways." This might have had some bearing on what Walker himself had done. He was hanged at Colquitt on June 17, 1872. Source: *Georgia Weekly Telegraph* (Macon), 12/26/71 (4:4) & 7/2/72 (8:3). *Savannah Morning News*, 4/22/72 (1:3) & 6/24/72 (1:3). The trial papers for this case were lost to fire a year later.

James C. Lloyd (white, age 61) and **John R. Holsenbake** (white, age 34). *Murder.* Their crime was committed on 2/28/1871 in Macon County. Both hanged for the shotgun slaying of 51-year-old George W. Fish (white), a newly appointed district court judge who was attacked in the doorway of his courthouse. Motive: Holsenbake thought that the judge had had sex with his wife, which was not only bad in itself but cast doubt on the paternity of a certain child. Lloyd was an accomplice in this assassination. A double execution ended the days of the guilty pair at Oglethorpe on June 28, 1872. Source: *Georgia Weekly Telegraph* (Macon), 7/2/72 (3:4). *Atlanta Constitution*, 7/1/72 (2:3). See also: 1870 U.S. Census (Macon Co., GA), which notes Holsenbake and Judge Fish.

Byrd Brooks (black, age 24). *Rape.* The crime was committed on 7/28/1872 in Hall County. Indecent assault on the person of about 30-year-old Sophia Hubbard (white), she having been dragged from her home by two burly intruders and raped on the bare earth by one of them while the other kept her pinned to the ground by means of a forked stick that was jammed around her neck. The woman was reported to have died from her injuries three months later. Byrd Brooks got caught. He was legally hanged at Gainesville on November 8, 1872. Source: *Atlanta Weekly Sun*, 11/13/72 (5:4). *Atlanta Constitution*, 11/9/72 (3:4). *Georgia*

Weekly Telegraph (Macon), 11/12/72 (8:7).

Ben Bacon (black, age 22). *Murder.* The crime was committed 10–30–1872 in Richmond County. Executed for the killing of 65-year-old James Hamilton Martin (white), a farmer whom he had approached under false pretenses. Motive: highway robbery. The homicide victim had been bludgeoned with a wooden wagon standard. The killer was described as a Savannah vagrant, a derelict and a public nuisance who had joined with others of his ilk to prey on the unwary. He saw Martin trade some of his crop at the Augusta Cotton Exchange for cash. Then he followed Martin through the streets. He overtook Martin as he was about to leave town and offered his services to him as a farmhand. Martin accepted this ostensible proposal. Bacon then got into the farm wagon that Martin was driving home. They rode to a point that was suitably remote for the killer's purpose. Bacon was nabbed the next day with money and a written receipt bearing Martin's name. He was probably too illiterate to recognize the latter item as a damning piece of evidence linking him to the crime. This mistake likely sealed Bacon's doom. He was legally hanged at Augusta on November 29, 1872. Source: *Daily Chronicle* (Augusta, GA), 11/1/72 (3:4) & 11/30/72 (3:2). *Savannah Morning News*, 11/30/72 (2:4). See also: 1860 U.S. Census (Richmond Co., GA), which notes Mr. Martin.

1873

Mike Dobbs (black, age 52). *Murder.* The crime was committed on 9/1/1872 in Fayette County. Fatal stabbing of another black man named James Swanson, age not recorded. Motive: rivalry for a female. Dobbs was described as a borderline idiot. He was hanged at Fayetteville on January 3, 1873. Source: *Atlanta Constitution*, 1/6/73 (1:1). See also: 1870 U.S. Census (Fayette Co., GA), which notes this killer.

Kenney Burns (black, age 22). *Rape.* The crime was committed on 8/3/1872 in Jackson County. Indecent assault on the person of Mrs. Elvira Wilson (white, age not recorded), a widow who was terrorized in her home by two assailants. They demanded that she submit to their concupiscence lest they murder her son, a lad aged 10–15. She bravely replied that she would rather that they murder her instead. The boy managed to jump out a window. The culprits then dragged Mrs. Wilson out of the house. They raped her in a nearby field. They also taunted her by saying that they cared not about the consequences. Both were subsequently sentenced to death. The accomplice, Lewis Pace (black, age 24), somehow got loose but was hunted down by vigilantes. He is presumed to have been lynched. Burns met his own fate pursuant to law when he was hanged at Jefferson on January 10, 1873. Elvira Wilson had been the wife of William C. Wilson. He was killed at Second Manassas on 8/30/62. Source: *Northeast Georgian* (Athens, GA), 11/29/72 (3:2) & 1/17/73 (2:1). *Baltimore Sun*, 1/14/73 (4:5). *New York Herald*, 1/12/73 (5:1). See also: 1870 U.S. Census (Jackson Co., GA), which notes Lewis Pace.

Steven Dunson (black, age 24). *Rape.* The crime was committed on 4/9/1872 in Jackson County. Indecent assault on the person of 30-year-old Nancy E. Dunson (white) and attempt to do the same to that woman's 13-year-old daughter named Georgia Dunson. The victims were dragged from their home by two assailants. Steven Dunson had formerly been a slave in that household. He and several like-minded cronies had reportedly been emboldened to commit such acts by the lax administration of justice under the preceding gubernatorial regime. Steven Dunson was legally hanged at Jefferson on January 10, 1873. Source: *Northeast Georgian* (Athens, GA), 1/17/73 (2:1). *New York Herald*, 1/12/73 (5:1). See also: 1870 U.S. Census (Jackson Co., GA), which notes all three Dunsons. Newspaper reports say "Dunston" whereas the census says "Dunson." Reporters also confused a local justice of the peace named "Hood" with the surname of the sexual assault victims. "Hood" had merely provided the newsmen with affidavits. Georgia Dunson was grossly mishandled by the rapists with every intention of doing the same to her as they had done to her mother. Their failure to actually penetrate her and "accomplish their purpose" was apparently due to the prohibitive size of their organs—or so the tactfully worded news accounts implied. See also: Crawford Norwood (executed 3/28/73).

Crawford Norwood (black, age 19). *Rape.* The crime was committed on 4/9/1872 in Jackson County. Accomplice in the forcible rape of 30-year-old Nancy Dunson (white) and attempt to do likewise to that woman's 13-year-old daughter. He was legally hanged at Jefferson on March 28, 1873. Source: *Northeast Georgia* (Athens, GA), 4/4/73 (3:4). See also: Steven Dunson (executed 1/10/73).

Enoch Ferdinand Spann (white, age 41). *Murder.* The crime was committed on 5/4/1872 in Webster County. Uxoricide. Executed for strangling his over-50-year-old wife (Sarah Spann) with a plow cord while his much younger female accomplice (Susan Eberhardt) stuffed a cotton handkerchief into the victim's mouth to staunch the bloody froth that issued therefrom. Motive: adultery turned deadly. Spann himself said that he had been "young and foolish" when he married the murdered woman, she being substantially older than he. She had also developed health problems that necessitated a leg amputation. The strain of caring for Sarah Spann gradually wore her husband down to a point where in December of 1871 he hired a live-in housekeeper named Susan Eberhardt. The caregiver entered into a relationship and decided to do away with the burdensome third party. Sarah Spann was found dead in her sickbed with the unmistakable mark of a lariat around her gullet. The guilty lovers were nabbed in Coffee Co., AL, nine days later. Enoch Spann was hanged at Preston on April 11, 1873. Source: *Savannah Morning News*, 5/18/72 (4:1), 6/3/72 (1:4) & 4/14/73 (1:4). *New York Herald*, 4/12/73 (3:3). *Daring Detective*, 1/36. *Dynamic Detective*, 3/39. The 1850 U.S. Census shows Spann's parents and younger siblings living in Stewart Co., GA. Enoch Spann was already "grown and flown" by then. His ill-fated marriage probably dates from then or shortly before. See also: Susan Eberhardt (executed 5/2/73).

Westley Tate (black, age 23). *Murder.* The crime was committed on 9–5–1871 in Elbert County. Ax murder of another black man named Jefferson Tate, age not recorded. Motive: an argument that had escalated. The killer was a plantation foreman. All parties lived and worked there. Westley's wife was soon to give birth. Jeff's wife had picked a quarrel with her, alleging that it was her brother rather than Westley who had sired the forthcoming child. Angered by this, Westley Tate said harsh words to the authoress of the gossip. Her husband (Jefferson Tate) then came to her defense and in so doing incurred Westley's fury as well. The men were not related to each other. The surname they shared was that of their former owner, Oliver Tate. A gallows made short work of Westley Tate at Elberton on April 25, 1873. Source: *Daily Chronicle & Sentinel* (Augusta, GA), 5/3/73 (1:4). Also: *Elbert County Superior Court Evidence Record* (1873–1874), 1–8. Microfilm drawer no. 2, reel no. 76, GA State Archives. See also: 1870 U.S. Census (Elbert Co., GA), which notes Westley Tate.

Susan Eberhardt (white, age 20). *Murder.* The crime was committed on 5/4/1872 in Webster County. Accomplice in the killing of over-50-year-old Sarah Spann (white), who was strangled in her sickbed. Motive: adultery with the victim's husband. She was hanged at Preston on May 2, 1873, and is primarily remembered as the only white female legally executed in Georgia after the War for Southern Independence. Several other white women were condemned to death by Georgia courts during that time, but all successfully played the "Southern chivalry" card to get their sentences reduced. Tremendous pressure was put on Governor James Milton Smith to commute Miss Eberhardt's sentence for the same reason, but he would not be swayed from his campaign pledge to reverse the hated soft-on-crime policy of his predecessor, Rufus Bullock. It can therefore be argued that Susan Eberhardt was as much a victim of politics as she was of her own transgressions. Source: *Savannah Morning News*, 5/5/73 (1:5) & (2:1). See also: 1870 U.S. Census (Webster Co., GA), which notes Miss Eberhardt. See also: Enoch Spann (executed 4/11/73).

Nick Boswell (black, age 22). *Murder.* The crime was committed on or about 1/25/1873 in Putnam County. Fatal stabbing of another black man named Robert Gadlin, age not recorded. Motive: fracas at a "negro festival" or all-black cookout, as it would nowadays be called. The killer was hanged at Eatonton on May 23, 1873. Source: *Atlanta Weekly Sun*, 6/3/73 (6:5). *Daily Chronicle & Sentinel* (Augusta, GA), 5/29/73 (1:4). See also: 1870 U.S. Census (Putnam Co., GA), which notes Boswell.

Isham O'Neil, alias "Benton O'Neal," alias "J. B. O'Neal" (white, age 29). *Murder.* The crime was committed on 9/8/1871 in Fulton County. Fatal stabbing (with a large Bowie knife) of 29-year-old James Little (white). Motive: acrimonious lawsuit. This killer was hanged at Atlanta on June 13, 1873. Source: *Atlanta Weekly Sun*, 9/9/71 (4:5). *Atlanta Constitution*, 6/14/73 (3:3). *New York Herald*, 6/14/73 (8:1). See also: 1870 U.S. Census (Fulton Co., GA), which notes both parties.

George Copeland (black, age 28). *Murder.* The crime was committed on or about 5/15/1871 in Greene County. Executed for the killing of 49-year-old Sarah Richards (white), a maiden woman. Motive: robbery and home invasion. Copeland confessed that he had acted alone when he forced his way into the woman's cottage and demanded money of her. He whacked her across the back of the head with a stick. Then he raped her right there on the floor. The victim remained conscious throughout her ordeal but was unable to escape. Copeland went on to pilfer a few coins, a watch, some articles of clothing and assorted edibles such as sugar, butter, flour and cured meat from the pantry. He also cut the woman's throat with a case knife and burned the place to the ground. The spinster's death was apparently attributed to accidental causes at the time. Somehow the truth leaked out two years later. It was probably the stolen watch that gave Copeland away—a watch that had been presumed lost in the fire and was later recognized and traced back to him. Copeland was hanged at Greensboro on October 24, 1873. Source: *Atlanta Daily Herald*, 10/28/73 (4:6). *Daily Telegraph & Messenger* (Macon), 10/30/73 (2:1). See also: 1870 U.S. Census (Greene Co., GA), which notes both parties.

Lee Smith (black, age not recorded). *Murder.* The crime was committed on or about 7/15/1872 in Webster County. Uxoricide. Most of the written record of this case is believed to have been lost to fire in 1914. Few other details survive. The condemned man was hanged at Preston on November 7, 1873. Source: *Weekly Sumter Bulletin* (Americus, GA), 3/21/73 (2:2) & 11/14/73 (3:3).

Gus Peterson (black, age not recorded). *Murder.* The crime was committed on 4/2/1872 in Dougherty County. Handgun slaying of John Simmons (black, age not recorded), his brother-in-law. Motive: the homicide victim had given refuge to the killer's estranged wife. The latter was hanged at Albany on November 21, 1873. Source: *Albany (GA) News*, 4/5/72 (3:3) & 11/27/73 (3:2).

Hudson Raiford (black, age not recorded). *Murder.* The crime was committed on an unknown date in Chattahoochee County. Shotgun slaying of a white man named Frank Galloway (age not recorded), who was hit by pellets meant for someone else. Raiford had fired over a fence with the intention of killing another black man whom he despised. The latter stepped into his cabin doorway at the critical moment so that Galloway caught the blast instead. Clemency was denied on the grounds of *malice prepense*. The culprit was hanged at Cusseta on November 21, 1873. Source: *Macon (GA) Telegraph & Messenger*, 11/25/73 (1:4). *Evening Star* (Wash., DC), 12/1/73 (1:5). *Louisville (KY) Courier Journal*, 9/29/73 (2:1) & 11/25/73 (3:2), for accounts taken from a lost Columbus newspaper.

John Killen (black, age not recorded). *Murder.* The crime was committed on 3/29/1873 in Pulaski County. Shotgun slaying of another black man named Jerry Mabin, age not recorded. Motive: card game fracas. The killer was hanged at Hawkinsville on November 28, 1873. Source: *Savannah Morning News*, 12/8/73 (1:2). Appeal: 50 GA 223–231.

1874

Richard General (black, age 22). *Murder.* The crime was committed on an unknown date in Lowndes County. Executed for the killing of another black man named William Boyson under unknown circumstances. The court record for this case has not survived. The condemned man was hanged at Valdosta on January 16, 1874. Source: *Savannah Morning News*, 1/26/74 (1:2). See also: 1870 U.S.

Census (Lowndes Co., GA), which notes General.

Nimrod Austin (black, age 31), **Emanuel McCormick**, alias "Dollman" (black, age 27) and **Charles Ponder**, alias "Walker" (black, age 43). *Murder.* Their crime was committed on 11/25/1873 in Thomas County. All three executed for the killing of 55-year-old Juniper Hall (white), their employer. They strangled Mr. Hall with their bare hands and then made sure that he was dead by ramming a flaming torch into his mouth. Motive: they felt cheated. Hall was described as a prewar plantation owner who had been ruined by economic hardship. Alcoholism was also a contributing factor to his decline. He was share-cropping cotton when his final crisis came. Five of his hired hands (all black men) had helped him bring a load to market on the above date. All expected a handsome payday, but Hall barely broke even when all was sold. This sorely disappointed the five black men. They fell to grumbling. To make matters worse, Hall got drunk and harangued his aforesaid employees, saying that it was they who had eroded his profit margin. He also added insult to injury by accusing them of stealing his pigs—or so they later said—for which they deserved to be mulcted anyway. Hall's skeletal remains were found three months later by wildcat hunters prowling the woods. The only flesh that remained to him was that of his feet inside of his shoes. The three killers were hanged at Thomasville on April 17, 1874. Source: *Thomasville (GA) Times*, 4/18/74 (3:2) & *New York Herald*, 4/18/74 (5:1). See also: 1870 U.S. Census (Thomas Co., GA), which notes Juniper Hall.

Webster Lyons (black, age 32). *Murder.* The crime was committed on 1/10/1874 in Thomas County. Uxoricide. Fatal and deliberate poisoning of 31-year-old Eliza Lyons (black) by putting strychnine in her cough syrup. Motive: so he could be free to pursue another woman. This wife killer was hanged at Thomasville on April 17, 1874. Source: *Thomasville (GA) Times*, 1/31/74 (3:3) & 4/18/74 (3:2). *New York Herald*, 4/18/74 (5:1). See also: 1870 U.S. Census (Jefferson Co., FL), which notes both parties.

Ann Hunt (black, age 22). *Murder.* Her crime was committed on 1–24–1874 in Elbert County. Fatal and deliberate poisoning of 27-year-old Eliza Brawner (black). Motive: jealousy and personal resentment. The sheer ferocity of this young woman's personality was demonstrated by an incident two or three weeks prior to the date of the murder itself. Acting out of pure spite, Ann (or "Anna," as the 1870 census taker called her) had run into Eliza Brawner's modest house during an unguarded moment. She herded Brawner's little children into a bedroom, deliberately set the bed ablaze and locked them therein with the intention that they be burned alive. All this was just to get her digs in at their mother. The latter was thereafter on the alert and let it be known in the black community what Ann Hunt had done. Slyly, the murderess recruited a mentally challenged girl to serve as an additional tool of her malice. She gave the girl a small bottle of whiskey (into which she had poured a lethal dose of strychnine) and instructed her to offer some to Eliza Brawner. The gullible girl did this at a fiddle dance that Ann made it a point not to attend. The unsuspecting Eliza Brawner imbibed the poisoned whiskey and was dead a few minutes later. The contortions she suffered were so agonizing that death came to her only as a blessed relief. Suspicion of foul play led a surgeon to remove the contents of the decedent's stomach. A tenth part of this was given to a dog, which promptly died. Ann Hunt went on to admit that she had made away with three other persons by similar means. This could well have been true, since poisoners often rack up several victims before they overplay their hands. This one legally paid the price at the end of a rope at Elberton on May 1, 1874. Source: *Atlanta (GA) Herald*, 2/8/74 (7:1) & 3/21/74 (1:6). *Daily Chronicle* (Augusta, GA), 5/3/74 (1:5). *Georgia Weekly Telegraph* (Macon), 5/19/74 (8:3). See also: 1870 U.S. Census (Elbert Co., GA), which notes both parties.

Primus Edwards (black, age not recorded). *Murder.* The crime was committed on 3/30/1874 in Sumter County. Executed for the malicious killing (by undisclosed means) of 25-year-old Berry Adams (black). Motive: the homicide victim had accused Edwards of ogling his woman. The condemned man was hanged at Americus on November 13, 1874. Source: *Weekly Sumter Republican* (Americus, GA), 4/3/74 (3:2) & 11/20/74 (3:4). See also: 1870 U.S. Census (Sumter Co., GA), which notes Adams.

Louis Armstrong, alias "Strickland" (black, age not recorded). *Murder.* The crime was committed on 6/29/1874 in Franklin County. Handgun slaying of 51-year-old Willis Dickson (white), who was shot through the right eye. Motive: resisting capture. The culprit had escaped from the Cobb County jail where he was being held on a charge of forcible rape. A substantial reward had been offered for his capture. Bounty hunters traced him to a cabin near Toccoa where the fugitive got the drop on them with a pistol. He was legally hanged at Carnesville on November 27, 1874. Source: *Northeast Georgian* (Athens, GA), 7/8/74 (2:3), 10/21/74 (3:3) & 12/2/74 (3:4). See also: 1870 U.S. Census (Franklin Co., GA), which notes Mr. Dickson.

George Simms (black, age 19). *Rape.* The crime was committed on 11/2/1873 in Newton County. Incipient serial rapist. Executed for an indecent assault on the person of a married white female identified only as "Mrs. Wallace." She was walking home in company with her little boy when Simms accosted her. He physically threw the kid down an embankment (giving him a nasty head injury in the process) and then forced himself on the mother. It is noteworthy that Simms had previously been run out of Elbert County for "a similar crime." He was legally hanged at Covington on November 27, 1874. Source: *Atlanta Constitution* (Daily) 11/28/74 (3:2) and (Weekly) 12/1/74 (6:6). *Georgia Weekly Telegraph* (Macon), 11/18/73 (8:5).

1875

Bill Roseman (black, age not recorded). *Murder.* The crime was committed on 12/15/1873 in Calhoun County. Musket slaying of another black man named Luke Crawford, age not recorded. Motive: the homicide victim owed him money, or so the killer said. Roseman was hanged at Morgan on January 29, 1875. Source: *Calhoun County Superior Court Minutes* (Sept. Adjourned Term, 1874), 63. Microfilm drawer no. 143, reel no. 25, GA State Archives. *Macon (GA) Telegraph & Messenger*, 1/31/75 (4:1).

Isaac Hooper (black, age 28). *Murder.* The crime was committed on 12/12/1873 in Richmond County. Fatal stabbing of another black man named Howard Satterwhite, age not recorded. Motive: big attitude. Both men were performing in a brass band at the time. Hooper became disruptive for some reason. Satterwhite told him that he should obey the directions of the band leader. Hooper then yelled, "What's it to you? You damned son of a bitch!" and attacked Satterwhite with a knife. Further insight into Hooper's character can be gleaned from a courtroom incident the previous summer. He was so pig-headed that he chose to serve 30 days on the chain gang during the hottest time of the year rather than pay a small fine for being drunk in public. He was hanged at Augusta on February 19, 1875. Source: *Augusta (GA) Chronicle*, 7/3/73 (4:2), 12/14/73 (4:2), 12/24/73 (4:1) & 2/20/75 (4:1). See also: 1870 U.S. Census (Richmond Co., GA), which notes Hooper.

Henry Jackson (black, age 19). *Murder.* The crime was committed on 8/21/1873 in Lee County. Child killer. Executed for the slaying (by undisclosed means) of 15-year-old Joseph Johnson (white), a novice store clerk. Motive: robbery and burglary. "I never saw a more brutal countenance than Jackson's," said one newspaper correspondent. "He looks more like a chimpanzee than a man." He was legally hanged at Leesburg on April 30, 1875. Source: *Georgia Weekly Telegraph* (Macon), 8/27/73 (1:4), 9/2/73 (4:4), 9/2/73 (5:1), 3/27/75 (4:2) & 5/4/75 (3:7). See also: 1870 U.S. Census (Lee Co., GA), which notes both parties.

Jim Cooper (black, age not recorded) and **Pomp Haney** (black, age not recorded). *Murder.* Their crime was committed on 12/27/1874 in Heard County. Both hanged for the fatal beating of 64-year-old Webb Summerlin (black, a cobbler) and the ransacking of his cabin. Motive: robbery. The culprits had approached the aging shoemaker under the pretense of getting their soles mended. They battered him on the head (probably with the tools of his trade) and absconded with what was called "a considerable amount of gold." The homicide victim had apparently been a miser by habit. His killers were executed at Franklin on May 14, 1875. Source: *Georgia Weekly Telegraph* (Macon), 1/19/75 (4:6). *Augusta (GA) Constitutionalist*, 5/16/75 (3:1). *Daily Enquirer-Sun* (Columbus, GA), 4/2/75 (2:3). See also: 1870 U.S. Census (Heard Co., GA), which notes Summerlin.

Elisha Yarbrough (white, age 17). *Murder.* The crime was committed on 10–30–1874 in Carroll County. Hanged for the ax murder of Henry W. Smith (white), a rural storekeeper who was hacked to death in his bed. Motive: robbery and mendacity. Described as a "prepossessing" lad in terms of his looks and ostensible deportment, Yarbrough had either left or run away from his father's DeKalb County farm. He showed up in Carroll County a day or two before the end of October and there asked aid of Mr. Smith. The latter took him in, gave him a job, fed him well and even shared the same bed with him. Yarbrough repaid his benefactor by murdering him in that same bed. The records are silent as to whether Smith made what might be called "unwelcome advances" while sharing the same bed with his new hire, but it is known that Yarbrough ransacked the place before absconding to his grandfather's home in Randolph Co., AL. Subsequently extradited back to Georgia, this young killer was hanged at Carrollton on May 28, 1875. Source: *Daily Enquirer* (Columbus, GA), 6/1/75 (2:3). *Savannah Morning News*, 6/8/75 (1:1). *Georgia Weekly Telegraph* (Macon), 11/1/74 (1:4). See also: *Herald and Torchlight* (Hagerstown, MD), 6/23/75 (1:4) for a detailed account apparently copied from a lost issue of the *Carroll County Times*. See also: 1860 U.S. Census (Randolph Co., AL) and 1870 U.S. Census (DeKalb Co., GA), which note Yarbrough.

Alfred Orange (black, age abt. 26). *Murder.* The crime was committed on 3/8/1875 in Fulton County. Hanged for the ax murder of about 23-year-old Joe Mayfield (black), the killer having lain in wait with deliberate intent. Motive: rivalry for a female. This ax man was executed at Atlanta on June 4, 1875. Source: *Daily Chronicle* (Augusta, GA), 6/5/75 (1:2). *Atlanta Constitution*, 6/5/75 (1:2).

John Purlfoy (black, age abt. 40). *Murder.* The crime was committed on 1/26/1875 in Fulton County. Executed for the killing of John Casey (white, age not recorded), a liquor merchant who was struck down from behind with an iron bar. His throat was mutilated by a dull knife. Motive: robbery. The homicide victim was described as a rum character who had been selling his slop in an area inhabited almost entirely by negroes. Some of them thought that he had a monetary cache to match his bottled one. Purlfoy reaped his reward when he was hanged at Atlanta on June 25, 1875. Source: *Daily Chronicle* (Augusta, GA), 1/29/75 (1:6) & 6/5/75 (1:1). *Atlanta Constitution*, 6/26/75 (1:2).

George Speer (black, age 33). *Rape.* The crime was committed on 5/30/1875 in Fayette County. Indecent assault on the person of 15-year-old Margaret Millsaps (white), she having been pounced on and dragged into woods, where she was manually throttled and then sexually violated at knifepoint. George Speer was legally hanged at Fayetteville on October 8, 1875. This case had an equally unpleasant sequel. A brother of the executed man named Clarke Edmundson, seething with resentment, deliberately went out and raped the first white woman to cross his path, a Mrs. Kennedy. That act proved suicidal. Outraged locals hunted down the offender and strung him up from the same gallows on which his brother had been legally hanged four days earlier. Source: *Georgia Weekly Telegraph* (Macon), 6/8/75 (6:4). *Savannah Morning News*, 10/9/75 (2:4), 10/11/75 (1:5) & 10/19/75 (1:5). See also: 1870 U.S. Census (Fayette Co., GA), which notes both parties.

Rufus Evans (black, age not recorded) and **Edward Williams** (black, age not recorded). *Murder.* Their crime was committed on 7/31/1875 in Camden County. Shotgun slaying of 25-year-old Charles Lang (white), a storekeeper. Motive: armed robbery. Both of these killers were hanged at St. Mary's on December 17, 1875. Source: *Augusta (GA) Chronicle*, 8/11/75 (1:2). *Savannah Morning News*, 12/24/75 (1:5). See also: 1860 U.S. Census (Camden Co., GA), which notes the murdered man.

John B. Petty (white, age 22). *Murder.* The crime was committed on 12/7/1864 in Camden County. Rifle slaying of 44-year-old Elbert Allen (white), who was bushwhacked as he drove his wagon along a public road. Motive: uncertain. Petty was a deserter from the 4th Georgia Volunteer Cavalry under the command of Lt. Col. John Lewis Harris (CSA). Whether he gunned down Elbert Allen for the purpose of highway robbery or because he mistook him for a bounty hunter is not specified in surviving accounts. Petty was caught in Florida eleven years after the crime. His former C. O. (John Lewis Harris) had since then been appointed circuit judge for Brunswick and adjacent counties. Thus did Petty's wartime commanding officer come to be the same judge who presided at his peacetime trial. Harris became emotionally overwrought as he sentenced Petty to death. He recounted the condemned man's service record up until the time of his desertion plus the fact that he had been a combat veteran. Nobody thought to call this a conflict of interest. Even so, the fact that Judge Harris did pronounce the death sentence on Petty proved that he was impartial. The worst indignity of all, however (in the minds of many), came when Petty was made to share the same gallows with three former slaves. This was a gross violation of the Jim Crow ethic and it can be argued that it was meant to stigmatize him in a manner deemed even worse than hanging itself because of his wartime transgression. He was executed at St. Mary's on December 17, 1875. Source: *Savannah Morning News*, 11/23/75 (1:1) & 12/24/75 (1:5). *Georgia Weekly Telegraph* (Macon), 11/30/75 (8:5). See also: O. J. Hickox Jr., "A Brief History of Clinch's Regiment, 4th Georgia Volunteer Cavalry" (2011). Also: 1850 U.S. Census (Nash Co., NC) and 1860 U.S. Census (Camden Co., GA), which note Mr. Allen.

Joshua Pinckney (black, age not recorded). *Murder.* The crime was committed on 6/20/1866 in Camden County. Shotgun slaying of 34-year-old R. H. Eaton (white, a physician, full name not indicated). Motive: apparent spitefulness. Pinckney was among a group of so-called "belligerent freedmen" who surrounded Dr. Eaton's residence at night on the above date. They had interpreted Emancipation as a license to run wild. They lured Dr. Eaton out onto his veranda and then blasted away at him. Eaton reportedly had had one of this rabble arrested some days earlier. Several of the offenders were rounded up and brought to trial. Three of them (including Pinckney) were sentenced to death. All broke jail before the time of execution. Pinckney was nabbed nine years later by a policeman of his own color. He was hanged at St. Mary's on December 17, 1875. Source: *Daily Sun* (Columbus, GA), 7/6/66 (3:2) & 7/11/66 (1:4). *Georgia Weekly Telegraph* (Macon), 11/30/75 (8:5). *Savannah Morning News*, 12/24/75 (1:5). See also: 1860 U.S. Census (Thomas Co., GA), which notes Dr. Eaton.

Nick Thompson (black, age 24). *Murder.* The crime was committed on 10/7/1874 in Brooks County. Fatal stabbing of 42-year-old James H. Hunter (white) who was attacked directly in front of the Brooks County courthouse. Motive: election-day violence. This was a racially charged affair with black folks practicing their own brand of voter intimidation. Thompson happened to be one of a group of young hotheads (all black) who were loitering around the public water pump that stood opposite the courthouse. Ballots were being cast there that day in a statewide election. Thompson and his cronies took it upon themselves to selectively screen those wishing to exercise their right to vote—especially black voters. They saw an elderly black man walking toward the voting place along with Capt. James H. Hunter. The latter was acting as the former's escort at his own request because it was known among the blacks that this particular voter was independent minded and could not be relied on adhere to their party line. The old black man feared that his own people might beat him up or worse. Nick Thompson confronted this odd-looking pair and demanded to know their intentions. The black man said that he was going to vote the Conservative ticket. An argument ensued. Capt. Hunter said that the black man who he was escorting to the polling place had a legal right to vote however he saw fit. Thompson then shouted: "Damned I'll be if I don't see all white men in hell!!!" whereupon he pulled out a knife and plunged its blade into Hunter's chest. He wound up with a rope around his neck and a trap door beneath his feet at Quitman on December 17, 1875. Source: *Thomasville (GA) Times*, 10/10/74 (2:2) & 12/18/75 (2:1). *Bainbridge (GA) Weekly Democrat*, 10/15/74 (1:2) & 9/23/75 (1:2). *Savannah Morning News*, 12/20/75 (1:5). See also: 1850, 1860 and 1870 U.S. Censuses (Brooks Co., GA), which note Capt. Hunter.

1876

Edward Sally (black, age not recorded). *Murder.* The crime was committed on or about 10/15/1875 in Talbot County. Ax murder of John Sally (black, age not recorded, his stepfather), who was butchered in his bed and then secretly buried. Motive: the homicide victim had scolded him for not properly tending their livestock. Edward Sally was hanged for this misdeed at Talbotton on April 29, 1876. Source: *Weekly Telegraph* (Macon, GA), 11/2/75 (2:3). *Atlanta Constitution*, 4/30/76 (2:4).

Bob Jackson (black, age not recorded). *Murder.* The crime was committed on or about 8/15/1875 in Dooly County. Executed for the malicious killing of another black man named Edward Clarke. No further details are preserved except for the fact that Bob Jackson was legally hanged at Vienna on May 5, 1876. Source: *Weekly Telegraph* (Macon, GA), 5/16/76 (2:7). *Savannah Morning News*, 5/22/76 (1:1).

Paul Campbell (black, age not recorded) and **Prince Robertson** (black, age not recorded). *Murder.* Their crime was committed on 1/14/1876 in Effingham County. Child killers, etc. Handgun slayings of 38-year-old Isabelle Davis Cochran and 7-year-old Isabelle Cochran the younger (whites, a mother and daughter) whose bodies were found in their farmhouse with their heads literally shot to pieces. Motive: robbery and home invasion. The culprits were legally hanged at Springfield on May 15, 1876. Source: *Atlanta Constitution*, 5/16/76 (2:2). *Savannah Morning News*, 1/15/76 (3:4), 1/17/76 (3:6), 4/13/76 (1:5), 4/14/76 (1:4) & 5/16/76 (3:4). See also: 1850 U.S. Census (Effingham Co., GA), which notes Mrs. Cochran by her maiden name as well as 1870 U.S. Census (same county), which notes mother and child as "I. Cochran."

Haywood Grant (black, age 32). *Arson.* The crime was committed on 3/14/1876 in Floyd County. Specifically executed for firing the storehouse of Benjamin Winslow (white, age not recorded), a structure that was within the city limits of Rome. This felonious act met the legal definition of "Arson Within a Town" under the statute then in force and could be punished with death at the trial court's discretion.

Grant did not help his case by confessing to also having murdered five people during the preceding decade. One of these was the unsolved slaying of a former CSA general in Arkansas in 1868. It could not be independently confirmed that Grant had or had not actually perpetrated those purported homicides or whether his acknowledgment of them was just another case of jailhouse bravado. He was hanged at Rome on July 14, 1876. Source: *Atlanta Constitution*, 7/15/76 (1:2). *Rome (GA) Tri-Weekly Courier*, 7/15/76 (3:4).

James Berry Phillips (black, age 19). *Murder.* The crime was committed on 12/12/1874 in Newton County. Executed for the malicious killing of a white peddler named James Gallagher, age not recorded. How he did it cannot be ascertained because the trial record was lost to fire in 1883. The motive was almost certainly robbery. Phillips was hanged for this crime at Covington on November 24, 1876. Source: *Atlanta Constitution*, 11/25/76 (4:2). See also: *Executive Minutes of the Governor of Georgia*, entry dated 12/29/74.

1877

George Williams (black, age 24). *Murder.* The crime was committed on 8–5–1875 in Effingham County. Filicide. Executed for the killing of 2-year-old Willie Williams (black, his son), the little victim having been "burned, beaten and suffocated." Motive: unfit parent. The killer had become enraged when the baby could not walk without stumbling. He beat it mercilessly with a barrel stave and then thrust one of its tiny legs into his cooking fire until that limb was consumed up to the knee. He was hanged for this atrocity at Springfield on April 24, 1877. Source: *Savannah Morning News*, 4/25/77 (3:7). *New York Herald*, 4/25/77 (3:2).

David L. Beck (white, age 38). *Murder.* The crime was committed on 10/28/1875 in Chattooga County. Police killer. Shotgun slaying of 31-year-old Russell H. Shamblin (white), a constable with whom he had made a business deal. Motive: deal gone sour. Shamblin had previously arrested Beck on some charge necessitating incarceration for 30 days or so. Beck in the meantime had a crop in his fields that required his attention lest it rot. Sympathetic to Beck's dilemma, Shamblin offered to buy the harvest rights thereto. Beck agreed to partial payment with the balance to be paid at a later date. Beck returned home after his release from jail. Shamblin then offered him a promissory note on the remainder of the crop but Beck demanded cash. The two men quarreled at that point and Beck settled matters with a shotgun. He was hanged at Summerville on April 27, 1877. Source: *Atlanta Constitution*, 4/28/77 (1:2). *New York Herald*, 4/28/77 (7:4). Appeal: 57 GA 351–352. See also 1850 and 1860 U.S. Census (Chattooga Co., GA), which note Shamblin, and 1860 U.S. Census (Lumpkin Co., GA), which notes Beck.

William Meeks (white, age not recorded). *Murder.* The crime was committed on 9/6/1875 in Polk County. Handgun slaying of 31-year-old John McCormack (white). Motive: adultery and home wrecking. The killer was said to have seduced the victim's wife, resulting in the breakup of the McCormack household. Mrs. McCormack then took their child and moved in with her mother. John McCormack tried to forcibly take custody of the child because the house of his mother-in-law bore a bad reputation. The two women then appealed to Meeks, who responded by gunning down the betrayed husband. Meeks was hanged for this at Cedartown on May 4, 1877. Public opinion ran strongly against him. The two females were thereafter accorded the status of prostitutes. Source: *Atlanta Constitution*, 5/5/77 (2:2). *New York Herald*, 5/5/77 (3:2). See also: 1870 U.S. Census (Polk Co., GA), which notes "McCormick."

Charles Toomey, alias "Thomas" (black, age 39). *Murder.* The crime was committed on 4/15/1877 in Sumter County. Executed for the killing of 41-year-old Benetah Caraway (white), the wife of James Caraway. She was attacked in her own home (while her husband was at work in the fields) and later found "in the middle of the floor entirely unconscious with her skull badly mashed and blood and brains scattered about the premises." Motive: plunder. The miscreant was hanged at Americus on May 18, 1877. Source: *Sumter Weekly Republican*, 4/20/77 (3:4) & 5/25/77 (3:3). *Savannah Morning News*, 5/19/77 (1:3). See also Mrs. Caraway's well-preserved gravestone in Williams Cemetery, Smithville.

Stephen Brinkley (white, age 44). *Murder.* The crime was committed on 5/13/1874 in Coweta County. Uxoricide. Executed for the killing of 32-year-old Elizabeth Brinkley (white) who was slashed to death with a pocket knife. Motive: acrimonious divorce. Possibly deranged. This case was so hard fought that Brinkley had seven trials. He also underwent extensive psychiatric evaluations. The governors of Tennessee and Mississippi both urged clemency, as did no less a personage than General Nathan Bedford Forrest (the condemned man's commander during the late war), who had discharged him from CSA service on the grounds of mental illness. The governor of Georgia, however, refused to intervene because Brinkley had violated a protective order when he killed his estranged spouse. It would have established a dangerous precedent (he reasoned) to spare a murderer under such circumstances. As a result, Stephen Brinkley was hanged at Newnan on June 15, 1877. Source: *Atlanta Constitution*, 6/17/77 (1:4). *New York Herald*, 6/16/77 (8:3). See also: 1870 U.S. Census (Tishomingo Co., MS), which notes the Brinkleys before they came to Georgia.

Anthony Goble (white, age 27). *Murder.* The crime was committed on 11/2/1876 in Gilmer County. Executed for the killing of Charles Brown (white), age 50+, who was struck down from behind with a knotty walking stick and beaten almost beyond recognition. A rock was used to further mash the victim's head, but that did not satisfy the killer. Goble then rousted out the denizens of a nearby whorehouse and herded them over to the scene of the crime. Finding Brown to still be alive, he then stomped up and down on the man's face (his boots having heavy wooden heels) until it was a lifeless pulp. This was too much even for the wide-eyed scum of the county to endure. Goble's forced audience overpowered him and called for the sheriff. Motive: Brown had accused Goble's father of robbing his smokehouse more than a decade earlier. Goble was hanged for what he did at Ellijay on June 22, 1877. Source: *Atlanta Constitution*, 6/24/77 (1:5) & 6/26/77 (1:2). *New York Herald*, 6/24/77 (7:5). See also: 1870 U.S. Census (Pickens Co., GA), which notes Goble.

Jack Thomasson (black, age 15). *Murder.* The crime was committed on 12/18/1876 in Troup County. Child killer. Executed for the killings of 8-year-old Rebecca Miller and 2-year-old Melvina Miller (blacks), the daughters of a share-cropping couple named Charles and Amanda Miller. The older girl had the top of her head torn away by a shotgun blast. The rest of her corpse was then deliberately propped up to present a horrid spectacle. The 2-year-old was brained with an ax. Her throat was also cut from ear to ear. Motive: apparent spite. Thomasson had begrudged the mother of the homicide victims because she had forbidden him to come near her cabin or her kids. This was because Thomasson already had an extant reputation for sadistic acts against small children. He was hanged at La Grange on July 6, 1877. Source: *Atlanta Constitution*, 7/5/77 (4:2) & 7/7/77 (1:2). *New York Herald*, 7/7/77 (6:1).

Frank Jones (black, age not recorded). *Murder.* The crime was committed on an unknown date in Twiggs County. Executed for the unmitigated killing of another black man named Peyton Chapman, age not recorded. Further details of this case are lost to history save for the fact that Jones was legally hanged at Jeffersonville on October 5, 1877. Source: *Savannah Morning News*, 10/6/77 (1:2).

Alfred Marshall (black, age 39). *Murder.* The crime was committed on 5/5/1877 in Randolph County. Handgun slaying of 28-year-old S. A. White (white, full name not specified). Motive: obnoxious drunk. Marshall committed one of the most senseless murders on record. He had come to town (Cuthbert, GA) on market day bearing a basket of eggs. He succeeded in selling them all. Then he went to a saloon and drank the proceeds of those sales. Another saloon patron (Mr. White) asked what Marshall had in his basket. The latter replied that it had contained eggs that he had sold. White asked what price he had charged. Marshall named the price, whereupon White remarked that he would have offered him more. This angered Marshall (a one-armed man), who then pulled out a pistol and shot the other man dead. Marshall was legally hanged for this at Cuthbert on December 19, 1877. Source: *Cuthbert (GA) Appeal*, 5/11/77 (3:2) & 12/21/77 (3:2). *Daily Enquirer-Sun* (Columbus, GA), 12/21/77 (4:5).

1878

Augustus Johnson (white, age 24). *Murder.* The crime was committed on 8/24/1876 in Floyd County. Possible serial killer. Executed for the shotgun slaying of 46-year-old Alfred McCarver (black), a ferryman along the Coosa River. Motive: possibly deranged. Johnson was described as an ardent member of the KKK and a psychopathic killer. He had a particularly virulent hatred for "Niggers," as he called them. Several horrific atrocities were attributed to him, but it is difficult to discern truth from propaganda. One of these stories concerned an alleged horse thief named Hunt (first name not recorded) who ran afoul of him. The owner of the missing horse had offered a $25 reward for recovery of the animal. Gus Johnson made good on this and collected the bounty. Then he demanded an additional $25 for the thief himself. Challenged to produce, Johnson came back a short time later and displayed a severed human ear purportedly belonging to the thief. Confirmation was had when Hunt's mutilated remains were found minus an ear. He had also been shot twice in the head and his ripped-open belly had been stuffed with rocks. Another story concerned a young black child of toddling age. Johnson's buddies played a prank on him by inducing the so-called "pickaninny" to call him "papa." This reportedly sent Johnson into such a rage that he hacked the tot into little pieces and used those gory bits to bait his fishing lines.

Better substantiated was the story of what Johnson did to a bedridden ex-slave named Squire Foster. This happened one night as Johnson and his cronies were on the prowl for mischief. Johnson proposed that they "have some fun with" the elderly invalid because he had dared to vote the "Radical" ticket. The Klan declined to go along with this because they saw it as stooping low and needlessly cruel. Johnson was not deterred. He went to Foster's cabin and kicked in the door. Then he terrorized the helpless occupant by threatening him with death if he did not immediately rise up from his sickbed and dance a Highland fling. Alas, this was impossible for the crippled man. The pitiless intruder then shot old Foster in the head and hacked him into little chunks with an army saber that the victim had heretofore used as a fireplace poker. The insanity dodge saved Johnson when he was called to account for this.

The murder of Alfred McCarver (erroneously called Daniel Alford in many news accounts) was occasioned when an equestrian Johnson came to a ford on the Coosa river. A flatbed ferry (operated by McCarver) was then at the far bank, much to Johnson's annoyance. He barked a command to McCarver that lacked even the rudiments of common courtesy: "Get your black ass over here PDQ!!!" or words to that effect. "I'se comin', boss!" replied McCarver. "Faster! Damn you!!!" yelled Johnson. "I'se comin' fast as I can!" McCarver said. Johnson regarded this as insolence. He raised his shotgun, took careful aim, and killed the ferryman at mid-stream with a well placed blast. There was no insanity dodge this time. Johnson had been pronounced "cured" after being institutionalized in the aftermath of the Squire Foster affair. In addition, many people—white and black—were revolted by Johnson's misbehavior. He was hanged at Rome on March 15, 1878. Source: *Weekly Constitution* (Atlanta), 8/29/76 (1:7). *Daily Constitution* (Atlanta), 3/16/78 (1:1). *New York Herald*, 3/16/78 (5:3). See also: 1870 U.S. Census (Floyd Co., GA), which notes McCarver.

Frank Perry (black, age 18). *Murder.* The crime was committed on 4/18/1878 in Chatham County. Musket slaying of 33-year-old Frank J. Lee (white), a Bulloch County farmer who was shot in the face as he drove his wagon home from market. Motive: highway robbery. The killer was hanged at Savannah on June 26, 1878. Source: *Savannah Morning News*, 4/19/78 (3:4) & 6/27/78 (3:4).

Dick Dawson (black, age 27). *Murder.* The crime was committed on an unknown date in Upson County. Executed for the killing (by unspecified means) of 27-year-old Frank Cunningham (black), his brother-in-law. Motive: adultery. Dawson had been meddling with Cunningham's wife. He tried to justify himself by claiming that Cunningham had hexed him. This killer was hanged at Thomaston on July 5, 1878. Source: *Savannah Morning News*, 7/6/78 (2:3) & 7/8/78 (1:1) &

(1:5). *Columbus (GA) Daily Enquirer-Sun*, 7/6/78 (1:4).

Michael Shaw (white, age 25). *Murder.* The crime was committed on 4/30/1877 in Baldwin County. Uxoricide. Executed for the killing of 25-year-old Ardecia Moore Shaw (white), who was battered with a pine knot and then finished off by a pistol shot to the head. Motive: marital discord. Shaw was also a suspected klansman who had been indicted for the murders of two black men named James Bostwick and Edward Smith. He was hanged at Milledgeville on July 12, 1878. Source: *Union and Recorder* (Milledgeville, GA), 5/1/77 (3:2), 5/8/77 (3:2) & 7/16/78 (3:2). See also: 1870 U.S. Census (Baldwin Co., GA), which notes Mrs. Shaw by her maiden name.

Moses Allen (black, age not recorded). *Murder.* The crime was committed on 12/15/1877 in Glascock County. Executed for the killing of 44-year-old Benjamin Ivey (white), a former sheriff of that county who was slashed to death in a brawl with two black men. Moses Allen was apprehended and made to "dance on air." He was legally hanged at Gibson on November 1, 1878. Source: *Atlanta Constitution*, 11/3/78 (1:4). *Macon (GA) Weekly Telegraph*, 11/5/78 (2:7). See also: 1870 U.S. Census (Glascock Co., GA), which notes Benjamin "Ivy."

1879

Thomas Jones, alias "Satherwhite" (black, age 54). *Murder.* The crime was committed on 12/26/1876 in Columbia County. Shotgun slaying of Mary Jones (black, age not recorded), they apparently being unrelated because she was described as his "concubine" rather than as his wife. Motive: suspicion of infidelity. The killer purposefully blasted Mary in the crotch for that reason. Jones blamed his fellow blacks for his predicament, saying that they had falsely sworn his life away because of his refusal to follow the herd at election time. He was hanged at Appling on May 9, 1879. Source: *Savannah Morning News*, 5/10/79 (1:1). *Georgia Weekly Telegraph* (Macon), 5/20/79 (3:8). *New York Herald*, 5/10/79 (3:5).

Henry McSeed, alias "Cantello" (black, age 60+). *Murder.* The crime was committed on 11/18/1878 in Columbia County. Filicide. Shotgun slaying of Henry McSeed Jr. (black, his own son, age not recorded) who was purposely ambushed along a rural lane. Motive: a grouchy old reprobate. Papa McSeed had reportedly murdered two other black men prior to Emancipation. His owner used bribery and influence to save him on those occasions because he regarded McSeed as too valuable an asset to risk losing. Freedom did nothing to improve McSeed's personality. He bore the reputation of a dangerous man, especially among those of his own color. He was also a habitual bully and wife beater. In 1878 McSeed's second wife left him on account of intolerable cruelty. McSeed blamed his own son and namesake for this because the latter had often tried to defend his stepmother. McSeed self-pitied his way right onto the gallows platform at Appling on May 9, 1879. Source: *Savannah Morning News*, 5/10/79 (1:1). *New York Herald*, 5/10/79 (3:4).

Anthony Collins (black, age not recorded). *Murder.* The crime was committed on an unknown date in Tattnall County. Baby killer. Few details survive of this black-on-black infanticide. Collins wanted to marry a certain unwed mother of his acquaintance but did not want to get stuck raising another man's child. So he made away with the baby by some undisclosed means and then pressed his marriage suit. Things didn't work out the way Collins had hoped. He was hanged at Reidsville on May 16, 1879. Source: *Savannah Morning News*, 5/30/79 (1:1).

Robert Skelly (white, age 41). *Murder.* The crime was committed on 12/13/1878 in Pierce County. Uxoricide. Fatal beating of his wife (name and age not specified in surviving accounts), she having been battered with a wooden stool "and her mangled remains pitched into the road." Motive: adultery on her part. This wife-killer was hanged at Blackshear on May 23, 1879. Source: *Savannah Morning News*, 5/24/79 (2:4). *New York Herald*, 5/24/79 (3:6).

Jordan Sheats (black, age not recorded). *Murder.* The crime was committed on 2/24/1879 in Madison County. Shotgun slaying of 31-year-old John T. Ledbetter (white). Motive: the homicide victim had butted into an argument between the killer and his employer. Sheats was legally hanged for this at Danielsville on November 14, 1879. Source: *Savannah Morning News*, 11/15/79 (2:4) & 11/17/79 (1:2). *Atlanta Constitution*, 11/15/79 (1:1). See also: 1870 U.S. Census (Madison Co., GA), which notes the murdered man.

Drew Holloway (black, age 20). *Murder.* The crime was committed on 12/24/1878 in Bulloch County. Fatal stabbing of about 30-year-old Benson Brown (black). Motive: obnoxious drunk. This Christmas Eve killer was hanged at Statesboro on December 19, 1879. Source: *Savannah Morning News*, 12/20/79 (3:4). *New York Herald*, 12/20/79 (6:5).

1880

John Henry Johnson (black, age 31). *Murder.* The crime was committed on 3/16/1878 in Chatham County. Fatal stabbing of Daniel McDermott (white, age not recorded), a sailor. Motive: mugging in the red light district. McDermott was a Labradorian serving aboard the British bark *Tikoma.* The man who knifed him was hanged at Savannah on February 27, 1880. Source: *Savannah Morning News*, 3/18/78 (3:4) & 2/28/80 (3:4).

Daniel Brigherty (black, age 22). *Rape.* The crime was committed on 10/22/1879 in Thomas County. Indecent assault on the person of an adult white female identified only as "Mrs. Futch." She was attacked in her home and later found staggering along a country lane with a baby in her arms. Her physical condition bespoke what had happened. The culprit was legally hanged at Thomasville on March 12, 1880. Source: *Thomasville (GA) Times*, 3/13/80 (3:4). *New York Herald*, 3/13/80 (5:5).

George Jackson (black, age not recorded). *Murder.* The crime was committed on or about 10/15/1879 in Paulding County. Executed for the killing of another black man named Jack Moss, age not recorded. The homicide victim was beaten on the head with a stick until the killer thought him dead. All of his money was stolen. Returning to the scene sometime afterward, Jackson found Moss still breathing and then finished him off by cutting his throat. Motive:

gambling dispute. Jackson was hanged at Dallas on March 26, 1880. Source: *Savannah Morning News*, 3/29/80 (1:1). *Marietta (GA) Journal*, 4/1/80 (3:3). *Paulding New Era* (Dallas, GA), 7/25/84 in retrospect.

Henry Ryan (black, age 34). *Murder.* The crime was committed on 12/24/1879 in Burke County. Hanged for the callous murder of Mary Thomas (black), age 50+, who was lashed to a tree on Christmas Eve and left to die of exposure. Motive: robbery. Both parties were cotton pickers on the James Dye plantation. Ryan was described as an idler who drew only $1.30 when the workers were paid on the above date. Mary Thomas by contrast drew the more substantial sum of $6.50 plus a holiday bonus of corn meal and a large slab of bacon. Jealous thereof, Ryan stalked Mary Thomas and felled her with a club. Then he dragged the stunned woman into some woods where he bound her upright to a tree, using his suspenders in lieu of rope. He stole both her money and her food. Mary Thomas remained in that position throughout the ensuing night. Ryan returned to the scene on Christmas morning and found her still there. He tortured her by poking, prodding and pulling her body parts. Then he left her immobile for a second night. Mary Thomas was found the following day crawling along on her hands and knees barely alive. She succumbed to internal injuries about a week later. The tree to which she had been tied was denuded of its bark to the height of about 6' on account of her "frantic attempts to release herself." More than 7,000 angry blacks witnessed the execution of this killer at Waynesboro on July 9, 1880. They were ready to tear Ryan limb from limb in the event of a reprieve. Source: *Savannah Morning News*, 7/10/80 (1:3). *New York Herald*, 7/10/80 (6:3). See also: 1880 U.S. Census (Burke Co., GA), which notes Ryan.

Jim Morgan (black, age not recorded). *Murder.* The crime was committed on an unknown date in Emanuel County. Legally executed for the malicious killing of another black man named Bill Smith, age not recorded. The superior court file for this case is inaccessible. All that is further known at this point is that Morgan was hanged at Swainsboro on December 3, 1880. Source: *Savannah Morning News*, 12/4/80 (1:3).

1881

Mose Twiggs (black, age 24). *Murder.* The crime was committed on 11/18/1880 in Burke County. Shotgun slaying of William Driscoll (white, age not recorded), a plantation overseer who was murdered in his bed. The homicide victim was found with his guts blown out and his bedclothes aflame. Motive: Twiggs and his brother resented a reprimand they had received for shoddy work. Mose Twiggs was hanged at Waynesboro on January 28, 1881. Source: *Augusta (GA) Chronicle*, 11/23/80 (1:3). *New York Herald*, 1/29/81 (4:1). See also: 1880 U.S. Census (Burke Co., GA), which notes the killers. See also: Frank Twiggs (executed 2/18/81).

Frank Twiggs (black, age 37). *Murder.* The crime was committed on 11/18/1880 in Burke County. Accomplice in the shotgun slaying of William Driscoll (white, age not recorded), a plantation overseer who was murdered in his bed. Motive: resentment for a reprimand. Frank Twiggs was hanged at Waynesboro on February 18, 1881.

Source: *Savannah Morning News*, 2/19/81 (1:4). See also: Mose Twiggs (executed 1/28/81).

Pink Pratt (black, age 21). *Rape.* The crime was committed on 9/24/1880 in Cobb County. Incipient serial rapist. Executed for an indecent assault on the person of 11-year-old Margaret Watkins (white), who was attacked while walking to school. Pratt had also made attempts on at least two other young girls during the preceding weeks. His father was nearly dealt with summarily when he was heard to say: "My Pink won't be hung for no white trash!" The younger Pratt was hung—legally—at Marietta on March 4, 1881. Source: *Atlanta Constitution*, 3/5/81 (4:3). *Savannah Morning News*, 3/5/81 (1:8).

Henry Hill (black, age 49). *Murder.* The crime was committed on 2/23/1881 in Hart County. Prison-guard killer. Executed for the assassination of 29-year-old Thomas N. Skelton (white), the official jailor for Hart County. The homicide victim was battered to death with a wooden plank, his head having been "literally beat to pieces." Motive: jailbreak. Henry Hill was hanged at Hartwell on April 22, 1881. Source: *Savannah Morning News*, 3/8/81 (1:1) & 4/25/81 (1:2). *New York Herald*, 4/23/81 (8:3).

Frank Hudson (black, age 28). *Murder.* The crime was committed on 8/16/1881 in Terrell County. Executed for the infamous killings of 63-year-old David M. Lee, 65-year-old Mary Lee (whites, a married couple) and their household employee (black, age abt. 60) named Sallie Johnson. Motive: plunder. Said the killer: "I heard that Mr. Lee kept a large sum of money in his house. Being in want, and not being able to earn more than a miserable living by work, I deliberately determined to have that money even if I had to wade through blood to get it." Hudson initially decoyed Mr. Lee out of his residence by setting fire to some nearby woods. Then he struck the man down from behind with a fence rail, knocking his brains out. Next, he went to Lee's house and told Mrs. Lee that her husband was in distress. She then came outdoors only to be struck down from behind with an ax. The killer went into the house and frightfully maimed a 16-year-old black girl, leaving her for dead. He also found Sallie Johnson (the family cook) asleep on her pallet by the kitchen and beheaded her with one swing of his ax. This done, Hudson tore the house apart in a maniacal search for money. He was legally hanged at Dawson on October 14, 1881. Source: *Macon (GA) Telegraph & Messenger*, 8/20/81 (1:1), 8/21/81 (1:1) & 9/14/81 (4:2). *Atlanta Constitution*, 10/15/81 (1:5). *New York Herald*, 10/15/81 (8:3). See also: 1880 U.S. Census (Terrell Co., GA), which notes Mr. & Mrs. Lee.

Tom Betts (black, age 25). *Murder.* The crime was committed on 9/28/1880 in Clayton County. Executed for the killing of 68-year-old Hilliard Judge Moore (white), who was struck on the head with a wooden maul. Motive: Betts thought that he had been shorted in his wages. He did not satisfy himself with taking only the disputed amount but went on to steal all the money that he found on the homicide victim's person. Tom Betts was legally hanged for this at Jonesboro on November 4, 1881. Source: *Georgia Weekly Telegraph* (Macon), 10/5/80 (2:3). *Atlanta Constitution*, 11/5/81 (1:5). See also: 1880 U.S. Census (Clayton Co., GA), which notes H. J. Moore.

Joe Harris (black, age 22). *Murder.* The crime was committed on 5/12/1881 in Greene County. Prison guard killer. Shotgun slaying of 29-year-old Ezekiel T. Langston (white). Motive: escape from custody. Harris had been put on the county farm for rifling a woman's pocketbook. He conspired with another convict to break out. One of them hit the guard on the head with a hoe. Harris then snatched the guard's shotgun and used it to blow his head off. The killers took to the woods, but only Harris was caught. He was hanged at Greensboro on November 11, 1881. Source: *Augusta (GA) Chronicle,* 5/15/81 (4:2). *Atlanta Constitution,* 11/12/81 (1:3). *New York Herald,* 11/12/81 (4:1). See also: 1880 U.S. Census (Oconee Co., GA), which notes Langston.

Levi Sparks (black, age 37). *Rape.* The crime was committed on 10/5/1881 in Stewart County. Indecent assault on the person of 22-year-old Ida Pope (white), who was forcibly stupefied with ether and then left infected with venereal disease. The victim had been caregiver for her invalid father (age 60) who suffered from "mental impairment" in addition to other infirmities of a physical nature. Sparks was a quack doctor and herbalist who had ingratiated himself to these rather naïve people with a pledge to cure the father. The latter wound up getting chloroformed in his sickbed. Then his daughter was attacked. Ether burns on her face combined with genital putrescence substantiated the charges as set forth in the indictment. Levi Sparks was legally hanged for this at Lumpkin on November 18, 1881. Source: *Columbus (GA) Daily Enquirer-Sun,* 10/20/81 (4:4), 11/1/81 (4:3), 11/18/81 (4:3) & 11/19/81 (4:3). *New York Herald,* 11/19/81 (8:2). See also: 1880 U.S. Census (Stewart Co., GA), which notes the Popes, and 1870 U.S. Census (Marion Co., GA), which notes Levi Sparks.

Sang Armor (black, age 41). *Murder.* The crime was committed on 4/6/1881 in Taliaferro County. Executed for the killing of 58-year-old Amos Ellington (white), who was struck down from behind with an ax and then finished off by a pistol shot behind the left ear, execution style. Motive: land acquisition. An unmarried man, Ellington owned 425 acres of prime woodland from which he derived his livelihood. He employed Sang Armor as his general assistant. He also reportedly used Armor's wife as a concubine with her husband's consent. Armor had a self-serving reason for tolerating this. It so happened that the adulterous pair had spawned a mulatto son (named Edgar Ellington) who by the age of 17 was his white father's only heir. Sang Armor saw this situation as a chance to wrest control of the aforesaid 425 acres because if Amos Ellington was eliminated, title to the property would pass to the son (Edgar), who would in turn pass it along (by pre-design) to his mother, who was Sang's wife. The latter got more than he bargained for when he was hanged at Crawfordville on November 25, 1881. Source: *Savannah Morning News,* 11/26/81 (1:4). See also: 1880 U.S. Census (Taliaferro Co., GA), which notes all parties.

1882

Jesse Williams (black, age 17). *Murder.* The crime was committed on 6/11/1881 in Chatham County. Executed for the killing of Toby Lark (black), age 90+, a watchman at a woodlot. The nonagenarian was apparently beaten to death; "his skull was fractured and his body mangled," according to one report. Motive: robbery. This gratuitously brutal slayer was hanged at Savannah on January 16, 1882. Source: *Savannah Morning News*, 1/17/82 (4:3).

Anderson Jones (black, age abt. 28). *Murder.* The crime was committed on 12/15/1879 in Richmond County. Ax murder of about 20-year-old John G. Harralson (white), a storekeeper. Motive: robbery and reneging on a debt. The killer owed the victim seven dollars. He had no intention of paying. He solved the problem by feigning a desire to do so and (with clear premeditation) smuggled an ax into Harralson's place of business. Then he waited for an unguarded moment before striking unawares and stealing whatever cash ($42) was there. Anderson Jones met the rope for this (legally) at Augusta on January 20, 1882. Source: *Augusta (GA) Chronicle*, 12/17/79 (4:3), 12/23/79 (4:2) & 1/21/82 (1:2).

James E. Hanvey (white, age 23). *Murder.* The crime was committed on 7/2/1881 in Carroll County. Fatal stabbing of 48-year-old Arthur McMullen (white). Motive: obnoxious drunk. This killer was hanged at Carrollton on June 2, 1882. Source: *Macon (GA) Telegraph & Messenger*, 6/4/82 (1:1). See also: 1880 U.S. Census (Carroll Co., GA), which notes McMullen.

William L. Moon (white, age 38). *Murder.* The crime was committed on 1/4/1881 in Carroll County. Shotgun slaying of 28-year-old John B. Ward (white). Motive: fracas in a boarding house. Moon was supposed to be executed side-by-side with James Hanvey, but a messy suicide attempt resulted in a 24-hour postponement. He was hanged at Carrollton on June 3, 1882. Source: *Macon (GA) Telegraph & Messenger*, 6/4/82 (1:1). See also: 1880 U.S. Census (Carroll Co., GA), which notes Ward.

Robert Donaldson (black, age 37), **Joseph King** (black, age 39), **Ella Moore** (black, age 32), **Riddick Powell** (black, age 24) and **Simon Quinn** (black, age 60). *Murder.* Their crime was committed on 8/6/1882 in Dodge County. All five executed for the mutilation murder of 21-year-old James Quinn Harvard (white). Motive: race riot. The morning of the above date (it being a Sunday) saw thousands of black folks swarm the town of Eastman for a huge outdoor revival meeting sponsored by an evangelical religious sect. In addition to those who came by wagon and on foot, many came by special passenger trains from counties near and far. Along with this throng came a parasite element consisting of gamblers, pickpockets and whiskey peddlers. Among these was a hustler from Macon named Jake Johnson, alias "Jake Terrapin," who was notorious among his fellow blacks as a swindler, thief and card sharp. He wasted no time in cheating one of the so-called "country negroes" out of his watch by means of a rigged card game. Some of the other blacks complained to the town marshal and one of his deputies, both of whom were white men. The latter arrested Johnson and was in the act of walking him to the local jail when the suspect broke free and made a run for it, hoping to lose himself in the enormous crowd. Johnson ignored warnings to halt, whereupon the deputy brought him down with a well-aimed gunshot. Then hell broke loose. The body of the already dead criminal (who up until then had been despised by his own people) was carried through the camp grounds for all to see. Ella Moore whipped up the crowd by screaming banshee-like for blood and vengeance. No one had to second her motion. These so-called churchgoers rampaged through the town beating up and shooting any white person they found. One of these was young James Q. Harvard. The mob mistook him for the deputy who had shot Jake Johnson and determined that he must die. Harvard ran for dear life. He tried to hide in a certain house. The place was carried by storm. Harvard (whose only crime was not heeding a warning to stay home that day) was dragged from the house. He was beaten without mercy. The assailants tore wooden pickets from a fence and used them to hack and batter Harvard almost beyond recognition. Ella Moore once again made herself conspicuous by her frenzied attempts to cut Harvard's throat. Somebody finally finished off the young man by firing a pistol shot through his head. Not satisfied, the infuriated rioters continued their path of mayhem. They were hankering for trouble. Armed whites began to fight back by shooting into the human stampede. There is no accurate count of the dead and wounded. Suddenly the mood changed from rage to panic. The out-of-town blacks fled in every direction. They had been seized by the sudden realization that they had better get out of there before well-armed whites got organized. Swarms of them flung themselves into and onto the waiting excursion trains that had brought them there. They trampled each other in the process. The passenger cars were crammed beyond capacity in the midsummer heat with arms, legs and heads flailing wildly from the burst windows. No one knows how many were crushed and suffocated as the trains rolled out of town. Many arrests were made in the aftermath of this debacle. Trials followed, with the result that dozens were sent to the mines. The five most aggressive offenders (above named) were legally hanged on a specially constructed gallows at Eastman on October 20, 1882, their racist rants choked out of them by five snugly fitted nooses. Source: *Macon (GA) Telegraph & Messenger*, 8/8/82 (1:1). *Atlanta Constitution*, 10/21/82 (1:1). *Savannah Morning News*, 10/21/82 (1:3). See also: 1880 U.S. Census (Pulaski Co., GA), which notes Donaldson, Harvard and Moore plus 1880 U.S. Census (McIntosh Co., GA), which notes King.

Edward Conyers (black, age 23). *Murder.* The crime was committed on 4/19/1882 in Emanuel County. Handgun slaying of about 50-year-old Northen Pierce (black). Motive: an argument about a marauding dog. This black-on-black killer was hanged at Swainsboro on December 8, 1882. Source: *Savannah Morning News*, 12/9/82 (1:3).

William Porter (black, age 25). *Murder.* The crime was committed on 9/13/1882 in Houston County. Executed for the killing of 16-year-old Bill Swift (black), who was beaten on the head with a stick and his body left naked on a roadside. Motive: highway robbery. This black-on-black killer was hanged at Perry on December 8, 1882. Source: *Savannah Morning News*, 12/9/82 (1:3). See also: 1880 U.S. Census (Houston Co., GA), which notes Porter.

1883

William Barks (black, age abt. 22) and **Green Cunningham** (black, age abt. 26). *Murder.* Their crime was committed on 1/23/1883 in Walker County. Both hanged for the ax murder of 68-year-old Herod Herman Rudd (white). Motive: robbery and home invasion. The gallows marked their exit from this world at La Fayette on March 23, 1883. Source: *Marietta (GA) Journal*, 2/1/83 (3:5). *Savannah Morning News*, 3/24/83 (1:3). *Atlanta Constitution*, 1/26/83 (1:3) & 3/24/83 (1:3). *New York Herald*, 3/24/83 (6:2). See also: 1880 U.S. Census (Walker Co., GA), which notes Mr. Rudd.

Daniel T. Walker (white, age not recorded). *Murder.* The crime was committed on 10/5/1882 in Dade County. Executed for the killing of 47-year-old Samuel S. Hardberger (white), who was blasted by a shotgun and then finished off with a pistol shot fired point blank into his head. Motive: highway robbery. Walker was reported to be a roving bad man from Mississippi. He was hanged at Trenton on May 4, 1883. Source: *Telegraph & Messenger* (Macon) 5/5/83 (1:2). *Savannah Morning News*, 5/5/83 (1:5). See also: 1880 U.S. Census (Marion Co., TN), which notes the murdered man.

James C. Jones, née "Joseph C. Cohen" (white, age 25). *Murder.* The crime was committed on 3/16/1883 in Oglethorpe County. Uxoricide. Handgun slaying of 16-year-old Surilla Matthews Jones (white), who was shot three times despite her pleas for mercy. The killer had originally been a Jewish orphan, or so it would appear based on his personal history. Much was written about his personality, all of it bad. His wife was 12 years old at the time of their marriage. She had also been reduced to a terrified, cringing wreck before their honeymoon was over. Jones tried to rape his mother-in-law when she gave refuge to her wretched child. Then he fled town only to reappear three years later. The refusal of his wife to be reconciled with him (or so he reasoned) justified killing her. A superior court jury disagreed. As a result, Jones was hanged at Lexington on May 18, 1883. Source: *Banner-Watchman* (Athens, GA), 3/20/83 (3:7). *Savannah Morning News*, 5/19/83 (1:3).

Henry Knight (black, age 22). *Murder.* The crime was committed on 7/1/1882 in Ware County. Shotgun slaying of 26-year-old Edward Hunter (black). Motive: Hunter (as the foreman of a turpentine camp) had asked Knight to pay his employee membership dues in an extracurricular club that he had joined, in this case a brass band. Knight was executed at Waycross on May 18, 1883. "His hanging was accepted by the colored people as a just retribution," said the *Savannah Morning News*, 5/19/83 (1:5). Also: *Telegraph & Messenger* (Macon), 5/19/83 (1:5). See also: 1870 U.S. Census (Dougherty Co., GA), which notes Hunter before he came to Ware County.

John Bailey (black, age 27). *Murder.* The crime was committed on 6/20/1882 in Bibb County. Handgun slaying of 54-year-old Paris Tatman (black) in a dispute over a silver dollar. The homicide victim was a bartender. Bailey insisted that he had given the coin to Tatman to be changed into nickels and dimes. Tatman reportedly took the silver dollar and then stalled Bailey for a few minutes before saying that his cash drawer had been pilfered and that he had not been given any such coin. One of these men was a glib hustler who was trying to cheat the other. Both wound up dying for it: Tatman at the scene and Bailey on the gallows. The latter was executed at Macon on June 1, 1883. Source: *Macon Telegraph &*

Messenger, 7/2/82 (4:4). *Savannah Morning News*, 6/2/83 (1:3). See also: 1880 U.S. Census (Macon, GA), which notes Tatman.

Henry Wimbish (black, age 30). *Murder.* The crime was committed on 6/7/1882 in Bibb County. Fatal stabbing of 21-year-old Morgan Washington (black), who was knifed multiple times. Motive: workplace violence. Both parties had been employed on a gravel train. Wimbish was hanged at Macon on June 1, 1883. Source: *Macon Telegraph & Messenger*, 6/8/82 (1:2). *Savannah Morning News*, 6/2/83 (1:3). See also: 1880 U.S. Census (Macon, GA), which notes Washington.

Elbert M. Stevenson (white, age 31). *Murder.* The crime was committed on 8/13/1881 in Gwinnett County. Rifle slaying of 46-year-old Selina Clementine Jackson Stevenson (white, his paternal aunt by marriage), who was shot four times and died after eight weeks in agony with a mutilated spine. Her husband–Van R. Stevenson—had died on 1/8/1867. He had served with honor in the 42nd Georgia Infantry and was among the very last to lay down his arms on 4/26/1865, a true Southern patriot. His widow chose to remain so for the rest of her life and was by all accounts a remarkably well preserved woman in terms of her appearance. It was this latter fact that inspired an abnormal obsession on the part of Elbert Stevenson, her late husband's nephew. He sought to marry her but was told that such was impossible. Elbert refused to take no for an answer despite already having a wife of his own. Then he took recourse in the old "If I can't have you then neither will anyone else" line of reasoning. He was hanged at Lawrenceville on June 8, 1883. Source: *Macon Weekly Telegraph*, 8/26/81 (2:3). *Atlanta Constitution*, 6/9/83 (1:1). *Savannah Morning News*, 6/9/83 (1:3). See also: Mrs. Stevenson's gravestone in Prospect Methodist Church Cemetery, Lawrenceville. The killer is also interred there, but his grave was left unmarked.

Tony James (black, age 20). *Murder.* The crime was committed on 8/5/1882 in McIntosh County. Handgun slaying of 21-year-old Prince Anderson (black). Motive: obnoxious drunk. Buddies since childhood, these young males (with their respective girlfriends) had planned a picnic excursion to Champney Island. Trouble began during the boat ride thither when James splashed water on Anderson's girl. Once ashore, the argument escalated until James pulled out a weapon and started shooting. James was hanged for this at Darien on June 29, 1883. Source: *Savannah Morning News*, 6/30/83 (1:3). See also: 1870 U.S. Census (Liberty Co., GA), which notes both parties.

George Wallace (black, age 35). *Murder.* The crime was committed on 3/18/1882 in Chatham County. Handgun slaying of Martin Jansen (white, age not recorded), a Norwegian sailor. Motive: fracas in a waterfront dive. The killer was a Guyanese who had himself lived a seafaring life. He was hanged at Savannah on September 28, 1883. Source: *Savannah Morning News*, 3/20/82 (4:3), 3/21/82 (4:5) & 9/29/83 (4:3). *New York Herald*, 9/29/83 (4:1).

Taylor Bryant (black, age 27). *Rape.* The crime was committed on 8/29/1883 in Walton County. Indecent assault on the person of Elizabeth V. Swords (white, age not recorded), who was attacked in her home. The woman tried to defend herself with a handgun but the weapon misfired. The culprit then pounced on her. He had been released from prison but a short time earlier, having served "a long term for the same offense." This supposedly rehabilitated sex offender was legally hanged at Monroe on October 19, 1883. Source: *Savannah Morning News*, 10/20/83 (1:3). See also: 1880 U.S. Census (Walton Co., GA), which notes Bryant.

Margaret Harris (black, age 18). *Murder.* The crime was committed on 8/19/1883 in Gordon County. Child killer. Executed for the fatal and deliberate poisoning of 8-year-old Leila Lewis (white) as part of a common plan to wipe out her entire household. The poison was poured from a bottle into a pot of boiling rice that was then served up as part of a meal. It was purposefully prepared in advance, apparently from a native plant of the Solanaceae family. Motive: the murderess did not want to wait until the age of 21 to be free from the terms of her indentured servitude. A young man who was thought to have put the idea into Margaret's head (and to have actually supplied the poison) was sentenced to life at hard labor. Margaret Harris was legally hanged at Calhoun on October 19, 1883. Source: *Marietta (GA) Journal*, 9/6/83 (2:3). *Savannah Morning News*, 10/20/83 (1:3).

Ambrose West (black, age 18). *Murder.* The crime was committed on 9/17/1883 in Worth County. Executed for the killing of James Monroe (black, age not recorded), whose skull was smashed with a wooden maul. Motive: not specified in surviving accounts. Ambrose West was hanged at Sylvester on November 30, 1883. Source: *Savannah Morning News*, 12/1/83 (1:5).

1884

James Crummidy (black, age not recorded). *Murder.* The crime was committed on 9/8/1883 in Dodge County. Handgun slaying of James A. Mitchell (white, age not recorded). Motive: obnoxious drunk. This killer was hanged at Eastman on January 4, 1884. Source: *Telegraph & Messenger* (Macon, GA), 9/15/83 (1:4) & 1/5/84 (1:5). *New York Herald*, 1/5/84 (10:1). *Eastman (GA) Times*, 9/13/83 (3:2) & 1/10/84 (3:2).

David McLain (white, age 38). *Murder.* The crime was committed on 2/3/1879 in Charlton County. Shotgun slaying of 27-year-old William Freeman Sexton (white), who was wounded in the back and died three weeks later. Motive: dispute over property rights. The killer took to the swamps but turned up four years later. He was executed at Folkston on March 7, 1884. Source: *Savannah Morning News*, 3/7/84 (4:2) & 3/8/84 (1:4). Appeal: 71 GA 279–286. See also: 1870 U.S. Census (Charlton Co., GA), which notes Sexton.

Willis Hodges (black, age abt. 23). *Murder.* The crime was committed on 12/25/1883 in Dodge County. Handgun slaying of Lizzie Jones (black, age not recorded). Motive: lovers' quarrel. This Christmas Day killer was hanged at Eastman on April 18, 1884. Source: *Savannah Morning News*, 4/19/84 (1:5). *Atlanta Constitution*, 4/19/84 (1:6).

Thomas Henry Curry (black, age 21). *Murder.* The crime was committed on 10/15/1882 in Walton County. Ax murder of 22-year-old Powell Reid (black), who was butchered in his bed. Motive: rivalry for a female. Curry fled but was caught exactly one year later.

He collected his prize (in the form of a rope necklace and a cheap pine coffin) at Monroe on April 25, 1884. Source: *Macon (GA) Telegraph & Messenger*, 10/16/83 (1:1) & 4/26/84 (1:2). *Savannah Morning News*, 4/26/84 (1:5). See also: 1880 U.S. Census (Rockdale Co., GA), which notes "Powell Reed."

Leonidas Johnson (black, age 21). *Rape.* The crime was committed on 2/2/1883 in Henry County. Serial rapist. Executed for an indecent assault on the person of a married white female, identified only as "Mrs. Cook," who was attacked in her home while attending her small children. Johnson already had an extant record for sex crimes and burglary. He was also a chain-gang alumnus. Still, he was given perhaps the best of court-appointed lawyers in the person of James Stoddard Boynton, who served as governor of Georgia that same year. The weight of the evidence proved insurmountable even for this personage, and Leonidas Johnson paid the death penalty at McDonough on May 23, 1884. Source: *Telegraph & Messenger* (Macon, GA), 4/22/83 (1:7), 10/31/83 (3:3) & 5/24/84 (1:1). *Atlanta Constitution*, 5/24/84 (1:5).

John McKeithan (black, age 21). *Murder.* The crime was committed on 1/5/1884 in Ware County. Ax murder of Tom McCrimmon (black, age not recorded) who succumbed after 18 excruciating days. Motive: rivalry for a female. He paid the price on the gallows at Waycross on May 23, 1884. Source: *Savannah Morning News*, 5/24/84 (1:5). *Atlanta Constitution*, 5/24/84 (5:3).

Fletcher Lowery (black, age 27). *Murder.* The crime was committed on 6/16/1883 in Appling County. Handgun slaying of John Brimage (black, age not recorded), whose person was also rifled for valuables and then dumped in a creek. Motive: possibly a badger game; the homicide victim had been caught necking with the killer's female lover. Whatever the truth, Fletcher Lowery was hanged for murder with malice at Baxley on July 11, 1884. Source: *Telegraph & Messenger* (Macon, GA), 6/22/83 (1:6). *Atlanta Constitution*, 7/12/84 (4:4). Appeal: 72 GA 649–654.

Sam Williams (black, age not recorded). *Murder.* The crime was committed on 10/20/1883 in Burke County. Shotgun slaying of Clem Bush (black, age not recorded). Motive: rivalry for a female. Score another one for the hangman—this time at Waynesboro–on July 18, 1884. Source: *Chronicle & Constitutionalist* (Augusta, GA), 5/31/84 (1:4). *Savannah Morning News*, 7/19/84 (4:5). *The True Citizen* (Waynesboro, GA), 10/26/83 (3:3) & 7/18/84 (3:3).

George Clarke, alias "Jones" (black, age not recorded). *Rape.* The crime was committed on 7/22/1884 in Terrell County. Indecent assault on the person of 57-year-old Julia Ann Jennings (white). She died in 1893. Her attacker was legally hanged at Dawson on August 25, 1884. Source: *Atlanta Constitution*, 7/24/84 (2:2), 7/26/84 (2:3) & 8/26/84 (2:3). *Atlanta Journal*, 8/25/84 (1:7). *New York Herald*, 8/26/84 (10:3). See also the gravestone of Mrs. Jennings at Chickasawhatchee Primitive Baptist Church, Dawson.

George Hill (black, age 35). *Murder.* The crime was committed on 2/7/1883 in Cherokee County. Ax murder of William Bryant (black, age not recorded). Motive: the homicide victim had interfered in an argument between the killer and a third man while attending a private house party. Another one who paid the forfeit of his life for a stupid reason, George Hill was hanged at Canton on October 31, 1884. Source: *Marietta (GA) Journal*, 2/15/83 (2:4). *Savannah Morning News*, 11/1/84 (1:7).

Homer Perry (black, age 15). *Rape.* The crime was committed on 6/9/1884 in Newton County. Indecent assault on the person of 10-year-old Sissy Perry (black) under circumstances that were described as "brutal and diabolical" by newspaper correspondents who dared not say anymore. It is unclear if these Perrys were related. The ravisher was hanged at Covington on November 7, 1884. Source: *Macon (GA) Telegraph*, 11/2/84 (3:3). *Savannah Morning News*, 11/8/84 (1:9). See also: 1870 and 1880 U.S. Census (Newton Co., GA), which respectively note the culprit and the little girl.

Warren James Price (white, age 42). *Murder.* The crime was committed on 8/27/1882 in Johnson County. Shotgun slaying of 24-year-old Romanus F. Perry (white), his son-in-law. Motive: the homicide victim had attempted to visit his estranged wife, to whom the killer had given refuge. Price was hanged at Wrightsville on December 12, 1884. Source: *Macon (GA) Telegraph & Messenger*, 9/3/82 (3:3). *Savannah Morning News*, 12/13/84 (1:5). See also: 1880 U.S. Census (Johnson Co., GA), which notes Price. Also see Perry's gravestone in Oaky Grove Primitive Baptist Church Cemetery, Wrightsville.

1885

Peter Johnson (black, age 71) and **Moses Keaton** (black, age 64). *Murder.* Their crime was committed on 12/2/1884 in Mitchell County. Both executed for the ax murders of 28-year-old Stephen Godwin, 39-year-old Malinda Gregory and 18-year-old Richard Gregory (whites), the latter two being a mother and her son. Their throats were also cut to make sure that they were dead. Motive: robbery and mendacity. Keaton confessed that murderous thoughts had first entered their minds when Mr. Godwin took some of their hogs in lieu of rent. They acted on a particularly cold night, using the weather as a pretext to gain entry to Godwin's house by asking and receiving permission to warm themselves by the homeowner's fire. Then they butchered the three inhabitants and plundered the premises. These killers were hanged high at Camilla on April 17, 1885. Source: *Americus (GA) Recorder* (Weekly) 12/26/84 (3:1) and (Daily) 4/21/85 (1:5). See also: 1880 U.S. Census (Mitchell Co., GA), which notes all parties.

Henry Etheridge (black, age 23). *Murder.* The crime was committed on 6/8/1884 in Jones County. Handgun slaying of Tom Clements (black, age not recorded), who was killed on the day that he was to have been married. Motive: rivalry for a female. This jealous suitor was hanged at Gray on June 19, 1885. Source: *Telegraph & Messenger* (Macon, GA), 6/20/85 (1:3). *Savannah Morning News*, 6/20/85 (1:7), which gives the homicide victim's name as "Thomas Clemons."

Robert McCoy (black, age abt. 30). *Murder.* The crime was committed on 11/20/1884 in Screven County. Police killer. Executed for the assassination of James Miller (white, age not specified), the assigned constable for the 80th District of Screven County. He was beaten on the head with a white pine board. Motive: a grudge stemming from a prior arrest. Forensic examination of the decedent proved that he had been struck down from behind. The killer was hanged at Sylvania on June 26, 1885. Source: *Savannah Morning News*, 6/27/85 (1:5). *Atlanta Constitution*, 6/27/85 (1:3).

William McGaughey (black, age not recorded). *Murder.* The crime was committed on 2/12/1885 in Walton County. Uxoricide. Executed for the killing of Mollie McGaughey (black, age not recorded), who was attacked with an ax and a razor and succumbed to her injuries after eighteen agonizing days. Rural Walton County had its third legal hanging in as many years when this killer swung from the gallows there on October 16, 1885. Source: *Weekly Banner-Watchman* (Athens, GA), 2/24/85 (1:3). *Savannah Morning News*, 10/17/85 (1:3).

1886

John Drake (black, age 19). *Murder.* The crime was committed on 12/27/1884 in Upson County. Uxoricide. Executed for the ax murder of Ella Drake (black, age not recorded) and the burning of their cabin with her body inside. Motive: suspected infidelity. This young wife-killer was hanged at Thomaston on March 26, 1886. Source: *Middle Georgia Times* (Thomaston, GA), 3/27/86 (3:3). *Macon (GA) Telegraph*, 3/27/86 (4:4).

Richard Townsend (black, age 22). The crime was committed on 12/25/1885 in Lowndes County. Police killer, etc. Gunshot slaying of 53-year-old George Washington Epperson (white), the sheriff of Bradford Co., FL. Motive: resisting arrest. Epperson had traced Townsend to a cabin four miles north of Valdosta. Townsend was at that time the prime suspect in the murder and robbery of a Jewish man near Starke, FL. He was subsequently executed at Valdosta on July 16, 1886. Source: *Waycross (GA) Headlight*, 1/6/86 (1:5). *Atlanta Constitution*, 7/17/86 (5:1). See also: 1880 U.S. Census (Bradford Co., FL), which notes G. W. Epperson.

Willis Hudson (white, age 28). *Murder.* The crime was committed on 8/2/1885 in Clay County. Shotgun slaying of Marion Millirons (white, age not recorded). Motive: brawling on a plantation. The killer was executed at Fort Gaines on August 7, 1886. Source: *Macon (GA) Telegraph*, 8/8/86 (4:4). See also: 1880 U.S. Census (Early Co., GA), which notes the killer as "Hutson."

Jesse Cook (black, age 25). *Murder.* The crime was committed on 4/30/1885 in Taylor County. Uxoricide. Ax murder of 28-year-old Delia Fowler Cook (black). Motive: she had refused to abscond with him to Alabama in the face of impending court action. This wife killer was hanged at Butler on September 17, 1886. Source: *Macon (GA) Telegraph*, 9/18/86 (4:3). See also: 1880 U.S. Census (Marion Co., GA), which notes both parties.

Frank Humphries (white, age 30). *Murder.* The crime was committed on 3/5/1886 in Baldwin County. Shotgun slayings of 32-year-old Ella Humphries and 43-year-old Carrie Raines (whites), they respectively being his niece and his sister-in-law. Motive: sexual assault. This offender was hanged at Milledgeville on September 24, 1886. Source: *Union and Recorder* (Milledgeville), 3/9/86 (2:2) & 9/28/86 (2:1). *Savannah Morning News*, 9/25/86 (1:5). See also:

1880 U.S. Census (Baldwin Co., GA), which notes all parties.

Henry Norris (white, age 36). *Murder.* The crime was committed on 3/2/1886 in Haralson County. Executed for the malicious killing of George Elliott (white, age not recorded), who was battered to death with a hoe and a shovel. Motive: intellectually and emotionally stunted personality. Both of these men were dirt-poor road sweepers employed at salaries of six dollars per month. They were also described as dullards suited to little else. Norris begrudged Elliott because of an incident that had occurred three years earlier. Elliott had asked Norris for a chew of tobacco. Norris agreed but Elliott spat out the chew, saying that it was of poor quality. This irked Norris, who brooded thereafter for the loss. Three years later the incident was repeated. This time Norris went berserk. He struck Elliott with the hoe with which he had been grubbing along the roadside. He kept up a maniacal hacking with that implement until it broke. Then he snatched up the shovel with which Elliott had been working and used it the same way. The question of the killer's sanity was thoroughly investigated. Rather than crazy, Norris was found to be merely stupid and ill-bred. He was hanged at Buchanan on October 15, 1886. Source: *Macon (GA) Telegraph*, 9/16/86 (4:1). *Savannah Morning News*, 10/16/86 (2:1).

1887

Preston Valentine (black, age 30). *Murder.* The crime was committed on 9/12/1884 in Richmond County. Executed for the killing of 68-year-old William Vales (white), night watchman at the stables of the Augusta Street Railway Company, or horse drawn trolleys as they were then known. Vales was beaten beyond recognition and then set afire while still breathing, the killer having poured kerosene all over him. Motive: burglary. Death on the gallows was the fate of this killer at Augusta on January 21, 1887. Source: *Augusta (GA) Chronicle*, 3/30/86 (8:2) & 1/22/87 (7:1). *Savannah Morning News*, 1/22/87 (1:7). See also: 1880 U.S. Census (Columbia Co., GA), which notes the culprit as "Presley" Valentine.

Jacob Leggett (black, age 19). *Murder.* The crime was committed on 2/21/1887 in Tattnall County. Fatal stabbing of Lillie Grigdon (black, age not recorded), she having been knifed multiple times in the back and sides. Motive: distraught lover. Leggett was hanged at Reidsville on June 17, 1887. Source: *Savannah Morning News*, 6/18/87 (1:4), *Augusta (GA) Chronicle*, 6/16/87 (2:1). See also: 1880 U.S. Census (Beaufort Co., NC), which notes the killer before he came to Georgia.

Fred Morgan (black, age 25). *Murder.* The crime was committed on 12/25/1886 in Jefferson County. Executed for the killing of 24-year-old Emma Lewis (black), who had the back of her head blown off by a shotgun blast and her belly ripped open with a knife. Motive: she had dared to walk out on him. Fred Morgan was hanged at Louisville on June 17, 1887. Source: *Savannah Morning News*, 6/18/87 (1:3). See also: 1880 U.S. Census (Jefferson Co., GA), which notes both parties.

John W. Smith (white, age 33). *Murder.* The crime was committed on 12/31/1884 in Heard County. Handgun slaying of 25-year-old Samuel Bonner Barker (white), who was taken unawares while feeding his livestock and in the presence of his horrified wife. Motive:

feuding. This killer was hanged at Franklin on June 17, 1887. Source: *Savannah Morning News*, 6/18/87 (1:3). See also original trial transcript (State vs. Smith), Heard Superior Court (Sept. Term, 1885), GA State Archives.

Charles Edwards (black, age 30). *Murder.* The crime was committed on 5/29/1887 in Habersham County. Executed for the killing of 23-year-old William Echols (white), who was shot multiple times with a handgun and his head mashed with a club. Motive: rivalry for a prostitute. Edwards was legally hanged at Clarkesville on October 14, 1887. Source: *Macon (GA) Daily Telegraph*, 9/11/87 (3:2). *Savannah Morning News*, 10/15/87 (1:5). See also: 1880 U.S. Census (Habersham Co., GA), which notes Edwards, and 1870 U.S. Census (Habersham Co., GA), which notes Echols.

Tillman C. Justice (white, age 29). *Murder.* The crime was committed on 1/14/1887 in Towns County. Shotgun slaying of 68-year-old James B. Goddard (white), who was blasted in the face (as he knelt begging for his life) and then had his head further mashed with a rock. Motive: Goddard had voiced disapproval of the illicit liquor trade thereabouts. This killer was hanged at Hiawassee on November 18, 1887. Source: *Savannah Morning News*, 11/19/87 (2:2). See also: 1880 U.S. Census (Towns Co., GA), which notes Goddard, plus 1860, 1870 and 1880 U.S. Censuses (Rabun Co., GA), which note "Justis."

1888

Lewis Moore (black, age 26). *Murder.* The crime was committed on 10/2/1887 in Quitman County. Executed for the killing of Ransom Wright (black, age not recorded) who was slashed on the neck, chased down and then finished off by being shot point-blank in the face with a pistol. Motive: rivalry for a female. This black-on-black killer was hanged at Georgetown on February 23, 1888. Source: *Columbus (GA) Enquirer-Sun*, 12/24/87 (1:2) & 2/24/88 (3:1). See also: 1880 U.S. Census (Quitman Co., GA), which notes Moore.

George McDuffie (black, age 39). *Murder.* The crime was committed on 9/13/1887 in Greene County. Shotgun slaying of William Cheney (black, age not recorded), who was ambushed with deliberate purpose. Motive: rivalry for a female. This all-too-common brand of killer was hanged at Greensboro on May 11, 1888. Source: *Macon (GA) Telegraph*, 5/12/88 (1:5). See also: 1880 U.S. Census (Greene Co., GA), which notes McDuffie.

Henry Weaver (black, age not recorded). *Murder.* The crime was committed on 12/29/1887 in Early County. Executed for the malicious killing of another black man named Miles West (age not specified) for the purpose of robbery. Further details of this case are obscure save for the fact that the killer was hanged at Blakely on May 31, 1888. Source: *Macon (GA) Weekly Telegraph*, 1/10/88 (9:1) & 6/5/88 (12:2).

1889

Charles Blackman (black, age 20). *Murder.* The crime was committed on 9/5/1885 in Schley County. Shotgun slaying of 23-year-old Stonewall Jackson Tondee (white), a store clerk who was blasted in the back. Motive: jealousy, or so it was reported. The killer was hanged at Ellaville on January 25, 1889. Source: *Weekly Telegraph & Messenger* (Macon, GA), 9/11/85 (5:3). *Savannah Morning News*, 1/26/89 (2:1). See also: 1880 U.S. Census (Schley Co., GA), which notes both parties.

Edward Williams, alias "Ed Frey" (black, age not recorded). *Murder.* The crime was committed on 7/1/1888 in Cobb County. Uxoricide. Fatal stabbing of Patsy Williams (black, age not recorded). Motive: drunken brutality. Reported to have been a lush and an idler, Williams awoke on the above date to find that no breakfast had been prepared for him. Patsy Williams refused to feed him, saying that he did not deserve it on account of his dissipated ways. An enraged Ed then attacked Patsy with a knife. "I'll kill any damned woman that won't work for me!" shouted Williams when asked why he had done this. He was hanged at Marietta on January 25, 1889. Source: *Marietta (GA) Journal*, 7/5/88 (3:4) & 1/31/89 (1:1).

Will Debill, alias "Joe Dorr" (black, age 28). *Murder.* The crime was committed on 12/12/1888 in Thomas County. Ax murder of Walter Long (black, age not recorded), who was struck down in his own residence while in the act of eating his supper. Motive: jealousy and mendacity. The killer had been a boarder in the victim's home. He was hanged at Thomasville on June 14, 1889. Source: *Thomasville (GA) Times*, 12/15/88 (3:5), 6/8/89 (1:2) & 6/22/89 (1:4).

Alexander Henderson (black, age 27). *Murder.* The crime was committed on 2/16/1889 in DeCatur County. Child killer, etc. Rifle slayings of 34-year-old Amos Jackson and 8-year-old Hettie Jackson (blacks), they being a father and his daughter. Both bodies were thrown into the Flint River, where they were found three weeks later at a point forty miles downstream. Motive: black-on-black hatred. Henderson was hanged at Bainbridge on June 14, 1889. Source: *Bainbridge (GA) Democrat*, 2/21/89 (3:2), 3/14/89 (3:4), 5/30/89 (3:4) & 6/20/89 (3:5). See also: 1880 U.S. Census (DeCatur Co., GA), which notes the homicide victims, and 1880 U.S. Census (Mitchell Co., GA), which notes the killer as "Aleck" Henderson.

John Pickett, alias "Charlie Cooper" (black, age 19). *Murder.* The crime was committed on 2/26/1889 in Lee County. Executed for the ax murders of 49-year-old Nelson Brooks and 59-year-old Rhoda Brooks (blacks), a married couple. Motive: despoilment. Pickett was infatuated with 29-year-old Matilda Hicks (black), a young woman who was living with Nelson Brooks and wife as their foster daughter. Failing to entice her away, Pickett butchered her benefactors, plundered their home and carried off "Tilda" by force. He was legally hanged at Leesburg on June 14, 1889. Source: *Atlanta Constitution*, 6/15/89 (3:3). See also: 1880 U.S. Census (Lee Co., GA), which notes the homicide victims.

Hardy Hamilton (black, age not recorded). *Murder.* The crime was committed on 2/5/1889 in Floyd County. Executed for the ax murder of Joe Lee (Chinese, age not recorded), the owner of "a thriving laundry business" located at No. 5 Third Avenue in Rome. Motive: burglary. This killer was legally hanged in that city on June 19, 1889. Source: *Macon (GA) Telegraph*, 2/7/89 (1:6) & 6/20/89 (1:3).

Frank Blount (black, age 30). *Murder.* The crime was committed on

5/20/1889 in Lowndes County. Handgun slaying of another black man named William Miller (age not recorded), who was shot in the back in addition to being stabbed. It was the bullet that actually killed Miller. Motive: fracas on an excursion train. Blount was hanged for this felony at Valdosta on July 26, 1889. Source: *Savannah Morning News*, 5/22/89 (8:1). *Atlanta Constitution*, 7/27/89 (3:3). *Macon (GA) Telegraph*, 7/27/89 (2:5).

Willie Williams (black, age not recorded). *Murder.* The crime was committed on 6/12/1889 in Wilcox County. Handgun slaying of 28-year-old Bartow S. Whigham (white), a railroad conductor. Motive: the homicide victim had tried to stop the killer from stealing a ride on his train. Williams was a fugitive at that time. He had escaped from the Lake Co., Florida, jail where he was facing prosecution for another murder: that of a black man named Nelse Durham. He was hanged at Abbeville on November 8, 1889. Source: *Macon (GA) Telegraph*, 11/9/89 (2:3). Also see Whigham's gravestone in Mount Olive Cemetery, Cusseta.

James David Vann, known to some as "Pigg Vann" (white, age 30). *Murder.* The crime was committed on 5/1/1888 in Chattooga County. Handgun slaying of another white man named North H. White (age not recorded). Motive: the homicide victim said (or was reported to have said) that Vann had organized a lynching. This killer was legally hanged at Summerville on November 8, 1889. Source: *Macon (GA) Telegraph*, 5/1/88 (4:1), 5/2/88 (1:5), 5/7/88 (3:1) & 11/9/89 (2:3). See also Vann's rather well-preserved gravestone in the Vann Family Cemetery, Coosa.

1890

Philmore Bell (black, age 29). *Murder.* The crime was committed on 5/31/1889 in Jefferson County. Shotgun slaying of 22-year-old James L. Evans (white). Motive: Evans got in his way. The killer was really gunning for someone else. This proved a costly mistake indeed when Bell was legally hanged for it at Louisville on January 3, 1890. Source: *Savannah Morning News*, 1/4/90 (1:4). See also: 1870 U.S. Census (DeCatur Co., GA), which notes the executed man as "Fillmore" Bell and 1880 U.S. Census (McDuffie Co., GA), which notes Evans.

James Butts (black, age not recorded) and **Edward Johnson** (black, age not recorded). *Murder.* Their crime was committed on 10/26/1889 in Houston County. Ax murder of 61-year-old William Miller (white) and concomitant attempted murder of that man's wife. Motive: robbery and home invasion. Both offenders were described as "professional gamblers" (sometimes called "payday sharks") who used to go from work camp to work camp for the purpose of fleecing their fellow blacks out of their hard-earned pay packets. The homicide victim in this case was a farmer who was said to have drawn money from a nearby bank with the intention of using it to pay his laborers the following day. Butts and Johnson thought that it would be easier to steal that cash outright rather than go through the trouble of hustling for it. They were hanged at Perry on February 13, 1890. Source: *Macon (GA) Telegraph*, 10/28/89 (1:3), 11/3/89 (2:5), 1/12/90 (1:3) & 2/14/90 (1:3). See also: 1880 U.S. Census (Pulaski Co., GA), which notes Mr. Miller.

Will Hicks (black, age 21) and **Robert McCoy** (black, age 19). *Murder*. Their crime was committed on 11/6/1889 in Clinch County. Ax murders of 74-year-old William H. Hughes and 59-year-old Nellie Hughes (whites), a married couple. Motive: robbery and home invasion. These young predators were legally hanged at Homerville on April 3, 1890. Source: *Savannah Morning News*, 4/4/90 (2:1). See also: 1880 U.S. Census (Clinch Co., GA), which notes Mr. & Mrs. Hughes.

Robert Hill (black, age 32). *Murder.* The crime was committed on 2/6/1890 in Warren County. Handgun slaying of 29-year-old Alexander Rogers (white). Motive: burglar caught in the act. Hill was hanged at Warrenton on May 9, 1890. Source: *Macon Weekly Telegraph*, 5/14/90 (5:3). *Savannah Morning News*, 5/10/90 (1:5). See also: 1870 U.S. Census (Warren Co., GA), which notes Hill, and 1880 U.S. Census (Warrenton, GA), which notes Rogers.

Edward Morrison (black, age 18). *Murder.* The crime was committed on 8/16/1890 in Madison County. Handgun slaying of 20-year-old Henry Hunter (white). Motive: insolence. Hunter was in charge of the dray animals at a railroad work camp. He had reproved Morrison for ferociously whipping a mule. Morrison's reply was a tirade of foul language. Hunter approached Morrison several hours later and asked him if he really meant all the nasty things that he had said. Morrison's response to that was to pull out a pistol and shoot Hunter dead. He was legally hanged for this at Danielsville on October 17, 1890. Source: *Athens (GA) Weekly Banner*, 8/19/90 (1:6) & 8/26/90 (3:3). *Savannah Morning News*, 10/18/90 (2:1). See also: 1880 U.S. Census (Oconee Co., GA), which notes a very young Henry Hunter.

Thomas George Woolfolk (white, age 27). *Murder.* The crime was committed on 8/6/1887 in Bibb County. Mass killer. Patricide. Child killer. Baby killer. Executed for the massacre of nine people (with an ax) as they lay asleep in their beds. The victims (all white) consisted of his father: Richard Franklin Woolfolk (age 52), his stepmother Mattie Howard Woolfolk (age 40) and his six siblings of the half blood: Richard Franklin Woolfolk, Jr. (age 20), Pearl Woolfolk (age 17), Annie Woolfolk (age 10), Rosebud Woolfolk (age 7), Charles Woolfolk (age 5) and Mattie Woolfolk (age 18 months). The ninth homicide victim was a visiting aunt from Americus named Temperance West (age 84), who happened to be in the wrong place at the wrong time. Venue changed from Bibb County to Houston County. Motive: apparently a long-smoldering resentment. Woolfolk's father had been twice married. His first wife (with whom he had had Thomas) died in 1865. The elder Woolfolk soon remarried and produced six more children by his second spouse. Eldest son Thomas seems to have watched this scenario unfold with mounting disenchantment as the years went by. He did not get along with his stepmother. Thomas probably regarded her and her offspring as interlopers. She for her own part may well have regarded her stepson as an obstacle to the inheritance rights of her own brood. Whatever the case, this situation festered for 20 years before Thomas finally snapped. He never admitted his guilt, but revisionist attempts to exculpate him are not convincing. Tom Woolfolk was found to have flecks of blood in his ears and in his hair but none upon his clothes. It was determined that he had paused to wash the other parts of his person and to change his apparel before alerting the nearest neighbor on the night of the murders. The missing clothes were found in a weighted bundle at the bottom of the Woolfolk family well. They were putrid with what appeared to be bloody gore. These were not deemed to be the kinds of things that an innocent person would do. Furthermore, the suspect showed an emotional detachment to the entire situation, indeed to such a degree that he probably considered himself justified in doing what he was alleged to have done. The generally accepted version of events is that Tom Woolfolk grew to despise his father for raising a second family and felt himself being shunted further and further down the domestic pecking order. He also hated that second family itself and felt that it had no right to exist. Hence his motive for mass murder. He was hanged at Perry on October 29, 1890. Source: *Macon (GA) Telegraph*, 8/7/87 (1:1), 8/8/87 (1:1) & 10/30/90 (1:1). *Savannah Morning News*, 10/30/90 (1:1).

Will Bethea (black, age 26). *Murder.* The crime was committed on 3/18/1890 in Johnson County. Handgun slaying of Robert Raiford (white, age not recorded), a lumber inspector who was shot in the face at point-blank range. Motive: the killer resented having been fired from his job. Bethea was legally hanged at Wrightsville on November 7, 1890. Source: *Macon (GA) Telegraph*, 3/23/90 (1:1) & 11/8/90 (1:3). *Atlanta Constitution*, 3/19/90 (2:2) & 11/8/90 (1:4). See also: 1880 U.S. Census (Wash. Co., GA), which notes Bethea.

Alonzo Evans (black, age 28). *Murder.* The crime was committed on 6/26/1889 in Bulloch County. Gunshot slaying of 32-year-old Henry J. Dutton (white) in a work-related incident. Motive: he resented being fired from his job. This killer was legally hanged at Statesboro on November 21, 1890. Source: *Macon (GA) Weekly Telegraph*, 7/3/89 (6:4). *Augusta (GA) Chronicle*, 11/12/90 (5:6). *Savannah Morning News*, 11/22/90 (8:1). See also: 1880 U.S. Census (Screven Co., GA), which notes Evans, and 1880 U.S. Census (Bulloch Co., GA), which notes Dutton.

Henry Moore (black, age not recorded). *Murder.* The crime was committed on 2/2/1889 in Wayne County. Shotgun slaying of an unidentified wayfarer (white male, age unknown), who was a peddler to all appearances. The homicide victim was blasted from behind when he attempted to run away. Motive: enigmatic. There was no evidence of robbery. Moore's accomplice (who testified against him) claimed that they had mistaken the white man for a fugitive criminal. Exactly why they chose to shoot the man in the back, however, was never satisfactorily explained. Henry Moore was hanged for this crime at Jesup on November 21, 1890. Source: *Atlanta Constitution*, 2/5/89 (2:1). *Savannah Morning News*, 11/22/90 (1:7).

Lewis Watson (black, age not recorded). *Murder.* The crime was committed on 9/21/1890 in Worth County. Executed for the killing (by unspecified means) of another black man named Jack Curry (age not recorded). Motive: the homicide victim had slapped the killer's wife. The men's spouses had had an argument. Both women ran crying to their husbands. Curry got drawn into the spat and defended his own wife with the flat of his hand as well as the power of speech. Watson didn't like this and reacted with a physical display of his own. It earned him a long drop from the gallows at Sylvester on December 5, 1890. Source: *Savannah Morning News*, 12/6/90 (3:3). *Worth Local* (Sylvester, GA), 12/13/90 (3:2).

Charles Williams (black, age not recorded). *Murder.* The crime was committed sometime during the year 1890 in Charlton County. Uxoricide. This man was legally hanged at Folkston on December 19, 1890, for the killing of his wife. She was presumably a black female. The trial record is lost and no further details have been forthcoming. Source: *Savannah Morning News*, 12/20/90 (2:3).

1891

Charles Reeves (black, age not recorded). *Murder.* The crime was committed on 2/1/1890 in McIntosh County. Shotgun slaying of 45-year-old Theodore Gronwald (white), a storekeeper. Motive: a dispute about store credit. Reeves had only one arm but was still able to heft a double-barreled breech loader. The gallows gave him its own brand of equal justice for the handicapped when he was hanged at Darien on January 15, 1891. Source: *Macon (GA) Telegraph*, 2/22/90 (2:4). *Savannah Morning News*, 1/16/91 (2:1). *Darien (GA) Timber Gazette*, 2/8/90 (3:2) & 1/17/91 (3:4). See also: Mr. Gronwald's burial record: St. Andrew's Cemetery, Darien.

Rena Turner (black, age 20). *Murder.* The crime was committed on 10/20/1890 in Clay County. Handgun slaying of 22-year-old Thomas Glenn (black). Motive: obnoxious drunk. Turner had swaggered through the streets of Fort Gaines barking defiance at anyone who crossed his path. Thomas Glenn did not move fast enough to get out of his way. Turner made his last public appearance in that same town when he was hanged there on April 21, 1891. Source: *Atlanta Constitution*, 4/22/91 (2:1). See also: 1880 U.S. Census (Clay Co., GA), which notes both parties as minors.

Rufus Moore (black, age 20). *Murder.* The crime was committed on 6/29/1890 in Dade County. Executed for the killing (by unspecified means) of another black man named Henry Slade (age not recorded). Motive: rivalry for a female. No further details of this case have been forthcoming save for the fact that Rufus Moore was hanged at Trenton on May 15, 1891. Source: *Atlanta Constitution*, 5/16/91 (2:4).

Benjamin Chambers (black, age not recorded). *Murder.* The crime was committed on 11/23/1890 in Ware County. Ax murder of another black man named Samuel Strother (age not recorded), who was treacherously attacked from behind. Motive: reneging on a deal. Both men were laborers at a turpentine camp. Chambers quit the job and bartered his cabin furnishings to Strother. However, when Strother came to collect the goods, Chambers abruptly changed his mind. He lost his temper when Strother said that the deal was irrevocable. Then he took up an ax when Strother momentarily turned his back. Chambers was hanged for this homicide at Waycross on May 22, 1891. Source: *Columbus (GA) Enquirer-Sun*, 11/26/90 (2:3). *Savannah Morning News*, 5/23/91 (2:1). *Macon (GA) Telegraph*, 4/18/91 (3:3) & 5/23/91 (1:5).

Samuel Snelling (black, age 20). *Murder.* The crime was committed on 4/14/1884 in Randolph County. Executed for the killing of 32-year-old Seaborn Batts (black), who was struck on the head with the blade of a hoe, the culprit lying in wait. Motive: Snelling didn't take to being scolded about the way he had yoked some oxen. Snelling fled in the aftermath of this crime. He remained at large for six years. Lawmen almost caught him on 5/18/1887 when he was traced to a Randolph County shanty. But Snelling got the drop on his pursuers by opening fire on them with a .32-caliber pistol. Slain on that occasion was Edward B. Skipper (white, age 40), a bailiff who was in quest of a $150 reward that had been posted for the fugitive. Snelling was finally nabbed at Albany on 6/17/1890. He was legally hanged at Cuthbert on May 28, 1891. Source: *Macon (GA) Telegraph*, 5/29/91 (1:5). See also: 1870 U.S. Census (Quitman Co., GA), which notes Snelling. Also: 1880 U.S. Census (Randolph Co., GA), which notes Batts and 1880 U.S. Census (Taylor Co., GA), which notes Skipper. See also: *Executive Minutes of the Governor of Georgia* (1884), 420.

Sherman Brookins (black, age 24). *Murder.* The crime was committed on 5/1/1890 in Jefferson County. Rifle slaying of 22-year-old Simon Kelley (black). Motive: workplace violence. Brookins was a railroad section hand who couldn't get along with his fellow workers. He went to their trackside camp armed with a borrowed Winchester and climbed up onto a flat car that was on a siding there. Then he started shooting indiscriminately into the crowd, fatally wounding Kelley. The rifleman (Brookins) was hanged for this at Louisville on June 19, 1891. Source: *Savannah Morning News*, 6/20/91 (1:7). See also: 1880 U.S. Census (Wash. Co., GA), which notes Brookins and 1880 U.S. Census (Jefferson Co., GA), which notes Kelley.

Ezekiel Lemox (white, age 31). *Murder.* The crime was committed on 3/22/1891 in DeCatur County. Uxoricide. Executed for the killing of 32-year-old Georgia Willis Lemox (white), who was gagged and purposely smothered in a rolled-up mattress. Motive: marital breakdown, the killer being a drunk and a loser. He was hanged at Bainbridge on June 26, 1891. Source: *Bainbridge (GA) Democrat*, 3/26/91 (3:3) & 7/2/91 (3:2). See also: 1880 U.S. Census (Colquitt Co., GA), which notes both parties.

George Washington (black, age 24). *Murder.* The crime was committed on 10/7/1890 in Fulton County. Rifle slaying of 25-year-old Ben Oliver (black), who was gunned down on a public street. Motive: big attitude. The killer was a habitual bully who used to brazenly stride through "colored" neighborhoods with a Winchester slung over his shoulder. His particular penchant was to saunter into any "colored" home or business (like he owned the place), brandish his rifle and demand whatever goods or services he desired at gunpoint. This obnoxious character finally went too far on the above date when he gunned down Ben Oliver for no apparent reason. Then true to form, he barged into the nearest "negro dwelling" and ordered the housewife there to cook him a meal while all the while aiming his rifle at her head. The astonished woman dared not refuse because she knew that Washington meant business. It was that delay which enabled police to catch the killer. The black population of Atlanta shed no tears when Washington was hanged there on July 3, 1891. Source: *Atlanta Constitution*, 7/4/91 (6:1). *Columbus (GA) Enquirer-Sun*, 7/4/91 (1:5). *Savannah Morning News*, 7/4/91 (2:1). See also: 1880 U.S. Census (Atlanta, GA), which notes Oliver.

Charles M. Ozburn (white, age 31). *Murder.* The crime was committed on 5/5/1890 in Fulton County. Handgun slaying of 45-year-old John M. Bradley (white), a grocer who was shot six times. Motive: a dispute over 5 pounds of potatoes. This itchy-fingered triggerman was hanged at Atlanta on July 24, 1891. Source: *Atlanta Constitution*, 5/6/90 (7:1). *Macon (GA) Telegraph*, 5/6/90 (2:1). *Savannah Morning News*, 7/25/91 (2:3). See also Mr. Bradley's gravestone in Stone Mountain Cemetery.

Frank Danforth (black, age not recorded). *Murder.* The crime was committed on 6/28/1891 in Richmond County. Executed for the killing of Lizzie Gray (black female, age not recorded), who was found floating in the Savannah River with her throat cut. Motive: lovers' quarrel. A razor was the instrument of death. The slayer was hanged at Augusta on September 4, 1891. Source: *Augusta (GA) Chronicle*, 6/30/91 (5:1). *Savannah Morning News*, 7/4/91 (2:2) & 9/5/91 (1:7).

Albert Morea Ketchen, alias "Albert Grant Morea" (black, age 31). *Murder.* The crime was committed on 3/2/1891 in Chatham County. Uxoricide, etc. Executed for the killing of 20-year-old Rhena Singleton, a.k.a. "Gallie Ketchen" (black), who was fatally slashed with a razor. Motive: she was a grifter. This offender had also murdered his actual wife, Rhena Ketchen (black, age 21), by the same means at Savannah on 11/7/1889. Motive in that case: brutish male jealousy. Ketchen was a fugitive when he slew the second woman (also named Rhena), they having met at Charleston, SC. He was hanged at Savannah on September 18, 1891. Source: *Savannah Morning News*, 11/8/89 (8:1) & 9/19/91 (8:1). See also: 1880 U.S. Census (Beaufort Co. SC), which notes "Rhina" Singleton.

Samuel Greer (black, age 20). *Murder.* The crime was committed on 5/4/1890 in Butts County. Handgun slaying of 19-year-old Wade Yancey (black), who was shot dead at a church service. Motive: the killer's sister had complained to him about the homicide victim's behavior toward her. This irreverent young man was hanged at Jackson on October 16, 1891. Source: *Middle Georgia Argus* (Jackson, GA), 5/6/90 (3:1) & 10/20/91 (2:4). See also: 1880 U.S. Census (Butts Co., GA), which notes both parties.

Alexander Morris (black, age not recorded). *Murder.* The crime was committed on 10/1/1887 in Morgan County. Executed for the killings of 53-year-old Daniel Lockett and 51-year-old Lucy Lockett (blacks), his in-laws. The male victim had the back of his head blown off by a shotgun blast. The woman's throat was cut from ear to ear. Motive: the Locketts had given refuge to the killer's estranged wife. Alexander Morris was hanged at Madison on October 16, 1891. Source: *Macon (GA) Telegraph*, 10/3/87 (1:1). *Savannah Morning News*, 10/17/91 (2:1). See also: 1880 U.S. Census (Morgan Co., GA), which notes the murdered couple.

Abe Wayman (black, age 23). *Murder.* The crime was committed on 6/22/1891 in Dade County. Prison guard killer. Executed for the shotgun slayings of 22-year-old Jesse Rankin and about-30-year-old Patrick Rawlin, a.k.a. "Rowland" (whites), two convict guards (not "trustys") at the Cole City labor camp. Motive: attempted breakout. Recidivist Killer. Wayman was already serving a life sentence for a previous murder when the two guards were assassinated. This had occurred at Savannah on 9/19/1885, the homicide victim being a 27-year-old Greek fruit-monger named John Russo. The Greek gentleman's wife had denounced Wayman (then aged 19) for stealing an apple from their sidewalk array. Hearing of this, the brazen thief returned to the scene and deliberately stabbed Mr. Russo in the heart, killing him instantly. Wayman avoided the gallows probably because he was young and physically fit. He was instead condemned to a lifetime of thralldom in the Dade County mines. This "mercy" wound up costing society two more innocent lives, as noted above. Wayman did not dodge the gallows a second time. He was hanged at Trenton on November 6, 1891. Source: *Macon (GA) Telegraph*, 9/22/85 (6:1). *Knoxville (TN) Journal*, 6/23/91 (1:6). *Atlanta Constitution*, 6/23/91 (5:2), 6/26/91 (1:2) & 6/28/91 (18:4). *Savannah Morning News*, 11/7/91 (1:7) & 11/8/91 (8:2). *State of Dade News* (Trenton, GA), 11/6/91 (3:3). See also: 1880 U.S. Census (Bibb Co., GA), which notes Wayman as a minor. See also: John Rutherford (executed 11/17/93).

Tom Webb (black, age 22). *Rape.* The crime was committed on 7/6/1891 in Washington County. Incipient serial rapist. Executed for an indecent assault on the person of 10-year-old Fannie Smith (white, the daughter of Jasper N. Smith), who was brazenly attacked while hoeing turnips in a field together with her siblings. The culprit fled the scene but turned up in Johnson County eleven days later where he did the same thing to a 10-year-old black girl. Tom Webb was legally hanged at Sandersville on November 6, 1891. Source: *Macon (GA) Weekly Telegraph*, 7/29/91 (3:3) & (6:4). *Savannah Morning News*, 11/7/91 (1:7).

William Blash (black, age 24). *Murder.* The crime was committed on 10/24/1891 in Montgomery County. Shotgun slaying of 49-year-old Thomas Richard Bone (white), who was blasted in the back. Motive: robbery and home invasion. Justice moved with uncommon speed in this case. The killer was legally hanged at Mount Vernon on November 21, 1891. Source: *Macon (GA) Telegraph*, 11/20/91 (2:2) & 11/22/91 (1:5). *Savannah Morning News*, 11/22/91 (1:7). See also: 1850 U.S. Census (Bibb Co., GA), which notes the murdered man as a minor, the son of Richard and Isabella Bone.

1892

Allen Bray (black, age 43). *Murder.* The crime was committed on 9/23/1891 in Troup County. Executed for the beating and manual strangulation of 61-year-old Mary B. Prather (white), allegedly with the aid of two female accomplices. Motive: plunder. Allen Bray was hanged at La Grange on January 8, 1892. Source: *Columbus (GA) Enquirer-Sun*, 9/27/91 (5:1). *Savannah Morning News*, 1/9/92 (2:1). See also: 1880 U.S. Census (Troup Co., GA), which notes both parties.

William McCoy (black, age 22). *Murder.* The crime was committed on or about 9/15/1891 in Liberty County. Handgun slaying of another black man named John W. Bowie (age not recorded), who was shot in his own house. Motive: party crashing. This black-on-black killer was hanged at Hinesville on January 8, 1892. Source: *Savannah Morning News*, 1/9/92 (8:1). See also: Pardon Files Box 80, GA State Archives.

Sol Rowell (black, age 17) and **Bob Richards** (black, age not recorded). *Murder.* Their crime was committed on 1/28/1890 in Calhoun County. Both executed for the handgun slaying of 23-year-old John W. Arnold (white). Motive: race riot. It was on the above date that between 5,000 and 7,000 blacks swarmed the little town of Morgan. They were in an expectant mood. All had come to see the public execution of 21-year-old Polk Newton, a "very likely young negro" who had gunned down another youthful male of his own race who had dared to flirt with his girlfriend. Whiskey wagons dispensed their slop unrestrained during the hours preceding the anticipated public spectacle. Then at a late hour the sheriff received a telegram from the governor of Georgia informing him that Polk Newton's death sentence had been commuted to life at hard labor. The mood of the crowd turned ugly when this news was announced. It was not the fact that they had been deprived of their entertainment that riled this multitude but a belief that the governor's action was a cynical ploy that had nothing to do with mercy. Polk Newton was now headed for a living death in the Dade County mines, a penal colony that made Devil's Island look like a luxury resort. This dreaded abode had a reputation among Georgia blacks for being an accursed place of no return where physically fit young men were sent for the express purpose of working them to death in what amounted to a thinly veiled continuum of slavery. Murmurs of this sort escalated among the crowd at Morgan. Racial lines were drawn. Then fights broke out. So did vandalism. One group of rowdy blacks attacked some white boys, who included the aforenamed John W. Arnold and his two younger brothers. Pistols, knives, brass knuckles and anything else that could be used as weapons came into play. Many people were wounded to varying degrees. John Arnold succumbed to a bullet wound one week later. Several other persons either died or disappeared over the course of the next two years as tension remained high. These subsequent events included the burning of the Calhoun County courthouse on 12/11/1891. Two of the principal rioters—Rowell and Richards—were legally hanged in that county on January 8, 1892. Source: *Macon (GA) Telegraph*, 1/30/90 (1:3) & 2/6/90 (1:5). *Columbus (GA) Enquirer-Sun*, 1/31/90 (1:2) & 2/19/90 (1:5). *Macon Weekly Telegraph*, 12/23/91 (2:4). *Atlanta Constitution*, 1/9/92 (2:1). See also: 1880 U.S. Census (Calhoun Co., GA), which notes Arnold and Newton. Also 1880 U.S. Census (Baker Co., GA), which notes Sol Rowell as "Saul Rowell."

Lucius Dotson (black, age 28). *Murder.* The crime was committed on 9/13/1890 in Chatham County. Executed for the handgun slaying of another black man named Jeff Coates (age not recorded) during the course of a saloon brawl. The case was a clear-cut one with no extenuating circumstances. The killer was hanged at Savannah on January 22, 1892. Source: *Savannah Morning News*, 9/14/90 (8:1) & 1/23/92 (8:1). *Savannah Press*, 1/22/92 (1:2). Pardons Files Box 34, GA State Archives. Also: 1880 U.S. Census (Aiken Co. SC), which notes Dotson.

Charles C. Cummings (black, age 30). *Murder.* The crime was committed on 11/22/1890 in Chatham County. Handgun slaying of about 20-year-old David Williams (black) who was described as "a crippled colored boy." Motive: hard to say. Cummings had come upon a group of blacks who were warming themselves at a campfire. He drove them away for no apparent reason by brandishing a stick and a loaded pistol. Williams did not move fast enough to suit Cummings. The latter then shot Williams in the back. This killer was hanged at Savannah on February 19, 1892. Source: *Savannah Morning News*, 11/24/90 (8:3) & 2/20/92 (8:1).

Walter Cook (black, age 19). *Murder.* The crime was committed on 10/20/1891 in Campbell County. Ax murder of 18-year-old Andrew Kiser (white), whose body was found sprawled on a public road with its head chopped off. Motive: highway robbery. In addition to a rope necklace this crime netted the killer exactly 15 cents. Walter Cook was hanged at Fairburn on April 1, 1892. Source: *Macon (GA) Telegraph*, 10/23/91 (1:4). *Atlanta Journal*, 4/1/92 (1:7). *Atlanta Constitution*, 10/23/91 (7:1) & 10/22/91 (4:6).

Elijah Cheavers (black, age not recorded). *Murder.* The crime was committed on 6/17/1890 in Ware County. Police killer. Rifle slaying of H.A. "Aleck" Culpepper (white, age not recorded), a Ware County deputy. Motive: resisting arrest. Cheavers was legally hanged at Waycross on May 13, 1892. Source: *Macon Weekly Telegraph*, 6/25/90 (6:4). *Savannah Morning News*, 5/14/92 (2:1).

Coleman Wilson (black, age not recorded). *Murder.* The crime was committed on 12/4/1891 in McDuffie County. Ax murder of 58-year-old Daniel Tice Adkins (white). Motive: highway robbery. This killer was sent through the gallows trap at Thomson on May 13, 1892. Source: *The State* (Columbia, SC), 12/15/91 (4:4). *Savannah Morning News*, 5/14/92 (2:2). See also: 1880 U.S. Census (McDuffie Co., GA), which notes Mr. Adkins.

Seaborn Smith (black, age 22). *Rape.* The crime was committed on 12/30/1890 in Newton County. Indecent assault on the person of 12-year-old Leila Aiken (black) under circumstances that were deemed sufficiently depraved to warrant the death penalty. This black-on-black child rapist was legally hanged at Covington on May 20, 1892. Source: *Savannah Morning News*, 5/21/92 (1:7). See also: 1880 U.S. Census (Wilkes Co., GA), which notes the culprit, and 1880 U.S. Census (Newton Co., GA), which notes Miss Aiken.

Edward Banks (black, age 19). *Murder.* The crime was committed on 10/18/1889 in Macon County. Fatal stabbing of 21-year-old William Belvin (black), who was run through the heart with a butcher knife. Motive: fracas in a "colored" diner. Subsequently convicted of capital murder, Edward Banks was hanged at Oglethorpe on June 30, 1892. Source: *Atlanta Constitution*, 10/19/89 (1:4) & 7/1/92 (2:3). See also: 1880 U.S. Census (Macon Co., GA), which notes both parties.

Peter Daniels (black, age not recorded). *Murder.* The crime was committed on 8/5/1891 in Fulton County. Handgun slaying of Sylvia Lyle (black, age not recorded). Motive: jealous suitor. This woman-killer was hanged at Atlanta on July 15, 1892.

Source: *Savannah Morning News*, 7/16/92 (1:4). Pardons Files Box 30, GA State Archives.

Gus Williams (black, age not recorded). *Murder.* The crime was committed on 1/24/1892 in Chatham County. Executed for the murder of August W. Meyer (white), who was set upon by more than five attackers (all black), beaten and stabbed multiple times. At least two of the miscreants were female. Motive: mugging. Williams was the one that didn't get away. He was hanged at Savannah on July 22, 1892. Source: *Savannah (GA) Tribune*, 1/30/92 (3:2). *Savannah Morning News*, 7/23/92 (8:1).

Joe Thomas (black, age 27). *Murder.* The crime was committed on or about 11/30/1891 in Jasper County. Handgun slaying of 51-year-old Wilkes Walker (black). Motive: fracas at a "negro frolic" or social event attended exclusively by black folks. Thomas paid for this at the end of a rope at Monticello on August 19, 1892. Source: *Macon (GA) Telegraph*, 4/4/92 (2:2) & 8/21/92 (1:2). See also: 1880 U.S. Census (Jasper Co., GA), which notes Walker.

Edmond Green (white, age 23). *Murder.* The crime was committed on 8/12/1890 in Fannin County. Gunshot slaying of 32-year-old William O. Keener (white), who was attacked by a four-man hit team wielding rifles and shotguns. Motive: to prevent the homicide victim from testifying in a pending arson case. Edmond Green was the one that didn't get away. He was hanged at Blue Ridge on August 26, 1892. The execution scene was marred when the rope broke and the crowd stampeded. Source: *Marietta (GA) Journal*, 6/4/91 (1:5). *Atlanta Constitution*, 8/27/92 (1:5). See also: 1880 U.S. Census (Fannin Co., GA), which notes Keener.

Roscoe Marable (black, age 24). *Murder.* The crime was committed on 1/17/1891 in Walker County. Executed for the killing of 56-year-old Nehemiah Evitt (white), a storekeeper who was battered to death with a hammer. Motive: robbery. Marable was legally hanged for this at La Fayette on October 6, 1892. Source: *Walker County Messenger*, 1/22/91 (1:6) & 10/13/92 (1:1). See also: 1880 U.S. Census (Sampson Co. NC), which notes the perpetrator before he came to Georgia.

Oran Coney (black, age 34). *Murder.* The crime was committed on 6/8/1891 in Dooly County. Handgun slaying of 35-year-old Moses Morgan (black). Motive: rivalry for a female. This black-on-black killer was hanged at Vienna on October 28, 1892. Source: *Savannah Morning News*, 10/29/92 (2:1). See also: 1880 U.S. Census (Dodge Co., GA), which notes Coney, and 1880 U.S. Census (Macon Co., GA), which notes Morgan.

Willie Bell (black, age 14). *Murder.* The crime was committed on 5/26/1892 in Bibb County. Police killer. Handgun slaying of 33-year-old Benjamin F. Wilder (white), a magistrate's deputy. Motive: resisting arrest. This precocious offender was legally hanged at Macon on November 29, 1892. Source: *Macon (GA) Weekly Telegraph*, 6/15/92 (5:3) & 12/5/92 (3:2). See also Mr. Wilder's gravestone in Ebenezer U.M.C. Cemetery, Macon.

1893

Louis Lewis (black, age abt. 30). *Murder.* The crime was committed on

9/16/1890 in Bibb County. Uxoricide. Handgun slaying of Melinda Lewis (black, age not recorded), the fatal bullet having literally gone in one ear and out the other. Motive: she had sassed him. This wife-killer was hanged at Macon on March 31, 1893. Source: *Weekly Telegraph* (Macon, GA), 9/24/90 (6:5) & 4/3/93 (7:1).

Nathan Smith (black, age not recorded). *Murder.* The crime was committed on 2/2/1893 in Crawford County. Rifle slayings of two black men named Randall Bell (age 51) and Dow Walker (age not recorded). Motive: robbery and home invasion. The shooter was hanged for this at Knoxville on April 28, 1893. Source: *Weekly Telegraph* (Macon, GA), 3/27/93 (8:1). *Savannah Morning News*, 5/1/93 (6:1). *Macon (GA) Telegraph*, 4/29/93 (6:4). See also: 1880 U.S. Census (Crawford Co., GA), which notes "Randal" Bell.

Jesse Yarbrough (black, age not recorded). *Murder.* The crime was committed on or about 11/15/1892 in Columbia County. Shotgun slaying of 17-year-old Jabez Williams (black), who was blasted in the back. Motive: attempted highway robbery. Williams was homeward bound from having sold a wagonload of baled cotton at the Augusta Cotton Exchange. Yarbrough wanted to steal the proceeds of that sale. So he ambushed young Williams on the road only to be prevented from plundering the homicide victim's person because the wagon horses bolted at the sound of the shotgun blast and carried that conveyance (with Williams in it) away beyond his reach. Yarbrough was hanged for this at Appling on May 5, 1893. Source: *Atlanta Constitution*, 5/6/93 (2:3). *Augusta (GA) Chronicle*, 5/6/93 (1:4). See also: 1880 U.S. Census (Columbia Co., GA), which notes Williams as a small child.

Nick Nutting (black, age 19). *Murder.* The crime was committed on 3/21/1893 in Montgomery County. Child killer and police killer. Executed for the fatal shooting of 5-year-old Zerilda Neal (black) during a siege of her family's cabin by two assailants firing a handgun and a Winchester rifle. It is not known exactly which weapon killed the little girl. Motive: an attempt to forcibly collect a small debt. Nutting is confirmed to have also fatally shot town marshal Redd C. Harris (white, age 40) of Forsyth 11 days later while resisting arrest. He was not tried in that case. Nick Nutting was legally hanged at Mount Vernon on May 26, 1893. Source: *Americus (GA) Times-Recorder*, 4/5/93 (4:5) & 5/27/93 (1:7). *Weekly Telegraph* (Macon, GA), 4/10/93 (2:5). *Montgomery Monitor* (Mt. Vernon, GA), 6/1/93 (2:1). See also: 1880 U.S. Census (Montgomery Co., GA), which notes Nutting and "R. C. Harris." See also: Weldon Gordon (executed 9/29/93).

Henry Ramsey (black, age 39). *Murder.* The crime was committed on 10/2/1892 in Richmond County. Police killer. Shotgun slaying of Robert Y. Harris (white, age not recorded), the marshal of Summerville. Motive: resisting arrest. Ramsey died on the gallows for this at Augusta on May 26, 1893. Source: *The State* (Columbia SC), 10/3/92 (1:3). *Savannah Morning News*, 5/27/93 (1:6). See also: 1880 U.S. Census (Richmond Co., GA), which notes the killer.

James Lamar (black, age abt. 30). *Murder.* The crime was committed on 11/23/1892 in McIntosh County. Handgun slaying of 29-year-old Archie Bird (black), who was shot three times in the back. Motive: the homicide victim was slow to pay a 50-cent gambling debt. Lamar came from Laurens County. He was hanged at Darien on June 30, 1893. Source: *Darien (GA) Timber Gazette*, 11/26/92 (3:3). *Darien (GA) Gazette*, 7/1/93 (3:2). *Savannah Morning News*, 7/1/93 (1:5). See also: 1880 U.S. Census (Montgomery Co., GA), which notes the murdered man.

Sumner Racken (black, age not recorded). *Murder.* The crime was committed on 4/27/1893 in Burke County. Executed for the killing of 40-year-old Franklin Moses Francis (white), who was struck down from behind with a wooden singletree; his throat was then cut from ear to ear. Motive: tenant-landlord dispute. Racken was legally hanged for this at Waynesboro on June 30, 1893. Source: *Middle Georgia Progress* (Sandersville, GA), 5/2/93 (1:4). *Savannah Morning News*, 7/1/93 (1:5). *The True Citizen* (Waynesboro, GA), 4/29/93 (3:6) & 7/1/93 (3:3) describes Racken as "a black, slick, greasy villain."

Samuel Thorpe, alias "Sammy the Kid" (black, age 18). *Murder.* The crime was committed on 12/31/1892 in Chatham County. Handgun slaying of a black man named Charles Brinson (age not recorded). Motive: fracas in a "colored gambling house." It was Thorpe's reaction to having lost 50 cents. He was hanged at Savannah on June 30, 1893. Source: *Savannah Morning News*, 7/1/93 (5:1).

Jim Courney, alias "John Lewis" (black, age 28). *Murder.* The crime was committed on 4/2/1893 in Ware County. Fatal stabbing of another black man named Jake Smith (age not recorded). Motive: gambling dispute. This time eight cents was the disputed amount. Jim Courney went to the gallows for this at Waycross on July 28, 1893. Source: *Savannah Morning News*, 7/29/93 (1:5). *Waycross (GA) Weekly Herald*, 8/5/93 (3:3).

Weldon Gordon (black, age 29). *Murder.* The crime was committed on 3/21/1893 in Montgomery County. Child killer. Accomplice in the firearm slaying of 5-year-old Zerilda Neal (black, the daughter of Barney Neal), who was struck in the face by a bullet while her father's cabin was under siege. Motive: strong-arm collection methods. Gordon was hanged for his part in this tragedy at Mount Vernon on September 29, 1893. Source: *Savannah Morning News*, 9/30/93 (1:5). See also: Nick Nutting (executed 5/26/93).

Lucian Manuel (black, age 22), **Hyre Brewington** (black, age 19) and **Hiram Jackson**, alias "Jacobs" (black, age 24). *Murder.* They were also described as "half breed Indians from North Carolina." Their crime was committed on 7/20/1893 in Montgomery County. Handgun slaying of 35-year-old Alexander Peterson (white), a storekeeper who was shot four times. Motive: armed robbery. These three bandits were hanged for this crime against the common peace at Mount Vernon on September 29, 1893. Source: *Montgomery Monitor* (Mt. Vernon, GA), 7/27/93 (2:2). *Macon (GA) Telegraph*, 9/30/93 (1:1). See also Mr. Peterson's gravestone in Peterson Cemetery, Ailey.

Purse Strickland (black, age 20). *Murder.* The crime was committed on 7/18/1893 in Montgomery County. Shotgun slaying of another black man named Jim Locklear (age not recorded), who was blasted in the back as he sat eating his supper. Motive: the killer felt threatened, or so he said. Strickland's dog had gotten into Locklear's cabin and made a mess by rooting up the ashes in the fireplace. Locklear came home to find these strewn all over his floor. Enraged, he fired several shots at the dog with a pistol and said that he would serve its owner the same way. Strickland heard of this and went on the offensive. Strickland was described as a "mongrel" from Robeson Co., NC, with white, black and Native American blood in him. He was hanged at Mount Vernon on September 29, 1893. Source: *Macon (GA) Telegraph*, 9/30/93 (1:1). *Savannah Morning News*, 9/9/93 (3:1) & 9/30/93 (1:5). *Montgomery Monitor* (Mt. Vernon, GA), 7/20/93 (2:1).

John Will Dutton (white, age 36). *Murder*. The crime was committed on 10/29/1890 in Bartow County. Executed for the killing of 20-year-old Sallie Mobbs (white), whose body was found on a roadside stabbed multiple times and with its head knocked in. Motive: unclear. Dutton was a pathological liar and womanizer who played cards for a living. He never admitted his guilt but did acknowledge being present when Mrs. Mobbs was slain. He was hanged at Cartersville on October 20, 1893. Source: *Atlanta Constitution*, 10/1/93 (16:4), 10/20/93 (7:3) & 10/21/93 (4:1). *Courant American* (Cartersville, GA), 10/26/93 (1:1). See also the burial record for Sallie Mobbs at Oak Hill Cemetery, Cartersville.

Isaac Williams (black, age 48). *Murder*. The crime was committed on 3/31/1893 in Morgan County. Shotgun slaying of 35-year-old Harriet Williams (black), his former lover. She was marched along at the point of the murder weapon "in broad daylight" for a considerable distance. Then when she refused to go any further, the killer opened fire with both barrels, blowing off her left breast and the back of her head. He also battered what remained of her mangled person with the stock of that same weapon until it broke in pieces. Motive: the homicide victim had jilted him. Isaac Williams was hanged for this public outrage at Madison on October 27, 1893. Source: *Weekly Banner* (Athens, GA), 10/31/93 (1:5). *Executive Minutes of the Governor of Georgia*, entry dated 4/7/93. Also: 1880 U.S. Census (Morgan Co., GA), which notes both parties.

John Rutherford (black, age 39). *Murder*. The crime was committed on 6/22/1891 in Dade County. Prison guard killer. Accomplice in the shotgun slayings of 22-year-old Jesse Rankin (white) and a second white man named Patrick Rawlin, a.k.a. "Rowland" (age not recorded) at the Cole City penal colony. Motive: attempted breakout. Rutherford was hanged for the part he played in this matter at Trenton on November 17, 1893. Source: *Dade News* (Trenton, GA), 11/17/93 (2:1). *Atlanta Constitution*, 11/18/93 (1:7). See: Abe Wayman (executed 11/6/91).

Will Stanley (black, age 25). *Murder*. The crime was committed on 11/29/1892 in Pike County. Handgun slaying of 32-year-old Martin Thomas (black), who was made to kneel in prayer before being shot. Motive: sore loser in a card game. This black-on-black killer was hanged at Zebulon on November 24, 1893. Source: *Pike County Journal*, 12/2/92 (3:2) & 11/24/93 (3:2). *Atlanta Constitution*, 11/25/93 (3:1). See also: 1880 U.S. Census (Pike Co., GA), which notes Thomas.

Charles Johnston (black, age not recorded). *Murder*. The crime was committed on an unknown date in Emanuel County. Executed for the malicious killing of another black man named William Shields (age not recorded). Motive: rivalry for a female. This is another case for which the court papers seem to be lost. No further details are known except for the fact that Charles Johnston was legally hanged for his crime at Swainsboro on December 1, 1893. Source: *Savannah Morning News*, 12/2/93 (1:5).

1894

Jerry Mumford (black, age abt. 21). *Murder.* The crime was committed on or about 2/15/1890 in Wayne County. Handgun slaying of James Roberts (black, age unknown) in a fit of pique. Motive: the homicide victim had refused to fetch a pail of water for him. Mumford was hanged for this at Jesup on January 26, 1894. Source: *Atlanta Constitution*, 1/27/94 (3:2). *Savannah Morning News*, 1/27/94 (2:3).

Henry Spencer (black, age abt. 35). *Murder*. The crime was committed on 6/28/1893 in Thomas County. Rifle slaying of about 38-year-old Mose Green (black), his brother-in-law. Motive: there are two versions. The first says that Green was slow to pay a dime that he owed to Spencer. The second says that there were hard feelings between the two men because Green suspected Spencer of molesting his daughter. Whatever the case, Henry Spencer was hanged for the crime of capital murder at Thomasville on March 1, 1894. Source: *Daily Times-Enterprise* (Thomasville, GA), 7/11/93 (1:4) & 10/25/93 (1:4). *Weekly Times-Enterprise* (Thomasville, GA), 3/3/94 (3:3).

Henry Miller (black, age 25). *Murder.* The crime was committed on 9/19/1893 in Bibb County. Shotgun slaying of 47-year-old John Braswell (white) as he was homeward bound in his wagon. Motive: highway robbery. The proceeds of this misdeed were a sack of flour, some butcher's meat, a razor and the dead man's eyeglasses. The killer was legally hanged at Macon on May 25, 1894. Source: *Macon Weekly Telegraph*, 9/25/93 (5:4). *Savannah Morning News*, 5/26/94 (1:7). See also: 1880 U.S. Census (Bibb Co., GA), which notes Mr. Braswell.

Frank Coleman (black, age not recorded). *Murder.* The crime was committed on or about 11/30/1893 in Jasper County. Handgun slaying of another black man named William Smith (age not recorded) during the course of a dancehall brawl. This proved a costly mistake for Coleman when he was hanged at Monticello on June 15, 1894. Source: *Atlanta Constitution*, 6/16/94 (3:2). *Jasper County News*, 6/21/94 (3:2). Pardon Files Box 25, GA State Archives.

Alexander Williams (black, age 25). *Murder.* The crime was committed on 7/23/1894 in Elbert County. Handgun slaying of 23-year-old Newton Hampton (black). Motive: rivalry for a female. This black-on-black killer was hanged at Elberton on December 14, 1894. Source: *Elberton (GA) Star*, 7/27/94 (3:4) & 12/21/94 (1:3). *Atlanta Constitution*, 12/15/94 (3:2). *Savannah Morning News*, 12/15/94 (2:1). See also: 1880 U.S. Census (Abbeville Co., SC), which notes Hampton as a minor.

1895

Henry Archer (black, age not recorded). *Murder.* The crime was committed on 5/15/1894 in Screven

County. Ax murder of 28-year-old John A. Jackson (white), a rural storekeeper. Motive: burglary. This ax man was legally hanged at Sylvania on January 11, 1895. Source: *Savannah Morning News*, 1/12/95 (2:4). See also: 1880 U.S. Census (Screven Co., GA), which notes Mr. Jackson as a minor.

Harrison Stevens (black, age 29). *Murder.* The crime was committed on or about 10/10/1894 in Terrell County. Executed for the killing of 36-year-old Jacob Greene Wells (white), who was found to have been shot more than 50 times with rifle bullets, handgun bullets and buckshot. He had apparently been abducted and brought to the edge of a swamp by more than one person for the deliberate purpose of murdering him. Early speculation was that Wells had paid the price for betraying the secrets of a Klan-like organization. Exactly how Stevens got blamed for it requires further research. Harrison Stevens was legally hanged at Dawson on January 30, 1895. Source: *Americus (GA) Times-Recorder*, 10/20/94 (5:3). *Dawson (GA) News*, 2/6/95 (1:1). See also: 1880 U.S. Census (Terrell Co., GA), which notes both parties.

Will Murray (black, age 25). *Murder.* The crime was committed on 8/9/1894 in Sumter County. Executed for the killing of 26-year-old Willie J. Sims (white), who was struck on the head with the blade of a hoe. Motive: big attitude. The homicide victim had been assigned to supervise a road crew. He reprimanded Murray for being "loud and boisterous." Murray's spiteful response to this was to strike at Sims from behind as soon as his back was turned. It proved to be the worst mistake he ever made. Will Murray was legally hanged at Americus on February 8, 1895. Source: *Americus Times-Recorder*, 8/10/94 (8:3), 8/17/94 (5:2) & 2/9/95 (4:3). See also: 1880 U.S. Census (Sumter Co., GA), which notes both parties as minors.

Jabez Wiggins (black, age not recorded). *Murder.* The crime was committed on 12/23/1894 in Richmond County. Police killer, etc. Executed for the handgun slaying of Joseph Murray (white, age not specified), an Augusta policeman. Motive: resisting arrest. Trouble had broken out the previous day in Edgefield Co., SC, when Wiggins waylaid and killed a 22-year-old fellow of his own color named Anderson Williams, presumably with one of the pistols that he was known to carry. He then fled across the river to Augusta and hid out there in the house of his sister. Angry blacks traced his whereabouts and reported the matter to local police. Officer Murray was sent to the scene. Wiggins dashed out the front door, firing as he ran. Two bullets hit Murray in the face, killing him instantly. The killer then ran up the street with a pistol in each hand. He fired indiscriminately at anything that moved. In so doing he fatally wounded a white man named John Davis, age 60+, who had come to town to visit his relatives for Christmas. This three-time killer was hanged at Augusta on February 8, 1895. Source: *The State* (Columbia, SC), 12/24/94 (1:6). *Savannah Morning News*, 2/9/95 (5:1). See also: 1880 U.S. Census (Edgefield Co., SC), which notes Williams.

George Egan, alias "Joe Dean" (black, age abt. 23). *Murder.* The crime was committed on 12/1/1894 in Campbell County. Mutilation killing of 55-year-old Anselm Leigh (white), a farmer who was lured from his house by means of a contrived story. The killer struck Mr. Leigh down from behind with a rock and then reportedly cut him up "Jack the Ripper" style. Motive: robbery and attempted home invasion. The gallows added this culprit to its tally at Fairburn on March 1, 1895. Source: *Macon (GA) Telegraph*, 12/3/94 (1:6) & 3/2/95 (1:5). *Executive Minutes of the Governor of Georgia*, entry dated 12/4/94. See also: 1880 U.S. Census (Campbell Co., GA), which notes Mr. Leigh.

Washington Strong (black, age 26). *Murder.* The crime was committed on 12/1/1890 in Pulaski County. Handgun slaying of 28-year-old Johnson Duncan (black). Motive: gambling dispute. This killer went through the gallows trap at Hawkinsville on March 15, 1895. Source: *Atlanta Constitution*, 12/8/90 (4:4). *Macon (GA) Telegraph*, 3/16/95 (1:6). See also: 1880 U.S. Census (Houston Co., GA), which notes Duncan, and 1880 U.S. Census (Pulaski Co., GA), which notes Strong.

Richard Gates (black, age not recorded). *Murder.* The crime was committed on an unknown date in Troup County. Executed for the unmitigated killing of another black man named Lee Sledge. Motive: speculative. Court papers for this case cannot be found, so details remain obscure. The condemned man was legally hanged at La Grange on April 5, 1895. Source: *Atlanta Constitution*, 4/6/95 (3:4).

Jerry Jeffries (black, age 22). *Murder.* The crime was committed on 12/1/1894 in Brooks County. Police killer. Rifle slaying of "Tip" Mauldin (white, age not specified), a Brooks County constable. Motive: racial antagonism. Payday at the turpentine camps found most of the laborers (nearly all of them black males) drinking and gambling their money. Constable Mauldin rode up to one such group on horseback and announced that he had an arrest warrant for one of their number. The crowd defied him with liquor-fueled bravado. Taunts of every kind were aimed at the lawman. Mauldin deemed it prudent to temporarily withdraw until he could summon assistance. As he turned to ride away, however, Jerry Jeffries shot him in the back with a Winchester rifle. This was bad enough, but a gang of blacks had the effrontery to return to the scene of the crime a day or two later and perform what was described as a "war dance" around the spot where Mauldin had been slain. The law-abiding segment of local citizenry could take no more. A three hundred-man posse was organized for the purpose of making these acts of belligerence very dear ones to the offenders. At least one white man and seven blacks are known to have been killed in the ensuing conflict. Jerry Jeffries was run to earth but spared from summary justice. He faced a court of law and had the sentence of death legally imposed on him. A huge assembly was on hand to watch him swing at Quitman on April 5, 1895. Source: *Daily Times-Enterprise* (Thomaston, GA), 12/6/94 (2:2). *Macon (GA) Telegraph*, 12/24/94 (1:3). *Atlanta Constitution*, 4/6/95 (3:3).

Eddie Westbrook (black, age 16). *Murder.* The crime was committed on 9/19/1894 in Sumter County. Shotgun slaying of 15-year-old Will Mixon (black), the blast having hit him in the eyes so that the upper half of his head was blown off. Motive: big attitude. Trigger-finger Westbrook was legally hanged at Americus on May 3, 1895. Source: *Americus Times-Recorder*, 9/21/94 (8:2) & 5/4/95 (4:5). *Atlanta Constitution*, 5/4/95 (3:3). See also: 1880 U.S. Census (Sumter Co., GA), which notes both parties as babies aged 2 and 1. The local newspaper erroneously gives "Nixon" as the killer's surname and "about 21" as his age.

Irwin Bush, alias "Birch" (black, age not recorded). *Murder.* The crime was committed on an unknown date in Tattnall County. Executed for the malicious killing of another black man named John Caldwell (age not specified). Motive: speculative. The court papers for this case are lost, but the condemned man is confirmed to have been legally hanged at Reidsville on May 31, 1895. Source: *Savannah Morning News*, 5/28/95 (2:2) & 6/1/95 (6:3).

George McCrary (black, age not recorded). *Murder.* The crime was committed on an unknown date in Meriwether County. This little-known case presents a puzzle. All that is certain about it is that McCrary was a black-on-black killer and that he was legally hanged at Greenville on October 25, 1895. One newspaper says that he murdered his wife while another one says that the homicide victim was a black man named Billy Mills, alias "Will Mims." Research efforts to sort this out were futile. Source: *Atlanta Constitution*, 10/26/95 (3:1). *Columbus (GA) Enquirer-Sun*, 10/26/95 (1:6).

Amanda Cody (black female, age not recorded) and **Florenz English** (black male, age not recorded). *Murder.* Their crime was committed on 5/13/1895 in Warren County. Ax murder of Cicero Cody (black, the husband of Amanda), who was butchered in his bed and buried in a shallow grave. Motive: adultery. These guilty lovers were hanged at Warrenton on November 22, 1895. Source: *Macon (GA) Telegraph*, 11/18/95 (4:2). *Savannah Morning News*, 11/23/95 (2:1).

1896

John Jackson (black, age not recorded). *Murder.* The crime was committed on 10/18/1895 in Randolph County. Executed for the killing of 39-year-old George Rawson (black), whose skull was fractured by the blade of a hoe. The two men had gotten into an argument while they were working the fields. Jackson chased Rawson until the latter got caught up in a wire fence. Then he hacked at him with the hoe. Rawson died at the scene. Jackson was hanged at Cuthbert on January 10, 1896. Source: *Americus (GA) Times-Recorder*, 10/20/95 (1:8) & *Atlanta Constitution*, 1/11/96 (3:3). See also: 1880 U.S. Census (Randolph Co., GA) which notes Geo. Rawson.

William Seymour Keener (white, age 27). *Murder.* The crime was committed on 6/23/1895 in Rabun County. Handgun slayings of 19-year-old Lilly Etta Moore and 17-year-old Laura Moore (whites, sisters), they being his cousins, or so it was reported. Motive: the older girl had refused to commit incest with him. Keener lay in wait for these females and sprang upon them with a pistol in each hand. Lilly Etta Moore was shot seven times. The killer was hanged at Clayton on February 14, 1896. Source: *Savannah (GA) Tribune*, 6/29/95 (4:3). *Atlanta Constitution*, 2/15/96 (1:4). See also: 1880 U.S. Census (Rabun Co., GA), which notes all parties.

Greene Waters (black, age not recorded). *Murder.* The crime was committed on 9/6/1895 in Meriwether County. Uxoricide. Fatal stabbing of Cindy Waters (black, age not recorded), she having been knifed multiple times. Motive: ongoing spousal abuse. The killer had very nearly done away with his wife on a prior occasion as well. In that incident he had used the butt of a shotgun to batter the harried woman on the head and body. The loaded weapon discharged, taking a chunk out of her rear end. Greene Waters finally succeeded in killing his wife. He was hanged at Greenville on April 24, 1896. Source: *Atlanta Constitution*, 4/25/96 (2:6). *Meriwether Vindicator* (Greenville, GA), 9/13/95 (4:2) & 5/1/96 (4:3).

Arthur Hanye (white, age 25). *Murder.* The crime was committed on 3/7/1896 in Fulton County. Executed for the fatal stabbing of 28-year-old Will Spinks (white), his longtime buddy. Motive: saloon brawl. On 11/12/1888 this same pair—Hanye and Spinks—had killed an Italian fruit vender named Amore Christofini (age not specified) on an Atlanta sidewalk by cracking him on the head with a heavy stick. The Italian man had caught them stealing his bananas. Both were acquitted at trial in an obvious case of jury nullification, the factors being their youth, the timely death of Hanye's mother that same week, and possibly anti–Catholic sentiment. It can be argued that justice did indeed overtake them, albeit perversely. Arthur Hanye was hanged by the neck until dead at Atlanta on September 4, 1896. Source: *Macon (GA) Telegraph*, 11/16/88 (2:1). *Atlanta Constitution*, 3/8/96 (20:6), 3/10/96 (2:5), 3/11/96 (5:3) & 9/5/96 (1:7).

1897

Sankey Cunningham (black, age not recorded). *Rape.* The crime was committed on 12/3/1896 in Dougherty County. Indecent assault on the person of 31-year-old Katie Camp (white), she having barely survived. The culprit was a so-called "trusty" on the Dougherty County chain gang. He took advantage of his privileged position to break into the woman's house, rape her in a particularly ferocious manner and beat her on the head with an iron pipe, leaving her for dead. He was legally hanged at Albany on New Year's Day 1897. Source: *Americus (GA) Times-Recorder*, 12/5/96 (4:4). *Macon (GA) Telegraph*, 1/2/97 (1:6). See also: 1900 U.S. Census (Baldwin Co., GA), which notes Katie Camp as an inmate of the Georgia State Sanitarium at Milledgeville. Her injuries had apparently left her brain damaged and unable to care for herself.

Jake Burney (black, age not recorded). *Murder.* The crime was committed on 1/18/1896 in Lowndes County. Executed for the fatal stabbing of another black man named Tom Butler (age not specified). Motive: speculative. Few details can now be confirmed other than the fact that Jake Burney was legally hanged at Valdosta on January 22, 1897. Source: *Tifton (GA) Gazette*, 1/31/96 (1:2). *Thomasville (GA) Times-Enterprise*, 1/24/97 (2:1).

William Deas (black, age 14). *Rape.* The crime was committed on 10/10/1896 in Jefferson County. Indecent assault on the person of a white female named Ella Lawson (age not specified), who was attacked as she walked along some railroad tracks. The precocious culprit had walked up to Miss Lawson and offered her a nickel for consensual sex. Appalled by such impudence, she indignantly rebuffed him. Deas then resorted to force. He was legally hanged for this at Louisville on February 26, 1897. Source: *News and Farmer* (Louisville, GA), 3/4/97 (1:5). *The State* (Columbia SC), 2/27/97 (8:3). Pardon Files Box 32, GA State Archives.

George Elder (black, age 31). *Murder.* The crime was committed on 4/17/1896 in Oconee County. Shotgun slaying of Robert Jones, a.k.a. "Bob Jeans" (black, age not recorded). Motive: the homicide victim had tried to shield his son from the killer's anger. George Elder was legally hanged at Watkinsville on March 26, 1897. Source: *Macon (GA) Telegraph*, 4/19/96 (2:4). *Atlanta Constitution* (Evening Edition), 3/26/97 (1:1). Appeal: 26 SE 80. See also: 1880 U.S. Census (Oconee Co., GA), which notes Elder.

Lovett Brookins (black, age not recorded). *Murder.* The crime was committed on 6/9/1896 in Jefferson County. Executed for the killings (by unknown means) of 39-year-old Sanders Oliphant (black) and a woman of the same color named Lelia McCrary (age not recorded). Motive: love triangle. This double murderer was hanged at Louisville on April 16, 1897. These matters were passed over in silence by this county's home newspaper (if it can be called such) because its editor did not regard black-on-black murders as worthy of note. Source: *Macon (GA) Telegraph*, 6/11/96 (2:3). *Atlanta Journal*, 4/17/97 (3:6). See also: 1880 U.S. Census (Jefferson Co., GA), which notes Sanders Oliphant.

Linton Finney, alias "Treadwell" (black, age not recorded). *Murder.* The crime was committed on 11/14/1896 in Oglethorpe County. Shotgun slaying of 25-year-old Julius Hardy (white), a storekeeper. Motive: robbery. Sentence of death was carried out in this case at Lexington on May 21, 1897. Source: *Oglethorpe Echo* (Lexington, GA), 11/20/96 (5:4), 12/5/96 (5:4) & 5/28/97 (5:4). *Columbus (GA) Enquirer-Sun*, 11/15/96 (4:4). *Atlanta Journal*, 5/21/97 (1:6). See also: 1880 U.S. Census (Chatham Co., GA), which notes Hardy as a young lad.

Elijah Morton (black, age not recorded). *Murder.* The crime was committed on 3/7/1897 in Telfair County. Rifle slayings of a married couple named Charles and Ellen Cromartie (blacks, ages not recorded), his in-laws. The woman was murdered in her bed. Motive: wrathful son-in-law. Morton blamed the homicide victims for the breakup of his marriage rather than his own abusive ways. He was hanged at MacRae on May 21, 1897. Source: *Macon (GA) Telegraph*, 5/22/97 (3:1). *New York Times*, 5/5/97 (3:2) & 5/22/97 (3:7).

Henry White (white, age 19). *Murder.* The crime was committed on 10/14/1896 in Muscogee County. Police killer. Executed for the rifle slaying of William Jackson (white, age not specified), a Columbus policeman. Two other officers were also slain relative to the same incident. Trouble began when James A. White (age 44) and Henry White (father and son) strode into a Columbus saloon, hankering for conflict. The elder White was a former police officer of that city who had been "dismissed from the force" some years earlier and had borne a grudge about it ever since. Somebody in the saloon called the police. Officers Richard M. Adams (white, age 49) and William Jackson responded to the call. They were shot dead by the rifle-toting Whites as they approached the swinging doors of the saloon. An angry crowd then chased these killers through the streets until the Whites gained the refuge of their home. A furious gun battle erupted as the crowd besieged the place. A third Columbus policeman named Charles J. Roberts (white, age not specified) was slain in this melee, as was James A. White. The mob dragged the latter's body out of the bullet-riddled house and vented their fury on it. Henry White somehow managed to slip away and get across the river to Alabama. He was caught a few hours later. The three dead policemen were buried in Linwood Cemetery. Henry White was hanged by the neck until dead at the Muscogee County jail on June 4, 1897. Source: *Columbus (GA) Enquirer-Sun*, 10/16/96 (3:1). *Atlanta Constitution*, 6/5/97 (1:5). See also: 1880 U.S. Census (Muscogee Co., GA), which notes Officer Adams and the killers.

Thomas Delk (white, age 24). *Murder.* The crime was committed on 4/2/1896 in Pike County. Police killer. Executed for the rifle slaying of 53-year-old William O. Gwyn (white), the sheriff of Pike County. Motive: resisting arrest. Members of the so-called "Delk Gang" (headed by family patriarch Taylor Delk) were described as bandits and cattle rustlers who would stoop to any level no matter how dastardly. In one noted incident they were reported to have invaded the home of a one-legged CSA veteran and ransacked the place to the tune of $4.75. The loot included a nickel that someone had given the homeowner's grandchild. Lawman-killer Thomas Delk was hanged at Zebulon on June 18, 1897. Source: *Macon (GA) Telegraph*, 4/4/96 (1:3). *Atlanta Constitution*, 6/19/97 (1:1). See also: 1880 U.S. Census (Pike Co., GA), which notes W.O. Gwyn, and 1880 U.S. Census (Calhoun Co. AL), which notes the Delks.

Terrell Hudson (black, age 19). *Murder.* The crime was committed on 11/13/1896 in DeKalb County. Handgun slaying of another young black man named Seaborn Malcolm (age not specified). Motive: a dispute over a hunting dog. Terrell Hudson paid with his life for this rash act when he was hanged at Decatur on June 25, 1897. Source: *Macon (GA) Telegraph*, 6/12/97 (1:4) & 6/26/97 (2:1). *Atlanta Constitution*, 5/12/97 (12:2), 6/10/97 (3:2) & 6/26/97 (5:1). Appeal: 101 GA 520–526. See also: 1880 U.S. Census (Newton Co., GA), which notes Hudson as a small child.

Jonas Jones (black, age 21). *Murder.* The crime was committed on 4/24/1897 in McIntosh County. Handgun slaying of another young black man named Luke King (age not specified) in a railroad passenger car as it was passing through McIntosh County. A card game had started the trouble. The shooter was hanged at Darien on July 9, 1897. Source: *Darien (GA) Gazette*, 7/10/97 (3:2). *Savannah (GA) Tribune*, 5/1/97 (3:3). *Atlanta Constitution*, 7/10/97 (2:1).

Horace Stephen Perry (white, age not recorded). *Murder.* The crime was committed on 3/8/1897 in DeKalb County. Handgun slaying of another white man identified only as N. B. "Bely" Lanier, who was shot down inside the DeKalb County courthouse. Motive: the homicide victim had exposed the killer for cheating on his wife. Perry came from Walton County. He was formerly the police chief at Winder. He died a disgraceful death by hanging at Decatur on September 8, 1897. Source: *Macon (GA) Telegraph*, 8/18/97 (5:3) & 9/9/97 (1:1). *Atlanta Journal*, 9/8/97 (1:5). Appeal: 102 GA 367–386.

Erastus Brown (black, age 31). *Murder.* The crime was committed on or about 5/15/1897 in Bulloch County. Gunshot slaying of another black man named Ben Alexander (age not recorded), the victim having been murdered in his bed. Motive: wife stealing. This black-on-black killer was legally hanged at Statesboro on December 10, 1897. Source: *Atlanta Constitution*, 12/11/97 (3:5). *Savannah Morning News*, 12/11/97 (2:3).

Henry Nesbitt (black, age not recorded). *Murder.* The crime was committed on 6/1/1897 in Irwin County. Possible serial killer. Executed for the handgun slaying of another black man named James Arlington (age not specified). Motive: the homicide victim had informed on him for stealing another man's money. Nesbitt was described as a self-hating negro who had reportedly killed several other men of his own color. He admitted to three such incidents (including that of a one-legged fellow named Dick Wright in Coffee County two days after Arlington), while his wife told of six others. Said Nesbitt: "I have shot three niggers dead and have wounded four but during this time have never had any trouble with a white man. If I was turned loose I would kill every nigger that came within reach of my gun!" This multiple killer was legally hanged at Ocilla on December 10, 1897. Source: *Atlanta Constitution*, 12/11/97 (3:4). *Columbus (GA) Enquirer-Sun*, 12/11/97 (6:2). *Savannah Morning News*, 12/11/97 (2:1).

Addison D. Brooks, alias "Bud Brooks" (white, age 33) and **Grady Reynolds** (white, age 35). *Murder.* Their crime was committed on 2/15/1897 in Jackson County. Both were executed for the killing of 41-year-old Millard C. Hunt (white), a retail merchant who was struck down from behind with a rock, shot in the back of the head execution-style (with his own pistol) and then dumped into the Oconee River. Motive: robbery, despoilment and mendacity. These killers were hanged at Jefferson on December 17, 1897. Source: *Jackson County Historical Society News* (May, August & November 2004), which presents an excellent account of this case based on original records. *True Police Cases*, 3/50. See also Mr. Hunt's gravestone in Barker's Creek Baptist Church Cemetery, Honea Path, SC.

1898

Tom Cyrus (black, age not recorded). *Murder.* The crime was committed on 6/2/1897 in Fulton County. Handgun slaying of Annie Johnson (black, age not recorded), a chambermaid in the governor's mansion. She was shot three times. Motive: jealous lover. Tom Cyrus was hanged at Atlanta on January 7, 1898. Source: *Atlanta Constitution*, 6/2/97 (1:6), 6/3/97 (7:2) & 1/8/98 (7:3). *Atlanta Journal*, 6/2/97 (8:3). Appeal: 29 SE 917–918.

Simon Hopkins (black, age 22). *Murder.* The crime was committed on 9/28/1897 in Decatur County. Shotgun slaying of John Harris (black, age not recorded), who was deliberately lured into the swamps and then gunned down from behind for the sake of his watch, knife and pocket money. All of the stolen items were found in the killer's possession. Simon Hopkins was hanged at Bainbridge on January 7, 1898. Source: *Macon (GA) Telegraph*, 12/11/97 (5:2). *Atlanta Constitution*, 9/30/97 (3:1), 12/9/97 (3:5) & 1/8/98 (3:5). *Bainbridge (GA) Democrat*, 9/30/97 (3:4) & 1/13/98 (3:4). See also: 1880 U.S. Census (Decatur Co., GA), which notes Hopkins as a minor.

Christopher Luby (white, age 38). *Murder.* The crime was committed on 4/8/1897 in Early County. Uxoricide. Fatal beating of Mrs. Flora E. Luby (white, age uncertain). Motive: alcoholic brutality. Luby can be described as a "Chattahoochee river rat" who spent his entire life in southwest Georgia. He was living in a tent and fishing for his meals when tragedy overtook him. The murdered woman was apparently his second wife. He was hanged at Blakely on February 18, 1898. Source: *Atlanta Constitution*, 4/11/97 (15:4) & 2/19/98 (1:5). See also: 1860 U.S. Census (Randolph Co., GA) and 1870 U.S. Census (Clay Co., GA), which note "C. C. Luby."

Isaiah Thomas (black, age 18). *Rape.* The crime was committed on 11/21/1897 in Hancock County. Incipient serial rapist. Specifically executed for an indecent assault on the person of 31-year-old Effie Hawkins (black). Thomas had already been notorious among the African American population as a sex offender. He had come close to being lynched by his own people on two prior occasions. He was legally hanged at Sparta on March 11, 1898. Source: *The Ishmaelite* (Sparta, GA), 11/26/97 (3:3) & 2/25/98 (3:4). *Atlanta Journal*, 3/11/98 (3:4). *Atlanta Constitution*, 3/12/98 (3:1). See also: 1900 U.S. Census (Hancock Co., GA), which notes Effie Hawkins, and 1880 U.S. Census (Hancock Co., GA), which notes the culprit as a baby.

Bristow Graham (black, age 23). *Murder.* The crime was committed on 9/1/1896 in Chatham County. Shotgun slaying of another black man named Ben Wilson (age not recorded) who was mostly decapitated when he tried to jump out a window. Motive: uproar in a "negro gambling house." The killer was hanged at Savannah on April 8, 1898. Source: *Savannah Morning News*, 4/9/98 (8:3).

Zach Holmes (black, age not recorded). *Murder.* The crime was committed on 5/3/1893 in Coffee County. Rifle slaying of 33-year-old James Nathaniel Blitch (white), a turpentine distiller. Motive: dispute over wages. Holmes had had five dollars withheld from his pay for violating company rules. He then picked an argument with his boss (Mr. Blitch) about it, and both of them wound up dead. Blitch died at the scene. Holmes died on the gallows at Douglas on April 29, 1898. Source: *Atlanta Constitution*, 5/6/93 (3:1), 5/20/93 (1:4) & 4/8/98 (3:2). *Savannah Morning News*, 5/6/93 (1:3). *Douglas (GA) Breeze*, 4/30/98 (3:2). See also the gravestone of Mr. Blitch in Old Bethel Cemetery, Jesup.

Asbury Mills (black, age 26). *Murder.* The crime was committed sometime during the year 1895 in Dooly County. Executed for the mutilation murder of a young black woman named Rena McKenzie (age not specified). A load of buckshot had been fired into her face. Then she was stabbed multiple times with a pair of scissors. Still not satisfied, the killer beheaded her next with an ax. He was also officially reported to "have eaten a meal over the dead body of his victim." Motive: the woman had dared to walk out on their abusive relationship. Asbury Mills was hanged at Vienna on June 16, 1898. Source: *Charlotte (NC) Daily Observer*, 6/17/98 (5:3). Appeal: 104 GA 502–505. See also: 1880 U.S. Census (Sumter Co., GA), which notes Mills as a minor.

John Weaver (black, age 22). *Rape.* The crime was committed on 3/7/1898 in Upson County. Indecent assault on the person of 19-year-old Jennie Gunn (white), she having been "seized by the throat and thrown to the ground," incurring injuries that disproved any question of consent. The attacker was legally hanged at Thomaston on July 29, 1898. Source: *Augusta (GA) Chronicle*, 3/11/98 (8:5). *Thomaston (GA) Times*, 8/5/98 (2:1).

Wade Hampton (black, age 19). *Murder.* The crime was committed on 9/21/1898 in Fulton County. Executed for the killing of 16-year-old George Loftin (black), a one-legged prisoner who "was hacked almost to pieces with a knife." Motive: violence among convicts. The scene was a labor camp for young offenders under the old Convict Lease System, in this case the Chattahoochee Brick Company of Atlanta. The killer in this case (Wade Hampton) had already been characterized as vicious by nature. He was legally hanged at Atlanta on November 9, 1898. Source: *Atlanta Constitution*, 9/23/98 (7:5) & 11/10/98 (5:1). *Augusta (GA) Chronicle*, 11/10/98 (2:4).

Willie Brown (black, age 17). *Murder.* The crime was committed on 4/25/1898 in Bryan County. Fatal stabbing of 16-year-old Thomas Benton (white). Motive: highway robbery. Willie Brown was legally hanged at Pembroke on December 9, 1898. Source: *Atlanta Constitution*, 12/11/98 (40:1). Appeal: 105 GA 640–646.

Reuben Battle (black, age 17). *Murder.* The crime was committed on 4/12/1898 in Greene County. Shotgun slaying of James Davis (black, age not recorded) by deliberately firing through his cabin window. Motive: he felt threatened, or so the killer said. Premeditation being clearly proven, Reuben Battle was capitally convicted. He was hanged at Greensboro on December 16, 1898. Source: *Greensboro (GA) Herald-Journal*, 4/15/98 (4:4) & 12/16/98 (6:1). *Atlanta Constitution*, 12/17/98 (3:1). Appeal: 105 GA 703–709.

Abner L. Taylor (white, age 29). *Murder.* The crime was committed on 7/10/1898 in Bibb County. Uxoricide. Executed for the killing of 21-year-old Minnie Lee Logue Taylor (white), who was stabbed eight times with a bone-handled knife and shot twice with a handgun. Motive: marital estrangement. Abner Taylor was hanged at Macon on December 16, 1898. Source: *Atlanta Constitution*, 12/17/98 (3:1). Appeal: 105 GA 746–783. See also: 1880 U.S. Census (Bibb Co., GA), which notes Taylor. Also see the gravestone of Mrs. Taylor in Bethel Baptist Church Cemetery, Lizella.

1899

Abram Smalls (black, age 22). *Murder.* The crime was committed on 2/10/1894 in Chatham County. Police killer. Rifle slaying of 42-year-old Jensen Christian Neve (white), who was shot in the back. Motive: resisting arrest. This assassin was hanged at Savannah on January 13, 1899. Source: *Savannah Morning News*, 2/11/94 (8:1) & 1/14/99 (8:3). See also: 1880 U.S. Census (Chatham Co., GA), which notes Neve, and *City of Savannah Death Register* (Jan. 1899), which notes "Small."

Jefferson Hicks (black, age not recorded). *Murder.* The crime was committed on 4/24/1897 in Macon County. Uxoricide. Fatal and deliberate strangulation of Mary Hicks (black, age not recorded). Motive: marital estrangement. Wife-killer Hicks was hanged at Oglethorpe on January 31, 1899. Source: *Atlanta Journal*, 1/31/99 (3:5). *Macon (GA) Telegraph*, 2/1/99 (4:5).

John Charlon (black, age 29). *Murder.* The crime was committed on 9/9/1898 in Chatham County. Handgun slaying of 40-year-old Harry A. McLeod (white), an unintended victim who got in the way. Motive: saloon brawl. John Charlon went the "rope route" (legally) at Savannah on March 10, 1899. Source: *Savannah Morning News*, 3/11/99 (8:3). See also: *City of Savannah Death Register*, entries at date.

Robert Lewis (white, age 24). *Murder.* The crime was committed on 7/29/1898 in Fulton County. Handgun slaying of Charles Haynes (white), the foreman at a building construction jobsite. Motive: revenge for having been fired. This rash act cost Lewis his life when he was hanged at Atlanta on March 14, 1899. Source: *Atlanta Constitution*, 3/15/99 (7:1). Appeal: 32 SE 342–343.

Cassius Law (black, age not recorded). *Murder.* The crime was committed on 12/25/1898 in Hall County. Executed for the deliberate killing (by unspecified means) of a black woman named Sarah Curry (age not recorded), she having been murdered in her bed. Motive: indiscernible from surviving records. Christmas Day assassin Cassius Law was legally hanged at Gainesville on April 12, 1899. Source: *Atlanta Constitution*, 4/13/99 (3:5).

Frank Wright (black, age 34). *Murder.* The crime was committed on 2/15/1899 in Chatham County. Handgun slaying of 19-year-old Amos Moy (black), his stepson. Motive: obnoxious drunk. The death penalty being imposed in short order, Frank Wright was hanged at Savannah on April 28, 1899. Source: *Savannah Morning News*, 2/17/99 (3:2) & 4/29/99 (8:3). See also: *City of Savannah Death Register*, entries at date.

William Embree (black, age 22). *Murder.* The crime was committed on 3/21/1898 in McDuffie County. Handgun slaying of 24-year-old Ellis Martin, Jr. (black), who was shot three times. Motive: obsessive jealousy. The homicide victim had courteously given Embree's wife a ride home from church. This was all it took to make the non-churchgoing husband go berserk. Embree beat his wife until she was more dead than alive. Then he hunted down Martin and shot him dead. The price he paid was a long drop from the gallows at Thomson on May 3, 1899. Source: *Augusta (GA) Chronicle*, 3/22/98 (5:3) & 5/4/99 (1:3). See also: 1880 U.S. Census (McDuffie Co., GA) and 1880 U.S. Census (Warren Co., GA), which note both men as minors.

Toby Bowens (black, age 25). *Murder.* The crime was committed on 8/30/1898 in Chatham County. Uxoricide. Executed for the killing of 19-year-old Rosa Bowens (black), who was battered to death with an iron fish plate. Motive: suspicion of infidelity. Wife-killer Bowens was hanged at Savannah on May 12, 1899. Source: *Atlanta Constitution*, 5/13/99 (3:3). *Savannah Morning News*, 5/13/99 (8:1). Appeal: 106 GA 760–765. See also: *City of Savannah Death Register*, entries dated 9/1/98 (Rosa "Bolian") and 5/12/99 (Bowens).

Will Williams (black, age not recorded). *Murder.* The crime was committed on 10/15/1898 in Telfair County. Shotgun slaying of 47-year-old Lovett P. Peacock (white), the commissary manager at a turpentine camp. Motive: revenge for having been fired from his job. Williams was legally hanged for this at MacRae on May 19, 1899. Source: *Augusta (GA) Chronicle*, 12/4/98 (3:3). *Macon (GA) Telegraph*, 5/20/99 (8:1). *Times-Journal* (Eastman, GA), 10/21/98 (3:4), 12/9/98 (4:4) & 5/25/99 (5:3). See also: 1880 U.S. Census (Twiggs Co., GA), which notes Mr. Peacock.

Crawford Mobley (black, age not recorded). *Murder.* The crime was committed on 1/15/1899 in Burke County. Shotgun slaying of 43-year-old Edward Lovett (black), his stepfather. The homicide victim was felled by a sniper who fired through the rear window of his cabin. Motive: personal resentment. Mobley legally paid the death penalty for this dirty deed at Waynesboro on May 25, 1899. "We venture to remark," wrote the reporter for the local Waynesboro newspaper, "that where one Negro is killed by a white person, ten are slain by the Negro. Let anyone who denies it go to the records and examine for themselves. The fact that they need more protection from themselves than from anything else remains to confront us as part of the Negro problem." Source: *The True Citizen* (Waynesboro, GA), 1/21/99 (3:5) & 5/27/99 (3:3). *Macon (GA) Telegraph*, 1/23/99 (1:2), 5/24/99 (6:4) & 5/26/99 (1:3). See also: 1880 U.S. Census (Burke Co., GA), which notes Edward Lovett.

Jim Rembart, alias "Jim Kimberly" (black, age not recorded). *Murder.* The crime was committed on an unspecified date in Mitchell County. Executed for the cruel killing of Amanda Smyles, age 80+, known to some as "Smike" but known to all as "Old Aunt Mandy" (black), she having been "knocked in the head" while puttering in her home lot and there "thrown into a hole about two feet deep and the dirt packed down on" her. Motive: plunder. The unnecessary brutality of this misdeed infuriated blacks and whites alike. The killer was legally hanged at Camilla on June 16, 1899. Source: *Bainbridge (GA) Democrat*, 5/4/99 (2:1). *Atlanta Constitution*, 6/17/99 (2:2). *Enquirer-Sun* (Columbus, GA), 6/17/99 (3:3).

Cain Stephens (black, age 22). *Murder.* The crime was committed on 1/31/1899 in Dodge County. Police killer. Executed for the handgun slaying of E. J. Osborn, age 50+ (white, full name not specified), the marshal of Chauncey. Motive: resisting arrest. The gallows claimed this assassin at Eastman on June 23, 1899. Source: *Times-Journal* (Eastman, GA), 2/2/99 (3:2) & 6/29/99 (1:4). *Macon (GA) Telegraph*, 2/1/99 (1:2), 2/26/99 (2:1:5) & 6/24/99 (8:1). See also: Will Wilson (executed 7/14/99).

Will Ables (black, age 17). *Rape.* The crime was committed on 6/4/1899 in Appling County. Indecent assault on the person of 35-year-old Vicey Edgerton (white) under circumstances that were deemed unfit for public disclosure. There was no appeal. The precocious culprit was legally hanged at Baxley on June 30, 1899. Source: *Macon (GA) Telegraph*, 6/9/99 (3:1). *Atlanta Constitution*, 6/9/99 (1:2) & 7/1/99 (3:5). See also: 1900 U.S. Census (Appling Co., GA), which notes the female party.

Will Wilson, alias "John Davis" (black, age 24). *Murder.* The crime was committed on 1/31/1899 in Dodge County. Police killer. Accomplice in the handgun slaying of E. J. Osborn, age 50+ (white), the marshal of Chauncey. Motive: resisting arrest. This party to that killing was legally hanged at Eastman on July 14, 1899. Source: *Times-Journal* (Eastman, GA), 7/20/99 (5:1). *Macon (GA) Telegraph*, 7/15/99 (3:1). See: Cain Stephens (executed 6/23/99).

Isaiah Scott (black, age abt. 26). *Murder.* The crime was committed on 5/5/1899 in Chatham County. Uxoricide. Executed for the ax murder of about 20-year-old Marie Scott (black), she having been slaughtered in her bed. Motive: unspecified by all accounts, although there appeared to have been another woman involved. This wife-killer was hanged at Savannah on July 21, 1899. Source: *Savannah Morning News*, 5/6/99 (8:1) & 7/22/99 (8:3).

Joe Carroll (black, age not recorded). *Murder.* The crime was committed on 5/6/1899 in Fulton County. Handgun slaying of a black woman named Josephine Alexander (age not specified) because she had dared to butt into a men's quarrel. The sentence of death being pronounced in this case, it was carried out at Atlanta on August 29, 1899. Source: *Atlanta Constitution*, 5/8/99 (7:1) & 8/30/99 (7:1). *Atlanta Journal*, 5/8/99 (10:4).

Hilliard Brooks (black, age not recorded). *Murder.* The crime was committed sometime during the year 1898 in Harris County. Handgun slaying of another black man named Will Bankston (age not specified). Motive: brawling. This killer (about whom little else is known) was legally hanged at Hamilton on September 15, 1899. Source: *Columbus (GA) Enquirer-Sun*, 9/16/99 (2:2). Appeal: 33 SE 812–813.

James Hall (black, age 21). *Rape.* The crime was committed on or about 7/15/1899 in Early County. Indecent assault on the person of 9-year-old Ella Brown (black), who was physically maimed in the process. This sexual predator was legally hanged at Blakely on September 28, 1899. Source: *Atlanta Constitution*, 9/29/99 (3:1). *Blakely (GA) Observer*, 9/27/99 (5:3) & 10/4/99 (5:3). Note: The rival *Early County News* did not report this matter even though the hanging took place less than a mile from its place of business.

Mack Cannon (black, age 26). *Murder.* The crime was committed on 5/2/1899 in Wilkinson County. Executed for the ax murder of another black man named John Briscoe (age not recorded), who was butchered in his bed. Motive: adultery with the homicide victim's wife. She got 99 years for complicity. Her lover was hanged at Irwinton on October 27, 1899. Source: *Macon (GA) Telegraph*, 5/6/99 (1:4), 10/7/99 (2:4) & 10/28/99 (1:3).

Richard Smith, alias "Alabama Red" (black, age 42). *Murder.* The crime was committed on 5/27/1899 in Houston County. Handgun slaying of 39-year-old Bob Pine (black), who was shot in the back. Motive: robbery. Despised by his fellow blacks, Smith went too far on the above date when he terrorized a well-attended "soul food" picnic. Bob Pine had asked him to change a five-dollar bill. Smith put the fiver in his pocket. Then he pulled a pistol out of his waistband and demanded every penny that Pine had on his person. The latter tried to run away but got gunned down from behind. Smith then rifled Pine's pockets to the tune of three more dollars. Next, he ran among the picnic crowd, brandishing his weapon and threatening to shoot anyone who dared to oppose him. A panic ensued, with the picnic-goers trampling each other in a mad dash to flee. The culprit was nabbed later that night. Black folks of Houston County petitioned for a special court so that "Red" could be brought to justice all the sooner. He was legally hanged at Perry on December 1, 1899. Source: *Macon (GA) Telegraph*, 5/29/99 (1:5) & 12/2/99 (1:3). See also: 1880 U.S. Census (Houston Co., GA), which notes Bob Pine.

Mack Taylor (black, age 27). *Murder.* The crime was committed on 8/11/1899 in Richmond County. Executed for the killing of 40-year-old Alfred A. Seago (white), a grocer and meat cutter who was slashed to death with one of his own butcher knives. Motive: robbery. The culprit was legally hanged at Augusta on December 6, 1899. Source: *Augusta (GA) Chronicle*, 12/3/99 (1:1) & 12/7/99 (2:3). *Atlanta Constitution*, 8/13/99 (4:2). See also: 1880 U.S. Census (Richmond Co., GA), which notes the murdered man as "A. A. Sego."

James Godding (black, age not recorded) and **Washington Powell** (black, age 23). *Murder.* Their crime was committed on 9/9/1899 in Lowndes County. Both executed for the mutilation murder of 26-year-old Henry Vickers (white), who was shot in the face with a handgun, slashed across the throat from ear to ear and then thrown down a 40' well with his head smashed in. Motive: robbery. These killers were legally hanged at Valdosta on December 13, 1899. Source: *Valdosta (GA) Times*, 9/12/99 (3:1) & 12/16/99 (5:1). *Atlanta Constitution*, 9/12/99 (3:4) & 12/14/99 (1:4). See also: 1880 U.S. Census (Lowndes Co., GA), which notes Powell and Vickers as minors.

W. J. Glaser (full name not recorded, white, age 47). *Murder.* The crime was committed on 8/1/1899 in Dougherty County. Uxoricide. Executed for the killing of Elizabeth Glaser (white, age not recorded), who was severely beaten before being stabbed multiple times. Motive: alcoholic brutality. This wife-killer was hanged at Albany on December 15, 1899. Source: *Columbus (GA) Enquirer-Sun*, 10/12/99 (3:4) & 12/16/99 (4:2). See also: *Sexton's Book for the City of Albany* (1899), entries at dates. Oakview Cemetery.

Wesley Tiller (black, age 22). *Murder.* The crime was committed on 3/14/1899 in Hart County. Uxoricide. Handgun slaying of about 18-year-old Vinie Myers Tiller (black), who was presumably the namesake of her mother. Motive: marital estrangement. This wife-killer was hanged at Hartwell on December 16, 1899. Source: *Hartwell (GA) Sun*, 3/24/99 (2:7) & 12/22/99 (3:6). *Elberton (GA) Star*, 3/23/99 (2:2) & 12/21/99 (6:3). *Atlanta Constitution*, 12/17/99 (2:6).

1900

Sam Harris, alias "Bud" Harris (black, age 19). *Murder.* The crime was committed on 12/24/1897 in Floyd County. Handgun slaying of 21-year-old David C. Erwin (black). Motive: rivalry for a female. This Christmas Eve killer was legally hanged at Rome on January 4, 1900. Source: *Atlanta Constitution*, 1/5/00 (3:3). See also: 1880 U.S. Census (Floyd Co., GA), which notes Erwin as a minor.

Ed Fields (black, age not recorded). *Murder.* The crime was committed on 8/21/1898 in Jackson County. Handgun slaying of a young black woman named

Virginia Griffith (age not specified). Motive: frustrated suitor. This all-too-common variety of killer was hanged at Jefferson on January 5, 1900. Source: *Jackson Herald* (Jefferson, GA), 8/26/98 (3:2), 1/5/00 (3:3) & 1/12/00 (3:2). *Atlanta Constitution*, 1/6/00 (3:2).

Sherman Rivers, alias "Sporty Bob" (black, age not recorded). *Murder.* The crime was committed on an unknown date in Emanuel County. Executed for the killing of another black man named George Perdue (age unknown). Motive: unclear. This case suffers from a dearth of surviving documentation, as do several others emanating from Emanuel County. All that is further known for certain is that "Sporty Bob" was legally hanged at Swainsboro on January 6, 1900. Source: *Macon (GA) Telegraph*, 1/7/00 (10:1).

Charlie Williams (black, age not recorded). *Murder.* The crime was committed on 6/9/1899 in Decatur County. Executed for the shotgun slaying of an unnamed black female who was described as his "concubine" because he was a married man. Motive: adultery turned deadly. The local newspaper was ambivalent about describing this sordid situation any further, save for the fact that Charlie Williams was hanged for his crime at Bainbridge on January 12, 1900. Source: *Bainbridge (GA) Democrat*, 6/15/99 (3:4) & 1/18/00 (3:6).

Philip Denson (black, age not recorded). *Murder.* The crime was committed on or about 11/15/1899 in Decatur County. Handgun slaying of another black man named Will Lane (age not recorded) during a showdown on a public street. Motive: a dispute over who should have 25 cents. Two lives for a quarter was the final tally when gunslinger Philip Denson was hanged at Bainbridge on January 19, 1900. Source: *Bainbridge (GA) Democrat*, 1/25/00 (3:3). *Atlanta Constitution*, 1/17/00 (7:6) & 1/20/00 (1:7). *Savannah Morning News*, 1/20/00 (7:3).

Will Leonard (black, age not recorded). *Murder.* The crime was committed on 12/24/1896 in Talbot County. Uxoricide, etc. Executed for the ax murders of 27-year-old Nora Dean Leonard and 64-year-old Frances Dean (blacks), they having respectively been his wife and his mother-in-law. Motive: presumably some kind of family tension. This ax man was hanged for what he did at Talbotton on March 2, 1900. Source: *Talbotton (GA) New Era*, 3/9/00 (6:4). *Atlanta Constitution*, 3/3/00 (3:2). *Columbus (GA) Enquirer-Sun*, 9/23/99 (2:1). See also: 1880 U.S. Census (Talbot Co., GA), which notes the homicide victims.

Allen Fuller (black, age not recorded). *Murder.* The crime was committed on 11/17/1899 in Bibb County. Executed for the killing of a white woman named Eugenia Hamilton Pottle (age not specified), whose head was battered in with a hickory stick and whose body was then dumped in a river. Motive: highway robbery. The homicide victim was driving homeward from a shopping trip when her buggy broke a wheel. She was unaccompanied at that time. Allen Fuller took cruel advantage of her plight to rob and murder her. Known as "the Jesse of the Roads," this daring man had long incurred the enmity of his own people (black folks) for his predatory nature. Few were sorry to see him swing. The gallows did its work in this case at Macon on April 2, 1900. Source: *Macon (GA) Telegraph*,

12/9/99 (5:2), 12/10/99 (11:1) & 4/3/00 (8:3).

Lewis Goolsby (black, age 17) and **King Goolsby** (black, age 15). *Murder.* Baby killers, etc. Their crime was committed on 3/5/1900 in Appling County. Both executed for the killing of 33-year-old Daniel A. Mims (white), who was jumped from behind, beaten with ax handles, stabbed through an eyeball and then finished off by having his throat cut. Motive: mendacity. The killers had gone to the homicide victim's home on the false pretense of looking for work. Mims agreed to hire them as cotton pickers. He was in the act of walking them over to the laborers' cabins when they turned on him. Seeing this, Mims' wife ran out of the farmhouse with a baby in her arms. She was then beaten with ax handles and left for dead. The baby (Pauline Mims, age 1) fell to the ground and died of a broken neck. The juvenile delinquents who did this were legally hanged at Baxley on April 6, 1900. Source: *Atlanta Constitution*, 3/7/00 (3:1), 3/8/00 (3:1) & 4/7/00 (3:4). *Macon (GA) Telegraph*, 4/7/00 (4:5). See also the Mims' gravestone in Mims Baptist Church Cemetery, Alma.

Homer Crawford (black, age 23). *Murder.* The crime was committed on 11/12/1899 in Pulaski County. Handgun slaying of 33-year-old Johnson Pate (black), whose "blood oozed from his wound like a beef stuck in the heart." Motive: obnoxious drunk. This killer was hanged at Hawkinsville on April 20, 1900. Source: *Macon (GA) Telegraph*, 11/13/99 (4:5) & 4/21/00 (4:5). See also: 1880 U.S. Census (Pulaski Co., GA) and 1880 U.S. Census (Houston Co., GA), which note each party as minors.

Dillard Herndon (white, age abt. 50). *Murder.* The crime was committed on 10/19/1899 in Wilkes County. Shotgun slaying of 26-year-old John J. Lovinggood (white), a storekeeper. Motive: armed robbery. The penalty was death by hanging. Herndon underwent that punishment at Washington on August 17, 1900. Source: *Augusta (GA) Chronicle*, 10/21/99 (1:7) & 10/22/99 (1:5). *Atlanta Constitution*, 11/3/99 (3:7) & 8/18/00 (2:3). *Washington (GA) Chronicle*, 10/23/99 (1:3). See also: 1880 U.S. Census (Wilkes Co., GA), which notes the homicide victim.

Hiram Sharpe (white, age 48). *Murder.* The crime was committed on 12/6/1899 in Decatur County. Uxoricide. Shotgun slaying of 45-year-old Clary Crosby Sharpe (white) plus the fearsome maiming of his mother-in-law in the same incident. Motive: family problems. This ill-fated couple had been married in Henry Co. on 3/16/1873. Hiram Sharpe was legally hanged at Bainbridge on August 28, 1900. Source: *Atlanta Constitution*, 12/7/99 (1:7) & 8/29/00 (7:1). *Bainbridge (GA) Democrat*, 12/14/99 (1:3). See also: 1900 U.S. Census (Decatur Co., GA), which notes Sharpe as a prisoner.

Sam Robinson (black, age 24). *Rape.* The crime was committed on 8/6/1900 in Cobb County. Indecent assault on the person of 18-year-old Ida V. Inzer (white), she having been chased down, severely beaten and then raped at knifepoint. The culprit was legally hanged at Marietta on September 1, 1900. There had apparently been no grounds for an appeal. Source: *Macon (GA) Telegraph*, 8/8/00 (6:3). *Atlanta Constitution*, 9/2/00 (4:1). *Marietta Journal*, 8/9/00 (4:2) & 9/6/00 (1:5). See also: 1900 U.S. Census (Cobb Co., GA), which notes the young lady.

William Branch (black, age 33). *Murder.* The crime was committed on 9/26/1900 in Elbert County. Shotgun slaying of 42-year-old George D. Bell (white). Motive: a cotton thief's reaction to a citizen arrest. As a result, Branch was held accountable for capital murder instead of simple larceny. He was legally hanged at Elberton on October 29, 1900. Source: *Macon (GA) Telegraph*, 9/28/00 (6:1). *Atlanta Constitution*, 10/30/00 (3:3). See also: 1900 U.S. Census (Elbert Co., GA), which notes both parties.

Manzo Glover (black, age 22). *Murder.* The crime was committed on 7/22/1900 in Newton County. Handgun slaying of 26-year-old Cary Henderson (black), who was shot in the back for the sake of seven pennies. Motive: gambling dispute. This seven-cent killer was hanged by the neck until dead at Covington on November 15, 1900. Source: *Atlanta Constitution*, 11/16/00 (2:5). *Jackson (GA) Argus*, 10/5/00 (4:4). *Georgia Enterprise* (Covington) 8/3/00 (1:5) & 11/16/00 (1:3). See also: 1880 U.S. Census (Newton Co., GA), which notes Henderson.

1901

Willis Hines (black, age 23). *Murder.* The crime was committed on an unknown date in Mitchell County. Executed for the killing (by uncertain means) of a young black woman named Minnie Walker. Motive: not specified. Additional details of this case could not be determined based on surviving documentation, but it is confirmed that Willis Hines was legally hanged at Camilla on January 10, 1901. Source: *Columbus (GA) Enquirer-Sun*, 1/11/01 (1:4). See also: 1900 U.S. Census (Mitchell Co., GA), which notes Hines.

Arnold Augustus (black, age 51), **Samuel Baldwin** (black, age not recorded), **Andrew Davis** (black, age 28), **William Hudson** (black, age 38) and **Richard Sanders** (black, age 24). *Murder.* Police killers, etc. Their crime was committed on 8/9/1900 in Screven County. All five executed for the barrage slayings of 34-year-old William Melton Mears and 44-year-old Richard Fillmore Herrington (whites), they respectively being a county peace officer and a posse man. Motive: contempt of authority with racial overtones. The murdered men had been detailed to arrest a member of the Sanders family. They were "shot to pieces" by rifle fire and shotgun blasts at the hands of the above-named men and possibly more. It was reported that the killers had previously bound themselves together by means of an occult oath for the purpose of assassinating white people in general, but this cannot be independently verified. This quintet dropped simultaneously from the same gallows at Sylvania on June 14, 1901. Source: *Atlanta Constitution*, 6/15/01 (1:6). *Savannah Morning News*, 6/15/01 (1:7). See also: 1900 U.S. Census (Screven Co., GA), which notes four of the killers as well as Mr. Herrington. See also the broken gravestone of W. M. Mears in Bethel Cemetery, Burton's Landing.

Tricey Griffin (black, age not recorded). *Murder.* The crime was committed on 10/7/1900 in Glynn County. Handgun slaying of 31-year-old Robert Marion Lattimer (white), a passenger train conductor. Motive: the homicide victim had caught him stealing a ride. This killer was legally hanged at Brunswick on June 14, 1901. Source: *Columbus (GA) Enquirer-Sun*, 10/9/00 (6:2) & 6/15/01 (2:4). *Brunswick (GA) Times-Call*, 10/9/00 (1:1). See also: 1900 U.S. Census (Atlanta, GA), which notes the murdered man.

George Mitchell (black, age 28). *Rape.* The crime was committed on 5/29/1901 in Chatham County. Indecent assault on the person of 34-year-old Patience Maxwell (black), she having been one of two black females on whom he had forced himself that day. This sex offender was legally hanged at Savannah on August 2, 1901. Source: *Atlanta Constitution*, 6/13/01 (2:4) & 8/3/01 (2:3). See also: 1900 U.S. Census (Savannah, GA), which notes both parties.

Edmond Scott (black, age 19). *Murder.* The crime was committed on 8/5/1900 in Troup County. Handgun slayings of two sisters: Carrie Huguley (black, age 33) and Lena Huguley (black, age 24), who were each shot through one of their eyeballs. Motive: fracas in a whorehouse. The killer's clemency petition stressed that the homicide victims were "notorious characters," i.e., trollops, who had corrupted a susceptible lad (Scott) and left him feeling ill-used. The guilt they shared—to whatever its degree—cost the lives of all three. The end came for Edmond Scott at La Grange on August 2, 1901, when he met a legally mandated death at the end of a rope. Source: *Columbus (GA) Enquirer-Sun*, 8/7/00 (2:2). *Atlanta Constitution*, 8/3/01 (2:3). *Augusta (GA) Chronicle*, 8/1/01 (2:2).

Raymond Ross (black, age 19). *Rape.* The crime was committed on 7/29/1901 in Cherokee County. Indecent assault on the person of 42-year-old Harriet Miller (white, a widow with three small children), who was terrorized in her little house after the culprit had broken into it and dragged her outside (by the neck), where she was further ravished. Raymond Ross paid with his life for this violent act when he was legally hanged at Canton on August 27, 1901. Source: *Atlanta Constitution*, 7/31/01 (2:3) & 8/28/01 (2:4). See also: 1900 U.S. Census (Cherokee Co., GA), which notes both parties.

Levi Carroll (black, age 24). *Murder.* The crime was committed on 2/28/1901 in Bibb County. Patricide, etc. Executed for the fatal stabbings of 53-year-old Hardy Carroll and 38-year-old Dinah Lockett (blacks), they being his father and that man's inamorata. The woman was murdered in her bed. Motive: sexual rivalry between the father and the son. Double killer Levi Carroll was legally hanged at Macon on September 5, 1901. Source: *Atlanta Constitution*, 3/15/01 (2:1) & 9/6/01 (2:3). *Macon (GA) Telegraph*, 3/1/01 (1:1).

John Romulus Williams (black, age not recorded). *Murder.* The crime was committed on 12/9/1900 in Houston County. Handgun slaying of 41-year-old Adam Hunnicutt (black), who was shot in the back. Motive: jealousy for the attention of a female. The killer was hanged at Perry on September 6, 1901. Source: *Houston Home Journal* (Perry, GA), 12/13/00 (3:4) & 9/12/01 (6:2). *Atlanta Constitution*, 4/12/01 (2:5) & 9/7/01 (8:7). Appeal: 113 GA 704–705. See also: 1900 U.S. Census (Houston Co., GA), which notes the homicide victim.

Neal Rylee (black, age 19). *Murder.* The crime was committed on 9/10/1901 in Banks County. Uxoricide.

Handgun slaying of Eliza Rylee (black, age not specified), who was shot in the head. Motive: connubial discord. This young wife-killer was hanged for this gross violation of his marriage vows at Homer on October 19, 1901. Source: *Atlanta Constitution*, 9/12/01 (5:6) & 10/20/01 (3:7). *Banks County Journal*, 10/24/01 (3:2). See also: 1900 U.S. Census (Banks Co., GA), which notes these newlyweds.

William Jackson (black, age abt. 25). *Rape.* The crime was committed on 10/7/1901 in Bartow County. Indecent assault on the person of 22-year-old Tiney Smith (white), who was attacked while picking cotton, the close proximity of her recently delivered baby adding to the pathos of the scene. She later had to be carried into the Bartow County courthouse seated in a chaise so a hushed panel could hear her testimony. She had been left unable to walk by the nature of her injuries. The person who did this to her was legally hanged at Cartersville on November 1, 1901. Source: *Atlanta Constitution*, 10/8/01 (5:4), 10/11/01 (3:5) & 11/2/01 (5:1). See also: 1900 U.S. Census (Bartow Co., GA), which notes Mrs. Smith.

1902

Ernest Outland (black, age 20). *Murder.* The crime was committed sometime early in the year 1901 in Screven County. Executed for the gunshot slaying of another black man named Thomas Mitchell (age not specified) in a dispute about a pair of pants. Surviving accounts give no further details save for the fact that Ernest Outland was legally hanged at Sylvania on January 3, 1902. Source: *Atlanta Constitution*, 1/4/02 (5:3). *Augusta (GA) Chronicle*, 1/4/02 (5:3). *Savannah Morning News*, 1/4/02 (2:3). See also: 1900 U.S. Census (Screven Co., GA), which notes the shooter.

John Robinson, alias "the Colored Ripper" (black, age not specified). *Murder.* The crime for which he was executed was committed on 5/24/1901 in Laurens County. Possible serial killer. Specifically hanged for the mutilation murder of a young black woman named Bertha Simmons (exact age not specified), who was strangled with a flour sack and eviscerated by means of a knife. Her gutted remains were dumped in a swamp. The sack fabric was knotted so tightly around the homicide victim's neck that her tongue was found protruding from her mouth. Most of her internal organs were never found. Motive: presumed sexual assault. Five other equally gory murders were attributed to Robinson, but they cannot be independently confirmed. Said this killer: "I will die like a brave coon!" as he walked up the thirteen steps of the gallows at Dublin on January 3, 1902. Source: *Augusta (GA) Chronicle*, 12/31/01 (1:1) & 1/4/02 (1:7). *Atlanta Constitution*, 1/4/02 (5:3). *Macon (GA) Telegraph*, 1/4/02 (3:2). *Dublin (GA) Courier-Dispatch*, 5/30/01 (1:1) & 1/2/02 (1:1). See also: Pardons Files Box 103, GA State Archives.

John Henry Peavy (black, age not recorded). *Murder.* The crime was committed on or about 7/15/1901 in Dooly County. Executed for the depraved killing of another black man named Jesse Ford (age not recorded) under circumstances that cannot be determined based on publicly accessible documentation. It is confirmed, however, that Peavy was legally hanged at Vienna on March 21, 1902. Source: *Atlanta Constitution*, 3/22/02 (5:2).

See also: Pardons Files Box 93, GA State Archives.

Arthur Price (black, age 22). *Murder.* The crime was committed on 12/5/1901 in Bibb County. Ax murder of 60-year-old Martha E. Rowland (white), a panic-stricken housewife. Motive: tragic mischance. Price had previously agreed to barter a handgun with Mrs. Rowland's 21-year-old son. The latter confirmed this. Price went to the Rowland residence to make the trade, carrying the aforesaid weapon in open view. Mama Rowland saw him coming and mistook his intention. She started screaming like a wild woman to rouse the neighborhood. Price tried to explain himself, but the old dame would have none of it. She continued acting hysterical. Price found himself in a no-win situation. He would almost certainly be accused (although incorrectly) of attacking Mrs. Rowland. She would be believed implicitly and he would then be hunted down like an animal. Exasperated, Price grabbed an ax and killed the woman with it because it seemed to be the only way to silence her. Mrs. Rowland's son was not there at the time, else the tragedy would have probably been avoided. Arthur Price was legally hanged at Macon on May 2, 1902. Source: *Savannah (GA) Tribune*, 12/14/01 (1:4). *Atlanta Constitution*, 5/3/02 (4:1). See also: 1900 U.S. Census (Bibb Co., GA), which notes the Rowlands.

Floyd Reese (black, age 62). *Murder.* The crime was committed on 4/5/1902 in Burke County. Shotgun slaying of 27-year-old Anthony Lane (white), whose entire face was blown off. Motive: thief caught in the act. The killer had been robbing corn cribs and getting away with it for a considerable length of time. Anthony Lane had been hired to lie in wait for the thief, but Reese got the drop on him. This earned Reese an appointment with the hangman. He kept that rendezvous at Waynesboro on May 23, 1902. Source: *Augusta (GA) Chronicle*, 4/6/02 (4:5), 4/10/02 (1:2) & 5/24/02 (2:3). See also: 1900 U.S. Census (Burke Co., GA), which notes both parties.

Joe E. Sparks (black, age not recorded). *Murder.* The crime was committed on 5/20/1902 in Decatur County. Uxoricide. Handgun slaying of Lula Sparks (black, age not recorded). Motive: the local newspaper described it in the following words: "An excursion train of niggers—male and female—was dumped into our town last Tuesday. The event was "Mancipation Day" [*sic*] and the manumits appeared to have a high old time. The thing wound up at night with the killing of one of "the sisterin" [*sic*], who met her death from a pistol ball fired by her escort. She was a Bainbridge "darkey." The slayer was promptly arrested and will be as promptly tried and hung on July 11th, the Superior Court being now in session." Joe Sparks was indeed hanged—legally—at Bainbridge on July 11, 1902. Source: *Atlanta Constitution*, 7/12/02 (5:2). *Thomasville (GA) Times-Enterprise*, 7/19/02 (1:7). *The Search Light* (Bainbridge, GA), 5/23/02 (1:4) & 7/18/02 (1:2).

William Roland Wells (white, age 55). *Murder.* The crime was committed on 2/1/1902 in Fulton County. Fatal stabbing of 47-year-old Frederick Pierce (white, a blind man), who was basely knifed in the back. Motive: sidewalk brawl. Wells was a firewood dealer. He also sold lumber. Financial reverses seem to have driven him to the brink. He had already attacked a garnishment bailiff with an ax but was granted a *nolle prosequi* out of pity for his wife and children. Then on the above date Wells went too far. He encountered sightless Fred Pierce on a public sidewalk being led by his 8-year-old son. Wells stopped them and demanded to know why the Pierce household had discontinued its regular delivery of firewood from his place of business. The blind man replied that he was not the one who made the buying decisions. Wells disliked that answer. He lost his temper and stabbed the helpless blind man in the back. Death by hanging was the fate of William Roland Wells at the Fulton County jail on July 21, 1902. Source: *Atlanta Constitution*, 2/3/02 (5:1), 2/4/02 (9:4) & 7/22/02 (7:1). See also: 1900 U.S. Census (Fulton Co., GA), which notes both parties.

Jesse Gibson, alias "John Mattox" (black, age 24). *Rape.* The crime was committed on 6/27/1902 in Warren County. Indecent assault on the person of 7-year-old Mary Lou Bacon (white), the daughter of Jerome Bartow Bacon. She never married, and she died young on 10/5/1931, quite possibly because she was never right after what Gibson had done to her. The gallows marked his end at Warrenton on August 8, 1902. Source: *Atlanta Constitution*, 6/28/02 (5:1), 7/8/02 (4:2) & 8/9/02 (4:5). See also: 1910, 1920 and 1930 U.S. Census (Warren Co., GA), which note the Bacons, and 1931 Warren Co. death cert. no. 29404.

Boisy Bryant (black, age 18). *Murder.* The crime was committed on 5/22/1902 in Berrien County. Police killer. Handgun slaying of about 54-year-old William A. Hyers (white), the marshal of Adel. Motive: resisting arrest. Death on the gallows was the fate of this young offender at Nashville on September 12, 1902. Source: *Macon (GA) Telegraph*, 5/24/02 (3:3) & 5/28/02 (4:5). *Atlanta Constitution*, 9/13/02 (4:1).

Henry Jones (black, age 22). *Rape.* The crime was committed on 8/3/1902 in Elbert County. Indecent assault on the person of 23-year-old Carrie Cleveland (white). He had climbed in her cabin window at 2 o'clock in the morning and forced himself on her irrespective of the presence of her sleeping husband (Jesse Cleveland) on the opposite side of the room. The latter was held to be a public laughing stock because he had slept through the whole thing. A court of law, however, took a more taciturn stance. The rapist was ordered for execution and the sentence was carried out at Elberton on October 10, 1902. Source: *Atlanta Constitution*, 9/14/02 (5:1), 10/10/02 (3:5) & 10/11/02 (4:3). *Hartwell (GA) Sun*, 8/8/02 (2:6), 9/19/02 (1:1) & 10/17/02 (1:1). Pardons Files Box 68, GA State Archives. See also: 1900 U.S. Census (Elbert Co., GA), which notes Mrs. Cleveland.

Goldy Tyus (black, age 19). *Murder.* The crime was committed on 8/24/1902 in Thomas County. Police killer, etc. Handgun slayings of 44-year-old Alexander Mathew Godwin (the town marshal of Cairo, GA) and his brother, 40-year-old Jefferson Davis Godwin (whites). Motive: resisting arrest. Double killer Goldy Tyus was legally hanged at Thomasville on December 12, 1902. Source: *Thomasville (GA) Times-Enterprise*, 8/30/02 (1:4), 9/6/02 (1:4) & 12/13/02 (3:3). See also: 1880 U.S. Census (Decatur Co., GA), which notes the Godwins. Their gravestones can still be seen in Godwin Cemetery, Route 111, Grady Co.

1903

Sol Dunn (black, age 26). *Murder.* The crime was committed on 12/9/1901 in Richmond County. Handgun slaying of 23-year-old Edward Springs (white), a bartender who had ejected him from his pub for being drunk and profane. This incident cost Dunn his life. He was legally hanged at Augusta on January 9, 1903. Source: *Augusta (GA) Chronicle*, 12/10/01 (1:1) & 1/10/03 (8:1). See also: 1900 U.S. Census (Richmond Co., GA), which notes the murdered man.

Robert Simmons (black, age not recorded). *Murder.* The crime was committed on 7/24/1902 in Chatham County. Handgun slaying of 35-year-old George Harris (black). Motive: rivalry for a female. This open-and-shut case of black-on-black homicide culminated on January 30, 1903, when Robert Simmons was hanged at the Savannah city jail. Source: *Savannah Morning News*, 7/26/02 (6:1) & 1/31/03 (12:3). *Atlanta Constitution*, 7/26/02 (2:5) & 1/31/03 (2:2).

Miles Johnson (black, age 27). *Rape.* The crime was committed on 11/29/1902 in Richmond County. Indecent assault on the person of a 6-year-old white female (name withheld), the news of which was not made public until the culprit had been brought to a secure location many miles away. He was legally hanged at Augusta on February 6, 1903. Source: *Augusta (GA) Chronicle*, 12/2/02 (8:5) & 2/7/03 (8:5).

Henry Steele (black, age 26). *Murder.* The crime was committed on 1/10/1903 in Thomas County. Handgun slaying of 21-year-old Goodman Pittman (white), who was shot in the crotch. Motive: apparently because the killer thought that Pittman had assisted police in breaking up an all-black social gathering. Steele became the central figure in another type of gathering when he was hanged for his crime at Thomasville on March 13, 1903. Source: *Thomasville (GA) Times-Enterprise*, 1/17/03 (1:3) & 3/14/03 (1:2). See also: 1880 and 1900 U.S. Census (Thomas Co., GA), which respectively note the killer and the homicide victim.

John Henry Bryant (black, age not recorded). *Murder.* The crime was committed on 7/15/1902 in Colquitt County. Handgun slaying of another black man named Dandy Buckner (age unknown). Motive: rivalry for a female. Score another one for the gallows at Moultrie on March 20, 1903. Source: *Atlanta Constitution*, 3/21/03 (4:3). *Moultrie (GA) Observer*, 7/18/02 (1:6), 8/8/02 (1:1) & 3/27/03 (8:3). Pardons Files Box 16, GA State Archives.

George Hamp, a.k.a. "Hampton" (black, age 27). *Murder.* The crime was committed on an unknown date in Morgan County. Executed for the ax murder of an unidentified black female who was presumably his lover. Motive: brutish male jealousy. This case is known only from a newspaper report, the court records being inaccessible. Hamp was hanged at Madison on April 10, 1903. Source: *Atlanta Constitution*, 4/11/03 (2:6). See also: 1900 U.S. Census (Morgan Co., GA), which notes this killer.

Charlie Phillips (black, age not recorded). *Murder.* The crime was committed on 3/13/1903 in Dade County. Executed for the willful killing of another black man named Ed Davis (age not recorded), who had the point of a pickaxe plunged through his back. Motive: prison violence. Recidivist killer. Phillips was already serving a life sentence in the Dade County mines when he killed Davis. The details of the earlier homicide that had landed him there are not specified in surviving accounts. He was legally hanged at Trenton on May 1, 1903. Source: *Dade County Sentinel* (Trenton, GA), 3/20/03 (3:3) & 5/1/03 (2:3). Pardons Files Box 95, GA State Archives. See also: *Acts and Resolutions of the General Assembly of the State of Georgia* (1904), 737.

Henry Owens (black, age not recorded). *Murder.* The crime was committed on 3/17/1903 in Charlton County. Uxoricide. This is another case that is known only from a thinly worded newspaper report. The actual court records perished long ago. Owens killed his wife (name not specified, presumably a black female) under unknown circumstances. He was legally hanged at Folkston on May 8, 1903. Source: *Savannah Morning News*, 5/9/03 (9:3).

Monroe Adams (black, age 41). *Murder.* The crime was committed on 7/23/1902 in Sumter County. Uxoricide and filicide. Executed for the shotgun slayings of 39-year-old Mollie Adams and 21-year-old Bobbie Adams (blacks), they respectively being his wife and his daughter. Motive: a sordid tale of incest. Adams was a cook by profession and a married father of seven. Some insight into his character can be gleaned from the fact that Adams sired his first child when its mother was twelve years old. Bobbie Adams (his second daughter) was due to be married on 7/24/1902. Black folks said that her papa would not hear of it because he was used to using the girl like a concubine and was loath to give her up. So he ran wild with a double barrel on the day before the wedding with an intention of exterminating anyone who had anything to do with its planning. He was legally hanged at Americus on May 15, 1903. Source: *Atlanta Constitution*, 7/25/02 (4:5) & 5/16/03 (12:2). See also: 1880 and 1900 U.S. Censuses (Sumter Co., GA), which notes all parties.

Oscar Cicero (black, age 30). *Murder.* The crime was committed on 2/27/1901 in Mitchell County. Handgun slaying of another black man called "Bud Battle" (age not specified). Motive: the homicide victim was wearing female apparel. Surviving records are coy about this in the manner of their wording, but it seems that Cicero had been duped by a cross-dresser. He was hanged for capital murder at Camilla on June 12, 1903. Source: *Columbus (GA) Ledger*, 6/12/03 (1:4). Pardons Files Box 23, GA State Archives. See also: 1880 U.S. Census (Mitchell Co., GA), which notes the killer.

Abe Cohen (black, age 27). *Murder.* The crime was committed on 7/3/1902 in Chatham County. Handgun slaying of 25-year-old Susie Rogers (black), she having been shot five times and then repeatedly kicked even as flames from the murder weapon ignited her clothes. Motive: wrathful lover. The killer had tracked his prey to the city from their usual abode in Brunswick. He was hanged for his misdeed at the Savannah city jail on July 10, 1903. Source: *Savannah Morning News*, 7/4/02 (10:1) & 7/11/03 (12:5).

Dennis Miller (black, age 21). *Murder.* The crime was committed on 6/4/1902 in Charlton County. Handgun slaying of another young black man named Lewis Strickland (exact age not recorded) in a dispute about a missing sack of rice. Dennis Miller learned the high cost of settling arguments with guns when he was hanged at Folkston on July 10, 1903. Source: *Atlanta Constitution*, 7/11/03 (2:2). Pardons Files Box 83, GA State Archives.

Millard Lee (white, age 22). *Murder.* The crime was committed on 5/25/1902 in Fulton County. Handgun slaying of 21-year-old Lilla Suttles (white), who was gunned down in a crowded church. Motive: thwarted lover. The fact that this young man had chosen to desecrate a church service in such a flagitious manner counted heavily against him. Millard Lee was hanged at the Fulton County Jail on October 30, 1903. Source: *Atlanta Constitution*, 5/26/02 (1:7) & 10/31/03 (1:4).

Robert Middlebrooks (black, age 63). *Murder.* The crime was committed on 6/27/1903 in Bartow County. Shotgun slaying of 38-year-old Robert L. Read (white), a court bailiff. Motive: resisting arrest. This assassin faced the hangman at Cartersville on December 11, 1903. Source: *Atlanta Constitution*, 7/1/03 (5:1) & 12/12/03 (2:5). See also: 1900 U.S. Census (Bartow Co., GA), which notes both parties.

Ned Jack Ferguson (black, age not recorded). *Murder.* The crime was committed on 10/20/1903 in Worth County. Executed for the fatal stabbing of 29-year-old Henry Tucker (black). Motive: prison violence. Recidivist killer. Ferguson was already serving a life sentence for an unrelated murder when he knifed Tucker. He had been sent up from Talbot County in 1895 for killing a black boy named Ben Bethel, circumstances unknown. The gallows marked Ferguson's end at Sylvester on December 17, 1903. Source: *Atlanta Constitution*, 10/23/03 (5:3) & 12/18/03 (9:5). *Atlanta Journal*, 12/18/03 (3:3). See also: 1900 U.S. Census (Sumter Co., GA), which notes Henry Tucker.

Lee W. Cribb (white, age 26). *Murder.* The crime was committed on 12/6/1902 in Coffee County. Police killer and child killer. Executed for the handgun slaying of 13-year-old Emmett White (white), who was randomly killed during an armed rampage on the streets of Nichols. Town Marshal Thomas Holton (white, age 38) was also killed by the same weapon, but Cribb was tried only for the boy's death. He was hanged at Douglas on December 18, 1903. Source: *Augusta (GA) Chronicle*, 11/1/03 (5:5) & 12/1/03 (2:6). *Macon (GA) Telegraph*, 12/19/03 (1:1). *Douglas (GA) Weekly Breeze*, 12/19/03 (1:4).

William Grant (black, age 23). *Murder.* The crime was committed on 12/26/1902 in Decatur County. Handgun slaying of 26-year-old James Byrd (white). Motive: insolence. A group of white folks and a group of black folks were walking along a rural road in oncoming directions. The latter were acting loud and smutty. Byrd asked them not to use obscene language in the presence of women—in this case, *white* women. William Grant's response was to pull out a pistol and start shooting. James Byrd fell dead in the road. Grant died twitching at the end of a rope following his conviction for capital murder. The location was Bainbridge. The date was December 18, 1903. Source: *The Search Light* (Bainbridge, GA), 1/2/03 (1:3) & 12/25/03 (1:5). *Atlanta Constitution*, 12/19/03 (5:3). See also: 1900 U.S. Census (Decatur Co., GA), which notes both parties.

Will Hardy (black, age 26). *Murder.* The crime was committed on 11/22/1903 in Mitchell County. Gunshot slaying of a young white man named Raymond Mullins (exact age uncertain), whose father was the mayor of Baconton. Motive: resisting arrest. The homicide victim in this case had been with a posse that was looking for Hardy at that time. The law made short work of this offender. He was legally hanged at Camilla on December 22, 1903. Source: *Vienna (GA) News*, 11/25/03 (1:5). *Atlanta Constitution*, 11/23/03 (3:1), 11/24/03 (9:7) & 12/23/03 (4:1). See also: 1900 U.S. Census (Mitchell Co., GA), which notes Hardy.

1904

John Harris (black, age abt. 45). *Murder.* The crime was committed on 10/3/1903 in Fulton County. Police killer. Fatal stabbing of 39-year-old Hans C. Drasbach (white). Motive: resisting arrest. Harris came from Abbeville, SC. It is not known why he was in Atlanta when he got into trouble. He was legally hanged there on January 15, 1904. Source: *Atlanta Constitution*, 10/5/03 (1:7), 10/6/03 (7:1), 10/19/03 (1:2) & 1/16/04 (7:3). *Atlanta News*, 1/15/04 (3:1). See also: 1900 U.S. Census (Fulton Co., GA), which notes "H. C. Drasbeck."

Tom Caruthis, alias "Caruthers," alias "Carithers" (black, age 27). *Murder.* The crime was committed on 6/15/1903 in Wilcox County. Handgun slaying of 37-year-old Henry L. Bird (white), a plantation overseer. Motive: the homicide victim had reproached Caruthis for being lazy. The killer's own father betrayed him into the hands of the law for the sake of a $150 reward. It is not known if Caruthis' father was among the spectators when his son was legally hanged at Abbeville on January 30, 1904. Source: *Atlanta Constitution*, 10/13/03 (2:1) & 1/31/04 (6:6). *Hawkinsville (GA) Dispatch*, 2/3/04 (1:2). *Abbeville (GA) Chronicle*, 6/18/03 (1:1) & 2/4/04 (1:3). See also: 1900 U.S. Census (Wilcox Co., GA), which notes Mr. Bird.

Will Strickland (black, age 30). *Murder.* The crime was committed on 1/31/1903 in Madison County. Handgun slaying of a young black woman named Dilsey Hudson (exact age uncertain). Motive: male bravado. The scene was an all-black dance. Dilsey had had a flower pinned to her blouse. The flower fell to the floor and Dilsey asked another black man to pin it back into place. Seeing this, Will Strickland became enraged. He felt slighted because Dilsey had not asked *him* to re-affix the flower. So he pulled out a pistol and started shooting. Strickland was hanged at Danielsville on March 11, 1904, with no one to blame but himself. Source: *Atlanta Constitution*, 3/26/03 (7:2). *Augusta (GA) Chronicle*, 2/5/04 (8:4) & 3/10/04 (5:5). *Atlanta Journal*, 3/11/04 (7:7). See also: 1900 U.S. Census (Madison Co., GA), which notes Strickland.

Jim Jenkins (black, age 29). *Murder.* The crime was committed on 8/1/1903 in Colquitt County. Hanged on his 30th birthday for the handgun slaying of a young black woman named Annie Taylor (exact age uncertain), whom he had shot three times in the head. Motive: jealous lover. Jim Jenkins faced the hangman at Moultrie on April 15, 1904. Source: *Macon (GA) Telegraph*, 8/30/03 (1:5) & 4/16/04 (3:4). *Moultrie (GA) Observer, 4/15/04 (1:6)*. Note: The issues of the *Moultrie Observer* that contained accounts of both the crime and the execution were stolen from their original folio volume sometime before the advent of microfilm.

Henry Curry (black, age not recorded). *Murder.* The crime was committed on or about 4/15/1904 in Wayne County. Executed for the gunshot slaying of another black man named Albert Smith (age unknown). Motive: bickering at a turpentine still. Little else is known about this case aside from the fact that Henry Curry was legally hanged at Jesup on June 15, 1904. Source: *Macon (GA) Telegraph,* 6/16/04 (2:5). *Jesup (GA) Sentinel,* 6/16/04 (8:6).

Willie Calvin (black, age not recorded). *Murder.* The crime was committed on 9/8/1902 in Chatham County. Executed for the frenzied killing of 32-year-old Rosa Pace (black), a.k.a. "Annie Pierce," who was slashed to death with a razor. Motive: adultery turned deadly. Calvin had abandoned his lawful spouse in Jacksonville, FL, and absconded to Savannah with the paramour that he killed. His new life there did not turn out to be what he had envisioned. He was hanged at the Savannah city jail on July 8, 1904. Source: *Savannah Morning News,* 9/9/02 (6:1) & 7/9/04 (3:1). See also: *Savannah Municipal Death Register,* entry dated 9/8/02.

Elton Attaway Gray (black, age 27). *Murder.* The crime was committed on 12/11/1903 in Dooly County. Uxoricide. Shotgun slaying of Rosa Gray (black, age not recorded). Motive: marital estrangement. Few other details are known of this case. Wife-killer Gray was hanged for what he did at Vienna on July 26, 1904. Source: *Atlanta Constitution,* 7/27/04 (9:4). *Vienna (GA) News,* 12/16/03 (1:1) & 7/27/04 (1:1). See also: 1900 U.S. Census (Burke Co., GA), which notes this husband-to-be.

Smith Brooks (black, age not recorded). *Murder.* The crime was committed on 6/25/1904 in Monroe County. Fatal stabbing of 45-year-old John M. Maddox (white), a storekeeper. Motive: a disagreement over a 50-cent store credit. The killer's temper cost him his life when he was hanged at Forsyth on September 19, 1904. Source: *Macon (GA) Telegraph,* 8/27/04 (6:4) & 9/20/04 (3:4). *Monroe Advertiser* (Forsyth, GA), 7/1/04 (3:5) & 9/23/04 (3:6). See also the gravestone of Mr. Maddox in McCowen Cemetery (McCowen Road), Monroe Co.

George Ponder (black, age 66). *Murder.* The crime was committed sometime during the year 1904 in Walton County. Executed for the ax murder of a black female who was known only as "Tip Davis" (age not specified). Motive: lovers' quarrel. Walton County courthouse personnel made an honest effort to locate the original file on this case for me, but without success. It is confirmed that George Ponder paid the death penalty there on September 23, 1904. Source: *Atlanta Constitution,* 8/20/04 (7:4) & 9/24/04 (2:1). See also: 1900 U.S. Census (Walton Co., GA), which notes this miscreant.

Alex Braddy (black, age 44). *Murder.* The crime was committed on 6/11/1904 in Warren County. Uxoricide. Executed for the killing of 32-year-old Vinie Braddy (black), whom he pulled from off of their wagon and attacked with a knife. She was found with her throat cut in addition to multiple stab wounds. Motive: domestic flare-up. This wife-killer was hanged at Warrenton on September 24, 1904. Source: *Augusta (GA) Chronicle*, 6/22/04 (2:2). *Atlanta Constitution*, 9/25/04 (5:4). See also: 1900 U.S. Census (Warren Co., GA), which notes both parties as "Brady."

Sampson Flournoy (black, age 33). *Murder.* The crime was committed on 7/23/1904 in Burke County. Shotgun slayings of 26-year-old James Minor and 18-year-old Evans Tomlin, and the severe wounding of 23-year-old Edward Minor (whites). Motive: a dispute over who should have access to a swimming hole. Flournoy had wanted to have a swim on this hot summer day. He went to a well-known pool but found three young white men there. They would not allow him access to the water because of the "Jim Crow" custom. Enraged at this, Flournoy fetched his shotgun. He then went back to the swimming hole and blasted away at every white man he saw. The local populace allowed the law to take its course. A trial court found that personal indignation in no way justified what Flournoy had done. He was legally hanged at Waynesboro on November 1, 1904. Source: *Atlanta Constitution*, 7/24/04 (24:3). *Augusta (GA) Chronicle*, 10/12/04 (8:4) & 11/2/04 (2:5). See also: 1900 U.S. Census (Burke Co., GA), which notes Flournoy and Tomlin.

John Butler (black, age 22) and **Guy Reid** (black, age abt. 20). *Murder.* Their crime was committed on 12/1/1904 in McDuffie County. Both executed for the ax murder of 46-year-old Radford Gunn Story (white), their employer. Motive: he would not let them have time off from work to attend a funeral, or so they said. The law took a fast track in this case. These killers were hanged at Thomson on December 27, 1904. Source: *Columbus (GA) Enquirer-Sun*, 12/3/04 (5:3), 12/4/04 (3:1:2) & 12/29/04 (1:2). *Atlanta Constitution*, 12/28/04 (1:3). *Atlanta Journal*, 12/27/04 (1:7). Also see Mr. Story's gravestone in Dunn's Chapel Cemetery, Leah.

1905

Whitley Williford (black, age not recorded). *Murder.* The crime was committed on 4/20/1903 in Mitchell County. Handgun slaying of 46-year-old Harmon West (white), a posse man. Motive: resisting capture. The killer was an escaped convict from Valdosta. He was traced to a cabin near Camilla, where the shooting took place. He was legally hanged there on January 13, 1905. Source: *Columbus (GA) Enquirer-Sun*, 4/21/03 (8:6) & 9/16/04 (5:5). *Atlanta Constitution*, 1/14/05 (4:7). Appeal: 121 GA 173–180. Pardons Files Box 133, GA State Archives. See also: 1880 U.S. Census (Mitchell Co., GA), which notes Harmon West.

Lige West (black, age 28). *Murder.* The crime was committed on 3/13/1904 in Houston County. Uxoricide. Executed for the gunshot slaying of 30-year-old Micky West (black), who was attacked while riding in a carriage with her sister and brother-in-law. Motive: presumably because the latter couple had dared to give the homicide victim sanctuary from her abusive spouse. He was hanged at Perry on January 20, 1905. Source: *The Home Journal* (Perry, GA), 3/17/04 (7:3), 6/30/04 (6:2) & 10/13/04 (6:2). *Atlanta Constitution*, 1/21/05 (1:2). See also: 1900 U.S. Census (Houston Co., GA), which notes both parties.

Charles "Bud" Hilburn (black, age 42). *Murder.* The crime was committed on 2/7/1904 in Emanuel County. Handgun slaying of 20-year-old Abraham H. Durden (white), a court bailiff. Motive: resisting arrest. Durden had a warrant to take Hilburn into custody. He traced him to an all-black gambling den that was crowded with gamesters. Perhaps overly eager to prove himself, Durden strode right into the place to make the collar without even calling for backup. Young Durden was carried dead from the dive. Bud Hilburn was carried dead from the gallows at Swainsboro on February 3, 1905. Source: *Macon (GA) Telegraph*, 2/9/04 (6:4), 2/12/04 (6:7) & 2/4/05 (1:1). See also: 1900 U.S. Census (Emanuel Co., GA), which notes Hilburn.

Courtney Baker (black, age not recorded). *Murder.* The crime was committed on 4/1/1904 in Floyd County. Uxoricide. Executed for the shotgun slaying of Carrie Garrett Baker (black, age not recorded). Motive: uncertain. Surviving accounts provide little insight into this case. It is confirmed, however, that this wife-killer was hanged at Rome on March 7, 1905. Source: *Rome (GA) Tribune*, 3/8/05 (8:1). See also: Floyd Co. marriage cert. no. 29 (dated 8/11/00). Microfilm drawer no. 162, reel no. 29, GA State Archives.

Bob Sutherland (black, age 18). *Murder.* The crime was committed on 6/4/1904 in Floyd County. Handgun slayings of two young blacks named James Bronner and Bettie Hadden (exact ages unknown) when this offender decided to shoot up a crowded dance hall for no apparent reason. "Because I couldn't resist the temptation to do so!" said Sutherland when questioned about his motive. He was hanged by the neck until dead at Rome on March 7, 1905. Source: *Rome (GA) Tribune*, 3/7/05 (8:1) & 3/8/05 (8:1). *Atlanta Constitution*, 3/8/05 (11:2). Pardon Files Box 117, GA State Archives.

Noah Anderson (black, age 33). *Murder.* The crime was committed on or about 8/25/1904 in Decatur County. Patricide. Executed for the handgun slaying of 64-year-old Henry Anderson (black). Motive: a stupid argument over who should be allowed to drink some whiskey. Another account says that they had fought over fifty cents. Whatever the circumstances, they were all the same to Noah Anderson when he dropped from the gallows at Bainbridge on March 22, 1905. Source: *Atlanta Journal*, 3/22/05 (5:2). *Vienna (GA) News*, 3/24/05 (1:4). Appeal: 122 GA 175–177. See also: 1880 and 1900 U.S. Censuses (Decatur Co., GA), which note both parties.

Tobe Thornton (black, age 24). *Rape.* The crime was committed on 1/1/1904 in Webster County. Indecent assault on the person of 51-year-old Margaret Dismukes (white, a maiden woman), who was beaten and traumatized to such a degree that she had to be institutionalized for the rest of her life. She died on 8/3/1927. Her attacker was legally hanged at Preston on April 27, 1905. Source: *Macon (GA) Telegraph*, 1/4/04 (6:4). *Augusta (GA) Chronicle*, 4/28/05 (1:6). See also: 1900 U.S. Census (Webster Co., GA), which notes the culprit, and 1910 U.S. Census (Baldwin Co., GA), which notes Miss Dismukes as an inmate of the state sanitarium.

Greeley Phillips (black, age 28). *Murder.* The crime was committed on

8/6/1904 in Coweta County. Handgun slaying of a young black woman named Mary Lasseter (exact age uncertain), who was shot five or six times at a picnic. Motive: she would not let herself be enticed away from her husband. The killer was hanged at Newnan on May 5, 1905. Source: *Herald & Advertiser* (Newnan, GA), 8/12/04 (7:5). *Macon (GA) Telegraph*, 5/5/05 (1:3) & 5/6/05 (1:2). See also: 1900 U.S. Census (Meriwether Co., GA), which notes Phillips.

Will Sims (black, age not recorded). *Murder.* The crime was committed on 4/11/1905 in Rockdale County. Uxoricide. Executed for the killing (by unspecified means) of Rosa Sims (black, age not recorded). The homicide was further aggravated by the fact that the decedent was in the act of nursing a baby when the killer struck. Motive: she had disobeyed her husband's order not to leave their home. He was legally hanged at Conyers on June 2, 1905. Source: *Augusta (GA) Chronicle*, 5/5/05 (3:4), 5/23/05 (3:7) & 6/3/05 (2:6).

Peter Thomas (black, age not recorded). *Murder.* The crime was committed on 4/15/1905 in Dougherty County. Police killer. Handgun slaying of John Manier (white, age uncertain), the marshal of Pretoria. Motive: resisting arrest. This homicide was further aggravated by the fact that the marshal was deliberately shot multiple times after he lay disabled on the ground. The assassin, Peter Thomas, was legally hanged at Albany on June 2, 1905. Source: *Augusta (GA) Chronicle*, 4/17/05 (2:1). *Savannah Morning News*, 6/3/05 (1:4). *Atlanta Constitution*, 6/3/05 (7:2).

Algernon Bachelor (black, age not recorded). *Murder.* The crime was committed on 10/14/1905 in Walton County. Police killer. Shotgun slaying of 27-year-old John Eugene Darby (white), a police constable who had come to levy a garnishment on the killer's cotton crop. Motive: contempt of authority. The assassin, "Algie" Bachelor, was legally hanged at Monroe on November 13, 1905. Little time was lost in bringing him to justice. Source: *Augusta (GA) Chronicle*, 10/16/05 (2:4) & 10/25/05 (1:6). *Athens (GA) Weekly Banner*, 10/27/05 (6:7). *Atlanta News*, 11/13/05 (11:3). See also: 1900 U.S. Census (Walton Co., GA), which notes Darby.

Jim Walker (black, age 23). *Rape.* The crime was committed on 10/26/1905 in Fulton County. Indecent assault on the person of 46-year-old Alice Moore (white), who was pounced on and nearly strangled in her vegetable garden by this roving sex offender. He was legally hanged at Atlanta on December 8, 1905. Source: *Atlanta Constitution*, 10/27/05 (1:7), 11/10/05 (1:7) & 12/9/05 (6:1). See also: 1900 U.S. Census (Atlanta, GA), which notes Mrs. Moore.

1906

William Aiken (black, age 44). *Murder.* The crime was committed at some point during the year 1905 in Tattnall County. Filicide. Executed for the unmitigated killing of 28-year-old Edwin Aiken (black), his own son. How he did it and why he did it are open questions because the original court papers are inaccessible. The elder Aiken was legally hanged at Reidsville on January 5, 1906. Source: *Savannah Morning News*, 1/6/06 (5:4). See also: 1900 U.S. Census (Tattnall Co., GA), which notes both parties as "Akin." Also note:

Tattnall County Superior Court Minutes (October Term, 1905), 130.

Dock Hardy (black, age not recorded). *Murder.* The crime was committed on 11/3/1905 in Heard County. Handgun slaying of a white man named Max Wilson (age unknown), who was shot in the back as he was sitting on a tree stump. Motive: vendetta. The homicide victim had reportedly killed Hardy's brother in self defense earlier that year. The only other thing that Dock Hardy secured by this self-defeating act was his own death as well. He was legally hanged at Franklin on January 12, 1906. Source: *Atlanta Constitution*, 11/4/05 (1:4), 11/5/05 (7:4), 11/6/05 (3:2) & 1/13/06 (4:5).

Essie Johnson (black, age 21). *Murder.* The crime was committed on 11/5/1905 in Terrell County. Handgun slaying of 82-year-old Eliza Banks (black), who was shot three times. Motive: chicken thief caught in the act. This black-on-black killer was hanged for what he did to a feeble old lady at Dawson on February 16, 1906. Source: *Dawson (GA) News*, 11/8/05 (9:2), 11/15/05 (9:2) & 2/21/06 (3:1). See also: 1900 U.S. Census (Terrell Co., GA), which notes Johnson.

Willie Richard Andrews (black, age 15). *Rape.* The crime was committed on 1/26/1906 in Wilkes County. Indecent assault on the person of 5-year-old Lucy Alva Roberts (white) under circumstances that were described as "peculiarly heinous." This precocious pervert was legally hanged at Washington on March 16, 1906. Source: *Augusta (GA) Chronicle*, 3/17/06 (2:4). See also: 1900 U.S. Census (Wilkes Co., GA), which notes that "Rich Andrews" had been born in the month of January 1891.

Will Gordon (black, age not recorded). *Murder.* The crime was committed on 2/23/1906 in Gwinnett County. Handgun slaying of 17-year-old Rachel Hunt (black). Motive: stupid male jealousy. Gordon had become enraged at the sight of Miss Hunt dancing with another man. Recidivist killer. Gordon had been previously convicted for murdering his wife in an unrelated incident. He was sentenced to a term of so-called "life imprisonment" but somehow wrangled a pardon. He then went on to make use of his new-found freedom in the manner described above. The hangman ensured that there would be no future offenses by this man when he sent him through the gallows trap at Lawrenceville on May 15, 1906. Source: *News Herald* (Lawrenceville, GA), 3/1/06 (1:5) & 5/17/06 (1:3). See also: 1900 U.S. Census (Gwinnett Co., GA), which notes Rachel Hunt.

George Broughton (black, age abt. 30). *Murder.* The crime was committed on 9/3/1904 in Sumter County. Shotgun slaying of 61-year-old Harry Horne (black), his father-in-law. Motive: family problems. The hangman exacted payment from George Broughton at Americus on May 18, 1906. Source: *Americus (GA) Weekly Times-Recorder*, 5/25/06 (6:3). *Macon (GA) Daily Telegraph*, 5/19/06 (1:6). Pardons Files Box 14, GA State Archives. See also: 1900 U.S. Census (Sumter Co., GA), which notes Harry Horne.

John Graham (black, age 28). *Murder.* The crime was committed on 9/3/1905 in Sumter County. Shotgun slaying of 55-year-old Horace Morgan (black). Motive: rivalry for a female. The killer had been accepted as a church congregant less than an hour before the crime. This was how he put his formalized Christianity into action. The gallows exacted penance from him at Americus on May 18, 1906. Source: *Macon (GA) Daily Telegraph*, 12/14/05 (1:4) & 5/19/06 (1:6). *Americus (GA) Weekly Times-Recorder*, 9/8/05 (5:2), 9/8/05 (8:2) & 5/25/06 (6:3). See also: 1900 U.S. Census (Sumter Co., GA), which notes both parties.

Huss Grant (black, age not recorded). *Murder.* The crime was committed on 8/12/1905 in Morgan County. Handgun slaying of a young black woman named Mary Johnson (exact age uncertain), who was shot multiple times in her bed. Motive: lovers' quarrel. The killer was hanged at Madison on May 18, 1906. Source: *Atlanta Constitution*, 5/18/06 (7:2). *Columbus (GA) Enquirer-Sun*, 5/19/06 (1:2). Pardons Files Box 47, GA State Archives.

Jonas Hicks (black, age not recorded). *Murder.* The crime was committed on 3/13/1906 in Sumter County. Handgun slaying of 43-year-old Jarrett J. Davis (white), his employer. Motive: big attitude. It was a strict rule of Mr. Davis that those who worked for him not carry firearms (either concealed or openly) while on duty. He found out that Jonas Hicks was toting a loaded .44-caliber pistol on the above date and demanded that its owner (Hicks) place it in his keeping until quitting time. Hicks replied to this by pulling said weapon from his waistband and shooting his boss dead. This earned him an appointment with the hangman. Hicks kept that date at Americus on September 7, 1906. Source: *Atlanta Constitution*, 3/14/06 (8:6), 3/15/06 (8:7) & 9/8/06 (5:6). *Americus (GA) Weekly Times-Recorder*, 3/16/06 (5:1). See also: 1880 U.S. Census (Sumter Co., GA), which notes Mr. Davis.

Jeff Hillhouse (black, age not recorded). *Murder.* The crime was committed on 6/20/1906 in Houston County. Child killer. Executed for the murder of 15-year-old Florida King (black female), whose skull was split open by the blade of a hoe. Motive: sexual assault. The homicide victim's little brother was also attacked in the same manner but survived with crippling injuries. Jeff Hillhouse was legally hanged with the full approval of the local black community at Perry on September 7, 1906. Source: *Macon (GA) Daily Telegraph*, 6/21/06 (1:6), 8/16/06 (4:5) & 9/8/06 (1:6).

Bob Moore (black, age abt. 40). *Rape.* The crime was committed on 8/17/1906 in White County. Indecent assault on the person of 7-year-old Annie Ruby Hood (white), who was ravished in a potato patch. No time was lost in adjudicating this case. Child predator Bob Moore was legally hanged at Cleveland on September 10, 1906. Source: *Atlanta Constitution*, 8/19/06 (3:3), 9/11/06 (3:6) & 9/17/06 (3:7). See also: 1900 U.S. Census (White Co., GA), which notes James C. Hood and family.

Bird Earl (black, age 36). *Murder.* The crime was committed sometime during the year 1906 in Morgan County. Uxoricide. Executed for the killing of Cora Jordan Earl (black, age not recorded) under circumstances that are difficult to discern because the original court papers are inaccessible. This wife-killer was legally hanged at Madison on October 19, 1906. Source: *Atlanta Constitution*, 10/20/06 (5:6). See also: 1900 U.S. Census (Morgan Co., GA), which notes Bird Earl. Also:

Morgan County Colored Marriage Register (1891–1904), 579, which notes the nuptials of this ill-fated couple on 12/4/1903.

Mims Devereaux (black, age not recorded). *Murder.* The crime was committed on 11/3/1905 in Baldwin County. Shotgun slaying of 58-year-old Jack Rushins (black). Motive: gambling dispute. This killer died hard. Devereaux held officers at bay for more than two hours when they came to escort him to the gallows at Milledgeville on November 16, 1906. Source: *Union-Recorder* (Milledgeville, GA), 11/7/05 (4:3) & 11/20/06 (1:5). *Atlanta Georgian*, 11/16/06 (1:6). Pardons Files Box 33, GA State Archives. Also: 1900 U.S. Census (Baldwin Co., GA), which notes Jack Rushins.

Joseph C. Rawlins (white, age 40) and **Alfred Moore** (black, age uncertain). *Murder.* Their crime was committed on 6/13/1905 in Lowndes County. Catalyst (Rawlins) and participant (Moore) in the killings of 16-year-old Annie Carter and 17-year-old Willie Carter (whites, siblings), who were gunned down by an organized assassination team. Motive: feuding. The so-called *Carter-Rawlins Feud* had been notorious in Lowndes County. It was said to have had its origin in some schoolhouse incident involving the children of each family. The parents were just as immature and spiteful as their kids. All declared war on each other. Joseph Rawlins either ordered or acquiesced to an armed attack on the Carter cabin by his three teenage sons: Milton (age 18), Leonard (age 17), Jesse (age 16) and a black adherent of theirs named Alfred Moore. All four took up concealed positions around the aforesaid premises. The Carter family dog barked an alarm so loud that three of the intended victims came outside to see what all the noise was about. The killers opened fire on them with rifles and shotguns, killing Annie and Willie Carter. The boy managed to crawl back into the cabin, where he died on the floor. The girl was singled out for special mistreatment because the killers hated her in particular. She was battered beyond recognition with rifle butts. She was also kicked and stomped so viciously that boot prints covered every inch of her person. All of these facts withstanding, the three Carter boys dodged the gallows through various stratagems of legalistic trickery. Their patriarch and their African American lackey were not so fortunate. The latter two perished by the noose at Valdosta on December 4, 1906. Source: *Columbus (GA) Enquirer-Sun*, 6/15/05 (1:3). *Macon (GA) Daily Telegraph*, 6/15/05 (1:1), 6/16/05 (1:5) & 12/5/06 (1:1). See also: 1900 U.S. Census (Lowndes Co., GA), which notes the family Rawlins.

Will Perkins (black, age not recorded). *Murder.* The crime was committed on 4/6/1906 in Effingham County. Shotgun slaying of Jesse Zeigler (black, age not recorded), who was blasted thrice with the same weapon. Motive: the killer felt threatened (or so he said), both parties having had harsh words with each other. Perkins met a felon's fate when he was hanged at Springfield on December 28, 1906. Source: *Atlanta Journal*, 12/29/06 (4:3). *Savannah Morning News*, 12/29/06 (5:1).

1907

John O. Bullard (white, age 40). *Murder.* The crime was committed on 9/24/1906 in Cobb County. Filicide. Handgun slaying of 17-year-old Ruby

Bullard (white), who was shot multiple times. Motive: incest turned deadly. The Cobb County Superior Court took a dim view of what Bullard had done as well as of what he had been in the habit of doing. It concluded that he should be hanged. That sentence was carried out at Marietta on March 1, 1907. Source: *Marietta (GA) Journal*, 9/27/06 (6:2) & 3/7/07 (1:3). See also: 1870 and 1880 U.S. Censuses (Paulding Co., GA), which note Bullard as a minor, one of the sons of James Madison Bullard.

Robert Henderson, alias "Will Ford" (black, age not recorded). *Murder.* The crime was committed on 3/5/1907 in Turner County. Ax murder of 55-year-old George W. May (white). Motive: highway robbery. There was no appeal. This public menace was legally hanged at Ashburn on May 23, 1907. Source: *Atlanta Constitution*, 3/7/07 (2:7) & 5/24/07 (8:4). See also: 1900 U.S. Census (Dooly Co., GA), which notes Mr. May.

Buck High (black, age 15). *Rape.* The crime was committed on 3/25/1907 in Henry County. Indecent assault on the person of 4-year-old Laura Daniel (white) under circumstances that are unfit for publication. This depraved sex offender was afforded no chance to repeat what he had done. He was legally put to death at McDonough on May 29, 1907. Source: *Columbus (GA) Daily Enquirer*, 3/27/07 (1:5). *Atlanta Journal*, 5/29/07 (3:1). See also: 1900 U.S. Census (Henry Co., GA) and 1910 U.S. Census (Cullman Co., AL), which note John Daniel and family.

Will Johnson (black, age uncertain). *Rape.* The crime was committed on 8/15/1906 in Fulton County. Serial rapist, killer, armed robber, and burglar. Specifically executed for an indecent assault on the person of 28-year-old Georgia Hembree (white), who was choked, beaten and raped by a purse snatcher later identified as Will Johnson. This was the opening act in a crime spree that terrorized the entire city of Atlanta. The marauder (Johnson) struck again three days later when he opened fire (with a shotgun) on a donkey wagon ambling its way along the Adamsville road. Its driver, Amos J. Moody (white, age 38), was found dead at the five-mile marker with his pockets pulled inside out. Two days after this (on August 20) Johnson attacked two white females who were gathering wild flowers. The elder of these, Ethel Lawrence (white, age 26), was beaten to within an inch of her life and raped. She was found at the scene with a broken arm, a fractured skull and one of her eyes gouged out. The young woman's niece, Mabel Lawrence (white, age 14), was also raped but managed to break free and raise an alarm. A month of heightened racial tension came next during which three more white women were reportedly attacked with varying degrees of brutality. Angry white men banded together to patrol the city. They beat up any black man who they deemed suspicious—especially vagrants, idlers and those who could not satisfactorily account for themselves. This situation reached a climax on the weekend of September 23–24 when a full-blown race riot erupted. At least fifteen people were reported to have been killed in the violence, including one police officer. The cause of it all (Johnson) lay low for a while thereafter. He reemerged on November 16 when he broke into the house of a white woman named Aletha Camp (age 30) and raped her on her kitchen floor. She was also beaten and garroted with a strip of rawhide. Then her house was ransacked. An innocent man was prosecuted for this last incident but was spared from further harm by the timely capture of the true miscreant. Will Johnson was sent through the gallows trap at the Fulton County Jail on June 14, 1907. Source: *Atlanta Constitution*, 8/16/06 (6:5), 8/19/06 (1:2), 8/24/06 (1:1), 8/25/06 (1:1), 9/24/06 (p. 1), 9/25/06 (p. 1), 11/14/06 (3:2), 11/17/06 (1:2) & 6/15/07 (1:2). See also: 1900 U.S. Census (Fulton Co., GA), which notes Hembree and Camp. Also 1900 U.S. Census (Douglas Co., GA), which notes Moody.

George W. Bundrick (white, age 37). *Murder.* The crime was committed on 9/24/1902 in Crisp County. Shotgun slaying of 26-year-old John H. Shrouder (white), who was bushwhacked on a public road while traveling with his wife. Bundrick thought that one of Mr. Shrouder's farm laborers (a black man) had stolen his pocket knife. He demanded satisfaction. Shrouder offered to pay for the missing knife, just to keep the peace, but Bundrick was not appeased. He accused Shrouder of "siding with niggers" (or words to that degree of vulgarity) and promised to make him regret it. So George Bundrick and his brother Andrew (who was a hothead like himself) lay in wait for Shrouder's buggy along a country lane. They peppered the conveyance with buckshot, killing John Shrouder and badly wounding his wife. Andrew Bundrick was sentenced to a long prison term. George Bundrick was caught in Louisiana five years later. He got the death penalty. He was hanged at Cordele on June 21, 1907. Source: *Augusta (GA) Chronicle*, 9/25/02 (4:4). *Macon (GA) Daily Telegraph*, 6/23/05 (6:1) & 6/25/05 (2:1:2). *Atlanta Constitution*, 6/22/07 (9:2). See also: 1900 U.S. Census (Dooly Co., GA), which notes all parties.

John Mitchell (black, age 26). *Murder.* The crime was committed on 5/1/1907 in Cobb County. Handgun slaying of another young black man named Nashmoore Johnson (exact age uncertain). Motive: rivalry for a female. The killer in this case was legally hanged at Marietta on June 21, 1907. Source: *Marietta Journal*, 5/16/07 (4:2) & 6/27/07 (1:4). *Atlanta Georgian*, 6/21/07 (6:3). Pardons Files Box 84, GA State Archives.

Will Price, alias "Buster" (black, age 30). *Rape.* The crime was committed on 7/6/1907 in Randolph County. Indecent assault on the person of 14-year-old Sarah Burks (white), who was attacked while walking along a rural lane with her 10-year-old brother. This sexual predator was legally hanged at Cuthbert on August 15, 1907. Source: *Atlanta Constitution*, 8/16/07 (2:3).

Will Nix (black, age not recorded). *Murder.* The crime was committed on 1/26/1907 in Washington County. Handgun slayings of 52-year-old Robert B. Jackson (white) and 18-year-old Aaron Daniel (black). Motive: a holiday brawl on the Taylor plantation. This double killer was hanged at Sandersville on August 16, 1907. Source: *Macon (GA) Daily Telegraph*, 1/28/07 (1:7). *Atlanta Constitution*, 8/17/07 (7:7). *Sandersville (GA) Progress*, 1/29/07 (1:3) & 8/20/07 (1:4). See also: 1900 U.S. Census (Wash. Co., GA), which notes Aaron Daniel, and 1860 U.S. Census (Wash. Co., GA), which notes Mr. Jackson as a minor.

Matthew Howell (black, age 19). *Murder.* The crime was committed on

10/4/1907 in Gwinnett County. Shotgun slaying of 45-year-old James B. Rainey (white), a court bailiff. Motive: resisting arrest. Howell was legally hanged at Lawrenceville on December 13, 1907. Source: *News-Herald* (Lawrenceville, GA), 10/10/07 (1:1) & 12/19/07 (1:4). *Columbus (GA) Daily Enquirer*, 10/6/07 (4:6). See also: 1900 U.S. Census (Gwinnett Co., GA), which notes Howell. Also see Mr. Rainey's gravestone in Duluth Cemetery, Duluth.

1908

Arthur Glover (white, age 37). *Murder.* The crime was committed on 10/19/1906 in Richmond County. Handgun slaying of 27-year-old Maude Dean Williamson (white), she having been shot three times in the back. Motive: adultery turned deadly. The killer was hanged at Augusta on January 31, 1908. Source: *Augusta (GA) Chronicle*, 10/20/06 (4:3), 1/31/08 (7:3) & 2/1/08 (3:2). See also: 1900 U.S. Census (Richmond Co., GA), which notes both parties.

Wesley Summerlin (black, age uncertain) and **Charles Summerlin** (black, age uncertain). *Murder.* Their crime was committed on 11/29/1907 in Carroll County. A father and son who were legally hanged for the shotgun slaying of 70-year-old Jethro Jones (white), a well-established planter. Motive: cotton stealing. These social liabilities were swung from the same gallows at Carrollton on February 14, 1908. Source: *Augusta (GA) Chronicle*, 12/1/07 (2:1). *Macon (GA) Daily Telegraph*, 2/15/08 (1:5). *Carroll Free Press* (Carrollton, GA), 12/5/07 (1:2) & 2/20/08 (1:1). See also: 1900 U.S. Census (Carroll Co., GA), which notes Mr. Jones.

William Rogers (white, age 25). *Murder.* The crime was committed on 9/30/1906 in Chatham County. Uxoricide. Handgun slaying of 28-year-old Ella Simmons Rogers (white), she having been shot in the back. Motive: recalcitrant bridegroom. This couple had been married four months. The murdered wife had two daughters (ages 16 and 9) by other men, meaning that she had already been a mother when only 12 years old. Husband Rogers changed his mind about this "ready-made family" and demanded that his wife put her offspring in an orphanage. Ella Simmons Rogers balked at this. Tension then steadily mounted. Rogers died the death of a condemned criminal at Savannah on February 25, 1908. Source: *Macon (GA) Daily Telegraph*, 10/2/06 (1:3), 10/20/06 (1:6) & 2/26/08 (3:3). *Savannah Morning News*, 10/1/06 (8:1) & 2/26/08 (12:4).

Lee Holmes (black, age 29). *Murder.* The crime was committed on 5/11/1907 in McIntosh County. Handgun slaying of 21-year-old Emery A. Sands (white). Motive: cocky attitude. The homicide victim was standing on a railroad station platform waiting for a train. Lee Holmes and some other black folks of his acquaintance were dancing and amusing themselves at a far end of the same platform. Holmes saw that Sands (a dental student) was watching them. He then walked up to Sands, pulled out a pistol, and shot him dead to demonstrate to everyone that no one should trifle with him. This earned Holmes a date with the hangman at Darien on February 28, 1908. He was carried from the gallows with a rope around his neck. Source: *Darien (GA) Gazette*, 5/18/07 (3:3), 2/29/08 (3:3) & 3/7/08 (3:2). See also: 1900 U.S. Census (Camden Co., GA), which notes Holmes, and 1900 U.S. Census (Tattnall Co., GA), which notes Sands.

Andrew Johnson, alias "Black Sport." (black, age uncertain). *Murder.* The crime was committed on 12/6/1907 in Fulton County. Police killer. Handgun slaying of 39-year-old James A. Manier (white). Motive: obnoxious drunk. "Black Sport" was in a reflective frame of mind as he fell through the gallows trap at the Fulton County Jail on March 18, 1908. Source: *Atlanta Constitution,* 12/7/07 (1:1) & 3/19/08 (6:4). Pardons Files Box 65, GA State Archives. See also: 1880 U.S. Census (Nashville, TN), which notes Policeman Manier as a minor.

Mack Brown (black, age uncertain). *Rape.* The crime was committed on 11/28/1907 in Mitchell County. Indecent assault on the person of 8-year-old Victoria Hollis (black) under circumstances that no one dared to describe in writing. The little girl must have been frightfully injured. Her attacker was legally hanged at Camilla on March 20, 1908. Source: *Atlanta Journal,* 3/21/08 (1:6). *Bainbridge (GA) Democrat,* 3/26/08 (1:5). Pardons Files Box 15, GA State Archives.

Ingram Canady Jr. (black, age 20). *Rape.* The crime was committed on 9/23/1907 in Troup County. Indecent assault on the person of 56-year-old Roxie Anna Hargett Jones (white), a respectable widow. The culprit broke into her home with this specific intention. He was legally hanged at La Grange on March 20, 1908. Source: *Macon Daily Telegraph,* 9/26/07 (1:4) & 3/21/08 (1:3). See also: 1900 U.S. Census (Harris Co., GA), which notes the felon. Also see the gravestone of Mrs. Jones in Pinewood Cemetery, West Point. She died in 1936.

Robert Golatt (black, age 41). *Murder.* The crime was committed on 7/2/1907 in Columbia County. Executed for the ax murder of 32-year-old Edie Moore (black), his so-called common-law wife. Motive: she had complained about his brutality to their landlord. This killer was hanged at Appling on April 17, 1908. Source: *Atlanta Journal,* 9/28/07 (2:7). *Augusta (GA) Chronicle,* 2/1/08 (1:5). *Atlanta Constitution,* 4/18/08 (7:2). Appeal: 130 GA 18–21. See also: 1900 U.S. Census (Columbia Co., GA), which notes Edie Moore.

Henry Campbell (black, age 54). *Murder.* The crime was committed on 1/2/1908 in Gwinnett County. Baby killer, etc. Executed for the killings of 27-year-old Ella Hudson and her 3-month-old baby (blacks). The mother had her head dashed in. Then she was slashed across the belly multiple times and left to be partially cremated in her burning house. The baby perished in the flames. Its name and gender are not specified in surviving accounts. Motive: the killer wanted to clear the way for Ella Hudson's husband to marry his daughter and thereby legitimize their adulterous relationship. The final scene in this tragic soap opera was played out at Lawrenceville on May 8, 1908, when Henry Campbell was hanged by the neck until dead. Source: *News-Herald* (Lawrenceville, GA), 1/9/08 (1:1) & 5/14/08 (1:3). *Atlanta Constitution,* 5/9/08 (4:4). See also: 1900 U.S. Census (Gwinnett Co., GA), which notes Ella Hudson.

Porter Cooper (black, age not recorded). *Murder.* The crime was committed on 3/23/1908 in Hancock County. Uxoricide. Executed for the ax murder and dismemberment of Sissy Tallington Cooper (black, age not recorded), who he chopped into small chunks and buried piecemeal in the surrounding woods. He also burned down their cabin. Motive: possibly deranged. Porter Cooper was legally hanged at Sparta on May 15, 1908. Source: *Augusta (GA) Chronicle*, 3/26/08 (10:1) & 5/16/08 (3:5). Pardons Files Box 26, GA State Archives.

Sonnie Williams (black, age not recorded). *Murder.* The crime was committed on 8/25/1907 in Mitchell County. Executed for the killing of another black man named Almond Ward (age not recorded), who was fatally slashed in a knife fight. Motive: the theft of a watermelon. Williams wound up paying a substantially higher price for that 15-cent melon when he was hanged at Camilla on June 19, 1908. Source: *Macon (GA) Daily Telegraph*, 6/20/08 (1:6). Appeal: 130 GA 400–406. Pardons Files Box 132, GA State Archives.

Harry E. Lyles (white, age 25). *Murder.* The crime was committed on 1/30/1907 in Ware County. Uxoricide, filicide and baby killer. Executed for the shotgun slayings of 17-year-old Eula Johnson Lyles and their 4-month-old child, whose name and gender are not specified in readily accessible records. Motive: alcoholism and immaturity. The couple had wed on 12/11/1905. The baby was born on 9/12/1906. Its father was hanged at Waycross on June 23, 1908. Source: *Atlanta Constitution*, 6/24/08 (7:2). *Macon (GA) Daily Telegraph*, 5/16/07 (2:5), 5/18/07 (1:6) & 6/24/08 (1:7). *Waycross (GA) Journal*, 2/1/07 (1:1), 2/5/07 (1:3) & 6/27/08 (3:1). Pardons Files Box 77, GA State Archives.

Neal Ryals (black, age 41). *Rape.* The crime was committed on 9/18/1907 in Appling County. Indecent assault on the person of 37-year-old Lizzie Middleton Overstreet (white). The culprit first overpowered her by throwing sand in her eyes. Then after he had actually raped her he attempted to murder the woman by smashing every bone in her face with an iron tool called a "turpentine puller." She survived but was horribly disfigured. The attacker was legally hanged at Baxley on September 11, 1908. Source: *Macon (GA) Daily Telegraph*, 9/19/07 (1:3) & 9/12/08 (2:3). *Augusta (GA) Chronicle*, 9/24/07 (1:2) & 9/26/07 (2:6). See also: 1910 U.S. Census (Appling Co., GA), which notes Lizzie Overstreet.

Leon Harrison (black, age 23). *Murder.* The crime was committed on or about 7/10/1908 in Jackson County. Gunshot slaying of 28-year-old Lina Daniel (black female) under circumstances that are difficult to discern based on surviving reports. Harrison was legally hanged at Jefferson on October 9, 1908. Source: *Jackson Herald* (Jefferson, GA) 8/13/08 (1:2) & 10/15/08 (6:3). *Atlanta Journal*, 10/10/08 (2:3). See also: 1900 U.S. Census (Jackson Co., GA), which notes both parties.

Jim Bennett (black, age 22). *Murder.* The crime was committed on 9/16/1908 in Fayette County. Handgun slaying of 48-year-old Daniel McEachern (white). Motive: tenant-landlord dispute. This young man with a trigger finger was legally hanged at Fayetteville on October 15, 1908. The law had functioned with alacrity in his case. Source: *Atlanta Constitution*, 9/17/08 (2:7) & 10/16/08 (5:2).

George Joiner (black, age 21). *Murder.* The crime was committed on 5/8/1908 in Emanuel County. Uxoricide. Executed for the killing of Mary Almeda Ricks Joiner, known to some as "Meta" Joiner (black, age uncertain), who was lured from their home under false pretenses, "beaten into insensibility" with an ax handle, shot through the head with a handgun, stripped naked and then dumped into a creek with a weight around her neck. Motive: suspicion of infidelity. This wife-killer was hanged at Swainsboro on December 11, 1908. Source: *The Forest Blade* (Swainsboro, GA), 12/17/08 (1:3). *Macon (GA) Daily Telegraph*, 5/25/08 (1:5). *Augusta (GA) Chronicle*, 5/29/08 (4:5) & 12/12/08 (10:4). Pardons Files Box 67, GA State Archives.

Fletcher Willis (black, age not recorded). *Murder.* The crime was committed on 11/14/1908 in Houston County. Shotgun slaying of 30-year-old James H. Hall (white), a rural storekeeper. Motive: armed robbery. The homicide victim was not even given a chance to comply with a demand for money. He was killed while in the act of lighting a lamp to accommodate what he thought was a late customer. The back of his head was blown off. Trial and sentence quickly followed. The hangman performed his official function in this case at Perry on December 28, 1908. Source: *Atlanta Constitution*, 11/15/08 (16:3) & 12/29/08 (12:4). *Marietta (GA) Journal*, 11/19/08 (2:4). *Vienna (GA) News*, 11/17/08 (1:6).

1909

Lucius Truitt (black, age not recorded). *Murder.* The crime was committed on or about 7/15/1908 in Troup County. Executed for the ax murder of 33-year-old Dock Tatum (black) during the course of a robbery and home invasion. There was no post-conviction appeal. Lucius Truitt expiated his crime against his fellow man in the manner required by law when he was hanged at La Grange on January 2, 1909. Source: *La Grange (GA) Reporter*, 1/8/09 (1:6). See also: 1900 U.S. Census (Troup Co., GA), which notes Tatum.

Isaiah Hicks (black, age 18). *Murder.* The crime was committed on 4/26/1909 in Macon County. Shotgun slaying of 34-year-old Thomas Banks Lofley (white) by lying in wait. Motive: tenant-landlord dispute. This teenage killer was legally hanged at Oglethorpe on June 1, 1909. Source: *Macon County Citizen*, 4/30/09 (5:2) & 6/4/09 (5:3). See also: 1900 U.S. Census (Macon Co., GA), which notes both parties.

James Jones (black, age not recorded). *Murder.* The crime was committed on 10/26/1907 in Jenkins County. Handgun slaying of another black man named James Brown (age not recorded), who was shot three times. Motive: he wanted to steal the homicide victim's wife. The only things that Jones accrued from this futile act were a rope around his neck and a trap door beneath his feet. He was legally hanged at Millen on June 11, 1909. Source: *Augusta (GA) Chronicle*, 6/12/09 (1:4). *Savannah Morning News*, 6/12/09 (1:4). Pardons Files Box 68, GA State Archives.

James Wiggins (black, age not recorded). *Murder.* The crime was committed sometime during the year 1905 in Dooly County. Uxoricide. Shotgun slaying of Belle Allen Wiggins (black, age not recorded) because she would not give him money to squander. The killer spent three years as a fugitive before being hunted down. He was legally hanged at Vienna on July 8,

1909. Source: *Vienna (GA) News*, 7/21/08 (1:1) & 7/9/09 (1:1). *Macon (GA) Daily Telegraph*, 7/9/09 (1:4). See also: *Dooly County Colored Marriage Register* (1899–1908), 258, which notes the nuptials of this ill-fated couple on 9/17/1903.

Ed Fallin (black, age 21). *Murder.* The crime was committed on 6/28/1908 in Wilkes County. Handgun slaying of another black man named Robert Johnson (age not recorded), the fatal shot having been fired through his cabin window. Motive: the killer coveted the homicide victim's wife. Fallin was legally hanged at Washington on July 9, 1909. Source: *Gazette-Chronicle* (Washington, GA), 7/1/08 (1:4) & 7/14/09 (1:5).

Marshall Lewis (black, age 23). *Murder.* The crime was committed on 4/26/1909 in Berrien County. Handgun slaying of 26-year-old Robert Clifford Rutherford (white), who was shot twice in the head. Motive: fleeing from the scene of a burglary. This thief-turned-killer was legally hanged at Nashville on July 9, 1909. Source: *Macon (GA) Daily Telegraph*, 4/27/09 (1:7) & 7/10/09 (1:3). See also: 1900 U.S. Census (Worth Co., GA), which notes Lewis. Also see Mr. Rutherford's gravestone in Pine Grove Baptist Church Cemetery, Nashville.

William Hawkins (black, age not recorded). *Murder.* The crime was committed on 3/23/1909 in Clarke County. Uxoricide. Executed for the killing of Mary Hawkins (black, age not recorded) who was slashed with a razor and shot five times with a handgun. Motive: impending divorce. This wrathful husband was hanged at Athens on October 1, 1909. Source: *Athens (GA) Banner*, 3/24/09 (1:3). *Augusta (GA) Chronicle*, 3/25/09 (3:5) & 4/21/09 (1:5). *Atlanta Constitution*, 10/2/09 (7:3).

Sylvester Bynum (black, age 20). *Murder.* The crime was committed on 7/10/1909 in Clay County. Shotgun slaying of 41-year-old John B. Turner (black), a rural storekeeper who was decoyed out of his house and then deliberately blasted in the back. Motive: a grudge concerning a small store purchase. This killer was hanged at Fort Gaines on October 27, 1909. Source: *Fort Gaines (GA) Sentinel*, 7/16/09 (1:1) & 10/29/09 (1:3). *Atlanta Journal*, 10/28/09 (4:1). See also: 1900 U.S. Census (Clay Co., GA), which notes Turner.

Bud Whitman (black, age not recorded). *Murder.* The crime was committed on 9/25/1909 in Clarke County. Executed for the ax killing of 25-year-old Vonderau Kennon (white), whose head was split open and whose body was dumped in the Oconee River. Motive: mugging. The college town of Athens breathed a little easier after Bud Whitman was legally hanged there on November 5, 1909. Source: *Athens (GA) Banner*, 10/8/09 (2:1) & 11/6/09 (1:3). *Augusta (GA) Chronicle*, 10/5/09 (1:4). *Atlanta Constitution*, 10/6/09 (2:5) & 11/6/09 (2:1).

Jebe Kellogg (black, age 20). *Murder.* The crime was committed on 8/28/1909 in Cherokee County. Handgun slaying of 25-year-old James E. Landers (white). Motive: gambling dispute. The homicide victim was literally shot dead for a dime. The killer had just completed a 1-year stint on the chain gang for shooting another person under similar circumstances. He was legally hanged at Canton on November 19, 1909. Source: *Marietta*

(GA) Journal, 9/3/09 (8:6). *Atlanta Constitution*, 11/20/09 (1:4). See also: 1900 U.S. Census (Cherokee Co., GA), which notes Kellogg, and 1900 U.S. Census (Towns Co., GA), which notes Landers.

Henry Bell (black, age 20). *Murder.* The crime was committed on 9/19/1908 in Terrell County. Handgun slaying of 24-year-old Willie Jackson (black). Motive: fracas at a card game. There were no winners in this matter. Henry Bell faced the hangman at Dawson on December 30, 1909. He wound up in a pine box just like the man he shot. Source: *Dawson (GA) News*, 9/23/08 (11:2) & 1/5/10 (3:4). See also: 1900 U.S. Census (Terrell Co., GA), which notes both parties.

1910

Willard Webb (black, age 29). *Rape.* The crime was committed on 7/20/1909 in Cobb County. Indecent assault on the person of 18-year-old Exie Brown (white), who was pounced on as she emerged from an outhouse. Her attacker was legally hanged at Marietta on February 18, 1910. Source: *Marietta Journal*, 7/22/09 (1:3), 7/29/09 (8:3) & 2/25/10 (3:3). Appeal: 133 GA 585–587. See also: 1880 U.S. Census (Cobb Co., GA), which notes the rapist as a baby.

George E. Burge (white, age 32). *Murder.* The crime was committed on 5/17/1909 in Fulton County. Uxoricide. Fatal stabbing of 32-year-old Mary Lovie Sikes Britton Burge (white), she having been murdered in her bed. Motive: spousal abuse. The homicide victim had already obtained a protective order against her husband. The latter demonstrated the efficacy of that piece of paper in the manner described above. George Burge atoned for this on the gallows. He was executed at the Fulton County Jail on April 15, 1910. Source: *Atlanta Constitution*, 5/18/09 (7:2) & 4/16/10 (7:3). See also: 1900 U.S. Census (Milton Co., GA), which notes Geo. Burge and 1880 U.S. Census (Randolph Co., AL), which notes his wife as a minor.

Julius Daggett (black, age 64). *Murder.* The crime was committed on 12/8/1909 in Columbia County. Executed for the killing of 78-year-old Zachariah Kendrick (white), a country store proprietor who was battered about the face and head with a knotty wooden stick. Motive: attempted robbery. This transgressor was legally hanged at Appling on April 19, 1910. Source: *Augusta (GA) Chronicle*, 12/10/09 (1:7). *Atlanta Constitution*, 4/20/10 (4:5). See also: 1880 U.S. Census (Columbia Co., GA), which notes Mr. Kendrick, and 1900 U.S. Census (Columbia Co., GA), which notes Daggett.

John Suple (black, age 24). *Murder.* The crime was committed on 12/12/1908 in Jeff Davis County. Handgun slaying of another black man named Simon Lee (age not recorded). Motive: drinking and gambling. Suple was hanged at Hazlehurst on May 6, 1910. Source: *Atlanta Journal*, 5/7/10 (7:4). Appeal: 133 GA 601–605. Pardons Files Box 117, GA State Archives. See also: 1910 U.S. Census (Appling Co., GA), which notes "Supple" as a prisoner.

Henry Patterson (black, age 44). *Murder.* The crime was committed on 7/6/1909 in Sumter County. Handgun slaying of about 45-year-old W. F. McRae (white, full name not recorded), the manager of a large plantation. Motive: evading arrest. The homicide victim came from Pike Co., AL. The killer was legally hanged at Americus on May 13, 1910. Source: *Americus (GA) Weekly Times-Recorder*, 7/8/09 (5:6), 7/15/09 (3:4) & 5/19/10 (3:4). *Atlanta Constitution*, 7/8/09 (3:2), 7/9/09 (5:1) & 5/14/10 (5:3). Appeal: 134 GA 264–268. Pardons Files Box 93, GA State Archives. See also: 1900 and 1910 U.S. Census (Sumter Co., GA), which notes Patterson.

Howard Harris (black, age 21). *Rape.* The crime was committed on 3/25/1910 in Thomas County. Indecent assault on the person of 17-year-old Effie McMillan Dutton (white), the culprit having accomplished his purpose at gunpoint. He was legally hanged at Thomasville on May 20, 1910. Source: *Daily Times-Enterprise* (Thomasville, GA), 4/28/10 (1:1) & 5/20/10 (1:3). *Thomasville (GA) Press*, 3/30/10 (1:3) & 5/21/10 (1:1). See also: 1910 U.S. Census (Thomas Co., GA), which notes "Effie McMillan," and 1900 U.S. Census (Thomas Co., GA), which notes Harris.

Walter Thomas (black, age not recorded). *Rape.* The crime was committed on 9/20/1909 in Troup County. Indecent assault on the person of 7-year-old Leola King (black), whom he also knowingly infected with a foul disease. The culprit had previously sought treatment for his condition at an Atlanta clinic. There is no way that he could have deluded himself into thinking that he was cured, because his symptoms were plainly evident when he attacked the little girl. Walter Thomas was legally hanged at La Grange on June 10, 1910. Source: *La Grange (GA) Reporter*, 6/17/10 (1:6). Pardons Files Box 120, GA State Archives.

Frank Brooks (black, age 19). *Murder.* The crime was committed on 11/3/1909 in Fulton County. Serial burglar and killer. Executed for the handgun slaying of 28-year-old Steve Morris (black) during the course of a burglary. Brooks had broken into the servants' quarters of twenty upscale homes during the weeks preceding this homicide. He always made it a point to avoid those parts of such residences that were inhabited by white people. His fellow blacks—reasoned Brooks—were easier prey whom the authorities would be less inclined to care about. His twentieth such break-in proved to be Brooks' undoing when a black man named Steve Morris confronted him. The hangman put a final end to this black-on-black crime spree when he sent Frank Brooks through the gallows trap at Atlanta on June 17, 1910. Source: *Atlanta Constitution*, 11/4/09 (2:4) & 6/18/10 (1:2). *Macon (GA) Daily Telegraph*, 11/14/09 (1:6).

Jesse Cook (black, age 18). *Murder.* The crime was committed on 12/20/1909 in Bartow County. Shotgun slaying of 52-year-old Joseph C. Cannon (black). Motive: robbery and mendacity. The subsequent sentence of death by hanging was carried out in this case at Cartersville on June 17, 1910. Source: *Macon (GA) Daily Telegraph*, 6/17/10 (3:2). *Atlanta Journal*, 6/17/10 (9:7). *Cartersville (GA) News*, 12/23/09 (1:4) & 6/23/10 (21:1). See also: 1900 U.S. Census (Bartow Co., GA), which notes Cannon, and 1910 U.S. Census (Bartow Co., GA), which notes Cook two days before his execution.

Charles Walker (black, age 24). *Murder.* The crime was committed on 4/23/1910 in DeKalb County. Handgun slaying of 27-year-old Samuel Thomas Brown (white), a trolley motorman who was shot point blank in the face. Motive: armed robbery. There being no post-conviction appeal in this case (nor grounds for one), the killer was legally hanged at Decatur on July 29, 1910. Source: *Atlanta Constitution*, 4/24/10 (C:1:1), 4/25/10 (1:2), 5/8/10 (8:1) & 7/30/10 (5:6). See also: 1910 U.S. Census (Atlanta, GA), which notes Walker. See also Mr. Brown's gravestone in Old Roswell Cemetery, Roswell. See also: Edward Weaver (executed 4/14/11).

Charles Scott, alias "Church Scott" (black, age 22). *Murder.* The crime was committed on 11/6/1909 in Washington County. Handgun slaying of 21-year-old Henry Harris (black), the killer having strode right into the homicide victim's house like he owned the place. Motive: Harris had slapped the killer's brother-in-law. Charles Scott learned the high cost of a high attitude when he was sentenced to death for what he had done. He was hanged at Sandersville on October 28, 1910. Source: *Macon (GA) Daily Telegraph*, 10/29/10 (6:6). *Sandersville Georgian*, 11/2/10 (1:1). Appeal: 135 GA 29. See also: 1900 U.S. Census (Wash. Co., GA), which notes Harris, and 1910 U.S. Census (Wash. Co., GA), which notes Scott.

Jake DeVauss (black, age not recorded). *Murder.* The crime was committed on 7/8/1901 in Coffee County. Rifle slaying of a white man named Charles McKinnon (age uncertain). Motive: temper tantrum. The concerned parties in this case were farm folks. The killer had previously bought a mule from the homicide victim's uncle. The mule became stubborn as DeVauss was using it to pull his plow on the above date. Enraged, DeVauss took up his rifle and shot the animal dead. Then he stomped over to the McKinnon farm and demanded a refund, saying that the mule was useless. An argument flared in which McKinnon took his uncle's side. He told DeVauss that a good plowman should be patient with mules, or words to that effect. The angry DeVauss then turned his weapon on McKinnon and gunned him down. This made DeVauss a murderer as well as an animal abuser. He took to the swamps and evaded capture for nine years. He was legally hanged at Douglas on November 10, 1910. Source: *Atlanta Constitution*, 7/16/01 (7:3) & 11/11/10 (12:1). *Macon (GA) Daily Telegraph*, 11/10/10 (3:4) & 11/12/10 (3:5).

John McKenzie (black, age 21). *Murder.* The crime was committed on 3/12/1910 in Upson County. Gunshot slaying of 66-year-old Lewis Ellerbee (black). Motive: a disagreement over 20 cents. This two-dime killer was legally hanged at Thomaston on December 6, 1910. Source: *Thomaston (GA) Times*, 3/18/10 (1:5) & 12/9/10 (1:4). See also: 1900 U.S. Census (Upson Co., GA), which notes both parties, the homicide victim as "Ellaby."

Charlie Whitfield, known to some as "Willie Whitfield" (black, age 20). *Murder.* The crime was committed on 6/1/1909 in Washington County. Handgun slaying of a young black woman named Maggie Lula Babb (exact age uncertain). Motive: jealous suitor. Whitfield was legally hanged at Sandersville on December 10, 1910. The local newspaper there commented as follows: "There have been many Negroes shot to death in Washington county within the past 20 years, the total number being estimated at about 300 which is nearly accurate. Many of them have no regard whatever for human life and use their weapons indiscriminately like savages." Source: *Sandersville Georgian*, 3/15/10 (1:3) & 12/14/10 (Sec. 2) (1:1). *Columbus (GA) Enquirer-Sun*, 12/11/10 (1:2). Appeal: 135 GA 248–249. Pardons Files Box 129, GA State Archives.

1911

Calvin Johnston (black, age 19). *Murder.* The crime was committed on 1/10/1911 in Burke County. Rifle slaying of 61-year-old Harvey Jones (white), a grocer. Motive: armed robbery. Johnston was legally hanged at Waynesboro on February 8, 1911. No time was lost in bringing him to justice. Source: *The True Citizen* (Waynesboro, GA), 1/14/11 (5:5) & 2/11/11 (2:3). *Macon (GA) Daily Telegraph*, 1/12/11 (3:4) & 1/18/11 (1:6). *Atlanta Constitution*, 2/9/11 (6:3). See also: 1910 U.S. Census (Burke Co., GA), which notes Mr. Jones.

Edward Weaver (black, age 30). *Murder.* The crime was committed on 4/23/1910 in DeKalb County. Accomplice in the handgun slaying of 27-year-old Samuel Thomas Brown (white), a motorman on a trolley car. Motive: armed robbery. Weaver went through the gallows trap in the same manner as his erstwhile partner at Decatur on April 14, 1911. Source: *Atlanta Constitution*, 4/15/11 (2:6). See also: Charles Walker (executed 7/29/10).

Ed Jones (black, age not recorded). *Murder.* The crime was committed on 3/25/1910 in Baker County. Handgun slaying of 19-year-old Green Key (black). Motive: none apparent. The homicide happened at an all-black festival where liquor flowed aplenty. Green Key (such being his name) got so drunk that he fell to the floor of a dance hall with his head obstructing its doorway. Ed Jones walked through the door. He had to step over Key's head to do so. He said not a word but turned around, pulled a revolver from his waistband and blew the inebriate's brains out. The black folks said that neither man had ever had trouble with the other up until then. Jones was hanged for this seemingly senseless act at Newton on June 9, 1911. Source: *Albany (GA) Herald*, 9/21/10 (1:6). *Atlanta Constitution*, 9/23/10 (6:6), 6/9/11 (5:5) & 6/10/11 (3:3). Appeal: 136 GA 157. See also: 1900 U.S. Census (Baker Co., GA), which notes Green Key.

Harry Paschal (black, age not recorded). *Murder.* The crime was committed on 4/29/1910 in Lincoln County. Shotgun slaying of 29-year-old Jim Jones (black). Motive: rivalry for a female. Exit another black-on-black killer pursuant to law. This one was legally hanged at Lincolnton on June 9, 1911. Source: *Atlanta Journal*, 6/12/11 (6:3). *Lincoln Journal* (Lincolnton, GA), 6/15/11 (4:3). Appeal: 135 GA 660. See also: 1910 U.S. Census (Lincoln Co., GA), which notes Jones.

John Withrow (white, age 21). *Murder.* The crime was committed on or about 7/20/1910 in Fannin County. Handgun slaying of pregnant 19-year-old Callie Withrow (white). Motive: obnoxious drunk. A disgusted court of law sentenced this young husband to death. He was hanged at Blue Ridge on June 9, 1911. Source: *Sylvan Valley News* (Brevard, NC), 6/16/11 (1:1). *Atlanta Constitution*, 6/10/11 (3:2). Pardons Files Box 134, GA State Archives.

Sam Swatson, alias "Shropshire" (black, age not recorded). *Rape.* The crime was committed on 12/6/1910 in

Muscogee County. Indecent assault on the person of 16-year-old Carrie Lee Watkins (white), who was dragged for 150 yards along railroad tracks, beaten up, bitten in a maniacal manner and raped beneath a boxcar. Venue changed from Muscogee County to Fulton County. The attacker was legally hanged at Atlanta on June 16, 1911. Source: *Columbus (GA) Enquirer-Sun*, 12/7/10 (5:3). *Macon (GA) Daily Telegraph*, 12/8/10 (1:6). *Columbus (GA) Ledger*, 1/24/11 (1:1). *Atlanta Constitution*, 6/17/11 (7:4). *Atlanta Georgian*, 6/16/11 (7:5).

Thomas Webster, alias "Wright" (black, age not recorded). *Rape*. The crime was committed on 6/6/1911 in Jackson County. Indecent assault on the person of 37-year-old Dora Neese (white), who was purposely attacked during her husband's absence. The crime being premeditated as well as unmitigated, the wheels of justice moved quickly. This sexual predator was legally hanged at Jefferson on July 17, 1911. Source: *Augusta (GA) Chronicle*, 6/14/11 (3:5). *Macon (GA) Daily Telegraph*, 6/27/11 (3:5). *Atlanta Constitution*, 7/18/11 (15:7). *Jackson Herald* (Jefferson, GA), 6/8/11 (4:2) & 7/20/11 (1:1). See also: 1910 U.S. Census (Jackson Co., GA), which notes Mrs. Neese. The local newspaper said that she was "aged about 23."

William Rouse (white, age 47). *Murder*. The crime was committed on 9/4/1909 in Worth County. Executed for the killing of 43-year-old William Bailey (white) under the following circumstances: Both men having disagreed over some matter, Bailey went to the Rouse residence to seek redress. A pistol shot was fired (presumably by Rouse), which broke one of Bailey's arms. The latter man was unarmed. Not satisfied with the injury already inflicted, Rouse then attacked the wounded man with a knife, stabbing him and cutting his throat. That done, the killer put the aforesaid pistol in the dead man's right hand (it being the same limb that was broken) and tried to fake a scene of self-defense. This wore thin when Rouse was found sitting upon the body of the murdered man celebrating his death with a bottle of whiskey. Nor could Rouse explain how Bailey had allegedly tried to shoot him and/or grip a pistol with the same arm broken. William Rouse was hanged for capital murder at Sylvester on September 1, 1911. Source: *Augusta (GA) Chronicle*, 9/5/09 (11:6), 9/21/09 (2:2) & 9/2/11 (1:6). See also: 1880 U.S. Census (Worth Co., GA), which notes "Baily" and 1900 U.S. Census (Worth Co., GA), which notes Rouse.

Albert Matthews (black, age 24). *Murder*. The crime was committed on 6/9/1911 in Monroe County. Uxoricide. Shotgun slaying of 21-year-old Minnie Stephens Matthews (black), she having been blasted in the back by the contents of two barrels as she stood with a baby in her arms. Motive: she had dared to walk out on him. It was the depraved indifference to human life as evinced by the presence of a baby in the woman's arms that neutralized any defense based on extreme emotional duress. As a result, Albert Matthews was legally hanged for what he had done at Forsyth on October 26, 1911. Source: *Macon (GA) Daily Telegraph*, 6/10/11 (2:7) & 10/27/11 (8:5). *Monroe (GA) Advertiser*, 6/16/11 (2:2) & 10/27/11 (5:2). See also: 1910 U.S. Census (Monroe Co., GA), which notes both parties.

Andrew Davis (black, age not recorded). *Murder*. The crime was committed on 8/18/1910 in Calhoun County. Uxoricide. Handgun slaying of Lonsie Davis (black, age not recorded), who was shot dead on the town square at Leary. Motive: she had dared to walk out on him. The homicide victim had originally come from Slocomb, AL. Her estranged husband was hanged at Morgan on November 11, 1911. Source: *Calhoun County Courier* (Arlington, GA), 8/26/10 (1:2) & 11/17/11 (1:3). *Atlanta Journal*, 11/11/11 (4:2). Appeal: 136 GA 798.

James W. Gatlin, alias "J. A. O'Berry" (white, age 26). *Murder*. The crime was committed on 8/15/1911 in Camden County. Child killer, etc. Executed for the shotgun slayings of a mother and daughter named Mary Randolph (black, age not recorded) and Mary (?) Randolph the younger (black, age 13), who were purposefully massacred in their cabin. Motive: robbery. The killer must have borne an especially low character because his own relatives refused to help him mount a legal defense. He said that he had seen the elder of the two homicide victims receive a "substantial" sum of money from a storekeeper that day and felt that "niggers" should not possess such sums. A posse later found Gatlin with some of the stolen cash literally in his mouth. He was legally hanged at St. Mary's on November 27, 1911. Source: *Savannah Morning News*, 8/17/11 (1:6). *Macon (GA) Daily Telegraph*, 11/27/11 (6:4) & 11/28/11 (1:3). *Atlanta Constitution*, 9/10/11 (10:5), 10/20/11 (8:3), 10/27/11 (5:3), 11/27/11 (2:6) & 11/28/11 (3:4).

Dave Walker, alias "T. B. Walker" (black, age not recorded). *Murder*. The crime was committed on 10/28/1911 in Wilkes County. Shotgun slaying of 50-year-old Charles S. Hollenshead (white, a storekeeper) by means of a sniper blast fired through his display window. Motive: twofold. The homicide victim had turned Walker's wife out of his employ; also, Walker saw this as a way to get out of paying money owed for store credit. He wound up face to face with the hangman at Washington on December 5, 1911. Source: *Macon (GA) Daily Telegraph*, 10/29/11 (4:1:1), 11/8/11 (1:1). *Columbus (GA) Ledger*, 12/6/11 (7:4). See also: 1910 U.S. Census (Wilkes Co., GA), which notes Mr. Hollenshead.

Thomas Jackson (black, age not recorded). *Murder*. The crime was committed on 3/5/1910 in Lowndes County. Uxoricide, etc. Executed for the killings of Gertrude Jason Jackson (black, age not recorded) and Hannah Jason (black, age not recorded), they respectively being his wife and that woman's grandmother. Motive: wrathful husband. Jackson went loco when he saw his wife walking with another man. He shot her five times with a handgun and then stomped up and down "on her quivering body." The older woman was fatally pistol-whipped when she tried to intervene. Double killer Thomas Jackson was hanged by the neck until dead at Valdosta on December 8, 1911. Source: *Valdosta Daily Times*, 3/7/10 (3:1) & 12/8/11 (5:1). *Valdosta Times*, 6/17/11 (3:1). *Macon (GA) Daily Times*, 6/14/11 (6:2), 12/2/11 (6:2) & 12/9/11 (3:4). Pardons Files Box 64, GA State Archives.

William Turner (black, age 39). *Murder*. The crime was committed on 8/25/1911 in Butts County. Rifle slaying of 20-year-old Jesse Singley (white), who was shot down in a planned ambush. Motive: racial tension. Turner was employed as a butler at the Hotel Elder, a high-class resort that catered to summer vacationers. One of his sons (Alonzo Turner) was a bellboy there. Trouble began when the younger Turner got into an argument with another black employee over how they should split a gratuity that had been left by a hotel guest. The argument became so heated that the *maître d'hôtel* attempted to quell it by physical means. This person (a white man) pistol-whipped Alonzo Turner (who was loud and out of control) because he saw no other way of calming him down. The pistol fell to the floor during this altercation, causing a shot to fire by mischance. That was all it took to make the other black employees overreact. They immediately banded together and turned the situation into a white-versus-black conflict. Various reports had them rampaging through the hotel halls, vandalizing hotel fixtures and terrorizing hotel guests. An alarm spread to the adjacent town of Indian Springs. Heavily armed whites then converged on the hotel. They threatened to shoot any unruly person, especially black folks. Hotel management then announced that the entire place was to be immediately shut down for the duration of the season. This did not appease the Turners. They lay in ambush for a homeward-bound party of white men and opened fire on them. One of that number (Jesse Singley) was killed and several others were wounded. William "Bill" Turner was singled out as the person most responsible for the homicide. He was legally hanged at Jackson on December 14, 1911. It was too late that he learned the folly of allowing tribal instinct to cloud his better judgment. Source: *Butts County Progress* (Jackson, GA), 9/1/11 (1:1) & 12/15/11 (5:5). *Macon (GA) Daily Telegraph*, 8/28/11 (1:6) & 10/30/11 (2:4). *Columbus (GA) Ledger*, 8/27/11 (3:4). See also: 1910 U.S. Census (Butts Co., GA), which notes all parties.

Balus Merck (black, age 51). *Murder.* The crime was committed on 5/3/1911 in Hall County. Uxoricide. Shotgun slaying of 51-year-old Leah Merck (black). Motive: obnoxious drunk. This all-too-common type of wife killer was hanged at Gainesville on December 29, 1911. Source: *Atlanta Journal*, 5/4/11 (1:6) & 7/29/11 (2:6). *Gainesville (GA) News*, 1/3/12 (1:2). Appeal: 137 GA 89–90. See also: 1910 U.S. Census (Hall Co., GA), which notes both parties.

1912

"Kid Glover" (black, exact age uncertain). *Murder.* The crime was committed on 1/29/1911 in Crisp County. Shotgun slaying of another black man named Charles West (age not recorded) during a general brawl at an all-black pig roast. The killer is known only by his alias. His real name does not appear in any known record. He was hanged at Cordele on January 16, 1912. Source: *Macon (GA) Daily Telegraph*, 5/28/11 (B6:7) & 1/17/12 (2:5). Appeal: 137 GA 82–85. Pardons Files Box 46, GA State Archives.

Charles West (black, age not recorded). *Murder.* The crime was committed on 8/16/1911 in Early County. Police killer. Shotgun slaying of 31-year-old Henry W. Newberry (white), the town marshal of Jakin. Motive: resisting arrest. This offender swung from the gallows beam at Blakely on February 20, 1912. Source: *Early County News*, 8/24/11 (6:1) & 2/22/12 (1:1). *Daily Times-Enterprise* (Thomasville, GA), 8/18/11 (1:1). See also: 1910 U.S. Census (Early Co., GA), which notes Newberry.

William Simms (black, age not recorded). *Murder.* The crime was committed on 1/9/1912 in Early County. Handgun slaying of 25-year-old Freeman Spence (white) during the course of a burglary. There was no delay in adjudication. This killer was executed alongside Charles West at Blakely on February 20, 1912. Source: *Early County News*, 1/11/12 (3:4) & 2/22/12 (1:1). See also: 1900 U.S. Census (Early Co., GA), which notes Freeman Spence.

William B. Walker (white, age 34). *Murder.* The crime was committed on 8/21/1910 in Bibb County. Uxoricide. Executed for the killing of 24-year-old Alma Johnson Walker (white), who was splashed with gasoline as she worked at her kitchen stove. The flames from the old fashioned stove burners did the rest. Motive: spousal abuse. The woman's charred remains were laid to rest with great reverence. Her husband met an ignoble death on the gallows at Macon on March 8, 1912. Source: *Macon (GA) Daily Telegraph*, 8/22/10 (1:7) & 3/9/12 (1:7). See also: 1910 U.S. Census (Bibb Co., GA), which notes this ill-fated couple.

Willie Bell (black, age not recorded). *Murder.* The crime was committed on 2/12/1912 in Bibb County. Uxoricide. Fatal stabbing and slashing (with a butcher knife) of Emma Bell (black, age not recorded). Motive: drunken rage. The woman had tried to flee across the fields near her home. The killer chased her down and stomped on her like a maniac. The knife did the rest. Then it was the law's turn. Willie Bell was hanged at the Bibb County Jail on March 29, 1912. Source: *Macon (GA) Daily Telegraph*, 2/13/12 (9:2) & 3/30/12 (2:3).

Hezekiah Stevens (black, age 21). *Murder.* The crime was committed on 10/12/1911 in Clarke County. Uxoricide. Shotgun slaying of 21-year-old Essie M. Stevens (black). Motive: adultery on her part. Stevens may have been an aggrieved husband but his case showed that "the unwritten law" was a myth. No man was legally entitled to kill his wife for any reason. The hangman was accordingly called upon to render his services in the case of Hezekiah Stevens at Athens on March 29, 1912. Source: *Athens (GA) Banner*, 10/13/11 (1:3) & 3/30/12 (1:2). Appeal: 137 GA 520–522. See also: 1910 U.S. Census (Clarke Co., GA), which notes both parties.

Edward Alford (white, age 38). *Murder.* The crime was committed on 12/27/1909 in Bibb County. Uxoricide, etc. Handgun slayings of Carrie Exum Alford and an older woman named Martha Exum (whites, exact ages uncertain), they respectively being his wife and mother-in-law. Motive: alcoholism and self pity. The killer was essentially a drunk and a loser. He knew that his life was going nowhere and chose this means to assuage his dilemma. It is unclear whether he had also counted on being hanged. Edward Alford met that fate on the gallows at Macon on May 10, 1912. Source: *Macon Daily Telegraph*, 12/28/09 (1:7) & 5/11/12 (1:3). See also: 1910 U.S. Census (Macon, GA), which notes Alford as a prisoner. He had originally come from Washington County.

Tom McCrary (black, age 35). *Murder.* The crime was committed on 12/17/1910 in Crisp County. Handgun slaying of 18-year-old Clarence Beasley (white). Motive: workplace violence. The homicide victim came from Colquitt County. He and an older brother had either purchased or inherited some timberland in Crisp County and gone into the business of cutting railroad ties. They employed laborers for that purpose, Tom McCrary being one of them. An argument erupted when the Beasley brothers reproached McCrary for not hewing a certain quota of ties and piling them atop a certain railroad flatcar. McCrary pulled out a handgun and opened fire. Clarence Beasley was slain on the spot and his brother severely wounded. Trigger-finger McCrary was legally hanged for this at Cordele on May 14, 1912. Source: *Macon (GA) Daily Telegraph*, 12/18/10 (1:7) & 2/14/11 (3:4). *Columbus (GA) Ledger*, 12/18/10 (1:4). *Atlanta Journal*, 5/15/12 (28:2). Appeal: 137 GA 784. See also: 1900 U.S. Census (Dooly Co., GA), which notes McCrary, and 1910 U.S. Census (Colquitt Co., GA), which notes Clarence Beasley.

George Burdine, known to some as "Lige Burdine" (black, age 31). *Rape.* The crime was committed on 1/26/1912 in Thomas County. Indecent assault on the person of a 6-year-old black female (name withheld) under particularly nasty circumstances. Angry persons of his own color tried to murder him while he was in jail, the black folks having no qualms about lynching so long as it was kept among themselves. However, the due process of law prevailed in this case. Burdine was legally hanged at Thomasville on May 24, 1912. Source: *Weekly Times-Enterprise* (Thomasville, GA), 2/16/12 (3:6), 4/19/12 (3:1) & 5/31/12 (3:1). See also: 1910 U.S. Census (Ware Co., GA), which notes this black-on-black sex offender.

Mack Strickland (black, age 21). *Murder.* The crime was committed on 7/8/1912 in Gwinnett County. Child killer. Executed for the killing of 13-year-old Susie Parsons (black), who was beaten to death with a wood plank. Motive: sexual assault. Fifty-eight black men and seventy whites signed a petition requesting that a special court be convened to try this matter. The petition was granted and Mack Strickland stood trial ahead of the regularly scheduled autumn assize. He was legally hanged at Lawrenceville on August 23, 1912. Source: *News-Herald* (Lawrenceville, GA), 7/11/12 (1:1), 7/15/12 (1:1), 7/29/12 (1:1) & 8/26/12 (1:3). See also: 1910 U.S. Census (Milton Co., GA), which notes Strickland.

John Haywood, alias "Hegwood" (white, age 26). *Murder.* The crime was committed on 1/14/1912 in Habersham County. Shotgun slaying of another white man named John Whittemore (age uncertain) during the course of a drunken brawl. Nothing could be found to mitigate the degree of this man's guilt. So he was ordered for execution. The hangman performed his appointed task at Clarkesville on September 6, 1912. Source: *Atlanta Constitution*, 3/13/12 (1:4), 3/20/12 (6:1) & 9/7/12 (1:5). Appeal: 138 GA 274. Pardon Files Box 55, GA State Archives.

Oscar Daniels (black, age 17) and **Ernest Knox** (black, age 17). *Murder.* Their crime was committed on 9/8/1912 in Forsyth County. Both executed for the killing of 19-year-old Mae Crow (white), who was beaten to the limit of human endurance, gang raped and thrown into a ravine. She succumbed to massive injuries on 9/23/1912. Five black males were implicated in this atrocity. One was lynched, two were legally hanged and two fled to parts unknown. Daniels and Knox were the two who died pursuant to law. They met their ends at Cumming on October 25, 1912. Source: *Augusta*

(GA) Chronicle, 9/10/12 (1:6), 9/11/12 (1:1) & 10/26/12 (1:3). See also: 1910 U.S. Census (Forsyth Co., GA), which notes "Daniel" and Knox. See also Miss Crow's gravestone in Pleasant Grove Cemetery, northeast of Cumming.

Jack Baldwin (black, age 33). *Murder.* The crime was committed on 9/16/1911 in Stewart County. Fatal stabbing of 37-year-old Alice Scott (black), who was deliberately ambushed for that purpose. Motive: she had sought to end their romantic involvement, they having hitherto shared the same cabin. The killer was hanged at Lumpkin on November 8, 1912. Source: *Macon (GA) Daily Telegraph,* 9/26/11 (6:3). *Columbus (GA) Enquirer-Sun,* 11/9/12 (1:2). See also: 1910 U.S. Census (Stewart Co., GA), which notes both parties as a purportedly married couple.

Leonard Lewis (black, age not recorded). *Murder.* The crime was committed sometime during the year 1912 in Douglas County. Executed for the handgun slaying of another black man (name and age unknown) in a gambling dispute. Further details of this case are elusive because the original court file could not be located. It is historically certain, however, that Leonard Lewis was legally hanged at Douglasville on November 8, 1912. Source: *Atlanta Georgian,* 11/8/12 (4:2). *Atlanta Constitution,* 11/9/12 (2:3).

Oscar Clyde (black, age 25). *Murder.* The crime was committed on 9/3/1911 in Bibb County. Uxoricide, etc. Handgun slayings of 22-year-old Ophelia Howard Clyde and 26-year-old Charles Howard (blacks), they being his wife and brother-in-law. Motive: they were leaving town to get away from him. He was legally hanged at Macon on December 4, 1912. Source: *Macon Daily Telegraph,* 9/3/11 (1:3) & 12/5/12 (16:3). See also: 1900 U.S. Census (Bibb Co., GA), which notes the homicide victims in this case.

Robert L. Clay (white, age 27). *Murder.* The crime was committed on 5/12/1912 in Fulton County. Handgun slaying of 24-year-old Katherine Hughes Clay (white), she having been shot three times. Motive: impending divorce. Possibly deranged. Robert Clay was a professional scenic painter with a quirky personality. The couple had been married five years. They had separated nine times during that period. Robert bore a skull indentation that had been caused by a piece of iron that had fallen from a scaffold and struck him on the head. He had reportedly been prone to odd behavior from that time on. It was not enough to save him from the gallows. He was hanged at Atlanta on December 13, 1912. Source: *Atlanta Constitution,* 5/13/12 (1:1) & 12/14/12 (1:7).

Noble Walker (black, age 24). *Murder.* The crime was committed on 5/31/1912 in Thomas County. Uxoricide. Executed for the killing of Sarah Green Walker (black, age uncertain), who was stabbed, slashed and then finished off by being shot in the back of the head execution-style. Motive: marital estrangement. The couple had been wed in 1910. Its male half was legally hanged at Thomasville on December 13, 1912. Source: *Weekly Times-Enterprise* (Thomasville, GA), 6/7/12 (3:5) & 12/20/12 (3:1).

1913

Edward Brazell (white, age 43). *Murder.* The crime was committed on

11/15/1911 in Richmond County. Shotgun slaying of 17-year-old Carrie Belle Duncan (white), whom he gunned down in the presence of his convalescent wife, saying that she had come between them. Motive: tenement building soap opera. The protagonist (Edward Brazell) was hanged for this bizarre act at Augusta on January 3, 1913. Source: *Augusta (GA) Chronicle*, 11/16/11 (7:5) & 1/4/13 (4:4).

Solomon Williams (black, age 22). *Murder.* The crime was committed on 6/3/1912 in Chatham County. Fatal stabbing of 38-year-old Ann Rivers (black), his mother-in-law. Motive: family problems. This killer was hanged at Savannah on January 17, 1913. Source: *Savannah Morning News*, 1/18/13 (12:3). *Atlanta Constitution*, 1/18/13 (3:4). Also see: *Savannah Registry of Deaths*, entries at date.

John Phillips (black, age not recorded). *Murder.* The crime was committed on 4/14/1912 in Tift County. Rifle slaying of 17-year-old James Smith, alias "Kid Jelks" (black), during a row at a turpentine camp. Phillips came from Wilcox County. His fellow laborers resented him for being too cozy with the boss. The situation boiled over when Phillips opened fire on those he thought were critical of him. This wound up costing Phillips his life. He was hanged for capital murder at Tifton on February 7, 1913. Source: *Tifton (GA) Gazette*, 7/12/12 (1:7) & 2/7/13 (1:3). *Augusta (GA) Chronicle*, 2/8/13 (7:5). Appeal: 138 GA 815. Pardons Files Box 95, GA State Archives. See also: 1910 U.S. Census (Terrell Co., GA), which notes Smith.

William Thompson (black, age 23). *Murder.* The crime was committed on 1/21/1911 in Jefferson County. Handgun slaying of 27-year-old Claude Humphrey (white), a railroad baggage master. Motive: fracas at a train station. This killer was legally hanged at Louisville on May 2, 1913. Source: *Macon (GA) Daily Telegraph*, 1/24/11 (6:1), which erroneously reported that Thompson had been lynched. *Augusta (GA) Chronicle*, 8/8/11 (7:3). *Atlanta Constitution*, 5/3/13 (1:5). See also: 1910 U.S. Census (Jefferson Co., GA), which notes both parties.

Jake Crawford (black, age not recorded). *Murder.* The crime was committed on 4/7/1912 in Putnam County. Gunshot slaying of another black man named John Henry Powell, a.k.a. "Henry Mack Powell" (age unknown). Motive: unknown. Crawford was legally hanged at Eatonton on May 23, 1913. Source: *Eatonton (GA) Messenger*, 9/21/12 (1:1) & 5/24/13 (1:6). Appeal: 139 GA 612–613. Surviving documentation for this case is skimpy. The Bill of Exceptions that was filed with the state supreme court is inaccessible. There was also a folder on this case in Pardons Files Box 28, GA State Archives, but that too is missing.

Carter Tompkins (black, age 22). *Murder.* The crime was committed on or about 1/10/1913 in Putnam County. Executed for the ax killing of 31-year-old Jerry Price (black), whose butchered corpse was then wrapped in a fish blanket and dumped into a creek. The homicide was discovered on 1/19/1913 when grapplers snagged the gory bundle. Motive: adultery with the decedent's wife. Tompkins was hanged for what he had done at Eatonton on May 23, 1913. Source: *Eatonton (GA) Messenger*, 1/25/13 (1:3), 2/1/13 (1:1) & 5/24/13 (1:6). See also: 1910 U.S. Census (Putnam Co., GA), which notes both parties.

Oscar Dewberry (black, age 24). *Murder.* The crime was committed on 6/15/1912 in Fulton County. Child killer. Executed for the fatal and deliberate stabbing of 15-year-old Horace Dodson (white), who was attacked on a public sidewalk for no apparent reason. Motive: possibly deranged. The homicide victim was knifed in the back. He succumbed to his wound on 7/11/1912. The killer was hanged at Atlanta on July 11, 1913. Source: *Atlanta Constitution*, 7/12/12 (5:1) & 7/12/13 (5:3).

Frank Collier (black, age 24). *Murder.* The crime was committed on 4/13/1912 in Chatham County. Fatal stabbing of 26-year-old Morris Robinson (black). Motive: sidewalk brawl. The homicide victim felt that he had been slighted in the presence of a female companion. Words were exchanged and next came the knife. Frank Collier then found himself on a path to the gallows. He was executed at Savannah on August 22, 1913. Source: *Savannah Morning News*, 8/23/13 (12:6). *Atlanta Constitution*, 8/23/13 (6:7). Appeal: 140 GA 138. See also: 1910 U.S. Census (Savannah, GA), which notes both parties.

William Varner (black, age 28). *Murder.* The crime was committed on 4/5/1913 in Newton County. Child killer. Handgun slaying of 9-year-old Rufus James (black), his stepson. Motive: barnyard rampage. Varner had gone gunning for his estranged wife. He wound up shooting at everything that moved. This earned him a date with the hangman at Covington on September 26, 1913. Source: *Covington (GA) News*, 4/9/13 (1:4), 9/24/13 (1:2) & 10/1/13 (1:6). *Atlanta Constitution*, 9/27/13 (5:5). Pardons Files Box 124, GA State Archives. See also: 1910 U.S. Census (Newton Co., GA), which notes Varner.

Edd Kitchens (black, age 28). *Murder.* The crime was committed on 4/19/1913 in Washington County. Handgun slaying of 33-year-old Henry A. Brantley (white), who was shot five times in his doorway. Motive: big attitude. The homicide victim was a farm overseer who had reprimanded a member of the Kitchens family. Edd and his brother Robert Kitchens (executed 6/2/16) then confronted Mr. Brantley and riddled him with bullets. Edd Kitchens was legally hanged for this at Sandersville on October 17, 1913. Source: *Macon (GA) Daily Telegraph*, 4/20/13 (1:6). *Atlanta Constitution*, 10/18/13 (6:5). See also: Robert Henry Kitchens (executed 6/2/16).

William Gathright (black, age 35). *Murder.* The crime was committed on 5/1/1913 in Gwinnett County. Executed for the ax murder of 33-year-old George L. Seay (white). Motive: enmity between neighbors. This ax-wielding killer was legally hanged at Lawrenceville on November 14, 1913. Source: *Atlanta Constitution*, 5/3/13 (1:4), 11/14/13 (14:6) & 11/15/13 (12:4). See also: 1910 U.S. Census (Gwinnett Co., GA), which notes both parties.

1914

David McLaughlin, alias "Lewis Davis" (black, age not recorded). *Murder.* The crime was committed on 6/26/1904 in Laurens County. Handgun slaying of Selma Burney Davis (black), who was shot three times. Motive: a flare-up at the home of his purported in-laws. They had apparently gotten wise to the fact that "Davis" had married their daughter under an assumed name. He fled to parts unknown and remained at large for several years. The hangman caught up with him at Dublin on January 24, 1914. Source: *Augusta (GA) Chronicle*, 12/13/13 (4:4). *Dublin (GA) Courier-Herald*, 1/29/14 (1:1). Appeal: 141 GA 132–135. Pardons Files Box 32, GA State Archives.

George Smith (black, age 41). *Murder.* The crime was committed on 2/23/1913 in Lowndes County. Shotgun slaying of 34-year-old Jesse Simmons (black), who was assassinated in his own doorway, the top of his head blown off. Motive: rivalry for a female. The killer was hanged at Valdosta on February 6, 1914. Source: *Valdosta Daily Times*, 2/24/13 (5:3) & 2/6/14 (5:1). *Macon (GA) Daily Telegraph*, 2/25/13 (11:2) & 2/7/14 (1:5). Appeal: 140 GA 791. See also: 1910 U.S. Census (Lowndes Co., GA), which notes both parties.

William M. Duncan (black, age 23). *Murder.* The crime was committed on 11/28/1912 in Houston County. Handgun slaying of a young black woman named Pace Reed (exact age uncertain) during a fracas in a dancehall. Duncan wound up dancing on air with a rope around his neck (legally) at Perry on February 12, 1914. Source: *Atlanta Constitution*, 2/13/14 (5:4). Appeal: 141 GA 4–5. Pardons Files Box 35, GA State Archives. See also: 1910 U.S. Census (Houston Co., GA), which notes this killer.

John Nathaniel Wilburn, alias "Nick Wilburn" (white, age 25). *Murder.* The crime was committed on 12/12/1912 in Jones County. Shotgun slaying of 36-year-old James H. King (white). Motives: gross perfidy, insurance fraud, and adultery with the decedent's wife. Wilburn was hanged for the part he played in this farrago at Gray on June 12, 1914. Source: *Macon (GA) Daily Telegraph*, 12/28/12 (1:6). *Augusta (GA) Chronicle*, 10/26/13 (2:3), 6/13/14 (2:5) & 6/14/14 (5:2). See also: 1900 U.S. Census (Jones Co., GA), which notes both parties.

George Hart (black, age 14), **Willie Hart** (black, age 15) and **Robert Paschal** (black, age 16). *Murder.* Their crime was committed on 12/15/1913 in Jefferson County. All three executed for the decapitation murder of 25-year-old Ellie Irby (white), the wife of Mr. Seth Lee Irby. Motive: pure savagery. One of the killers was due a few cents for a sack of potatoes by prior arrangement with Mr. Irby. The trio went to that man's residence in anticipation of getting paid, only to find that Mr. Irby was not then at home. So they asked payment of Mrs. Irby instead. She replied that they would have to see her husband. This was not what the three boys wanted to hear. They immediately pounced on Mrs. Irby and cut off her head. Seth Irby later came home to find the massacred remains of his wife. Her head had been kicked and beaten to a point where it was hardly recognizable. Venue changed from Jefferson County to Fulton County. The three young killers were legally hanged at Atlanta on June 19, 1914. Source: *Atlanta Constitution*, 12/16/13 (1:2), 1/1/14 (1:1) & 6/20/14 (3:3). See also: 1910 U.S. Census (Jefferson Co., GA), which notes the Irbys and the Harts.

Bartow Cantrell (white, age 17) and **James Cantrell** (white, age 29). *Murder.* Their crime was committed on 5/29/1913 in Hall County. Shotgun slaying of a white man named Arthur C. Hawkins (age uncertain). Motive: a sordid tale of adultery. Bartow Cantrell was the triggerman. He had been put up to the deed by his elder brother (James Cantrell) and the dead man's conniving wife. She drew a sentence of life imprisonment thanks to the old "Southern chivalry" dodge. This was a nullifying double standard of that era that barred the execution of white women no matter how heinous their crimes. This one's lover and his little brother did not benefit from that custom, simply because they were male. Both were hanged at Gainesville on July 31, 1914. Source: *Atlanta Constitution*, 6/1/13 (17:4), 8/17/13 (p. G-2), 8/30/13 (5:1), 8/1/14 (9:2) & 8/3/14 (4:5). *Gainesville (GA) News*, 6/4/13 (1:3). *Gainesville (GA) Eagle*, 8/6/14 (1:7). Appeal: 141 GA 98–105. See also: 1900 U.S. Census (Rabun Co., GA), which notes the Cantrells. Also see Bartow Cantrell's gravestone in Alta Vista Cemetery, Gainesville which says that he was born on 9/27/1895.

John Davis (black, age 46). *Murder.* The crime was committed on 6/15/1914 in Muscogee County. Handgun slaying of 31-year-old Oscar McGinty (white), who was shot in the back. Motive: highway robbery. This killer was legally hanged at Columbus on September 4, 1914. Source: *Columbus (GA) Ledger*, 6/15/14 (1:1) & 9/4/14 (1:1). *Columbus (GA) Daily Enquirer*, 6/16/14 (6:1) & 7/14/14 (1:1). See also: 1900 and 1910 U.S. Censuses (Muscogee Co., GA), which respectively note McGinty and Davis.

Miles Cribb (white, age 31). *Murder.* The crime was committed on 11/7/1913 in Turner County. Uxoricide, etc. Handgun slayings of 27-year-old Viola L. Cribb and 59-year-old Mary Ann Hancock (whites), they having respectively been his wife and his mother-in-law. Motive: dispute over child custody. This double killer was legally hanged at Ashburn on September 11, 1914. Source: *Macon (GA) Daily Telegraph*, 11/8/13 (1:7). *Columbus (GA) Ledger*, 11/9/13 (1:5). *Augusta (GA) Chronicle*, 9/12/14 (3:2). See also: 1910 U.S. Census (Macon, GA), which notes the Cribbs, and 1910 U.S. Census (Turner Co., GA), which notes Mrs. Hancock.

William I. Umphrey (white, age 64). *Murder.* The crime was committed on 11/17/1913 in Whitfield County. Shotgun slaying of 63-year-old Joseph S. Pritchett (white). Motive: landlord-tenant dispute. This crotchety killer was hanged for his misdeed at Dalton on September 11, 1914. Source: *Columbus (GA) Daily Enquirer*, 11/19/13 (8:3). *Atlanta Constitution*, 9/12/14 (7:3). See also: 1910 U.S. Census (Whitfield Co., GA), which notes Wm. Umphrey. Also see the gravestone of Joseph Pritchett in Grove Level Cemetery, Dalton.

1915

Fleming Jackson (black, age 20). *Murder.* The crime was committed on 11/10/1914 in Mitchell County. Police killer. Shotgun slaying of 28-year-old Will Griner (white), a Mitchell County deputy. Motive: resisting arrest. This offender was legally hanged at Camilla on January 15, 1915. Source: *Macon (GA) Daily Telegraph*, 11/12/14 (2:3). *Atlanta Constitution*, 1/16/15 (9:1). See also: 1910 U.S. Census (Mitchell Co., GA), which notes both parties.

Ransom Williams (black, age not recorded). *Rape.* The crime was committed on or about 10/25/1914 in Calhoun County. Indecent assault on the person of an adult white female (name withheld) during the course of which she was throttled to within an inch of her life by means of a shoelace held firmly around her neck. Venue changed from Calhoun County to Dougherty County. The attacker was legally hanged at Albany on January 15, 1915. Source: *Macon (GA) Daily Telegraph*, 12/22/14 (1:3). *Atlanta Constitution*, 1/16/15 (9:1). *Albany (GA) Herald*, 1/15/15 (1:5). Williams came from Quincy, FL. He was caught there on 11/1/14.

Burret Hickman (black, age not recorded). *Murder*. The crime was committed on 2/21/1914 in Fulton County. Police killer. Handgun slaying of 24-year-old Howard G. Bennett (white), a railroad detective for the Seaboard Air Line, then a large-scale freight transport company. Motive: boxcar break in gone awry. The assassin was legally hanged at Atlanta on January 29, 1915. Source: *Atlanta Constitution*, 2/22/14 (6:4), 2/23/14 (12:5) & 1/30/15 (9:2).

James Hill, known to some as "Bunk Hill" (black, age 43). *Murder.* The crime was committed on 9/5/1914 in Crisp County. Handgun slaying of 19-year-old Donald Forehand (white). Motive: not discernible based on surviving accounts. Hill was legally hanged at Cordele on March 16, 1915. Source: *Macon (GA) Daily Telegraph*, 9/7/14 (1:1), 9/9/14 (6:3) & 3/17/15 (2:1). See also: 1900 U.S. Census (Dooly Co., GA), which notes Hill, and 1910 U.S. Census (Crisp Co., GA), which notes Forehand.

Luther Stephens (black, age 17). *Murder.* The crime was committed on 1/19/1915 in Crisp County. Handgun slaying of 59-year-old Thomas Ephraim Gleaton (white), who was killed by a shot fired through his bedroom window. Motive: not discernible based on surviving accounts. The killer was legally hanged at Cordele on March 18, 1915. Source: *Augusta (GA) Chronicle*, 1/21/15 (3:4). *Atlanta Constitution*, 3/19/15 (7:5). See also: 1900 U.S. Census (Dooly Co., GA), which notes the assassin as "Luther Steven." Also see Mr. Gleaton's gravestone inscription in Zion Hope Cemetery, Arabi.

Will Bird (black, age 24). *Murder.* The crime was committed on 2/21/1914 in Jasper County. Handgun slaying of a black woman named Sabrie "Sadie" Brunson (age not recorded). Motive: adultery turned deadly. The woman-killer Will Bird was hanged at Monticello on April 9, 1915. Source: *Monticello (GA) News*, 4/9/15 (1:6). *Atlanta Constitution*, 4/10/15 (1:5). Appeal: 142 GA 596–600. Pardon Files Box 9, GA State Archives.

Alfred Goolsby (black, age 61). *Murder.* The crime was committed on an unknown date in Brooks County. Executed for the killing (by unknown means) of 32-year-old Mitch Davis (black), his much younger brother-in-law. Motive: not discernible based on surviving accounts. It is confirmed, however, that Goolsby was hanged for this homicide at Quitman on June 11, 1915. Source: *Valdosta (GA) Daily Times*, 6/11/15 (1:2). *Atlanta Constitution*, 6/12/15 (1:5). See also: 1910 U.S. Census (Brooks Co., GA), which notes both parties.

Henry Floyd (black, age not recorded). *Murder.* The crime was committed at some point during the year 1914 in Jenkins County. Executed for the ax murder of a black woman named Bertha Perdue (age unknown). Motive: not discernible based on surviving accounts. The killer was legally hanged at Millen on August 6, 1915. Source: *Atlanta Journal*, 8/6/15 (7:4). *Savannah Morning News*, 8/7/15 (11:7).

William McGriff (black, age not recorded). *Murder.* The crime was committed on 7/11/1911 in Colquitt County. Handgun slayings of 31-year-old William S. Washington (white), a turpentine distiller, and two of his employees: Dan Showers and Sylvester Phinney (blacks, ages not recorded). Motive: workplace violence. The killer was nabbed in Oklahoma on 4/8/1915. Most of his lower jaw was shot away before he could be subdued. He went to the gallows in a horribly disfigured condition, his mind unaffected. McGriff claimed to have also killed seven other persons (all blacks) while on the run, but this was probably jailbird bravado. He was hanged at Moultrie on August 19, 1915. Source: *Daily Observer* (Moultrie, GA), 7/11/11 (1:3) & 8/19/15 (1:3). *Macon (GA) Daily Telegraph*, 4/9/15 (2:3), 4/13/15 (8:6) & 4/24/15 (2:3). *Atlanta Constitution*, 8/20/15 (6:2). See also: 1910 U.S. Census (Colquitt Co., GA), which notes "W. S. Washington."

Frank Northfoot (black, age 22). *Murder.* The crime was committed on 11/1/1913 in Early County. Uxoricide. Hanged on his 24th birthday for the handgun slaying of 19-year-old Hattie Northfoot (black), whom he deliberately hunted down and found at her grandmother's house. Motive: the homicide victim behaved like a whore, or so the killer said. He was hanged at Blakely on September 24, 1915. Source: *Atlanta Constitution*, 9/25/15 (3:5). *Macon (GA) Daily Telegraph*, 9/25/15 (3:4). Appeal: 142 GA 714. Pardon Files Box 89, GA State Archives. See also: 1910 U.S. Census (Early Co., GA), which notes both parties as "Norfoot."

Joe Persons (black, age 14). *Rape.* The crime was committed on 6/14/1915 in Butts County. Indecent assault on the person of an 8-year-old white female (name withheld) under circumstances so heinous that the culprit's own father said that he deserved to be hanged. A mercy petition said that this felon was aged 13 and weighed only 65 lb. He was executed in accordance with legal procedure at Jackson on September 24, 1915. Source: *Atlanta Constitution*, 8/23/15 (5:6) & 9/25/15 (3:5). *Macon (GA) Daily Telegraph*, 9/24/15 (12:5) & 9/25/15 (2:5). Pardon Files Box 94, GA State Archives.

Clifford Sims (black, age 27). *Murder.* The crime was committed on 2/15/1909 in Lee County. Executed for the shotgun slaying of a black woman named Catherine Boston (age not recorded) because she had called him "a drop lip son of a bitch." Sims met death at the hands of the hangman at Leesburg on October 26, 1915. Source: *Albany (GA) Herald*, 10/26/15 (2:3). *Macon (GA) Daily Telegraph*, 10/27/15 (6:5). Appeal: 144 GA 90–91. See also: 1900 U.S. Census (Lee Co., GA), which notes Sims.

Sam Hardin (black, age not recorded), **Jake Turner** (black, age not recorded) and **Guy Young** (black, age not recorded). *Murder.* Their crime was committed on 10/9/1915 in Taliaferro County. All three hanged for the shotgun slaying of 30-year-old Charles Rackley (white), a sawmill operator. Motive: workplace violence with a strong racial overtone. The homicide victim employed laborers regardless of their color. Trouble erupted among those persons when a white worker beat up a black boy. The other black employees became incensed at this. They armed themselves and marched on the sawmill, vowing that they would be the death of every white man there. Charles Rackley was the first one they encountered. The other white men fled into the pines. They lay low until order was restored. Jake Turner was identified as the triggerman. He and two of his disarmed cohorts were charged with capital murder. All three dropped from the same gallows at Crawfordville on November 8, 1915. Source: *Advocate-Democrat* (Crawfordville, GA), 10/15/15 (1:1) & 11/12/15 (1:1). *Augusta (GA) Chronicle*, 10/12/15 (6:6). *Macon (GA) Daily Telegraph*, 10/16/15 (7:1). *Atlanta Constitution*, 11/9/15 (7:3).

Will Johnson (black, age not recorded). *Murder.* The crime was committed on 7/23/1915 in Bulloch County. Shotgun slaying of 56-year-old Cuyler Green (black), the homicide victim having been deliberately lured to his doom. Motive: a festering grudge over who should have had the right to use a mule. The killer said that his real name was John Sconyers and that he came from Orangeburg, SC. He was hanged at Statesboro on December 17, 1915. Source: *Macon (GA) Daily Telegraph*, 8/6/15 (2:3). *Bulloch Times* (Statesboro, GA), 7/29/15 (1:1), 8/5/15 (1:3) & 12/23/15 (1:1). See also: 1910 U.S. Census (Bulloch Co., GA), which notes the murdered man.

Lee Ingram (black, age not recorded). *Murder.* The crime was committed on 1/29/1915 in Randolph County. Uxoricide. Handgun slaying of Eliza Ingram (black, age not recorded), who was shot twice at a church social, including one time after she had fallen to the ground. Motive: marital estrangement. This wife killer was hanged at Cuthbert on December 21, 1915. Source: *Macon (GA) Daily Telegraph*, 12/22/15 (1:6). *Liberal-Enterprise* (Cuthbert, GA), 12/24/15 (4:2). Appeal: 144 GA 216. Pardon Files Box 62, GA State Archives.

1916

Will Brown (black, age not recorded). *Murder.* The crime was committed on 4/30/1915 in Rabun County. Executed for the handgun slaying of another black man named Will Sweet (age not recorded), who was shot in the back. Motive: dancehall hubris. Recidivist killer. At the time of the Rabun County homicide, Brown was a fugitive from North Carolina. He had killed his wife there two years earlier and had been sentenced to 30-years imprisonment, but he escaped. He was hanged at Clayton on January 28, 1916. Source: *Clayton (GA) Tribune*, 2/4/16 (1:2). *Augusta (GA) Chronicle*, 1/11/16 (2:3). *Macon (GA) Daily Telegraph*, 1/16/16 (8:1). *Atlanta Constitution*, 1/29/16 (1:6). Appeal: 144 GA 216–219.

Lon Lindsey (white, age 34). *Murder.* The crime was committed on 7/26/1915 in Clay County. Uxoricide. Handgun slaying of 31-year-old Florence McCorkle Lindsey (white). Motive: domestic disturbance. An aggravating factor in this homicide was the fact that Lindsey had treacherously passed their infant child to its mother's arms in order to put her off guard for what he had in mind. He had immediately snatched up a pistol at that point and pulled the trigger. He was hanged for this at Fort Gaines on May 19, 1916. Source: *Macon (GA) Daily Telegraph*, 9/18/15 (3:3). *Atlanta Constitution*, 5/20/16 (4:4). See also: 1900 U.S. Census (Clay Co., GA), which notes both parties, the victim by her maiden name.

Gideon McKinney (black, age 23). *Murder.* The crime was committed on 8/16/1915 in Miller County. Uxoricide. Shotgun slaying of 16-year-old Susie McGriff McKinney (black), who was ambushed while walking home from church. Motive: marital estrangement. This wife-killer was hanged at Colquitt on May 19, 1916. Source: *Atlanta Constitution*, 5/20/16 (4:4). *Miller County Liberal*, 5/24/16 (1:4). Appeal: 144 GA 833. Pardon Files Box 81, GA State Archives.

Robert Henry Kitchens (black, age 25). *Murder.* The crime was committed on 4/19/1913 in Washington County. Accomplice in the handgun slaying of 33-year-old Henry A. Brantley (white), who was shot five times in his own doorway. Motive: big attitude. The hangman caught up with this offender at Sandersville on June 2, 1916. Source: *Atlanta Journal*, 6/2/16 (22:1). See also: Edd Kitchens (executed 10/17/13). See also: 1910 U.S. Census (Wash. Co., GA), which notes Kitchens.

Wes Story (black, age 53). *Murder.* The crime was committed on 7/11/1915 in Harris County. Handgun slaying of 26-year-old Cherry Huling (black female). Motive: possibly deranged. The killer "had asked her for a dip of snuff and as she was bending over her open trunk to get it Story shot off one side of her head, scattering brains, blood and bone all around on the floor, the wall and in the trunk." Wes Story went to his death on the gallows at Hamilton on July 14, 1916. Source: *Columbus (GA) Ledger*, 7/12/15 (8:1). *Columbus (GA) Daily Enquirer*, 10/15/15 (1:2) & 7/15/16 (2:6). Appeal: 145 GA 43–48. See also: 1910 U.S. Census (Harris Co., GA), which notes both parties.

Charlie Mosby (black, age not recorded). *Murder.* The crime was committed on 1/29/1907 in Calhoun County. Handgun slaying of 26-year-old Earl S. Cunningham (white), the foreman of a lumber-company work gang. Motive: disgruntled employee. The killer was a lumberjack. His pay had been withheld because he was in debt to the company store. Cunningham went to Mosby's cabin on the above date and told him to report for duty. Mosby refused, saying that he would not work for nothing. A few minutes later Mosby was summoned to the company office. He surmised (probably correctly) that Cunningham had reported him to management. His next act was to walk up to Mr. Cunningham with a loaded pistol and shoot him dead. Nine years slipped by before the law caught up with Charlie Mosby. He was legally hanged at Morgan on July 17, 1916. Source: *Macon (GA) Daily Telegraph*, 2/1/07 (3:3). *Calhoun County Courier*, 2/1/07 (1:3). *Albany (GA) Herald*, 7/17/16 (2:2). See also Mr. Cunningham's gravestone in Oak Grove Cemetery, Arlington.

Will Lampkin, alias "Peg Leg Lampkin" (black, age not recorded). *Murder.* The crime was committed on 7/5/1915 in Decatur County. Uxoricide. Executed for the shotgun slaying of Annie Lampkin (black, age not recorded). Motive: because she had turned lesbian. This wife-killer was a sorry sight as he hobbled his way to the gallows on a wooden leg at Bainbridge on August 4, 1916. Source: *Bainbridge (GA) Post-Searchlight*, 8/10/16 (1:5). Appeal: 145 GA 40–43. Pardon Files Box 72, GA State Archives.

John David Wright (black, age not recorded). *Murder.* The crime was committed sometime during the year

1915 in Harris County. Uxoricide. Executed for the killing of 35-year-old Annie Wright (black) under circumstances that cannot be ascertained because the original court papers are inaccessible. It is confirmed that this wife killer was legally hanged at Hamilton on October 20, 1916. Source: *Columbus (GA) Ledger*, 10/20/16 (1:2). Pardon Files Box 135, GA State Archives. See also: 1910 U.S. Census (Harris Co., GA), which notes both parties.

1917

Harris Sutton (black, age 13). *Rape.* The crime was committed on 12/3/1916 in Henry County. Indecent assault on the person of a 10-year-old white female (name withheld), the details being such that no newspaper dared to publicize them. Several requests for further information about this case (as well as other capital cases that occurred in Henry County) have gone unanswered by the Office of the Clerk of Henry County Superior Court. Harris Sutton was legally hanged at McDonough on January 12, 1917. Source: *Atlanta Journal*, 1/12/17 (9:7). *Henry County Weekly* (McDonough, GA), 1/19/17 (1:3). See also: 1910 U.S. Census (Henry Co., GA), which notes that this sex offender was born in 1903.

Will Miles (black, age not recorded). *Murder.* The crime was committed on 10/3/1916 in Fulton County. Handgun slaying of 41-year-old John H. Moore (white), a coal merchant who was shot in the back while he was talking on a wall phone in his office. Motive: none indicated. Miles was probably a juvenile offender. He was hanged at Atlanta on January 30, 1917. Source: *Atlanta Journal*, 1/30/17 (7:1). *Atlanta Constitution*, 1/31/17 (9:1). See also: Frank Hugle, executed 7/20/1917.

Tom Shirley (black, age 23). *Murder.* The crime was committed on 12/3/1915 in Franklin County. Handgun slaying of another black man named Otis Akerman (age uncertain) when trouble erupted at an all-black cookout. Motive: big attitude. Witnesses said that Shirley had deliberately picked a fight with Akerman. The former was hanged for this self-defeating act at Carnesville on February 9, 1917. Source: *Atlanta Constitution*, 2/10/17 (4:6). Appeal: 146 GA 9–10. See also: 1900 U.S. Census (Franklin Co., GA), which notes Shirley as a minor.

Clarence Dennis (black, age 32). *Murder.* The crime was committed on 2/5/1916 in Pike County. Patricide. Shotgun slaying of 59-year-old Sam Dennis (black) because the father had accused the son of siphoning his whiskey. The younger Dennis was hanged in accordance with the law in such cases at Zebulon on February 16, 1917. Source: *Atlanta Journal*, 2/15/17 (7:7) & 2/17/17 (11:6). *Pike County Journal*, 2/23/17 (1:1). Appeal: 146 GA 191–193. Pardon Files Box 33, GA State Archives. See also: 1900 U.S. Census (Meriwether Co., GA), which notes both parties.

Sam Couch, alias "Mose Couch" (black, age 32). *Murder.* The crime was committed on 8/8/1915 in Harris County. Handgun slaying of 16-year-old Hollis Dewberry (black), who was shot in a deliberate act of terrorism. Motive: disruption of a church service. The killer had previously quarreled with the elders of an all-black church. He may have been excommunicated from their congregation. Whatever the details, Couch burst into that house of worship with gun drawn during Sunday meeting and shot up the place. This man was not only vindictive but sacrilegious. He was legally hanged at Hamilton on May 25, 1917. Source: *Columbus (GA) Ledger*, 8/23/15 (8:4). *Columbus (GA) Daily Enquirer*, 10/15/15 (1:1), 4/19/17 (4:5) and 12/17/21 (1:1) in retrospect. See also: 1900 U.S. Census (Talbot Co., GA), which notes Couch, and 1910 U.S. Census (Harris Co., GA), which notes Dewberry.

Frank Hugle (black, age 14). *Murder.* The crime was committed on 10/3/1916 in Fulton County. Accomplice in the handgun slaying of 41-year-old John H. Moore (white), a coal merchant who was shot in the back while standing at a wall phone in his office. Motive: none indicated. This young offender was legally hanged at Atlanta on July 20, 1917. Source: *Atlanta Journal*, 7/20/17 (3:1). *Atlanta Constitution*, 7/21/17 (10:6). Pardon Files Box 61, GA State Archives. See also: 1910 U.S. Census (Hapeville, Fulton Co., GA), which notes Frank Hugle, the son of Mary Hugle. See also: Will Miles (executed 1/30/17).

Charlie Williams, alias "Smith" (black, age not recorded). *Murder*. The crime was committed on or about 7/26/1916 in Decatur County. Handgun slaying of 23-year-old Minnon "Willie" Edwards (black), whose rotting corpse was later found hidden beneath a sawdust pile. Motive: rivalry for a female, in this case the killer's stepdaughter. Charlie Williams was hanged by the neck until dead at Bainbridge on August 3, 1917. Source: *Post-Searchlight* (Bainbridge, GA), 8/3/16 (1:2). *Macon (GA) Daily Telegraph*, 8/1/16 (3:3), 11/21/16 (9:3) & 12/27/16 (9:5). *Atlanta Journal*, 8/3/17 (12:5). Appeal: 147 GA 53–55.

Oscar Allen (black, age not recorded). *Murder.* The crime was committed on 8/20/1917 in Taliaferro County. Executed for the malicious killings of 58-year-old Seaborn J. Jones (white) and 42-year-old Sarah Chester (black) during the course of a robbery and home invasion. Jones was a bachelor farmer who lived in a modest house. Sarah Chester was a tenant on his land. Allen came from parts unknown. He was toting a rifle when he walked into the farmer's house and shot that man with it. Allen then ransacked the place. He found a shotgun among the homeowner's effects. The intruder then discarded his own weapon and used this newer one to murder Sarah Chester. Then with no one else about the premises, Allen continued tearing the house apart in a frenzied search for valuables. He found farmer Jones still breathing at that point and finished him off by literally beating his brains out with an iron fireplace poker. The law moved quickly in the aftermath of this atrocity. Oscar Allen was legally hanged for what he had done at Crawfordville on September 18, 1917. Source: *Augusta (GA) Chronicle*, 8/22/17 (4:4) & 9/19/17 (6:5). *Advocate-Democrat* (Crawfordville, GA), 8/24/17 (1:3), 8/31/17 (1:1) & 9/21/17 (5:5). See also: 1860 U.S. Census (Taiaferro Co., GA), which notes Mr. Jones as a small child, and 1910 U.S. Census (Taliaferro Co., GA), which notes Sarah Chester.

1918

Ras Jones, alias "Rabbit Jones" (black, age not recorded). *Murder.* The crime was committed on 3/20/1917 in

Miller County. Handgun slaying of another black man named Richard Blackshear (age not recorded), who was shot multiple times and thrown from a moving train. Motive: rivalry for a female. This killer was hanged at Colquitt on May 24, 1918. Source: *Miller County Liberal*, 5/29/18 (2:2). Appeal: 147 GA 356–357. Pardon Files Box 69, GA State Archives.

John Marvin Thompson (white, age 22). *Murder.* The crime was committed on 2/26/1917 in Troup County. Police killer. Rifle slaying of 42-year-old William Brewer Shirey (white), the sheriff of Troup County. Motive: liquor raid turned deadly. This offender was hanged at La Grange on July 26, 1918. Thompson's father committed suicide in the aftermath of his son's execution. Source: *Columbus (GA) Daily Enquirer*, 2/28/17 (5:1) & 5/4/17 (8:4). *Macon (GA) Daily Telegraph*, 7/27/18 (3:3). *Atlanta Constitution*, 11/19/18 (13:3). See also: 1910 U.S. Census (Troup Co., GA), which notes both parties.

John Burke, alias "Chick Burke" (black, age not recorded). *Murder*. The crime was committed on 10/28/1917 in Macon County. Executed for the ax murder of another black man named Joe Crittle (age not recorded), with whom he shared a cabin. Motive: tension over living arrangements. The homicide victim was decapitated as he lay asleep. The killer then loaded the headless corpse onto a wheelbarrow and dumped it half a mile away. He was hanged for this at Oglethorpe on October 23, 1918. Source: *Macon County Citizen*, 11/9/17 (5:5) & 10/25/18 (8:1). Appeal: 148 GA 230–232. Pardon Files Box 17, GA State Archives.

Bart Goodwin (white, age 31). *Murder.* The crime was committed on 6/22/1917 in Polk County. Uxoricide. Shotgun slaying of pregnant 23-year-old Ella Stubbs Goodwin (white) for a reason that no one was ever able to explain. Goodwin had joined the army, leaving his in-laws to care for his wife. They had been married seven years earlier when the bride was aged 16. Their first child had died in a railroad mishap. Bart Goodwin went A.W.O.L. from his army base near Atlanta. He made his way to Polk County and spent the ensuing night with a woman of bad character. Then he went to the home of his father-in-law (William M. Stubbs) and took down a shotgun from its place above the door. Goodwin loaded that weapon with shells that he had brought along with him and murdered his spouse forthwith. He was hanged at Cedartown on November 8, 1918. Source: *Atlanta Constitution*, 11/9/18 (3:8). *Cedartown (GA) Standard*, 6/28/17 (1:1) & 11/14/18 (4:3). See also: 1910 U.S. Census (Polk Co., GA), which notes the homicide victim by her maiden name.

George Wilkerson (black, age 31). *Murder.* The crime was committed on 6/2/1917 in Burke County. Executed for the killing of 36-year-old Charlie Bradley (black), who was set upon by a four-man gang, shot multiple times with a pistol, viciously stomped and then finished off by having his throat cut. Motive: fracas at a church picnic. The Wilkerson family had begrudged Bradley ever since he had won a lawsuit against them concerning the ownership of a cow. George Wilkerson was hanged for the part that he played in this homicide at Waynesboro on November 22, 1918. Source: *Waynesboro (GA) True Citizen*, 10/6/17 (4:3) & 11/23/18 (2:4). *Atlanta Constitution*, 11/23/18 (5:7). Appeal: 148 GA 197. Pardon Files Box 130, GA State

Archives. See also Wilkerson's World War I draft registration card (Burke Co., GA), which notes 6/20/85 as his date of birth. See also: Henry Wilkerson (executed 12/6/18).

Clifford F. Polk (white, age 37). *Murder.* The crime was committed on 1/19/1915 in Baldwin County. Uxoricide. Handgun slaying of about 35-year-old Maude Roberts Polk (white). Motive: possibly because his mind had come unhinged. Polk was an employee at the Georgia State Insane Asylum. The horrors that he witnessed there seem to have placed a strain on both his marriage and his own mental health. Maude Polk sought advice on what to do. Clifford Polk learned of this and became greatly incensed. His next step was to track down his wife to the place where she had gone for such advice (a public pharmacy near the asylum) and shoot her dead. Nowadays sanitarium workers are routinely monitored for job-related stress. It is doubtful whether Polk's problem (possibly anxiety disorder) was ever recognized for what it really was. The law drew no distinctions in this case. Clifford Polk was convicted of murder and sentenced to death. He was hanged at Milledgeville on November 29, 1918. Source: *Augusta (GA) Chronicle*, 1/20/15 (1:3). *Macon (GA) Daily Telegraph*, 11/30/18 (2:3). Appeal: 148 GA 34–40. Pardon Files Box 96, GA State Archives. See also: 1900 U.S. Census (Jasper Co., GA), which notes Polk as a young bachelor.

Henry Wilkerson (black, age 26). *Murder.* The crime was committed on 6/2/1917 in Burke County. Accomplice in the killing of 36-year-old Charlie Bradley (black) during a gang assault at an outdoor barbecue. He was hanged for his part in that crime at Waynesboro on December 6, 1918. Source: *Waynesboro (GA) True Citizen*, 12/7/18 (5:2). See also Henry Wilkerson's World War I draft registration card (Burke Co., GA), which notes 6/23/90 as his date of birth. See also: George Wilkerson (executed 11/22/18).

1919

Joe West (black, age 20). *Rape.* The crime was committed on 8/29/1918 in Thomas County. Indecent assault on the person of 26-year-old Rosa L. Collins (white), who was attacked in her home and nearly killed when the culprit fired a shotgun in her bedroom. West was a convicted burglar who had escaped from the Webster County chain gang. He made his way to Thomas County, where he broke into three houses including that of the Collins woman. Initial reports discreetly omitted mention of the fact that Rosa Collins was ravished on her own bed. Her attacker was legally hanged at Thomasville on May 16, 1919. Source: *Macon (GA) Daily Telegraph*, 9/2/18 (10:6). *Daily Times-Enterprise* (Thomasville, GA), 5/16/19 (1:6). See also: 1910 U.S. Census (Thomas Co., GA), which notes the assault victim.

Paul Bates (black, age 23). *Murder.* The crime was committed on 10/12/1918 in Screven County. Handgun slaying of 25-year-old Willie Grady Oliver (white). Motive: surly attitude. Bates had neglected to properly stable some farm animals. He shot Mr. Oliver (his employer) rather than account for them. This killer did his accounting on the gallows instead at Sylvania on May 23, 1919. Source: *Atlanta Constitution*, 5/24/19 (14:6). *Sylvania (GA) Telephone*, 10/18/18 (1:6), 1/24/19 (1:3) & 5/23/19 (1:2). See also: 1910 U.S. Census (Screven Co., GA), which notes Mr. Oliver, and World War I draft registration cards (Screven Co., GA), which note both parties.

Tom Steele (black, age 27). *Murder.* The crime was committed on 7/27/1918 in Thomas County. Executed for the killing of 21-year-old James Anderson (black), who was slashed to death with a razor. Motive: obnoxious drunk. Steele was due to leave for military service the following day. He went to "Rat Row" (as the predominantly black vice district in Thomasville was then called) and drank himself into a temper. Then he strode down the middle of the street brandishing an open razor and vowing to kill "the first damned nigger that crosses my path" (to use his own words). It was James Anderson who ran afoul of him. Tom Steele never made it to the army induction center. He was hanged at Thomasville on September 5, 1919. Source: *Daily Times-Enterprise* (Thomasville, GA), 7/31/18 (4:5) & 9/5/19 (1:4). Appeal: 149 GA 134.

West E. Rountree (black, age 30). *Rape.* The crime was committed on 7/16/1919 in Brooks County. Indecent assault on the person of a 14-year-old white female (name withheld). This sex offender was a married man and a so-called preacher of the Gospel. He was legally hanged at Quitman on September 12, 1919. Source: *Daily Times-Enterprise* (Thomasville, GA), 8/23/19 (6:3). *Macon (GA) Daily Telegraph,* 9/13/19 (14:2).

Bartow Nix (white, age 31). *Murder.* The crime was committed on 12/20/1917 in Muscogee County. Executed for the murders of 41-year-old Leslie Alexander and 40-year-old Jesse Allen Everidge (whites), who were lured to their doom on the pretense of buying illicit whiskey. Alexander was shot behind one of his ears with a handgun. The skulls of both men were smashed with a hammer. Then they were buried atop each other in a shallow grave. Motive: robbery and dirty dealing. Recidivist killer. Bartow Nix had murdered two other men on a previous occasion. The date was 6/6/1903. He was aged 17 at the time. It so happened that his father had wrested control of some farmland from a neighbor named John T. Edwards in a hard-fought court case. Edwards had a crop on the disputed land before the case was decided and felt that he should still be allowed to harvest it. Papa Nix refused to grant this consolation. John T. Edwards (white, age 54) and his son Jeff Edwards (white, age 25) did so anyway. Bartow Nix then killed both of them with a shotgun. He was convicted on two counts of first degree murder but was spared the death penalty by a jury recommendation for mercy. Bartow Nix was then sentenced to a term of life imprisonment and packed off to the state penitentiary. Three years later the Georgia State Prison Commission recommended and obtained a gubernatorial pardon for Bartow Nix. This was based almost entirely on the overly refined notion that such a young, handsome, corn fed "Son of the South" had merely been defending the property rights of his family. So Nix went free and returned to Muscogee County. Ten years later he proved to everyone how truly worthy of a pardon he had been. No amount of influence or legalistic trickery availed him like before. The hangman broke his neck to general satisfaction at Columbus on November 7, 1919. Source: *Columbus (GA) Enquirer,* 6/7/03 (11:1), 11/25/03 (1:6), 11/27/03 (1:2), 3/16/07 (1:6) & 12/22/17 (1:6). *Macon (GA) Daily Telegraph,* 11/8/19

(1:4). See also: 1900 U.S. Census (Columbus, GA), which notes Alexander. Also see the gravestone of Jesse Allen Everidge in Riverdale Cemetery, Columbus.

1920

William Daniel, alias "Smokey Joe" (black, age 51). *Murder.* The crime was committed on 10/20/1916 in Pulaski County. Child killer. Executed for the murders of 14-year-old Cora Brown and 8-year-old Lewis Brown (blacks, siblings), who were lured to a pond under the pretense of going fishing and then forcibly drowned there. Motive: possibly deranged. Smokey Joe was hanged for this heinous act at Hawkinsville on January 2, 1920. Source: *Macon (GA) Daily Telegraph*, 10/27/16 (3:2), 12/17/16 (B:1:2), 1/2/20 (1:4) & 1/3/20 (1:2).

Hollis Landers (white, age 19). *Murder.* The crime was committed on 1/19/1919 in Jackson County. Police killer. Handgun slaying of 38-year-old Clifford David Barber (white), the sheriff of Jackson County. Motive: resisting arrest. This ill-fated young fellow was legally hanged at Jefferson on May 7, 1920. Source: *Macon (GA) Daily Telegraph*, 1/20/19 (1:2) & 5/8/20 (1:1). See also: 1910 U.S. Census (Jackson Co., GA), which notes both parties.

Charles Jasper (black, age 18). *Rape.* The crime was committed on 7/22/1920 in Fulton County. Indecent assault on the person of an adult white female (name withheld) who was attacked in her own home. The culprit had just finished serving a sentence in the Atlanta stockade when he forced an entry into the victim's residence for no good purpose. He was shot while fleeing the scene and desperately resisted arrest with a knife. He was legally hanged at Atlanta on August 20, 1920. Source: *Atlanta Constitution*, 7/23/20 (13:7), 7/24/20 (2:6) & 8/21/20 (4:3). *Atlanta Journal*, 7/23/20 (8:3) & 8/20/20 (12:2).

Israelite Jones (black, age 24). *Murder.* The crime was committed on 7/20/1919 in Richmond County. Executed for the killing of 71-year-old Owen Conlin (white), who was bludgeoned with an iron hoe of the kind used for spreading concrete. Motive: robbery. The homicide victim was night watchman at a cotton warehouse. The killer was a bale handler there. He had lost all of his money gambling and saw Conlin as an easy means to recoup his depleted funds. This got Jones a date with the hangman at Augusta on November 26, 1920. Source: *Augusta (GA) Chronicle*, 8/31/19 (1:2), 10/22/19 (12:6) & 11/27/20 (7:5). See also the killer's World War I draft registration card (Columbia Co., GA), which says that he was born in March 1895.

1921

Broughton Simon (black, age 24). *Rape.* The crime was committed on 7/25/1920 in Lowndes County. Executed for an indecent assault on the person of an adult white female (name withheld) who was attacked in her bedroom by a burglar subsequently identified as this sex offender. Simon had also done the exact same thing to a black woman that night. Few mourned for him when he was legally hanged at Valdosta on February 25, 1921. Source: *Macon (GA) Daily Telegraph*, 7/27/20 (16:4) & 2/1/21 (1:6). *Atlanta Constitution*, 2/26/21 (2:4).

See also: 1920 U.S. Census (Lowndes Co., GA), which notes Simon.

Israel Waters (black, age 25). *Rape.* The crime was committed on 2/14/1921 in Bryan County. Indecent assault on the person of a 13-year-old black female (name withheld) under circumstances that very nearly saw him lynched by men of his own race. He was legally hanged at Pembroke on June 3, 1921. Source: *Atlanta Constitution,* 2/16/21 (14:5). *Macon (GA) Daily Telegraph,* 6/4/21 (1:3).

Lemon Wright, better known as "Shorty Ford" (black, age 19). *Rape.* The crime was committed on 5/16/1918 in Brooks County. Executed for participating in the gang rape of pregnant 22-year-old Bertha Simmons Smith (white) during the course of a home invasion in which her husband was murdered. Three black males had attacked the house of Mr. C. Hampton Smith (white, age 25), a planter residing in Brooks County. One of them fatally shot Mr. Smith with a Winchester rifle that had previously been stolen from him. Then all three raped the farmer's wife, mindless of the fact that she was *enceinte.* They left her for dead, a rifle bullet having been fired through one of her breasts. They also ransacked the house from top to bottom. Retribution was swift in coming. Infuriated whites (believed to have been led by the homicide victim's father) went on a manhunt in which at least four (and possibly as many as ten or eleven) blacks were lynched. Some of these persons were killed in particularly grisly ways either for direct involvement in the initial atrocity or for what the vigilantes regarded as guilt by association. One of those lynched was a pregnant woman who had her unborn baby cut out of her as possible payback for Mrs. Smith having lost her own unborn baby when she was so brutally mauled. The man who actually shot Mr. Smith was among those who perished in this week-long reign of terror. So did a second participant in the gang rape. The third actual rapist—"Shorty Ford"—managed to slip away at that time. He was caught after the uproar had subsided and sent to Savannah to be legally tried there on a change of venue. He was legally hanged at the Chatham County jail on June 3, 1921. Source: *Daily Times-Enterprise* (Thomasville, GA), 5/18/18 (1:3), 7/2/20 (6:4) & 6/3/21 (1:2). *Columbus (GA) Ledger,* 5/17/18 (12:5) & 5/20/18 (3:4). *Macon (GA) Daily Telegraph,* 5/18/18 (1:2). *Savannah Morning News,* 5/17/18 (1:7). *Savannah (GA) Tribune,* 6/18/21 (4:1). See also: 1910 U.S. Census (Brooks Co., GA), which notes Mr. Smith and his parents. Also see Smith's World War I draft registration card (Brooks Co., GA) and his gravestone in Pauline Cemetery (Morven, GA), which both say that he was born on 1/4/93. The Smith family has long been maligned by political propagandists. For a more recent and unbiased account of the events of May 1918 see: *Lynching: American Mob Murder in Global Perspective* by Robert W. Thurston (Burlington, VT: Ashgate, 2011), 386–393, with special attention to errors in paragraph 2, p. 386.

Jack L. Kelloy (white, age 25). *Murder.* The crime was committed on 9/10/1920 in Spalding County. Handgun slaying of 28-year-old Leroy S. Trexler (white), a taxi driver who was shot in the back of the neck. Motive: robbery and carjacking. Killer Kelloy was hanged for this at Griffin on July 15, 1921. Source: *Macon (GA) Daily Telegraph,* 9/12/20 (1:5). *Atlanta Constitution,* 7/16/21 (3:2).

Julius King (black, age 18). *Murder.* The crime was committed on 2/28/1921 in Atkinson County. Executed for the fatal and deliberate poisoning (strychnine) of 59-year-old Seaborn Alonzo Lastinger (white), his employer. Motive: retaliation for ill-treatment, or so he said. The lethal substance had been put in a cup of coffee that the homicide victim drank. The killer was legally hanged at Pearson on July 19, 1921. Source: *Macon (GA) Telegraph*, 7/20/21 (2:3). *Columbus (GA) Ledger*, 7/20/21 (12:1). See also: 1920 U.S. Census (Taliaferro Co., GA), which notes King, a.k.a. "Claud King." Also see Mr. Lastinger's gravestone in Red Bluff Cemetery, Pearson.

Early Bradley (black, age 24). *Murder.* The crime was committed on 6/16/1920 in Stephens County. Child killer. Shotgun slaying of 13-year-old Charity Watson (black, his sister-in-law), who was murdered in her bed. Motive: mistaken identity; the killer was really gunning for his estranged wife. The hangman was subsequently called upon to act in this case at Toccoa on August 5, 1921. Source: *Toccoa (GA) Record*, 8/11/21 (1:5). Appeal: 151 GA 422–425.

Wesley Cooper (black, age 32). *Murder.* The crime was committed on 10/1/1921 in Gwinnett County. Handgun slaying of 45-year-old William A. Cooper (white), who was shot four times. Motive: landlord-tenant dispute. The homicide victim was described as "a prominent banker and farmer." The shooting took place at a syrup press when Mr. Cooper told Wesley Cooper to "quit pulling corn and start picking cotton." Wesley Cooper wound up on the gallows instead at Lawrenceville on November 18, 1921. Source: *Atlanta Constitution*, 10/23/21 (6:6) & 11/18/21 (1:4). *News-Herald* (Lawrenceville, GA), 11/21/21 (1:1).

Louis Murray (black, age abt. 20). *Murder.* The crime was committed on 4/25/1920 in Harris County. Executed for the killing of 50-year-old O. S. Williams (white), who was pistol whipped and bludgeoned with rocks. Motive: card game melee. It is unclear what led a white man of the homicide victim's age to gamble with a young black man who was 30 years his junior. The killer was convicted of capital felony and ordered for execution. He was legally hanged at Hamilton on December 16, 1921. Source: *Columbus (GA) Enquirer-Sun*, 4/26/20 (1:6) & 12/17/21 (1:1). *Columbus (GA) Ledger*, 12/16/21 (1:7). Appeal: 152 GA 206. See also: 1880 U.S. Census (Harris Co., GA), which notes the murdered man as "Doc Williams," the cognomen by which he was generally known.

John Henry Lacey (black, age 16). *Rape.* The crime was committed on 11/25/1921 in Richmond County. Indecent assault on the person of an 8-year-old white female (name withheld), the culprit having been caught in the very act. The trial jury was comprised of two blacks and ten whites. There were no grounds for an appeal due to the incontrovertible nature of the evidence. The law being well known in such cases, this young sex offender was condemned to suffer death. He was legally hanged at Augusta on December 21, 1921. Source: *Macon (GA) Daily Telegraph*, 12/2/21 (1:1). *Atlanta Constitution*, 12/1/21 (4:3) & 12/22/21 (13:8).

1922

Claude Dunn (black, age 42). *Murder.* The crime was committed on

12/6/1921 in McDuffie County. Shotgun slaying of 67-year-old Gustavius E. Reese (white), a farmer who employed him. Motive: disobedience; the killer had not picked a certain crop as he had been bidden to do. An argument flared and Dunn went for his weapon. He was legally hanged at Thomson on January 24, 1922. Source: *Macon (GA) Telegraph*, 12/8/21 (10:2) & 1/5/22 (1:5). *Augusta (GA) Chronicle*, 1/25/22 (2:3). *McDuffie (GA) Progress*, 12/9/21 (1:1) & 1/27/22 (1:3).

William Ravenal (black, age 51). *Rape.* The crime was committed on or about 10/5/1921 in Hart County. Indecent assault on the person of an elderly white female (name withheld), who was terrorized in her own home. Ravenal had previously been consigned to the Hart County chain gang for attempted robbery and the reckless discharge of firearms. He escaped after several months of bondage and became the focus of a concerted search by armed citizens and law enforcement officers alike. These flushed the fugitive from the thickets, but Ravenal outdistanced them. He made his way across the fields and through the woods until becoming desperate for a place of refuge. It was then when he spotted the solitary cottage where the old lady lived. He forced his way into that abode and then did the same thing to its terrified inhabitant after the searchers had passed by. Ravenal was legally hanged at Hartwell on May 5, 1922. Source: *Hartwell (GA) Sun*, 5/12/22 (1:5). The Clerk of Hart County Superior Court and I spent the good part of an afternoon (in December 2013) rummaging through his records room in search of the original case file for *State vs. Ravenal.* It was a difficult task due to the disorganized way in which most of the case files from that period had been piled up in cardboard boxes. We did find the original file for the court case that sent Ravenal to the chain gang. We also found the files for every other case that was adjudicated at the same term of court at which Ravenal had been sentenced to hang. Alas, we did not find the file that had spelled death for Ravenal. It had apparently vanished long ago.

Henry Langston (black, age 21). *Murder.* The crime was committed on 6/23/1920 in Morgan County. Executed for the gratuitously brutal killing of Henry Moody, age 70+ (black), a retired circus performer who lived as a hermit. The homicide victim was initially shot with a rifle. Then he was finished off with an ax. Motive: robbery and home invasion. Langston atoned for this on the gallows at Madison on May 12, 1922. Source: *Atlanta Constitution*, 5/13/22 (2:4). *Macon (GA) Daily Telegraph*, 5/13/22 (9:2). Appeal: 151 GA 388–393.

Jim Denson (black, age 18). *Rape.* The crime was committed at some point during the year 1919 in Wilkinson County. Indecent assault on the person of a 72-year-old white female (name withheld), the circumstances being too obscene for publication. Denson was legally hanged at Irwinton on June 16, 1922. Source: *Macon (GA) Daily Telegraph*, 5/24/22 (1:8), 5/25/22 (1:8) & 6/17/22 (1:8).

Frank Dupre (white, age 18). *Murder.* The crime was committed on 12/15/1921 in Fulton County. Executed for the handgun slaying of 28-year-old Irby C. Walker (white), a Pinkerton detective who was on his trail. Dupre was a love-struck lad in search of a high-class gift for his girlfriend. He was also slick, to say the least. He walked into one of Atlanta's most exclusive jewelry stores and engaged its top salesman in astute conversation. One unguarded moment was all it took for Dupre to glide out the door of that establishment with a diamond ring of enormous value. So great was the loss that the store owners engaged the services of the renowned Pinkerton Detective Agency to track down the thief and recover the diamond. This objective was attained but at the cost of two lives: that of the detective assigned to the case and that of the crafty young man who had initiated the pursuit. The latter was executed amid public fanfare at the Fulton County Jail on September 1, 1922. Dupre was allowed to wave to the crowd outside the jail from several windows as he was led down the long hallway from his cell to the gallows. It was impossible to count the number of young women who tearfully called their farewells to him. Source: *Atlanta Journal*, 9/1/22 (1:8). *Detective Tabloid*, 2/35. *Official Detective*, 1/41.

Luke McDonald (black, age 37). *Murder.* The crime was committed on 10/23/1921 in Fulton County. Handgun slaying of 24-year-old Minnie Cowan (black), who was shot in broad daylight at the corner of Piedmont Avenue and Gilmer Street in Atlanta. Motive: wrathful lover. There was no love lost for McDonald when he paid the death penalty (by legal hanging) at the Fulton County Jail on September 1, 1922. Source: *Atlanta Constitution*, 10/24/21 (2:6) & 9/2/22 (1:8).

1923

Ed Dunbar (black, age 37). *Murder.* The crime was committed on 12/24/1922 in Bryan County. Handgun slaying of 52-year-old Steven W. Phillips, Jr. (white), who was shot five times. Motive: a confrontation about hunting rights. This Christmas Eve killer was legally hanged at Pembroke on March 2, 1923. Source: *Macon (GA) Daily Telegraph*, 12/27/22 (1:4) & 12/29/22 (5:6). *Atlanta Journal*, 3/2/23 (14:2). See also: 1923 Bryan Co. death cert. no. 7091. Also: 1910 U.S. Census (Bryan Co., GA), which notes Mr. Phillips.

Buster Strickland (black, age 18). *Rape.* The crime was committed on 2/8/1923 in Hall County. Indecent assault on the person of a white female (name and age suppressed by authorities), the further details of which were kept from the public to forestall civil unrest. Strickland was legally hanged at Gainesville on March 9, 1923. Source: *Gainesville (GA) News*, 2/14/23 (1:6) & 3/14/23 (1:4). Pardon Files Box 115, GA State Archives.

George Baker (white, age 22). *Murder.* The crime was committed on 3/18/1922 in Walker County. Police killer. Handgun slaying of 66-year-old Joseph W. Morton (white), a Walker County deputy. Motive: provocateur. Three other lawmen of this county had been killed by bootleggers during the preceding 24 months. George and Ralph Baker (brothers) boldly walked up to Deputy Morton and asked if he had a warrant for their arrest. Then George Baker pulled out a pistol and shot Morton three times. Both of the Bakers were subsequently sentenced to hang. Ralph Baker wrangled a commutation on a plea that he had had no prior knowledge of his brother's intentions. George Baker faced the hangman alone at La Fayette on April 27, 1923. Source: *Columbus (GA) Enquirer-*

Sun, 3/19/22 (1:4). *Walker County Messenger*, 3/24/22 (1:1) & 5/4/23 (1:3). See also: 1920 U.S. Census (Walker Co., GA), which notes the Bakers.

Walter Lee (black, age 19). *Rape.* The crime was committed on 6/18/1923 in Chatham County. Indecent assault on the person of a 30-year-old white female (name withheld) under circumstances that were far from normal. The culprit was only 4'4" tall. What he did was so offensive to public sensitivities that more than 2,000 irate people stormed the Chatham County jail in an attempt to get their hands on him. One man was killed in this riot. Lee remained secure in his cell. A court of law sentenced him to death. He was legally hanged at Savannah on August 3, 1923. Source: *Augusta (GA) Chronicle*, 6/20/23 (1:1) & 6/21/23 (1:8). *Atlanta Constitution*, 8/4/23 (4:1).

Joe Bonner (black, age 30). *Murder.* The crime was committed on 12/23/1920 in Jones County. Executed for the ax murder of 58-year-old Albert Sidney Jones (white), who was attacked in his own house. Motive: robbery and home invasion. The killer said that he was desperate to get some Christmas spending money. He got an appointment with the hangman instead. Bonner was legally dropped to his death with a rope around his neck at Gray on August 3, 1923. Source: *Macon (GA) Daily Telegraph*, 1/1/21 (1:8). *Atlanta Constitution*, 8/4/23 (7:2). See also: Jones Co. 1920 death cert. no. 34616 and 1923 death cert. no. 23795. Also: 1870 U.S. Census (Jones Co., GA), which notes Mr. Jones as a minor.

Seab Johnston (black, age 21). *Murder.* The crime was committed on 5/29/1921 in Emanuel County. Uxoricide. Child killer, etc. Handgun slayings of 25-year-old Ethel Cowart Johnston, 18-year-old Mattie Cowart Phillips and 6-year-old Mary Walker (blacks), they respectively having been his wife, his sister-in-law and his niece. Motive: estranged husband gone crazy. This triple killer was hanged at Swainsboro on August 10, 1923. Source: *Atlanta Constitution*, 8/11/23 (2:5). *Swainsboro (GA) Forest Blade*, 6/2/21 (1:4) & 8/16/23 (1:5). See also: 1921 Emanuel Co. death cert. nos. 11641 and 11643. See also: 1920 U.S. Census (Emanuel Co., GA), which notes Johnston and wife.

John Henry Walker (black, age 21). *Murder.* The crime was committed on 3/10/1922 in Spalding County. Fatal stabbing of 27-year-old Frank Epps (black) during a fracas at a funeral. There seemed to have been some personal grudge that led up to this. Further details about the motive are obscure. The killer was hanged at Griffin on August 17, 1923. Source: *Macon (GA) Daily Telegraph*, 8/20/22 (5:6). *Atlanta Constitution*, 8/18/23 (4:1). See also: Spalding Co. 1922 death cert. no. 7830 and 1923 death cert. no. 24448.

Evans McDowell (black, age 23). *Murder.* The crime was committed on 7/21/1923 in Butts County. Executed for the killing of 68-year-old Charles Anderson Pittman (white), a storekeeper who was beaten to death by two attackers and then thrown into a nearby river. Motive: robbery. McDowell was legally hanged at Jackson on November 2, 1923. Source: *Jackson (GA) Progress-Argus*, 11/2/23 (1:1). See also: 1923 Butts Co. death cert. nos. 19333 and 34246. See Fleming Lynch (executed 7/25/24).

1924

James Brown Satterfield (white, age 42). *Murder.* The crime was committed on 12/27/1921 in Fulton County. Handgun slaying of 44-year-old Robert Henry Hart (white, his brother-in-law), who was shot in the back. Motive: fiduciary fraud. A widower, Satterfield was rankled by the fact that his wife had put money in a structured fund for their two daughters and named her brother (Hart) as the steward thereof instead of him. The woman had apparently seen some flaw in her husband's character that disinclined her to trust him with this kind of responsibility. Satterfield would have none of that. Jealousy and personal indignation gnawed at him until he could stand it no more. He resolved upon desperate means to wrest control of the money. It was then that he gunned down his hated brother-in-law from behind, this killer being too much of a sneak coward to do so up front. J. B. Satterfield was hanged by the neck until dead at the Fulton County jail on May 23, 1924. Source: *Atlanta Journal*, 5/23/24 (1:8). *Atlanta Constitution*, 12/28/21 (1:8) & 5/24/24 (1:8). Also see Mr. Hart's gravestone in Prospect Methodist Cemetery, Chamblee.

Fleming Lynch (black, age 21). *Murder.* The crime was committed on 7/21/1923 in Butts County. Accomplice in the fatal beating of 68-year-old Charles Anderson Pittman (white), a rural storekeeper. Motive: robbery. This killer was legally hanged at Jackson on July 25, 1924. Source: *Atlanta Constitution*, 7/26/24 (12:6). See also: Evans McDowell (executed 11/2/23).

Harrison Brown (black, age 15). *Murder.* The crime was committed on 2/11/1924 in Upson County. Shotgun slaying of 23-year-old Oscar Mann (black), a sawmill worker. Motive: a job-related conflict. This black-on-black killer was legally hanged at Thomaston on August 15, 1924. Source: *Thomaston (GA) Times*, 2/15/24 (1:4) & 8/22/24 (4:3). See also: 1920 U.S. Census (Upson Co., GA), which notes Mann. Also see: 1924 Upson Co. death cert. no. 25886, which notes that Brown was born on 11/4/1908.

Howard Hinton (black, age 20). *Rape.* The crime was committed on 8/16/1924 in DeKalb County. Indecent assault on the person of a "young" white female (name withheld) who was grossly mistreated while an accomplice held her boyfriend at gunpoint, threatening him with death if he dared to intervene. Howard Hinton was the one that didn't get away. His capital offense having been perpetrated after enactment of the Electrocution Act, he was sent to the state prison at Milledgeville to await execution by that means. There was no appeal. The sentence was carried out on September 13, 1924. Source: *Atlanta Constitution*, 8/18/24 (8:1), 8/23/24 (10:8) & 9/14/24 (B:1:6). *Augusta (GA) Chronicle*, 9/14/24 (1:2). *Macon (GA) News*, 9/13/24 (1:3). See also: 1920 U.S. Census (DeKalb Co., GA), which notes Hinton.

Warren Waters (white, age 56). *Murder.* The crime was committed on 12/9/1923 in Jeff Davis County. Police killer. Executed for the shotgun slaying of 47-year-old Thomas Jordan Kersey (white), the town marshal of Hazlehurst. Motive: liquor raid turned deadly. The lawman was decapitated by a second shotgun blast deliberately fired into him after he had fallen. Warren Waters was legally hanged at Hazlehurst on September 19, 1924. Source:

Daily Times-Enterprise (Thomasville, GA), 12/10/23 (3:4). *Atlanta Journal,* 9/19/24 (1:4). See also: 1920 U.S. Census (Jeff Davis Co., GA), which notes Waters. See also T. J. Kersey's gravestone in Lambs Chapel Cemetery, Swainsboro.

Will Hodge (black, age 25). *Murder.* The crime was committed on 4/2/1924 in Thomas County. Uxoricide. Shotgun slaying of 26-year-old Mattie Glenn Hodge (black). Motive: she had refused to accompany him in relocating to a Northern state and also because Will Hodge could not bear the thought of "leaving her behind for another man to enjoy." This wife-killer suffered death on the gallows at Thomasville on September 26, 1924. Source: *Daily Times-Enterprise* (Thomasville, GA), 4/5/24 (5:5), 4/30/24 (4:4) & 9/26/24 (4:5). See also: 1920 U.S. Census (Thomas Co., GA), which notes the homicide victim by her maiden name.

1925

Alex Williams (black, age 31). *Murder.* The crime was committed on 8/14/1924 in Jones County. Uxoricide. Shotgun slaying of pregnant 30-year-old Martha Pounds Williams (black), who was also partially cremated when the killer fired their house. Motive: uncertain. The Georgia electric chair made short work of Alex Williams on May 15, 1925. Source: *Jones County News* (Gray, GA), 8/21/24 (1:2). *Macon (GA) News,* 5/15/25 (1:2). Appeal: 160 GA 129–131. See also: *Georgia Deaths Index (1914–1927),* which notes the murdered woman.

Robert Lee Curry (white, age 23). *Murder.* The crime was committed on 2/19/1920 in Toombs County. Executed for the deliberate killing of 37-year-old Burleigh E. Phillips (white), a cabbie who was shot behind his right ear with a handgun and then reportedly buried alive in a cow pasture. Motive: robbery and carjacking. This transgressor dodged the gallows for five years. His time ran out at Lyons on May 21, 1925. Source: *Augusta (GA) Chronicle,* 2/26/20 (1:1) & 5/17/25 (C:1:6). *Atlanta Journal,* 5/21/25 (1:8). See also: 1920 U.S. Census (Toombs Co., GA), which notes "B. E. Phillips."

Frank Jackson (black, age not recorded). *Murder.* The crime was committed on 2/21/1925 in Rabun County. Executed for the fatal stabbing of another black man named Holt Allen (age not recorded). Motive: prison violence. Both men were serving time on the Rabun County chain gang. Jackson was a so-called trusty. He misused his position of trust to get his hands on a butcher knife and then go after Holt Allen. It is not known what caused the animosity between them. The electric chair finished off Frank Jackson on September 26, 1925. Source: *Augusta (GA) Chronicle,* 3/9/25 (1:6). *Macon (GA) News,* 9/26/25 (1:4). Appeal: 160 GA 565–570.

1926

Gervis Bloodworth (white, age 18) and **Willie Jones** (white, age 16). *Murder.* Their crime was committed on 12/3/1923 in Taylor County. Shotgun slaying of 52-year-old Howard F. Underwood (white). Motive: highway robbery. Venue changed from Taylor County to Muscogee County. This teenage pair met early death on the gallows at Columbus on January 29, 1926. Source: *Atlanta Constitution,* 1/30/26 (1:8). Appeal: 159 GA 67–76.

Charlie Walton (black, age 38). *Murder.* The crime was committed on 1/7/1925 in Fulton County. Executed for the ax murder of 28-year-old Fred L. James (white), who had gone slumming that night. Motive: robbery in the red light district. The killer took his last seat in the Georgia electric chair on March 11, 1926. Source: *Atlanta Constitution*, 1/9/25 (1:1) & 3/12/26 (6:8).

Theodore L. Coggeshall (white, age 20) and **Floyd W. McClelland** (white, age 19). *Murder.* Their crime was committed on 3/4/1925 in Putnam County. Both executed for the killing of 65-year-old William Crosby Wright (white), who was beaten on the head with a heavy automobile spring. Motive: robbery and carjacking. The Georgia electric chair did for them on March 25, 1926. Source: *Augusta (GA) Chronicle*, 5/5/25 (1:8), 5/6/25 (1:8), 5/7/25 (1:8) & 3/26/26 (1:8). Also see Mr. Wright's gravestone in Pine Grove Cemetery, Eatonton.

Mack Wooten (black, age 42). *Murder.* The crime was committed on 12/31/1922 in Fulton County. Handgun slaying of 35-year-old Dan Hall Williams (white). Motive: resisting a citizen's arrest. In March of 1910 this miscreant had been sent to the chain gang at Montgomery, AL, following multiple convictions for armed robbery and highway robbery. He escaped in December of 1922 and made his way to Atlanta, appearing at the servants' quarters of a wealthy lumber dealer named Dan Hall Williams. The fugitive asked for food and admitted to the black folks there that he was a chain gang escapee in order to curry their sympathy. But one of the servants informed Mr. Williams. The latter then went to the servants' quarters and was shot down as soon as he entered. Mack Wooten was legally hanged for this at the Fulton County Jail on May 18, 1926. Source: *Montgomery (AL) Advertiser*, 11/22/09 (8:2). *Atlanta Constitution*, 1/1/23 (1:1). *Thomasville (GA) Times-Enterprise*, 10/24/25 (6:6). *Augusta (GA) Chronicle*, 5/20/26 (10:2). See also: 1900 U.S. Census (Marengo Co., AL), which notes Wooten, and 1920 U.S. Census (Atlanta, GA), which notes Mr. Williams.

Amos Stewart (black, age 28). *Murder.* The crime was committed on 5/2/1926 in Worth County. Ax murder of 60-year-old Ashton T. Ford (white). Motive: landlord-tenant dispute. The Georgia electric chair accommodated Amos Stewart on June 18, 1926. Source: *Sylvester (GA) Local*, 5/6/26 (1:3) & 6/24/26 (1:1). See also: 1920 U.S. Census (Worth Co., GA), which notes both parties.

Ed Glover (black, age not recorded). *Murder.* The crime was committed on 7/10/1926 in Bibb County. Shotgun slayings of 22-year-old Elisha W. Wilson and 21-year-old Hilda Smith (whites, an affianced couple), who were attacked while seated in their parked automobile. Motive: lovers' lane robbery. The killer even stole the slippers off the dead girl's feet. He was electrocuted at Milledgeville on September 9, 1926. Source: *Augusta (GA) Chronicle*, 7/21/26 (1:1) & 7/28/26 (1:8). *Atlanta Constitution*, 7/13/26 (1:1). *Macon (GA) Daily Telegraph*, 7/13/26 (1:8), 7/17/26 (1:8) & 9/10/26 (1:3). *Macon (GA) News*, 9/9/26 (1:1).

Tom Johnson (black, age 48). *Murder.* The crime was committed on 4/4/1926 in Jefferson County. Shotgun slaying of 40-year-old Dessie Whigham

Stone (black), who had one of her arms blown off and died three days later. Motive: apparent revenge. Johnson was a so-called trusty on the Jefferson County chain gang. He was serving a one-year sentence for an unspecified offense. It seems likely that Dessie Stone had played a part in his commitment. Whatever the case, Johnson stole a shotgun and went looking for her. He burst into a church where she was attending services and terrorized the entire congregation. Dessie attempted to flee but was mortally wounded while so doing. Tom Johnson paid with his life for this in the Georgia electric chair on September 25, 1926. Source: *Augusta (GA) Chronicle*, 4/8/26 (3:4) & 4/18/26 (B:3:4). See also: 1900 U.S. Census (Jefferson Co., GA), which notes Dessie by her maiden name. Also: 1926 Baldwin Co. death cert. no. 32837.

Pringle Williams (black, age 17). *Rape.* The crime was committed on 8/1/1926 in Emanuel County. Indecent assault on the person of a 14-year-old white female (name withheld) under circumstances of such an aggravated nature that a special court had to be convened to adjudicate the matter. This sex offender was electrocuted on October 8, 1926. Source: *Swainsboro (GA) Forest Blade*, 8/19/26 (1:1) & 9/16/26 (1:3). *Thomasville (GA) Times-Enterprise*, 10/8/26 (6:4).

James Johnson (black, age not recorded). *Murder.* The crime was committed on 9/14/1926 in Fulton County. Executed for the beating and strangulation of 48-year-old Myrtle Amanda Tumlin (white), a maiden woman. A steel padlock in a sock was used to inflict traumatic injuries on the victim. Motive: robbery and home invasion. The Georgia electric chair rid society of James Johnson on November 13, 1926. Source: *Atlanta Constitution*, 9/15/26 (1:7), 9/29/26 (1:1), 10/1/26 (3:5) & 11/14/26 (4:6). Pardon Files Box 66, GA State Archives.

1927

Herbert Fennell (black, age 29). *Murder.* The crime was committed on 5/9/1926 in Liberty County. Uxoricide. Handgun slaying of 22-year-old Viola Darden Fennell (black). Motive: because she sassed him. The electric chair functioned in this case on June 3, 1927. Source: *Augusta (GA) Chronicle*, 6/4/27 (1:2). Appeal: 164 GA 59–64. See also: 1926 Liberty Co. death cert. no. 9930.

Merrell Minor Gore, known to some as "Mell Gore" (white, age 21). *Murder.* The crime was committed on 12/19/1925 in Fulton County. Handgun slaying of 37-year-old William Henry Cheek (white), a grocer. Motive: attempted armed robbery. This wayward young man met his end pursuant to law at the Georgia State Prison on June 3, 1927. Source: *Augusta (GA) Chronicle*, 12/23/25 (1:5) & 12/24/25 (1:4). *Atlanta Constitution*, 6/4/27 (1:3). Also see the killer's gravestone in County Line Baptist Church Cemetery, Douglasville.

Oscar Mars (white, age 43). *Murder.* The crime was committed on 7/26/1925 in Ben Hill County. Uxoricide. Handgun slaying of 40-year-old Jennie Belle Bentley Mars (white), who was shot six times. The killer had reportedly "held his estranged wife in close embrace in a friend's automobile and murmured endearing words of reconciliation to lull her suspicions so that he could empty the contents of a revolver into her body point blank." Motive: marital breakdown. Mars was an obsessively jealous type who imagined that every man in Georgia was trolling for his wife. The final crisis came when Mrs. Mars got her hair bobbed in the 1920s flapper style—an act that Oscar Mars regarded as intolerably *avant-garde*. He was executed on June 6, 1927. Source: *Augusta (GA) Chronicle*, 10/23/25 (1:1) & 6/7/27 (1:7). *Thomasville (GA) Times-Enterprise*, 6/6/27 (1:6).

John Rounsaville (black, age 18). *Murder.* The crime was committed on 9/22/1925 in Chattooga County. Baby killer. Executed for the cruel murder of 6-month-old George Rounsaville (black), his stepson, by deliberately punching him and breaking the baby's neck. Motive: he hated the child for not being his own and also because it wouldn't stop crying. Death in the electric chair was the fate of this offender on July 12, 1927. Source: *Atlanta Journal*, 3/11/26 (4:6). Appeal: 163 GA 391. See also: 1927 Baldwin Co. death cert. no. 15506.

Marcellus Stewart (black, age 33). *Murder.* The crime was committed on 4/4/1925 in Early County. Executed for the killing of 35-year-old Abbie Gay (black), whose week-old corpse was found in an outhouse with its throat cut. Motive: lovers' quarrel. Stewart was executed at the Georgia State Prison on July 15, 1927. Source: *Early County News*, 4/16/25 (2:2) & 12/23/26 (6:1). See also: 1920 U.S. Census (Early Co., GA), which notes Stewart, and *Georgia Death Index 1914–1927*, which notes Abbie Gay.

Lee Chamblee (black, age 25). *Murder.* The crime was committed on 6/22/1924 in Bartow County. Handgun slaying of 30-year-old Zack Gordon, alias "Zack Ware" (black), who was shot in a gambling dispute. The amount of money in question was a nickel that one of these men had wagered in a crap game. Five-cent killer Lee Chamblee died in the Georgia electric chair on October 14, 1927. Source: *Tribune-News* (Cartersville, GA), 6/26/24 (1:7) & 10/13/27 (1:6). *Augusta (GA) Chronicle*, 10/15/27 (1:7). See also: 1910 U.S. Census (Bartow Co., GA), which notes "Ware."

Wilmer Galloway (black, age 28). *Murder.* The crime was committed on 7/24/1927 in Dodge County. Executed for the handgun slayings of 27-year-old Will T. Andrews and 16-year-old Edna Wingo Andrews (whites), a married couple. Motive: highway robbery. The white man died at the scene. His young bride succumbed 30 days later. Recidivist killer. Galloway had previously been sentenced to a term of life imprisonment for the unrelated killing of another Dodge County man named Henry Trotman. He served 9 years and 12 days. Then he bamboozled the Georgia Board of Pardons and Paroles into turning him loose on society, thereby enabling him to go out and murder two more law-abiding citizens. Galloway died a searing death in the Georgia electric chair on October 14, 1927. Source: *Augusta (GA) Chronicle*, 10/15/27 (1:7). *Times-Journal* (Eastman, GA), 7/28/27 (1:1) & 8/4/27 (1:3). *Atlanta Journal*, 10/14/27 (48:3). Pardon Files Box 43, GA State Archives.

Mose Parker (black, age 46). *Murder.* The crime was committed on 6/20/1926 in Pike County. Filicide, etc. Executed for the handgun slayings of 20-year-old Cordelia Parker (his daughter) and pregnant 16-year-old Virginia Pierce (his niece), who both got in the way when he went gunning for his estranged wife. Mose Parker paid the death penalty at the Georgia State Prison on October 14, 1927. Source: 1926 Pike Co. death cert. nos. 15222 and 15223. Also: 1927 Baldwin Co. death cert. no. 23203. See also: 1920 U.S. Census (Pike Co., GA), which notes Mose Parker. The issues of the *Pike County Journal* that told about this case were torn from their original folio volume by some long-dead vandal.

Roy Pryor (black, age 24). *Rape.* The crime was committed on 9/26/1927 in Walton County. Indecent assault on the person of a white female, age 50+ (name withheld), who was attacked in her backyard garden. Pryor was a fugitive from the Walton County chain gang at the time of his capital offense. He was electrocuted on October 26, 1927. Source: *Atlanta Constitution*, 10/27/27 (3:8). See also: 1927 Baldwin Co. death cert. no. 23204.

George Clark (black, age 26). *Rape.* The crime was committed on 10/5/1927 in Jasper County. Indecent assault on the person of an adult white female (name withheld), described as "the wife of a prominent dairyman." The victim's husband had hired the culprit to work on his farm. Clark began that job on 10/3/1927. Two days later he attacked the farmer's wife in a barn. He choked her until she had a throat hemorrhage. Then he raped her irrespective of the bloody froth that matted both of them. Lastly, this uninhibited predator beat the woman with a plow handle (intending to kill her) and left her at the scene with both a fractured skull and a dangerous loss of blood. She barely survived. It is a hard sell to say that George Clark did what he did either with consent or because of enticement. Venue changed from Jasper County to Bibb County. Death by electrocution followed at the Georgia State Prison on November 11, 1927. Source: *Thomasville (GA) Times-Enterprise*, 10/6/27 (6:4), 10/7/27 (6:1) & 11/11/27 (5:4).

John Sanders (black, age 39). *Rape.* The crime was committed on 10/18/1927 in Fulton County. Indecent assault on the person of an adult white female (name withheld) who was attacked in her own home and "choked into insensibility." No other details of this case can be found in publicly accessible records other than the fact that Sanders died in the electric chair on November 18, 1927. Source: *Atlanta Georgian* (Final Home Edition), 11/18/27 (3:3). *Atlanta Constitution*, 10/19/27 (8:3) & 11/19/27 (8:3). See also: 1927 Baldwin Co. death cert. no. 26053.

1928

Garfield Fuller, alias "C. R. Davis," alias "Dad Davis" (black, age 39). *Murder.* The crime was committed on 11/28/1927 in Pike County. Executed for the killing of 22-year-old Lillie Belle McDowell Davis (black, no relation), who was bludgeoned with a heavy stick as she walked along a path near her home. Her skull was fractured in two places. Motive: mugged for her purse. This killer of a young woman was electrocuted on January 13, 1928. Source: *Pike County Journal*, 12/2/27 (1:1), 12/23/27 (1:1) & 1/20/28 (1:4). See also: 1920 U.S. Census (Tallapoosa Co., AL), which notes Fuller.

Albert Quinn (black, age 24). *Murder.* The crime was committed on

1/29/1927 in Terrell County. Executed for the killing of 44-year-old James W. Sutton (white), who was struck upside the head with an ax handle. Motive: dispute over back wages. Both men lost their lives because they were too cheap to come to terms over 50 cents. Albert Quinn was executed at the Georgia State Prison on January 20, 1928. Source: *Dawson (GA) News*, 2/1/27 (6:2), 2/8/27 (11:3) & 1/24/28 (8:4). Also see Mr. Sutton's gravestone in Bronwood Cemetery, Bronwood. The funeral and the monument surely cost more than half a dollar.

Robert Coates (black, age 34). *Murder.* The crime was committed on 11/20/1926 in Jefferson County. Uxoricide. Executed for the killing of 33-year-old Lilly Belle Coates (black), who was beaten with a heavy steel spring and then finished off by having her head mashed with a fireplace poker. Motive: marital estrangement. The homicide victim had fled from their home in Tuskegee, AL. Her wrathful husband then hunted her down. He was executed at the Georgia State Prison on February 21, 1928. Source: *News & Farmer* (Louisville, GA), 11/25/26 (1:8). *Augusta (GA) Chronicle*, 11/29/26 (3:6). See also: 1926 Jefferson Co. death cert. no. 27614 and 1928 Baldwin Co. death cert. no. 2888.

Henry Ellis (black, age 24). *Murder.* The crime was committed on 2/19/1927 in Fulton County. Executed for the unprovoked killing of 23-year-old John Taylor (black), whose throat was slashed at an all-black dance when he had the temerity to ask for a drink. The killer's brother (to whom the beverage belonged) had wanted to shoot Taylor, but Henry Ellis attacked him with a knife instead. Henry Ellis paid with his life at the Georgia State Prison on April 18, 1928. Source: *Atlanta Journal*, 4/18/28 (22:6). Appeal: 166 GA 115–120.

Edgar Price (black, age 22). *Murder.* The crime was committed on 12/25/1926 in Grady County. Executed for the Christmas Day killings of 35-year-old Buster Gurley and 50-year-old Jim Butler (blacks), they having both been blasted with a shotgun and their bodies castrated. Motive: an argument that had flared when Price demanded a dollar from these men for using his tractor to pull their car out of a ditch. Price subsequently went to the electric chair on May 4, 1928. Source: *Thomasville (GA) Times-Enterprise*, 3/14/28 (1:4) & 5/4/28 (4:2). Appeal: 166 GA 120–121. See also: 1928 Baldwin Co. death cert. no. 11788.

James E. Grant (black, age 26). *Murder.* The crime was committed on 5/22/1927 in Fulton County. Executed for the killing of 71-year-old Jesse L. Ferguson (white), a night watchman at an automobile factory. He was bludgeoned with a heavy iron spring and his body thrown down an elevator shaft. Motive: burglary. This assassin died in the Georgia electric chair on May 18, 1928. Source: *Atlanta Constitution*, 5/23/27 (1:7), 5/26/27 (1:5), 10/16/27 (7:1) & 5/19/28 (9:2). Appeal: 166 GA 274. See also: 1900, 1910 and 1920 U.S. Census (Huntsville, AL), which note the murdered man before he came to Atlanta. See also: Charlie Hicks (executed 6/8/28).

Charlie Hicks (black, age 20). *Murder.* The crime was committed on 5/22/1927 in Fulton County. Accomplice in the killing of 71-year-old Jesse L. Ferguson (white), a night watchman in an automobile assembly plant.

Motive: burglary. Hicks was executed on June 8, 1928. Source: *Atlanta Journal*, 5/23/27 (5:4). *Atlanta Constitution*, 6/9/28 (7:2). Appeal: 166 GA 200–201. See also: James E. Grant (executed 5/18/28).

Robert Jones (black, age 21). *Murder.* The crime was committed on 10/7/1927 in Bibb County. Executed for the killing of 72-year-old Wesley P. Short (white), the proprietor of a dry-cleaning establishment. Motive: robbery. Jones explained that he had brought a suit to Mr. Short to be cleaned and pressed. The suit got misplaced and the store owner offered one of inferior quality to rectify the loss. Jones was displeased. He asked for an additional $1.50 but was thenceforth treated in a dismissive manner, or so he said. Finally on the above date—to continue his account of these events—Jones tried once again to reason with Mr. Short. The latter ordered him to get out of his store. Jones then lost his temper and hit Mr. Short on the head with an iron door bar, calling him a "rotten old miser" or words to that effect. This was bad enough, but Jones also rifled the business owner's pockets, taking money in excess of the disputed amount. This made him guilty of concomitant felony murder (in this case robbery in addition to homicide) and as such cost him his own life. Robert Jones died in the Georgia electric chair on June 28, 1928. Source: *Augusta (GA) Chronicle*, 10/12/27 (1:6). See also: 1928 Baldwin Co. death cert. no. 14545.

Harold Hammond (white, age 35). *Murder.* The crime was committed on 2/4/1927 in Fulton County. Baby killer, etc. Executed for the murders of 19-year-old Lottie Belle Ingram and 14-month-old Lloyd Ingram (whites), a mother and her child. The woman was battered to death with a flatiron. The baby was strangled with a strip of cloth. Motive: possibly deranged. This man was put to death at the Georgia State Prison on July 6, 1928. Source: *Thomasville (GA) Times-Enterprise*, 2/4/27 (1:8), 3/14/27 (1:4) & 7/6/28 (1:7). *Atlanta Journal*, 7/6/28 (1:1). *Master Detective*, 11/33.

Medie McCloud (black, age 28). *Murder.* The crime was committed on 10/14/1927 in Decatur County. Police killer. Handgun slaying of 36-year-old Samuel Brinson Arline (white), a Bainbridge policeman who was shot three times. Motive: resisting arrest. McCloud went to the electric chair on July 6, 1928. Source: *Atlanta Journal*, 7/6/28 (1:1). Appeal: 166 GA 436–445. See also: 1928 Baldwin Co. death cert. no. 17411. Also see the slain officer's gravestone in Oak City Cemetery, Bainbridge.

Samuel B. Gower (white, age 41). *Murder.* The crime was committed on or about 12/15/1927 in Gwinnett County. Child killer, etc. Executed for the ax murders of 55-year-old James Benefield and 9-year-old John Benefield (whites), a father and son. Motive: robbery and home invasion. The victims were found in their ransacked cabin on 12/18/1927. Gower was put to death on July 13, 1928. Source: *Augusta (GA) Chronicle*, 12/20/27 (1:7) & 7/14/28 (1:6). See also: 1920 U.S. Census (Gwinnett Co., GA), which notes Gower.

Preddis Taylor (black, age 32). *Murder.* The crime was committed on 1/12/1928 in Fulton County. Handgun slaying of 58-year-old William H. Cleveland (white), a filling station operator. Motive: armed robbery. The killer was executed on July 13, 1928.

Source: *Atlanta Constitution,* 1/13/28 (1:7). *Atlanta Journal,* 7/13/28 (1:4). See also: 1920 U.S. Census (Fulton Co., GA), which notes Mr. Cleveland.

Clifford Thompson (white, age 21) and **James Hugh Moss** (black, age 26). *Murder.* Their crime was committed on 8/5/1927 in Murray County. Handgun slaying of 40-year-old James Coleman Osborn (white), a storekeeper. Motive: armed robbery, or so the official version said. Thompson was an illiterate from Etowah, TN. His accomplice (Moss) had been a professional baseball player (Negro Leagues) with the Chicago Giants. The presence of Thompson's wife at the crime scene fueled tales of a more sordid motive. Whatever the truth, it was all the same to these mismatched killers when they died in the Georgia electric chair on August 3, 1928. Source: *Augusta (GA) Chronicle,* 8/19/27 (1:3) & 8/4/28 (1:6). *Master Detective,* 2/34. See also: Mr. Osborn's World War I draft registration card (Murray Co., GA), which notes his personal information.

Richard Henry Sheppard (Native American, age 56). *Murder.* The crime was committed on 2/19/1927 in Fulton County. Executed for the ax murder of 33-year-old Homer Fowler (white). Motive: he didn't like the homicide victim's manner. Sheppard was reportedly born in Colorado. He claimed to be a full-blooded Blackfoot. He was executed at the Georgia State Prison on December 19, 1928. Source: *Augusta (GA) Chronicle,* 3/11/27 (1:6) & 12/19/28 (1:6). *Atlanta Journal,* 12/19/28 (1:8). Appeal: 167 GA 326–340.

1929

Ed Capers (black, age 18), **Will Clarence George** (black, age 22) and **Willie Gilliam** (black, age 20). *Murder.* Their crime was committed on 11/19/1927 in Fulton County. Handgun slaying of 46-year-old Pat Daugherty (black), who was struck down from behind with a rock and then shot four times. Motive: mugging. The homicide victim was robbed of his money, his signet ring and his life. The State of Georgia exacted three for one on January 18, 1929. Source: *Atlanta Constitution,* 1/19/29 (15:2). Appeal: 167 GA 532–535.

Marshall Redding (black, age 42). *Murder.* The crime was committed on 9/27/1927 in Meriwether County. Police killer. Shotgun slaying of 38-year-old William H. Callaway (white), the police chief of Manchester. Motive: the lawman had come to his house to arrest his son. Venue changed from Meriwether County to Coweta County. Marshall Redding died in the Georgia electric chair on January 18, 1929. Source: *Augusta (GA) Chronicle,* 9/28/27 (1:1). *Atlanta Journal,* 1/18/29 (2:1). See also: 1910 U.S. Census (Meriwether Co., GA), which notes both parties.

George Griffin Grinstead (white, age 52). *Murder.* The crime was committed on 7/13/1928 in Montgomery County. Police killer. Executed for the shotgun slaying of 39-year-old Homer Stuckey (white). Motive: resisting arrest. Prime suspect in the death of Montgomery County police officer Don Sheppard (white, age 35), whose body was found in a staged automobile wreck on 4/23/1927. Recidivist killer. Grinstead had been serving a life sentence at the Georgia State Prison (Milledgeville) for a previous murder when he somehow obtained a furlough to settle some business-related matters in Montgomery County. He skipped out on the furlough and was a fugitive from justice when he gunned down Homer Stuckey. The earlier murder was that of 17-year-old Alvah Burton (white), who was shot dead in a sniper incident on Christmas Day 1926. Grinstead finally faced the executioner on February 22, 1929. Source: *Montgomery Monitor* (Mt. Vernon, GA), 1/6/27 (1:6), 4/28/27 (1:3) & 7/26/28 (1:5). *Augusta (GA) Chronicle*, 7/16/28 (8:1). *Thomasville (GA) Times-Enterprise*, 2/7/29 (8:5) & 2/22/29 (2:4). Appeal: 167 GA 536–537. See also: World War I draft registration cards (Dodge Co., GA, and Montgomery Co., GA), which respectively note Stuckey and Grinstead. Also: 1910 U.S. Census (Montgomery Co., GA), which notes Burton, and 1910 U.S. Census (Telfair Co., GA), which notes Sheppard.

John Clark (black, age 43). *Murder.* The crime was committed on 4/23/1928 in McIntosh County. Executed for the ax murder of 22-year-old Clifford Anderson (black). Motive: chain gang violence. The homicide victim had previously thwarted an escape attempt. The price he paid was death at the hands of his fellow prisoners. John Clark was the one who had actually wielded the murder weapon. He died in the electric chair on March 20, 1929. Source: *Savannah Morning News*, 4/24/28 (15:2). Appeal: 167 GA 341–347. See also: 1928 McIntosh Co. death cert. no. 10660 and 1929 Baldwin Co. death cert. no. 14413.

James Crumady (black, age 24). *Murder.* The crime was committed on 10/7/1928 in Colquitt County. Executed for the foul killing of 22-year-old George Burt (white), a clerk in a country store, whose charred remains were found amid the ruins of that establishment. Crumady never acknowledged his guilt, although a considerable quantity of looted goods from the burnt store were found in his possession. These included the very pants that George Burt had been wearing that day and which had apparently been stripped from his body. Crumady tried to lie his way out of a corner by saying that he had purchased the pants from a peddler, but no such person could be found. This killer was still talking trash when he was led to the electric chair on May 17, 1929. Source: *Thomasville (GA) Times-Enterprise*, 1/26/29 (1:8), 5/16/29 (3:6) & 5/17/29 (1:7). Appeal: 168 GA 457–469. See also: 1928 Colquitt Co. death cert. no. 26310.

Jeff Dozier (black, age 56). *Murder.* The crime was committed on 1/1/1929 in Floyd County. Handgun slaying of 37-year-old Laura Arnold (black), his lover. Motive: she had wanted to end their relationship. Recidivist killer. On 7/29/1919 this same Jeff Dozier had thrust the business end of a shotgun into his wife's abdomen and literally blown her guts out. Her name was Mary J. Dozier. This earned him a life sentence on the Floyd County chain gang. By 1928 he was a so-called trusty with an elevated degree of latitude above his fellow grunts. Dozier then went on to demonstrate the efficacy of life imprisonment at the expense of Laura Arnold. The electric chair ensured that Dozier would commit no further offenses on July 12, 1929. Source: *Macon (GA) Telegraph*, 8/1/19 (13:4). *Thomasville (GA) Times-Enterprise*, 1/17/29 (4:2) & 7/12/29 (10:2). *Rome (GA) News-Tribune*, 1/1/29 (1:5) & 1/2/29 (2:7). Appeal: 168 GA 670–671. See also: 1920 U.S. Census (Floyd Co., GA), which notes Arnold and Dozier.

Malcolm Morrow (white, age 35) and **Homer C. Simpson** (white, age 38). *Murder.* Their crime was committed on 2/23/1928 in Glynn County. Handgun slaying of 44-year-old Carl Arp Perry (white), who was shot three times and later found in a wrecked automobile. Motive: bank robbery. The homicide victim was lured to a rendezvous with a contrived story. Then he was forced to bring the culprits to his place of business (a bank in Kingsland, GA) and open its safe for them. Simpson was a renegade police chief from Tennessee. He and his accomplice completed their fall from grace on September 11, 1929, when they were executed at the Georgia State Prison. Source: *Augusta (GA) Chronicle*, 2/26/28 (1:6) & 2/27/28 (1:7). *Thomasville (GA) Times-Enterprise*, 9/11/29 (1:8). See also Mr. Perry's gravestone in Oak Grove Cemetery, St. Mary's.

Willie Bryant (black, age 23). *Rape.* The crime was committed on 7/29/1929 in Ware County. Indecent assault on the person of an adult white female (name withheld) who was attacked in her own home during her husband's absence and beaten to within an inch of her life. The culprit then dragged her out of the house and into some woods, where she remained comatose for several hours. The black folks of that vicinity were instrumental in running down the rapist, they being "highly incensed" at what he had done. Willie Bryant found no one to stand by him, not even among black people. He was legally put to death on October 4, 1929. Source: *Waycross (GA) Journal-Herald*, 7/31/29 (1:1). *Thomasville (GA) Times-Enterprise*, 7/31/29 (5:4) & 10/4/29 (1:4).

Alvin Eugene Merritt (white, age 26). *Rape.* The crime for which he was executed was committed on 2/25/1928 in Fulton County. Serial rapist. He was dubbed "the Masked Marauder" and "the South End Fiend" by the terrified female population of Atlanta. He was condemned specifically for an indecent assault on the person of a 14-year-old white female (name withheld) who was violated in such a way that the details were censored to prevent a public panic. The culprit was subsequently linked to no less than 46 other such attacks on young women and girls during a yearlong spree that began on 1/31/1928 when an 18-year-old white female was ravished. An oppressive atmosphere of paranoia gripped all of Fulton County as the attacks increased. Many innocent men were roughly handled by vigilantes intent on catching the rapist. The full extent of the problem was not revealed until after Merritt had been securely locked up. Merritt was electrocuted in Georgia's electric chair on October 4, 1929. Source: Georgia Supreme Court Case no. 7216. *Augusta (GA) Chronicle*, 2/11/29 (2:6). *Atlanta Journal*, 10/4/29 (1:1). *Daring Detective*, 4/35.

1930

John Ellen (black, age 38). *Murder.* The crime was committed on 9/2/1928 in Floyd County. Executed for the mutilation murder of 57-year-old Emmett Puckett (black), who was stabbed 19 times and his body "literally cut to ribbons." Motive: personal grudge. The homicide victim was described as "a notorious gambler who preyed on members of his own race." Therein probably lay the basis for the motive. Even so, the law made no special provisions for sore losers. John Ellen was made to answer for his misdeed like any other killer. He was executed at the Georgia State Prison on January 27, 1930. Source: *Rome (GA) News-Tribune*, 9/3/28 (1:1), 9/4/28 (1:8) & 1/27/30 (1:7). Appeal: 169 GA 391. See also: 1920 U.S. Census (Floyd Co., GA), which notes Puckett.

James Barker (black, age 22). *Murder.* The crime was committed on 2/26/1929 in Bibb County. Handgun slaying of 58-year-old Cosby H. Oxley (white), a night watchman at a basket factory. Motive: burglary. The sentence of death by electrocution was carried out in this case on February 14, 1930. Source: 1930 Baldwin Co. death cert. no. 2536. Appeal: 169 GA 414. See also: 1880 U.S. Census (Houston Co., GA), which notes Mr. Oxley as a minor.

Edmond Kelly (black, age 26). *Murder.* The crime was committed on 7/14/1928 in Grady County. Executed for the deliberate killing of 63-year-old John Stephens (black), who was shot with a rifle and knocked in the head. His body was dumped in a creek. Motive: robbery and carjacking. The culprit was executed on February 21, 1930. Source: *Thomasville (GA) Times-Enterprise*, 7/20/28 (6:4) & 2/19/30 (5:4). See also: 1928 Grady Co. death cert. no. 21345 and 1930 Baldwin Co. death cert. no. 8388. Also: 1920 U.S. Census (Quincy, FL), which notes Stephens.

Renty Screven (black, age 46). *Murder.* The crime was committed on 9/3/1926 in Chatham County. Filicide. Handgun slaying of 22-year-old Rosa Screven (black, his daughter), who was shot three times. Motive: the homicide victim had had the temerity to bring a married man into their home and introduce him as her lover in open defiance of Papa Screven's prohibition against it. Neither father nor daughter made these same mistakes again. The law made no distinction in regard to the "honor killing" of errant offspring. Renty Screven learned this the hard way when he was led to the electric chair on March 21, 1930. Source: 1930 Baldwin Co. death cert. no. 5397. Appeal: 169 GA 384. Also: 1920 U.S. Census (Chatham Co., GA), which notes the slayer in this case.

Lucius Jolley (black, age 22). *Murder.* The crime was committed on 3/11/1929 in Bibb County. Uxoricide. Fatal stabbing of 25-year-old Angeline Jolley (black). Motive: marital estrangement. A spiteful young man, Lucius Jolley had set fire to his wife's hope chest. She then had a warrant sworn out against him charging willful destruction of private property. This sent Jolley over the edge. He was executed at the Georgia State Prison on June 20, 1930. Source: *Macon (GA) Telegraph*, 3/12/29 (9:3). *Augusta (GA) Chronicle*, 6/21/30 (1:2). Appeal: 170 GA 461. See also: 1929 Bibb Co. death cert. no. 7040.

Emory van Dusen (black, age 23). *Murder.* The crime was committed on 11/2/1929 in Fulton County. Handgun slaying of 29-year-old Sarah Edelstein Gould (white), a grocer's wife and store assistant. Motive: attempted armed robbery. The killer was executed on June 27, 1930. Source: *Thomasville (GA) Times-Enterprise*, 12/13/29 (1:6) & 12/14/29 (3:6). See also: 1929 Fulton Co. death cert. no. 29517K and 1930 Baldwin Co. death cert. no. 14483.

Wash Smith (white, age 17). *Murder.* The crime was committed on 1/3/1928 in Banks County. Shotgun slaying of 43-year-old Jutist Lispust Wells, known to some as "Judson L. Wells" (white), a storekeeper. Motive: Smith felt that he had been given short shrift and treated in a condescending manner. Venue changed from Banks County to Ben Hill County. This young killer had his own life cut short by the Georgia electric chair on November 22, 1930. Source: *Thomasville (GA) Times-Enterprise*, 11/22/30 (1:2). GA Supreme Court case nos. 6653 and 7800. See also the murdered man's gravestone in Level Grove Cemetery, Cornelia.

1931

Edgar Jenkins (black, age 22). *Rape.* The crime was committed on 12/14/1930 in Early County. Executed for indecently assaulting two white females (names withheld) ages 9 and 11. No other details were ever released about this except for the fact that Jenkins was legally executed for what he did on January 16, 1931. The injuries to the two girls must have been traumatic both physically and mentally. Source: *Augusta (GA) Chronicle*, 12/23/30 (1:4). *Thomasville (GA) Weekly Times-Enterprise*, 1/20/31 (2:6).

William Biggers (black, age 24). *Murder.* The crime was committed on 9/7/1929 in Fulton County. Handgun slaying of 65-year-old Frank E. Marlin (white). Motive: mugging. Final toll: two lives lost for a watch and a 50-cent piece. Biggers was escorted to the Georgia electric chair on January 27, 1931. Source: *Atlanta Journal*, 1/27/31 (2:3). Appeal: 171 GA 596–601. See also: 1920 U.S. Census (Atlanta, GA), which notes Mr. Marlin.

Henry West (black, age 21). *Murder.* The crime was committed on 12/20/1930 in Floyd County. Executed for the malicious killing of 58-year-old Robert L. Huggins (white), a storekeeper who was battered about the head and face with the butt of a shotgun and died four days later. Motive: armed robbery. The killer was executed on March 13, 1931. Source: *Rome (GA) News-Tribune*, 12/21/30 (1:4), 12/26/30 (1:8) & 3/13/31 (1:8). See also: 1930 U.S. Census (Floyd Co., GA), which notes Mr. Huggins.

Lewis B. Newsome (black, age 21). *Murder.* The crime was committed on 7/12/1930 in Peach County. Shotgun slaying of 13-year-old Tereseta Burnett (black), who was killed in a case of mistaken identity. Newsome said that he had been gunning for his wife in the aftermath of a heated argument. The Burnett girl meanwhile had seated herself in a high-backed chair situated on Newsome's porch. It was the same chair that Mrs. Newsome routinely used. This proved that Newsome had intended all along to shoot his wife in the back, because he would have seen that someone else was sitting in that chair had he approached it from the front. A death penalty verdict was returned based on clear evidence of premeditation. The killer met his own demise in a different kind of chair on March 27, 1931. Source: *Macon (GA) Evening News*, 3/27/31 (1:6). See also: 1930 Peach Co. death cert. no. 19745 and 1931 Baldwin Co. death cert. no. 5230.

Willie Lee Cox (black, age 26) and **Gilbert Glaze** (black, age 28). *Murder.* Their crime was committed on 9/8/1930 in Fulton County. Handgun slaying of 43-year-old John B. McWhorter (white), a trolley car motorman who was shot six times. Motive: armed robbery. These assassins were executed at the Georgia State Prison on April 17, 1931. Source: *Thomasville (GA) Times-Enterprise*,

9/10/30 (7:2). *Atlanta Journal*, 4/17/31 (9:3). See also: 1930 U.S. Census (Atlanta, GA), which notes McWhorter.

Marvin Berry (black, age 36). *Murder.* The crime was committed on 11/17/1929 in Early County. Handgun slaying of 65-year-old William Harper (black). Motive: the older man objected to Berry's sniffing around his granddaughter when he was a married man. The Georgia electric chair permanently chastened Marvin Berry on April 29, 1931. Source: *Early County News* (Blakely, GA), 11/21/29 (1:6). *Augusta (GA) Chronicle*, 4/30/31 (1:7). Appeal: 172 GA 482. See also: 1920 U.S. Census (Early Co., GA), which notes both parties.

Fred Griffin (black, age 18). *Murder.* The crime was committed on 4/3/1931 in Campbell County. Police killer. Executed for the handgun slaying of 48-year-old Thomas W. Camp (white, the sheriff of Campbell County), who was shot three times with his own service weapon after the culprit had wrested it from him. Motive: courthouse breakout. Recidivist killer. This same offender had previously escaped from the Morgan County chain gang, on which he had been serving a 20-year term for another homicide. The details thereof were not given in published accounts of this case, an almost certain indication that it was a black-on-black crime. On May 18, 1931, the Georgia electric chair ensured that Griffin would never get a chance to add to his score. Source: *Thomasville (GA) Times-Enterprise*, 4/4/31 (3:3) & 4/7/31 (3:3). See also: 1931 Baldwin Co. death cert. no. 10898. Also: 1930 U.S. Census (Campbell Co., GA), which notes Thomas Camp.

James Burley Adams (white, age 31). *Murder.* The crime was committed on 2/22/1928 in Columbia County. Police killer. Handgun slaying of 27-year-old Walter R. Tolbert (white), a federal prohibition agent. He and his party of fellow lawmen were ambushed by moonshiners along the Avondale road. Agent Tolbert was struck by one bullet fired from a .45-caliber automatic, a weapon that is powerful enough to bring down an elephant. Motive: "us versus them." The assassin (Adams) was executed at the Georgia State Prison on May 22, 1931. Source: *Augusta (GA) Chronicle*, 2/23/28 (1:8) & 5/23/31 (1:8).

Willie Greene (black, age 26). *Murder.* The crime was committed on 3/22/1930 in Richmond County. Handgun slaying of 20-year-old Alexander Adams (black). Motive: attempted mugging. Greene was legally put to death for this at the Georgia State Prison on May 22, 1931. Source: *Augusta (GA) Chronicle*, 3/24/30 (2:8), 6/11/30 (3:3), 1/5/31 (2:4) & 5/23/31 (1:8).

Arthur Meyers (black, age 28). *Murder.* The crime was committed on 3/6/1924 in Richmond County. Police killer. Handgun slaying of 30-year-old Robert Franklin Gunn (white), a railroad policeman. Motive: resisting arrest. Meyers was hanged at the Richmond County jail on June 12, 1931, his capital offense having been perpetrated prior to the effective date of the Electrocution Act. Source: *Augusta (GA) Chronicle*, 3/8/24 (7:1) & 6/13/31 (1:6). See also Gunn's gravestone in Johnson Methodist Cemetery, Warrenton. See also: Chatham Co. World War I draft registration card no. 209, which notes the killer's race as "Ethiopian."

Eugene Dudley (black, age 22). *Murder.* The crime was committed on

11/18/1930 in Walton County. Shotgun slaying of 29-year-old Jesse Williams (black). Motive: the killer felt that he had been ill-used. Dudley thought that Williams had barred him from retrieving some of his personal effects from a vacated tenant cabin. It was a mistake that cost Dudley his own life in addition to that of the person he shot. The end came for him at the Georgia State Prison on July 17, 1931. Source: 1930 Walton Co. death cert. no. 31155 and 1931 Baldwin Co. death cert. no. 16584. Appeal: 172 GA 873. See also: 1930 U.S. Census (Walton Co., GA), which notes both parties.

Willie Higgins (black, age 26). *Murder.* The crime was committed on 7/7/1929 in Fulton County. Executed for the killing of 20-year-old Bob Peyton (black), whose head was beaten in with a baseball bat. Motive: gambling dispute. Both men were serving time on the Fulton County chain gang. Sunday being their day of rest, the members of that road crew included dice games among their leisure time activities. One such event (on the above date) got out of hand, with fatal results for two. The first person died at the scene and the other died in the Georgia electric chair on September 11, 1931. Source: 1929 Fulton Co. death cert. no. 24015 and 1931 Baldwin Co. death cert. no. 21829. Appeal: 172 GA 221.

Robert L. Chisholm (black, age 20). *Rape.* The crime was committed on or about 6/15/1931 in Houston County. Executed for an indecent assault on the person of a white female (identity withheld) under circumstances that made it impossible to select an impartial jury in Houston County. The case had to be transferred to Peach County for proper adjudication. Little else is known about the parties involved. The local newspaper was too discreet to describe events and the original court papers are not publicly accessible. This sex offender was legally executed at the Georgia State Prison on October 16, 1931. Source: *Macon (GA) Telegraph*, 10/17/31 (3:2). See also: 1931 Baldwin Co. death cert. no. 24243.

Clark Stevens (black, age 16). *Murder.* The crime was committed on 8/18/1931 in Morgan County. Police killer, etc. Executed for the handgun slayings of 30-year-old Percy Quinton McAdams (white, the asst. police chief of Madison, GA) and 58-year-old Will Mallory (white), a bystander. The lawman was shot three times. The other man got a bullet in the back and succumbed to his wound on 9/3/1931. Motive: resisting arrest. Stevens was electrocuted at the Georgia State Prison on October 16, 1931. Source: *Thomasville (GA) Times-Enterprise*, 8/18/31 (3:3) & 10/16/31 (8:3). See also: 1930 U.S. Census (Morgan Co., GA), which notes McAdams and Stevens.

Oconee Hendrix (black, age 33). *Murder.* The crime was committed on 1/10/1930 in Fulton County. Handgun slaying of 43-year-old "Sam Nisson" (white), a Jewish grocer whose name had been anglicized from "Samuel Nissinowitz." Motive: armed robbery. The killer was executed at the Georgia State Prison on October 30, 1931. Source: *Atlanta Constitution*, 1/11/30 (1:5) & 1/13/30 (1:6). *Atlanta Journal*, 10/31/31 (5:1). Appeal: 173 GA 419. See also: 1930 U.S. Census (Atlanta, GA), which notes Hendrix, and 1900 U.S. Census (Oconee Co., SC), which notes him as a minor. Also see: Fulton County naturalization cert. no. 641284, issued on 3/24/17, which notes the homicide victim in this case.

William Searey (black, age 32). *Murder.* The crime was committed on 8/7/1931 in Talbot County. Uxoricide. Shotgun slaying of 31-year-old Annie Mae Searey (black), who was blasted dead in the presence of their two small children. Motive: the woman had refused to give him a dime with which to buy a pack of cigarettes. Searey was a notorious drunk and brawler within the black community. The manner of his death came as no surprise to those who knew him. The forfeit of his life was exacted by the State of Georgia on October 30, 1931. Source: *Talbotton (GA) New Era,* 8/13/31 (1:4), 9/10/31 (1:3) & 11/5/31 (1:3). See also: 1930 U.S. Census (Talbot Co., GA), which notes both parties as "Searcy."

English Gaskins (white, age 43). *Murder.* The crime was committed on 3/29/1930 in Candler County. Uxoricide. Fatal stabbing of 25-year-old Jessie Hamm Gaskins (white), his second wife. Motive: marital estrangement. This killer had originally come from Chesterfield, SC, where he already had a family. He does not seem to have stayed in any one place for long. Liberty County GA was his place of residence when he killed the former Jessie Hamm. She had had her fill of him by then and fled with their infant child to her father's house in Candler County. Gaskins tracked down the young woman and lured her from the aforesaid place of refuge with an offer to take a leisurely ride in his automobile and hopefully straighten out their differences. No sooner had Jessie Hamm Gaskins gotten into the passenger seat, however, than English Gaskins started stabbing her frenziedly with a knife. Her shredded body was left on the roadside directly in front of her father's house. She had been "literally cut to pieces," as one newspaper described it. The killer smeared himself with blackface in the aftermath of this event and tried to evade a dragnet by imitating a black man. It was a poor performance that fooled no one. English Gaskins was executed at the Georgia State Prison on December 21, 1931. Source: *Augusta (GA) Chronicle,* 4/1/30 (1:7) & 12/21/31 (1:1). *Macon (GA) Telegraph,* 10/25/31 (9:4). See also: 1924 City Directory (Deland, FL), which notes this couple.

1932

Major Johnson, alias "Slick Johnson" (white, age 38). *Murder.* The crime was committed on 2/28/1931 in Dougherty County. Handgun slaying of 35-year-old Tobe Roberts (white), his brother-in-law. Motive: disgust at the homicide victim's apparently incorrigible alcoholism. There was nothing illegal about Johnson disliking his brother-in-law's traits, but he arrogated far too much authority to himself when he killed the man for it. This put him outside the bounds of the law, to say the least. He was executed for capital murder on February 9, 1932. Source: *Thomasville (GA) Times-Enterprise,* 3/31/31 (3:2) & 2/9/32 (1:3). Appeal: 173 GA 734. See also: 1920 and 1930 U.S. Censuses (Dougherty Co., GA), which respectively note Johnson and Roberts.

Eddie Marsh (black, age 17). *Murder.* The crime was committed on 10/18/1930 in Dougherty County. Shotgun slaying of 53-year-old Walter E. Campbell (white), a large-scale pecan grower. Motive: robbery and grand theft auto. The age of this offender is variously reported as having been 15, 16 and 17. Odds favor the latter because understating the age of young miscreants has always been a common ploy to curry favor for them. This became a moot point in the case of Eddie Marsh after he was carried dead from the execution chamber at the Georgia State Prison Farm (Milledgeville) on February 9, 1932. Source: *Thomasville (GA) Times-Enterprise*, 10/21/30 (5:4), 12/16/30 (3:1) & 2/9/32 (1:3). See also: 1930 U.S. Census (Dougherty Co., GA), which notes Mr. Campbell.

James H. Parker (white, age 36). *Murder.* The crime was committed on or about 6/15/1930 in Ware County. Uxoricide and filicide. Executed for the murders of 25-year-old Ethel Johns Parker and 18-month-old Geraldine Parker (whites), they having been his wife and daughter. The woman was slain with an ax. The baby was callously beaten to death. Motive: philandering. Parker had run out on his wife and child. He turned up in Ware County with another female whom he tried to pass off as his wife. The legal spouse (Ethel) traced his whereabouts and showed up on his doorstep, baby and all. Suspicious neighbors found what was left of the bodies four months later by plowing up the fields around Parker's house. He was executed on April 8, 1932. Source: *Augusta (GA) Chronicle*, 10/20/30 (1:8), 10/21/30 (1:6), 12/5/30 (1:7) & 4/9/32 (1:1). See also: 1910 U.S. Census (Wayne Co., GA), which notes Mrs. Parker by her maiden name.

Willie Rounds, alias "Yank" (black, age 25). *Murder.* The crime was committed on 10/28/1930 in Houston County. Fatal stabbing of 45-year-old William Visco Gunter (white), a cattleman who was knifed multiple times. Motive: workplace dispute. The killer was executed on June 10, 1932. Source: *Thomasville (GA) Times-Enterprise*, 10/29/30 (3:1). See also: 1930 Houston Co. death cert. no. 27465 and 1932 Baldwin Co. death cert. no. 13111.

Willie Jones (black, age 20). *Murder.* The crime was committed on 4/3/1932 in Richmond County. Executed for the killing of 56-year-old Charles Henry Dunn (white, a night watchman at an icehouse), who was beaten on the head with a sash weight. Motive: burglary. The killer was electrocuted on August 8, 1932. Source: Augusta (GA) Chronicle, 4/4/32 (1:8), 6/7/32 (1:5) & 8/9/32 (3:8). See also: 1930 U.S. Census (Augusta, GA), which notes Mr. Dunn.

Albert Jackson (black, age 20). *Murder.* The crime was committed on 1/21/1930 in Peach County. Executed for the deliberately fatal beatings of 89-year-old Green M. Hartley and 80-year-old Jeffie Hartley (whites), a married couple. Motive: robbery and home invasion. These old folks were mercilessly massacred in their own home, their frail bones shattered by repeated blows from sticks, clubs and furniture legs. The Georgia electric chair saw to Albert Jackson on October 7, 1932. Source: 1932 Baldwin Co. death cert. no. 23084. Also: 1930 Peach Co. death cert. nos. 1889 and 1890. Appeal: 172 GA 575. See also: 1900 U.S. Census (Houston Co., GA), which notes the Hartleys.

Paschal Baker (black, age 32) and **Charlie Green Jr.** (black, age 32). *Rape.* Their crime was committed on 8/12/1932 in Webster County. Both executed for indecently assaulting a married white farm couple (identities withheld) who were beaten insensible in the bed they shared by two nocturnal intruders wielding a hoe and a rectangular chunk of pig iron. The battered pair regained consciousness several hours later to find that they had also been raped, the man as well as the woman. Their attackers were legally executed by the State of Georgia on October 28, 1932. Source: *Stewart-Webster Journal*, 10/7/32 (1:2) & 10/28/32 (8:2).

William Hulsey (white, age 53) and **Fred Hulsey** (white, age 27). *Murder.* Their crime was committed on 6/18/1930 in Polk County. Handgun slayings of 32-year-old Clifford Jones, 30-year-old Lige Harper and 26-year-old Ernest McCullough (whites), who were all shot in the backs of their heads. The bodies were then loaded onto a donkey wagon and carted for several miles before being dumped into an abandoned well. Motive: a crooked card game. The killers were both executed at the Georgia State Prison on November 4, 1932. Source: *Augusta (GA) Chronicle*, 6/21/30 (1:3) & 7/17/30 (1:3). See also: 1932 Baldwin Co. death cert. nos. 25571 and 25572. Also: 1930 U.S. Census (Polk Co., GA), which notes all parties.

John Lee Humphreys (black, age 20). *Murder.* The crime was committed on 10/14/1931 in Stewart County. Uxoricide. Shotgun slaying of 18-year-old Fannie Humphreys (black). Motive: acrimonious divorce. It is not known what led this young couple to marry in the first place, but the true character of at least one of them did not take long to emerge. This wife-killer was executed at the Georgia State Prison on November 5, 1932. Source: 1932 Baldwin Co. death cert. no. 25569. Appeal: 175 GA 705–714. See also: 1930 U.S. Census (Stewart Co., GA), which notes both parties.

James C. Jackson (black, age 23). *Murder.* The crime was committed on 10/8/1932 in Early County. Handgun slaying of 22-year-old Michael Davis (white). Motive: evading pursuit. Jackson was wanted by the police for burglary. He ran when confronted on a street. Davis (a stalwart baseball player who was quick on his feet) attempted to chase him down, only to get a bullet in the chest for his effort. The killer went to the electric chair on November 16, 1932. Source: *Early County News*, 10/13/32 (2:2) & 11/24/32 (2:1). See also: 1932 Baldwin Co. death cert. no. 25570.

1933

Lawrence Welch (black, age 41). *Murder.* The crime was committed on 6/15/1931 in Early County. Uxoricide. Executed for the shotgun slaying of 29-year-old Lucy Welch (black), she having also been battered about the head with the stock of that weapon. Motive: she had disobeyed his command to return with him to their home. The Georgia electric chair functioned in this case on April 4, 1933. Source: 1931 Early Co. death cert. no. 17313 and 1933 Baldwin Co. death cert. no. 6959. Appeal: 176 GA 410–415.

Johnny Todd (black, age 18). *Murder.* The crime was committed on 3/24/1933 in Greene County. Shotgun slaying of 35-year-old Willard Stephens Acree (white), a rural mail carrier whose head was also mashed with the butt of that weapon. Motive: robbery. There was no appeal in this case and no grounds for one. Johnny Todd was carried dead from the execution chamber at the Georgia State Prison Farm (Milledgeville) on May 19, 1933. Source: *Atlanta Constitution*, 5/20/33 (4:5). See also: 1933 Wilkes Co. death cert. no. 6850 as well as Mr. Acree's gravestone in Wisteria Cemetery, Union Point.

Pat Randall (black, age not recorded). *Murder.* The crime was committed on 2/27/1932 in Randolph County. Shotgun slaying of 46-year-old Uriah Harrell (black). Motive: Harrell had called Randall a "son of a bitch." Randall's reaction to this cost him his life. He was electrocuted on May 20, 1933. Source: 1932 Randolph Co. death cert. no. 3839 and 1933 Baldwin Co. death cert. no. 16989. Appeal: 176 GA 897–902. See also: 1910 U.S. Census (Randolph Co., GA), which notes Harrell.

Rader Davis (black, age 26). *Murder.* The crime was committed on 2/18/1933 in Fulton County. Incipient serial killer. Executed for the shotgun slaying of 25-year-old Annie L. Henderson (white) together with the grievous wounding of her husband and 2-year-old baby. Motive: burglary. Davis is confirmed to have also murdered two other persons: Hamp McGee (white, age 68), a jitney driver who was blasted in the back with a shotgun for the purpose of robbery on 1/27/1933 as he stood before a mirror shaving himself in his Fulton County home. Also: William E. Stanley (white, age 78), who perished by the same means at his residence in Rockdale County on 2/28/1933. Both men were solitary types suspected of having hoarded wealth. Davis was a sociopath who had become embittered by previous scrapes with the law and with people in general. He was executed on June 14, 1933. Source: *Thomasville (GA) Times-Enterprise*, 3/6/33 (6:5). *Atlanta Journal*, 6/14/33 (1:7). See also: 1930 U.S. Census (Fulton Co., GA), which notes McGee and the Hendersons. *Master Detective*, 7/34.

Richard Morris (black, age 18), **Richard Sims** (black, age 17) and **Mose White** (black, age 17). *Murder.* Their crime was committed on 3/16/1932 in Fulton County. Police killers. All three executed for the handgun slaying of 35-year-old Frank Clinton Foster (white). Motive: armed robbery gone awry. Three prospective criminal careers were precluded when this trio went to the electric chair on August 11, 1933. Source: *Atlanta Constitution*, 3/17/32 (1:4) & 8/12/33 (12:7). See also: 1930 U.S. Census (Fulton Co., GA), which notes the three miscreants, and 1900 U.S. Census (Jackson Co., GA), which notes Foster as a minor.

Eugene Key (black, age 25). *Murder.* The crime was committed on 10/25/1932 in Houston County. Uxoricide. Executed for the shotgun slaying of 17-year-old Katie Key (black). Motive: she had resolved to walk out of their abusive marriage. This wife-killer went to the Georgia electric chair on August 25, 1933. Source: *Atlanta Constitution*, 8/26/33 (2:3). Appeal: 177 GA 329–334. See also: 1930 U.S. Census (Monroe Co., GA), which notes both parties.

Thomas Andrew McCullough (white, age 57). *Murder.* The crime was committed on 9/25/1932 in Fayette County. Handgun slaying of 70-year-old William B. Baker (white), a plantation owner. Motive: obnoxious personality. Baker was one of the largest peach growers in the state of Georgia. He was gunned down when he went to see about a disturbance in his workers quarters. The killer died in the Georgia electric chair on August 25, 1933. Source: *Thomasville (GA) Times-Enterprise*, 9/26/32 (1:4). *Atlanta Constitution*, 8/26/33 (1:2). Appeal: 177 GA 315–318.

Rochelle Jackson (black, age 26). *Murder.* The crime was committed on 7/29/1932 in Worth County. Executed for the killing of 49-year-old Sarah Armstrong (black, his half sister), who was disabled by a shotgun blast that was fired through a window of her house and then pounced on and finished off with an ax. Motive: family feud. The murdered woman had charge of her late father's estate. Six other siblings resented this. Rochelle Jackson chafed under the situation so much that he resorted to drastic means. His reward for this was death by electrocution as administered at the Georgia State Prison on September 8, 1933. Source: *Sylvester (GA) Local,* 8/11/32 (1:1), 9/7/33 (1:1) & 9/14/33 (1:2).

Harry Simpson (black, age 34). *Murder.* The crime was committed on 10/17/1932 in Clinch County. Uxoricide. Shotgun slaying of Marie Simpson (black, age not recorded) amid circumstances that are uncertain based on surviving accounts. Simpson had come from Bay St. Louis, MS, six years earlier. It is not known if he was already married by then. This wife-killer met his own demise at the hands of the law on October 20, 1933, when he was electrocuted at the Georgia State Prison. Source: *Clinch County News,* 5/5/33 (1:1), 10/20/33 (1:3) & 10/27/33 (1:6). See also: 1933 Baldwin Co. death cert. no. 31351. Also: Original Superior Court Case File (*State vs. Simpson*), copy provided through courtesy of the present-day clerk of Clinch County Superior Court.

Grady Brooks (black, age 19) and **George Zuber** (black, age 29). *Murder.* Their crime was committed on 7/1/1933 in Pickens County. Prison-guard killers. Both were executed for the shotgun slaying of 61-year-old Lee Lindsey (white), an officer with the Pickens County chain gang. Motive: escape from their fetters. It was a desperate act that availed them not. The Georgia electric chair did a twosome in this case on October 27, 1933. Source: *Times-Enterprise* (Thomasville, GA), 10/27/33 (4:5). Appeal: 178 GA 663–668. See also: 1930 U.S. Census (Pickens Co., GA), which notes Mr. Lindsey. See also: Reese Castlebury (executed 6/15/34).

James F. Barbee (white, age 45). *Murder.* The crime was committed on 3/3/1931 in Pulaski County. Handgun slaying of 22-year-old Delmar Cannon (white), who was shot six times. Motive: the young man had dared to elope with the killer's daughter. Cannon was deceitfully lured to Barbee's house by means of a letter that was written in a conciliatory tone. Then as soon as he walked into the house Barbee fired the entire contents of a pistol into him. Barbee paid with his own life at the Georgia State Prison on December 29, 1933. Source: *Augusta (GA) Chronicle,* 3/4/31 (1:8) & 9/26/31 (2:7). See also: 1933 Baldwin Co. death cert. no. 27444.

1934

Albert Dobbs (black, age 18). *Rape.* The crime was committed on or about 11/1/1933 in Fulton County. Executed for an indecent assault on the person of an adult white female (name withheld) who was attacked in her own home. Dobbs admitted that he was a sneak thief who had stealthily slipped into the woman's residence to see what he could steal. Caught in the act, he hit the lady on the head with a blackjack and raped her as she lay unconscious. Dobbs was executed at the Georgia

State Prison Farm (Milledgeville) on January 12, 1934. Source: *Atlanta Daily World*, 12/7/33 (1:7). *Atlanta Constitution*, 1/13/34 (7:2).

Homer Lee Short (black, age 23). *Murder.* The crime was committed on 2/20/1933 in Marion County. Shotgun slaying of 35-year-old Mose W. Dabbs (white), who was blasted by a sniper as he sat in his parlor. Motive: an alleged murder-for-hire having to do with a feud between bootleggers. The triggerman in this case was executed at the Georgia State Prison Farm (Milledgeville) on March 2, 1934. Source: *Marion County Patriot* (Buena Vista, GA), 2/23/33 (1:3) & 3/8/34 (1:1).

John Downer (black, age 25). *Rape.* The crime was committed on 5/17/1931 in Elbert County. Indecent assault on the person of 20-year-old Hazel Craft (white), she and her fiancé having been accosted at gunpoint as they sat in a parked car. The young man who was forced to live through this outrage proved his devotion by marrying the victimized girl the following day. Their attacker died in the Georgia electric chair on March 16, 1934. Source: *Augusta (GA) Chronicle*, 5/19/31 (1:8), 5/27/31 (1:1) & 3/17/34 (1:2). See also: 1934 Baldwin Co. death cert. no. 5289 and 1940 U.S. Census (Oglethorpe Co., GA), which notes the former newlyweds.

Sandy Walker (black, age 46). *Murder.* The crime was committed on 12/18/1932 in Worth County. Executed for the deliberate killings of 68-year-old Cliff Kearce and 67-year-old Bettie Kearce (described as "a wealthy colored couple"), who both had their heads dashed in. The woman lingered until 1/3/1933. Motive: a sordid tale of avarice. Cliff Kearce's 75-year-old brother was sentenced to life imprisonment as an accessory. Violence even marked the slain man's funeral when a mourner named Gold Cobb fatally shot another mourner named Britt Combs. The Georgia electric chair accounted for Sandy Walker on March 16, 1934, and no amount of ill-gotten money was able to save him from it. Source: *The Sylvester (GA) Local*, 12/22/32 (1:1), 12/29/32 (1:3), 1/5/33 (1:5) & 3/22/34 (1:1). See also: 1930 U.S. Census (Worth Co., GA), which notes Cliff and Bettie "Kerce."

Miley W. Lively (white, age 46). *Murder.* The crime was committed on 7/26/1933 in Fulton County. Uxoricide, etc. Executed for the murders of about 32-year-old Rosa Kell Lively and 51-year-old Rettia "Rethey" Kell (whites, they respectively being his wife and mother-in-law), who were both slashed to death with a razor. Motive: the homicide victims had become aware of his duplicity. This double-dipper turned double killer was put to death at the Georgia State Prison Farm on April 20, 1934. Source: *Atlanta Constitution*, 7/27/33 (1:1). Appeal: 178 GA 693–700. See also: 1934 Baldwin Co. death cert. no. 8647. Also: 1920 U.S. Census (Fannin Co., GA), which notes the family Kell.

Mack James (black, age 28). *Murder.* The crime was committed on 9/13/1933 in Banks County. Executed for the mutilation murder of 23-year-old Ida Whitfield (white), who had been attacked while walking home from the local store. The culprit was a so-called trusty with the Banks County chain gang. He was also a known sex offender with at least two prior convictions for felonies of that nature.

James was then serving a 20-year sentence that had been imposed on him in Bibb County. The details of what he did to the homicide victim were such that great tact was used in reporting this case. Mack James died in the Georgia electric chair on May 11, 1934. Source: *Atlanta Constitution*, 9/15/33 (11:7). *Times-Enterprise* (Thomasville, GA), 9/25/33 (6:4) & 4/12/34 (8:1). Appeal: 178 GA 761–765. See also: 1930 U.S. Census (Banks Co., GA), which notes Miss Whitfield.

Claude Hicks (black, age 26) and **Hosea Patrick**, alias "Partridge" (black, age 29). *Murder.* Their crime was committed on 1/2/1933 in Fulton County. Both executed for the purposeful killing of 19-year-old Ray Schells, known to some as "Shell" (black), who was "taken for a ride" in an automobile with the culprits, shot three times with a handgun, pistol whipped and beaten on the head with that car's crank handle. Motive: insurance fraud. The guilty parties met their own inglorious fates in the execution chamber of the old Georgia State Prison on May 15, 1934. Source: *Atlanta Journal*, 5/15/34 (12:8). Appeal: 178 GA 561–566. See also: 1933 Fulton Co. death cert. no. 777.

Reese Castleberry (black, age 23). *Murder.* The crime was committed on 7/1/1933 in Pickens County. Prison-guard killer. Accomplice in the shotgun slaying of 61-year-old Lee Lindsey (white), an officer assigned to the Pickens County chain gang. Motive: breakout. Castleberry was put to death for his part in this misdeed on June 15, 1934. Source: *Times-Enterprise* (Thomasville, GA), 6/15/34 (1:7). Appeal: 178 GA 663–668. See: Grady Brooks and George Zuber (executed 10/27/33).

Floyd South (black, age 20). *Murder.* The crime was committed on 5/13/1933 in Fulton County. Accomplice in the handgun slaying of 44-year-old Benjamin Gadlin (white), who was shot in the back. Motive: attempted robbery. The actual shooter (Andrew Bostick) got away. South was held to be equally guilty under the law of accomplices because he had made no attempt to restrain the gunman. He was executed on June 15, 1934. Source: *Atlanta Constitution*, 5/14/33 (1:3) & 5/15/33 (1:5). Appeal: 178 GA 769–770. See also: 1934 Baldwin Co. death cert. no. 14471.

Clifford Duncan (black, age 27). *Rape.* The crime was committed on 11/21/1933 in Candler County. Indecent assault on the person of an 11-year-old white female (name withheld), the details of which are too obscene for recitation. The Georgia electric chair did its job in this case on September 14, 1934. Source: *Metter (GA) Advertiser*, 2/8/34 (1:1). *Times-Enterprise* (Thomasville, GA), 8/9/34 (5:8). Appeal: 179 GA 254. See also: 1934 Baldwin Co. death cert. no. 31236.

Frank Johnson (black, age 42). *Murder.* The crime was committed on 6/4/1934 in Washington County. Prison-guard killer. Executed for the murder of 47-year-old John Waller (white), a night guard at the Washington County convict camp, who was fatally clubbed during a breakout from that facility. Frank Johnson was executed in the electric chair on October 5, 1934. Source: *Augusta (GA) Chronicle*, 6/12/34 (6:5). *Sandersville (GA) Progress*, 6/14/34 (1:2) & 10/11/34 (1:2). See also: 1934 Baldwin Co. death cert. no. 25571. Also: 1930 U.S. Census (Wash. Co., GA), which notes Mr. Waller.

Mose Street (black, age 28). *Murder.* The crime was committed on 1/22/1934 in Chatham County. Police killer. Handgun slaying of 46-year-old James E. Roughen (white), who was shot in the back. Motive: resisting arrest. This willful assassin of a law enforcement officer was put to death at the Georgia State Prison Farm on November 15, 1934. Source: *Times-Enterprise* (Thomasville, GA), 11/15/34 (1:1). See also: 1934 Chatham Co. death cert. no. 493. Also: 1920 U.S. Census (Savannah, GA), which notes the slain policeman.

1935

Charlie Dodson (black, age 17). *Murder.* The crime was committed on 12/24/1934 in Schley County. Police killer. Handgun slaying of 41-year-old Wilbur B. Souter (white), the police chief of Ellaville. Motive: resisting arrest. The lawman had nabbed Dodson for shoplifting on Christmas Eve. The latter somehow wrested Souter's service weapon away from him and shot its owner dead. The Georgia electric chair did the rest on January 21, 1935. Source: *Times-Enterprise* (Thomasville, GA), 12/26/34 (4:4) & 1/1/35 (4:2). Also: 1935 Baldwin Co. death cert. no. 80. See also the police chief's gravestone in Ellaville (GA) Cemetery.

John T. Hammett (white, age 53). *Murder.* The crime was committed on 12/18/1933 in Troup County. Executed for the malicious killings of 43-year-old James Howard Boozer and 53-year-old Michael O. Bowman (whites), who were each blasted by a shotgun and battered about their faces and heads with a metal automobile jack. Motive: the homicide victims had gossiped about the killer's wife. She (Loretta Hammett) drew a life sentence for her own part in the crime. Her irate husband—whom she had goaded—died in the Georgia electric chair on February 11, 1935. Source: 1933 Troup Co. death cert. nos. 30016 (Boozer) and 30935 (Bowman) plus 1935 Baldwin Co. death cert. no. 2696 (Hammett). Appeal: 179 GA 776–782.

Archie Barfield (black, age 20). *Murder.* The crime was committed on 1/15/1933 in Clayton County. Handgun slaying of 44-year-old Eva Lamb Evans (white), who was shot dead in her sickbed by a home intruder (Barfield) intent on robbery. Venue changed from Clayton County to Gwinnett County. The killer paid with his life for this at the Georgia State Prison Farm on February 15, 1935. Source: 1935 Baldwin Co. death cert. at date. Appeal: 179 GA 293–301. See also the murdered woman's gravestone in New Hope United Methodist Church Cemetery, Clayton Co.

Rack Reese, alias "Bussey" (black, age 54) and **John Henry Wright** (black, age 32). *Murder.* Their crime was committed on 11/9/1934 in McDuffie County. Both executed for the willful killing of 42-year-old James Black Stone (white), who was struck on the head with a brick, an ax handle and "a section of iron wagon tire." Motive: mugging. This guilty pair died in the Georgia electric chair on March 1, 1935. Source: *Augusta (GA) Chronicle*, 11/11/34 (1:5), 12/4/34 (1:4), 12/5/34 (1:7) & 3/2/35 (6:7). See also: 1930 U.S. Census (McDuffie Co., GA), which notes Stone and Wright.

Joe Tucker (black, age 28). *Murder.* The crime was committed on 7/2/1934 in Meriwether County. Executed for the murders of 59-year-old Samuel

Hughes and 59-year-old Mary deLong Hughes (whites), a married couple. The woman was beaten to death with a heavy stick. The man was killed by a shotgun blast several hours later when he went looking for his missing spouse. The bodies of both were dumped in a swamp. Motive: disgruntled employee. Tucker paid the death penalty for this on March 5, 1935. Source: *Columbus (GA) Ledger*, 3/5/35 (1:8). Appeal: 180 GA 87–88. See also the modest but lovingly preserved gravestone of Mr. & Mrs. Hughes in Casey's Hill Cemetery, Atlanta.

Arthur Bell, alias "Wilbur," alias "Kid Wilbur" (black, age abt. 20) and **Daniel W. Brown** (black, age 25). *Murder.* Their crime was committed on 1/3/1935 in Webster County. Both executed for the killing of 67-year-old Joseph J. King (white), a storekeeper who was clubbed to death in his place of business. Motive: robbery. The Georgia electric chair did double duty in this case on March 7, 1935. Source: *Columbus (GA) Ledger*, 1/3/35 (1:3) & 3/7/35 (1:1). *Stewart-Webster Journal*, 3/15/35 (1:5). *Times-Enterprise* (Thomasville, GA), 3/7/35 (2:4). See also: 1935 Webster Co. death cert. no. 2551. Also: 1930 U.S. Census (Webster Co., GA), which notes Brown and Mr. King.

Robert Franklin Hargroves (white, age 24). *Murder.* The crime was committed on 5/6/1933 in Effingham County. Ax murder of 51-year-old James Zittrauer (white), whose mangled corpse was then wrapped in a blanket and shoved head-first down a gopher hole so that his feet protruded from the ground. Motive: moonshiners' squabble. Both men were due to appear in court for making illicit whiskey. Each dreaded what the other one might say. Hargroves got the drop on his rival. Then the State of Georgia got the drop on Hargroves. He was executed on March 15, 1935. Source: *Times-Enterprise* (Thomasville, GA) 5/9/33 (2:2) & 5/10/33 (1:1). See also: 1935 Baldwin Co. death cert. no. 5466. Also see the murdered man's gravestone in Zion Lutheran Cemetery, Guyton.

Victor Pierce (white, age 32). *Murder.* The crime was committed on 2/20/1934 in Clayton County. Handgun slaying of 30-year-old Stanley Dodge (white), the proprietor of a tourist camp, who was shot three times. Motive: armed robbery. The killer said that his real name was "Valmore Wilkerson" and that he came from Illinois. He died in the Georgia electric chair on March 29, 1935. Source: *Times-Enterprise* (Thomasville, GA), 2/20/34 (2:3). *Augusta (GA) Chronicle*, 11/27/34 (2:7). *Atlanta Journal*, 2/20/34 (1:2) & 3/29/35 (1:7). See also: 1930 U.S. Census (Atlanta, GA), which notes Pierce.

Isaiah Ashley (black, age 16). *Murder.* The crime was committed on 5/6/1934 in Appling County. Handgun slaying of 38-year-old John Wesley Holton (white). Motive: big attitude. He and his 20-year-old brother (Walter Ashley) were walking toward a so-called "Negro Row" (i.e., an all-black den of vice) when they encountered Mr. Holton, his wife and daughter walking in the opposite direction. The white man advised them that their destination was not a salubrious one. Isaiah Ashley's response was to pull out a pistol and start shooting. He was brought to the electric chair for this on April 5, 1935. Source: *News-Banner* (Baxley, GA), 5/9/34 (1:3). *Atlanta Constitution*, 4/6/35 (3:4). See also: 1930 U.S. Census (Appling Co., GA), which notes both parties.

Albert Rivers (black, age 23). *Rape.* The crime was committed on or about 2/1/1934 in Screven County. Indecent assault on the person of a 9-year-old white female (name withheld) under circumstances so repugnant that the perpetrator had to be held in a secret location for more than a year before tempers cooled to a point where he could be safely brought into court. Sex offender Albert Rivers was legally put to death at the Georgia State Prison Farm (Milledgeville) on April 5, 1935. Source: *Atlanta Daily World,* 4/5/35 (1:5) & 4/6/35 (1:7). *Augusta (GA) Chronicle,* 4/6/35 (10:1). See also: 1930 U.S. Census (Screven Co., GA), which notes Rivers.

Henry Harden (black, age 34). *Murder.* The crime was committed on 4/21/1934 in Washington County. Handgun slaying of 21-year-old John W. New (white). Motive: a dispute over a car repair bill. In doing this, the killer abrogated not only his right to drive a car but also his right to exist—at least in the eyes of the law. He was executed at the Georgia State Prison Farm on May 10, 1935. Source: *Sandersville (GA) Progress,* 4/26/34 (1:3) & 5/16/35 (1:2). Appeal: 180 GA 265–266. See also: 1930 U.S. Census (Wash. Co., GA), which notes both parties.

Charlie Stone, also known as "Marion Morris" (black, age 32). *Rape.* The crime was committed on 7/29/1933 in Fulton County. Indecent assault on the person of 43-year-old Jennie Pierce (white), who was attacked by a prowler (Stone) as she lay in her bed at 4 o'clock in the morning. An ice pick was held to the woman's breasts throughout this ordeal and the perpetrator pricked her with it numerous times (repeatedly drawing blood) lest she dare to resist. There was no question of consent in this case. The culprit was electrocuted pursuant to law on May 10, 1935. Source: *Atlanta Constitution,* 5/11/35 (6:4). Appeal: 180 GA 223–224. See also: 1930 U.S. Census (Fulton Co., GA), which notes both parties.

Charlie Beasley (black, age 45). *Murder.* The crime was committed on 3/7/1935 in Troup County. Executed for the ax murder of 64-year-old Dan Daniel (white), a farmer who was then in the act of scolding his employees. Motive: big attitude. The electric chair added this killer to its tally at the Georgia State Prison Farm on June 14, 1935. Source: *LaGrange (GA) Daily News,* 6/13/35 (1:6). *Columbus (GA) Ledger,* 6/14/35 (1:7). *Atlanta Constitution,* 6/15/35 (10:5). See also: 1935 Troup Co. death cert. no. 7535. Also: 1930 U.S. Census (Troup Co., GA), which notes the murdered planter.

Robert Mullinax (white, age 33). *Murder.* The crime was committed on 5/28/1934 in Floyd County. Shotgun slaying of 23-year-old Nevin P. Hancock (white), his stepson. Motive: obnoxious drunk. There had already been friction between these persons. Mullinax said that they had argued and that the homicide victim had hit him with a rock. It was a lame defense that saw the electric chair again called into service on June 14, 1935. Source: *Rome (GA) News-Tribune,* 5/29/34 (1:5) & 6/14/35 (1:7). Appeal: 180 GA 464–466.

Cleveland Hicks, alias "Bud Jones" (black, age 30). *Murder.* The crime was committed on 1/13/1935 in Mitchell County. Executed for the murder of 31-year-old Charles Edward Norris (white), a garage man. He was beaten on the head with a stout stick and succumbed to a fractured skull. Motive:

grand theft auto. All this killer wound up with was a seat in the Georgia electric chair on July 12, 1935. Source: *Camilla (GA) Enterprise*, 1/18/35 (1:4) & 7/19/35 (1:1). See also: 1930 U.S. Census (Mitchell Co., GA), which notes the homicide victim.

J. B. Reese, alias "J. B. Allen," alias "George Allen" (black, age not recorded). *Rape.* The crime was committed on 6/5/1935 in Jackson County. Indecent assault on the person of an adult white female (name withheld) who was attacked in her home near Nicholson. The culprit was an escapee from the Morgan County chain gang. The woman tried to defend herself by striking the assailant on the head with an antique iron shoe horn. This cut Reese in two or three places but did not inhibit him from his baser intention. It proved his undoing, however, when he was picked up later and could not satisfactorily account for his injuries. Reese was executed on July 19, 1935. Source: *Jackson Herald* (Jefferson, GA), 6/13/35 (8:6) & 6/27/35 (1:5). The death certificate in this case is missing. The official list of executions put out by the Georgia Dept. of Corrections is the only known confirmation that the death sentence was carried out.

Simmie Gaines (black, age 24). *Murder.* The crime was committed on 6/26/1935 in Oglethorpe County. Executed for the unmitigated killings of 73-year-old Ida E. Goolsby and 49-year-old Mettie Goolsby (whites), a mother and daughter who were clubbed to death in the home that they shared. Motive: robbery in a dwelling house. Gaines was a remorseless predator who saw these unassuming victims as easy prey. He met a searing end in the electric chair on October 10, 1935. Source: *Augusta (GA) Chronicle*, 9/17/35 (12:3). Also: 1935 Baldwin Co. death cert. no. 29392. See also: 1930 U.S. Census (Oglethorpe Co., GA), which notes the murdered ladies.

George P. McRae (white, age 23). *Murder.* The crime was committed on 9/16/1934 in Cherokee County. Handgun slaying of 21-year-old Virgil Turner (white), a taxi driver who was shot three times. Motive: carjacking. The killer was executed on October 18, 1935. Source: *North Georgia Tribune*, 9/21/34 (1:7). *Times-Enterprise* (Thomasville, GA), 9/17/34 (4:6) & 10/18/35 (3:8). Appeal: 181 GA 68–70.

Jack Mattox (black, age 29). *Murder.* The crime was committed on 3/24/1935 in Oglethorpe County. Handgun slaying of 40-year-old Ed Watkins (black), who was shot in the back. Motive: an argument over who was the better man. Mattox realized the error of what he had done when prison guards walked him to the electric chair on November 22, 1935. Source: *Oglethorpe (GA) Echo*, 3/28/35 (1:2) & 11/28/35 (1:2). Appeal: 181 GA 361–362. See also: 1930 U.S. Census (Oglethorpe Co., GA), which notes both parties.

Marvin Honea (white, age 27). *Murder.* The crime was committed on 12/20/1934 in Fulton County. Handgun slaying of 23-year-old David A. Lord (white). Motive: armed robbery gone awry. This stickup-man-turned-killer was executed on December 20, 1935. Source: *Atlanta Journal*, 12/25/34 (3:1) & 12/20/35 (1:2). Appeal: 181 GA 40–44. See also: 1910 U.S. Census (Fulton Co., GA), which notes Honea as a minor.

John Willie White (black, age 22). *Murder.* The crime was committed on

10/5/1935 in Cobb County. Executed for the ax murder of 32-year-old Orel C. Swanson (white), a filling station operator. Motive: robbery. Prime suspect in the 9/26/1935 killing of Marietta night watchman Wilburn P. Smith (white, age 66), who was struck down from behind with a heavy stick while making his rounds. John Willie White paid the death penalty at the Georgia State Prison Farm on December 20, 1935. Source: *Marietta (GA) Journal*, 10/3/35 (1:6), 10/10/35 (1:6), 10/17/35 (1:2) & 10/31/35 (1:2). *Times-Enterprise* (Thomasville, GA), 12/20/35 (1:6).

1936

Eddie B. Bowen (black, age 22). *Murder.* The crime was committed on 2/19/1935 in Douglas County. Handgun slaying of 42-year-old Joseph Carroll (white). Motive: burglary gone awry. Death in the electric chair was the fate of Eddie Bowen on March 6, 1936. Source: *Atlanta Journal*, 2/19/35 (1:2). *Atlanta Constitution*, 2/20/35 (19:5) & 3/8/35 (1:5). *Times-Enterprise* (Thomasville, GA), 3/8/35 (3:8) & 3/27/35 (6:8). *Savannah (GA) Evening Press*, 3/6/36 (5:3). Appeal: 181 GA 427–429.

Thomas Nelson, alias "Lincoln" (black, age 36) and **John Henry Simmons**, alias "Johnny Jones" (black, age 48). *Murder.* Their crime was committed on 9/20/1934 in Camden County. Shotgun slaying of 23-year-old Nicholas K. Perry (white). Motive: armed robbery. These killers entered the execution chamber at the Georgia State Prison Farm (Milledge ville) on March 20, 1936, and were carried out of it in pine boxes several minutes later. Source: 1936 Baldwin Co. death cert. nos. 5865 and 5866. Appeal: 181 GA 761–767. See also: 1930 U.S. Census (Camden Co., GA), which notes the homicide victim.

Julius Lowman (black, age 31). *Murder.* The crime was committed on 8/5/1935 in Chatham County. Fatal stabbing of 29-year-old Mabel Jones, alias "Helen Lowman," alias "Louise Williams" (black), who suffered multiple puncture wounds in addition to a severed neck. Motive: lovers' quarrel. The Georgia electric chair exacted retributive justice from Julius Lowman on March 25, 1936. Source: *Savannah Evening Press*, 8/5/35 (11:4) & 3/25/36 (11:2). Appeal: 181 GA 698. See also: *Savannah City Death Register*, entry dated 8/7/35, which notes the slain woman as "Louise Williams."

Hamp McLemore (black, age 19). *Rape.* The crime was committed on 8/11/1934 in Muscogee County. Indecent assault on the person of 25-year-old Ola Melton (white), she having been attacked while walking across a golf course with her 4-year-old daughter. The capital felony was perpetrated at knifepoint in the presence of the terrified toddler. McLemore was executed on April 10, 1936. Source: *Times-Enterprise* (Thomasville, GA), 4/10/36 (2:3). Appeal: 181 GA 462–471. See also: 1936 Baldwin Co. death cert. no. 9410.

John Henry Thomas (black, age 21). *Murder.* The crime was committed on 6/12/1936 in Clarke County. Handgun slaying of 48-year-old Charles Lewis Rice (white), a filling station operator. Motive: attempted armed robbery. The killer was executed on August 6, 1936. Source: *Times-Enterprise* (Thomasville, GA), 6/13/36 (8:4). See also: 1936 Baldwin Co. death cert. no. 21595. Also see the murdered man's gravestone in Oconee Hill Cemetery, Athens.

John Daniel (black, age 23) and **Demps Charles** (black, age 27). *Murder.* Their crime was committed on 7/5/1935 in Hall County. Both executed for the ax murder of 68-year-old Walter Simpson (white), who was butchered in his own house. Motive: robbery and home invasion. The Georgia electric chair functioned for a double event in the case of these killers on August 21, 1936. Source: *Times-Enterprise* (Thomasville, GA), 7/8/35 (1:7) & 7/12/35 (6:7). *Atlanta Constitution,* 8/22/36 (3:6). Appeal: 182 GA 359–360. See also the murdered man's gravestone in Redwine Cemetery, Oakwood.

Arthur Coombs, alias "Powell" (black, age 30). *Rape.* The crime was committed on an unknown date in Henry County. Very little is known about this case. It was ignored by the press, which is indicative (under the standards of that time) of its being a matter of black-on-black violence. It is also uncertain whether the indictment has survived, because three written requests for information about it (addressed to the Clerk of Henry County Superior Court) have all gone unanswered. A death certificate does, however, confirm that this offender died in the Georgia electric chair on November 12, 1936. Source: 1936 Baldwin Co. death cert. no. 29594.

Winton Boyer (black, age 24). *Murder.* The crime was committed on 11/17/1935 in Hancock County. Police killer. Handgun slaying of 23-year-old Maurice L. Stafford (white), a Sparta motorcycle patrolman. Motive: because he felt personally violated. The homicide victim (while in the performance of his duty) had pulled over an automobile occupied by six black males. He ordered all six to line up with their hands on the car and submit to being searched. Boyer's response was to pull out a pistol and start shooting. He was executed for this on December 4, 1936. Source: *Augusta (GA) Chronicle,* 10/18/35 (1:1) & 11/27/35 (2:1). See also: 1936 Baldwin Co. death cert. no. 36295. Also see the dead officer's gravestone in Sparta Cemetery, Sparta.

John Henry Sloan (black, age 23). *Murder.* The crime was committed on 10/15/1935 in Colquitt County. Shotgun slaying of 22-year-old Otis Gay (white) as he and his fiancée sat on a roadside embankment discussing their wedding plans. Motive: none apparent. Sloan suffered death by legal electrocution at the Georgia State Prison Farm on December 31, 1936. Source: *Augusta (GA) Chronicle,* 10/30/35 (3:1) & 11/15/35 (1:8). See also: 1936 Baldwin Co. death cert. no. 32862. Also: 1920 U.S. Census (Colquitt Co., GA), which notes the homicide victim as a minor.

1937

Arthur Burden (black, age 25). *Murder.* The crime was committed on 12/1/1934 in Bibb County. Shotgun slaying of 28-year-old Elizabeth Jones Henry (black), his sister-in-law. Motive: he had come to despise his wife's family. The homicide victim in this case was one of three female siblings then asleep in the same bed. These included the killer's wife. Burden fired his weapon through a window with an intention of killing them all. The price he paid was death by electrocution on February 24, 1937.

Source: *Macon (GA) Telegraph & News*, 12/2/34 (11:8). *Times-Enterprise* (Thomasville, GA), 2/24/37 (1:3). Appeal: 182 GA 533–535. See also: 1937 Baldwin Co. death cert. no. 2257.

James Burke (black, age 22). *Murder.* The crime was committed on 12/2/1935 in Richmond County. Executed for the killing of 67-year-old Patrick Joseph Collins (white), a grocer who was fatally beaten on the head. Motive: robbery. Burke had been a bad one from early youth, as his record attests. He was executed on April 19, 1937. Source: *Augusta (GA) Chronicle*, 12/6/35 (4:4), 12/18/35 (2:5), 3/10/36 (12:3) & 4/20/37 (3:6). See also: 1930 U.S. Census (Richmond Co., GA), which notes Burke as a juvenile delinquent.

John P. Goodman (black, age 20). *Murder.* The crime was committed on 8/30/1936 in DeKalb County. Handgun slaying of 20-year-old Willie Thomas (black), who was shot multiple times. Motive: a dispute about a liquor payment. Goodman had also robbed one female of his own color that night and attempted to rape another. He was executed at the Georgia State Prison Farm (Milledgeville) on May 14, 1937. Source: *Atlanta Daily World*, 9/1/36 (1:1) & 9/16/36 (1:6). See also: 1936 Fulton Co. death cert. at date. Also: 1937 Baldwin Co. death cert. no. 11262. See also: 1920 U.S. Census (DeKalb Co., GA), which notes Goodman as a minor.

Will Lacy, alias "Will Brown" (black, age 39). *Murder.* The crime was committed on 7/6/1935 in Cook County. Shotgun slayings of mother and daughter 49-year-old Donie Lockhart Mitchell and 26-year-old Nellie Ruth Harris (blacks). Motive: personal problems; exact details obscure. This double killer was executed on May 21, 1937. Source: *Adel (GA) News*, 7/12/35 (5:1), 5/7/37 (4:4) & 5/28/37 (5:3). See also: 1935 Cook Co. death cert. nos. 16955 and 19463.

Eli C. Melton (white, age 28). *Rape.* The crime was committed on 2/13/1936 in Muscogee County. Indecent assault on the person of an 18-year-old white female (name withheld) as part of a carjacking incident during which the girl's male escort was held at bay with a loaded pistol. This sex offender was executed on May 21, 1937. Source: *Times-Enterprise* (Thomasville, GA), 7/23/36 (5:4) & 5/21/37 (1:2). See also Melton's grave marker in Cemetery No. 5, Fort Benning.

Leonard Brown (black, age 16). *Murder.* The crime was committed on 7/16/1936 in Richmond County. Executed for the killing of 46-year-old Walter E. Barnard (white), a garage man who was hit between the eyes with a crowbar. The culprit then loaded the victim's body into his own automobile and drove with it for 15 miles before stashing the same in a deserted shack. Motive: robbery and ingratitude. This was the thanks that Mr. Barnard received for taking in a stray boy. The latter was executed on May 24, 1937. Source: *Augusta (GA) Chronicle*, 7/17/36 (1:7), 7/18/36 (1:1), 7/19/36 (1:1) & 5/25/37 (10:5). See also: 1930 U.S. Census (Augusta, GA), which notes Brown, and 1920 U.S. Census (Danville, VA), which notes Mr. Barnard before he came to Georgia.

Mose Trammell (black, age 35). *Murder.* The crime was committed on 4/2/1936 in Troup County. Uxoricide, etc. Executed for the murders of 24-year-old Willie Mae Palmore Trammell and 22-year-old Ella Pearl Palmore (blacks), they having respectively been his wife and his sister-in-law. Motive: irate husband. The killer's spouse had absented herself from their Atlanta home and taken refuge with relatives in Troup County. Enraged by this, Mose Trammell went there armed with a knife and attacked everyone he encountered at the home of his in-laws. The bodies of the two fatally slashed women were carried from the house. The body of Mose Trammell was later carried from the execution chamber at the Georgia State Prison Farm on May 28, 1937. Source: *LaGrange (GA) Daily News*, 5/13/36 (1:5) & 5/28/37 (1:3). Appeal: 183 GA 711–715. See also: 1936 Troup Co. death cert. nos. 12334 and 12335.

Willie Hopkins (black, age 21). *Rape.* The crime was committed on 4/26/1937 in Burke County. Indecent assault on the person of a 33-year-old white female (name withheld) described as "a Blythe area farm wife" under circumstances that had to be tamped down in local newspaper reports to prevent civil unrest. "I must've been crazy!" was all that Hopkins would say. He was executed at the Georgia State Prison Farm (Milledgeville) on June 14, 1937. Source: *The True Citizen* (Waynesboro, GA), 4/30/37 (1:7), 5/14/37 (1:7) & 6/18/37 (1:6).

Edgar Rose (white, age 20). *Murder.* The crime was committed on 12/29/1936 in Dougherty County. Prison-guard killer. Executed for the shotgun slaying of 50-year-old Thomas Levy Lewis (white) while attempting to escape from the Dougherty County chain gang. Rose had made the transition from minor offender to major offender, but he paid a non-refundable price for so doing. This was exacted from him by the State of Georgia on June 18, 1937. Source: *Albany (GA) Herald*, 12/29/36 (1:4) & 12/30/36 (1:2). *Times-Enterprise* (Thomasville, GA), 12/30/36 (1:4), 12/31/36 (1:4) & 6/18/37 (1:7).

James Worthy (black, age 23). *Murder.* The crime was committed on 10/10/1936 in Fulton County. Handgun slaying of 49-year-old Berry C. Dodson (white), a trolley motorman. Motive: the homicide victim would not allow Worthy to board his vehicle because of being drunk and disorderly. James Worthy walked to the Georgia electric chair on June 18, 1937. Source: *Atlanta Journal*, 6/18/37 (9:5). Appeal: 184 GA 402. See also: 1930 U.S. Census (Fulton Co., GA), which notes both parties.

Charlie Young (black, age 33). *Murder.* The crime was committed on 2/27/1937 in Burke County. Uxoricide. Fatal stabbing of 32-year-old Estella Smith Young (black), she having been pierced through the breasts. Motive: not discernible based on surviving documentation. The original court papers for this case are not publicly accessible. This wife-killer was executed at the Georgia State Prison Farm on June 25, 1937. Source: 1937 Baldwin Co. death cert. no. 14065. Also: 1937 Burke Co. death cert. no. 5339. See also: 1920 U.S. Census (Burke Co., GA), which notes the murdered woman by her maiden name.

Mitchell Jackson (black, age 26). *Murder.* The crime was committed on 5/29/1937 in Fulton County. Executed for the killing of 52-year-old Birdie Adele Doughty Fluker (white), who was battered on the head with a hammer, thrown into her china closet and there set ablaze after being doused with turpentine. Motive: temper tantrum. The homicide victim had employed the killer as a chauffeur. Her husband had fired Jackson from that position but Mrs. Fluker allowed herself to be sweet-talked into giving him another chance. Then a money matter arose. Jackson insisted that $1.50 was due him. The lady of the house balked at this and the culprit repaid her magnanimity in the manner described above. He was electrocuted on July 9, 1937. Source: *Augusta (GA) Chronicle,* 5/30/37 (1:8). *Marietta (GA) Journal,* 5/31/37 (1:1). *Atlanta Journal,* 7/9/37 (1:3).

Willie E. Douberly (white, age 25). *Murder.* The crime was committed on 6/7/1936 in Chatham County. Executed for the killing of 55-year-old Peter Carellas (white), an automobile parts salvage man who was battered to death in his scrap yard with a large iron cotter pin. The murdered man also had one of his eyes gouged out. Motive: apparent robbery, the decedent's pockets being turned inside out. The killer was executed at the Georgia State Prison Farm on July 30, 1937. Source: *Savannah Evening Press,* 6/8/36 (12:6) & 7/30/37 (1:1). Appeal: 184 GA 577.

Lawrence Ward (white, age 51). *Murder.* The crime was committed on 11/25/1936 in Jeff Davis County. Child killer. Executed for the murder of 14-year-old Maude Salters (white), his stepdaughter, whom he fatally beat and stomped on in the presence of her mother. The latter was bound with chains at first to render her helpless and unable to interfere. Motive: the girl had gone out on a date of which Ward did not approve. He was made to pay the death penalty for this excessive act of discipline on August 13, 1937. Source: *Times-Enterprise* (Thomasville, GA), 12/9/36 (1:2), 12/10/36 (1:2) & 8/13/37 (1:6).

Clinton Pinson (black, age 37). *Murder.* The crime was committed on 3/20/1934 in Fulton County. Handgun slaying of 26-year-old Roscoe Harbin (white), who was shot three times. Motive: vindictiveness. Harbin had previously struck Pinson in an argument. The latter did not stop to consider the repercussions of gunning down his antagonist. Nor was he the type to simply walk away. The Georgia electric chair put an end to Pinson's quandary on September 29, 1937. Source: *Atlanta Constitution,* 3/21/34 (5:3) & 9/30/37 (2:6). Appeal: 184 GA 333. See also: 1934 Fulton Co. death cert. no. 6769 and 1937 Baldwin Co. death cert. no. 22003.

Willie Frank Daniels (black, age 24). *Murder.* The crime was committed on 11/29/1936 in Clarke County. Police killer. Executed for the handgun slaying of 43-year-old Herman Karl Stein (white). Motive: resisting arrest. The trial court found no mitigating factors and Daniels was sentenced to death. The sentence was carried out at the Georgia State Prison Farm (Milledgeville) on December 27, 1937. It was the last execution there. Source: *Augusta (GA) Chronicle,* 11/30/36 (1:1). *Times-Enterprise* (Thomasville, GA), 12/27/37 (8:4). See also: 1930 U.S. Census (Clarke Co., GA), which notes the homicide victim.

1938

Archie Haywood (black, age 41). *Murder.* The crime was committed on 9/11/1937 in Worth County. Electrocuted for the ax murder of another black man named Will Robinson, whose exact age is not recorded. Motive: robbery. The former state prison complex at Milledgeville having been decommissioned by this time, death row had been relocated to a newer institution near Reidsville. This morgue-like, whitewashed edifice soon became notorious as "the Prison in the Pines" and continues in operation to this day. Archie Haywood became the first condemned inmate to be executed there on May 6, 1938. Source: *Sylvester (GA) Local*, 9/16/37 (1:5) & 5/12/38 (1:2). See also: 1938 Tattnall Co. death cert. no. 13409.

George Thomas (black, age 21). *Murder.* The crime was committed on 3/26/1938 in Fulton County. Executed for the shotgun slaying of 30-year-old Gordon Haston (white), who was grievously wounded on a shooting range and died eight days later. Motive: robbery and carjacking. The killer ended up in the Georgia electric chair on May 13, 1938. Source: *Atlanta Constitution*, 3/27/38 (1:4) & 5/14/38 (4:5).

Levy L. Rozier (white, age 40). *Rape.* The crime for which he was executed was committed on 2/16/1937 in Ware County. Serial child molester. Specifically condemned for indecently assaulting a 7-year-old white female (name withheld) under circumstances that are too appalling to allow further description. Additionally sentenced to 20 years' imprisonment for forcing himself on an 8-year-old black female in Laurens County. Rozier also faced prosecution for ravishing a 9-year-old black female on the same day that he attacked the 7-year-old white girl. Another very young white female was similarly mistreated by him on Easter Sunday 1937. He suffered death in the electric chair on June 17, 1938. Source: *Waycross (GA) Journal-Herald*, 4/30/37 (8:4). *Times-Enterprise* (Thomasville, GA), 4/30/37 (3:8). Appeal: 185 GA 317–321. Also: 1938 Tattnall Co. death cert. no. 16212 and Rozier's grave marker in Walnut Creek Baptist Church Cemetery, Wilkinson Co.

Ralph Benton (black, age 39). *Murder.* The crime was committed on 1/2/1937 in Fulton County. Fatal stabbing of 29-year-old John Jinks (black), a fellow convict then serving time on the Fulton County chain gang. Motive: prisoner violence. The life journey of Ralph Benton ended in the execution chamber at the new Georgia State Prison on October 28, 1938. Source: *Atlanta Constitution*, 1/3/37 (5:6) & 10/29/38 (4:4).

Walter Melton (black, age 30). *Murder.* The crime was committed on 1/1/1938 in Charlton County. Prison-guard killer. Executed for the murder of 58-year-old Pratt G. Mizell (white), who was gagged and tied up with a blanket over his face in such a manner that he was smothered thereby. Motive: jailbreak. Melton paid with his life for this at the new Georgia State Prison on October 28, 1938. Source: 1938 Tattnall Co. death cert. no. 26879. Appeal: 186 GA 660. See also: 1930 U.S. Census (Camden Co., GA), which notes Mr. Mizell.

Isaac McBride (black, age 30). *Murder.* The crime was committed on 1/14/1938 in Clinch County. Police killer. Handgun slaying of 32-year-old Carey A. Thomas (white), a Clinch County deputy who was shot three times. Motive: resisting arrest. The Georgia electric chair added Isaac McBride to its list of accomplishments on November 4, 1938. Source: *Augusta (GA) Chronicle*, 1/17/38 (1:6). *Times-Enterprise* (Thomasville, GA), 3/9/38

(8:2). See also: 1938 Tattnall Co. death cert. no. 29506. Also: 1930 U.S. Census (Clinch Co., GA), which notes "Cary" Thomas.

Buck Etheridge (black, age 19). *Murder.* The crime was committed on 2/1/1938 in Henry County. Executed for the deliberate killing of 68-year-old Will Combs (black), who was stabbed multiple times with an ice pick and set afire with kerosene. Motive: the homicide victim had intended to press charges against Etheridge for stealing a shotgun. The latter went to the electric chair on November 10, 1938. Source: 1938 Henry Co. death cert. no. 4042 and Tattnall Co. death cert. no. 29508. Appeal: 187 GA 30–40. See also: 1930 U.S. Census (Henry Co., GA), which notes Combs.

Frank Knight (black, age 26). *Rape.* The crime was committed on 2/24/1938 in Bryan County. Indecent assault on the person of a 14-year-old white female (name withheld), who was waylaid as she walked from her home to her family's woodlot. The attacker had been released from the county chain gang only a few days earlier after serving a 2-year stint for burglary. He had originally come from Edgefield, SC. The penalty of death by high voltage was carried out in this case on November 25, 1938. Source: *Butler (GA) Herald*, 12/1/38 (8:3). *Pembroke (GA) Journal*, 2/25/38 (1:3), 3/25/38 (1:1) & 11/25/38 (2:2).

George Gilbert (black, age 28). *Rape.* The crime was committed on 11/11/1937 in Troup County. Indecent assault on the person of an adult white female (name withheld) who was attacked in her own home. The woman did not hear him breaking into the place because she was deaf. She was therefore set upon without any inkling of impending danger. Gilbert was taken to the Georgia electric chair on November 30, 1938. Source: *La Grange (GA) Daily News*, 12/2/37 (1:4), 6/3/38 (1:8) & 10/27/38 (1:3). Also: 1938 Tattnall Co. death cert. no. 29513.

Raymond Carter (black, age 23), **Charlie Rucker** (black, age 18) and **Jim Henry Williams** (black, age 21). *Murder.* Their crime was committed on 10/25/1938 in Butts County. Police killers. All three executed for the handgun slaying of 55-year-old Charles T. Thornton (white), the police chief at Jackson. Motive: resisting interrogation. The lawman had sought to question this trio for suspicious activity. Williams pulled out a pistol and opened fire. The other two made no effort to restrain him. They all wound up dead for this when they went to the electric chair on December 9, 1938. Source: *Jackson (GA) Progress-Argus*, 10/27/38 (1:6). See also: 1938 Tattnall Co. death cert. nos. 32436, 32438 and 32441. Also: 1930 U.S. Census (Butts Co., GA), which notes the murdered police chief.

Arthur Mack (black, age 25) and **Arthur Perry** (black, age 24). *Murder.* Their crime was committed on 7/31/1937 in Muscogee County. Both executed for the killing of 47-year-old Charles R. Helton (white), whom they attacked with knives when he refused to sell them some beer. These stabbers died by high voltage at the Georgia State Prison on December 9, 1938. Source: *Times-Enterprise* (Thomasville, GA), 8/5/37 (8:6). See also: 1938 Tattnall Co. death cert. nos. 32439 and 32440. Also: 1930 U.S. Census (Harris Co., GA), which notes Mr. Helton.

Willie Russell (black, age 31). *Murder.* The crime was committed on

10/15/1938 in Cobb County. Executed for the murders of 66-year-old George Washington Camp and 26-year-old Christine Camp Pauls plus the grievous wounding of 9-year-old Cecil Pauls (whites), who were all traumatically beaten with an ax handle. The victims comprised three generations of the same family. Motive: a dispute over wages. The killer had previously worked for Mr. Camp. He felt that he was due five dollars. Camp offered him a quarter. It was a parsimonious gesture that made Willie Russell go berserk. He was legally put to death on December 9, 1938. Source: *Marietta (GA) Journal*, 10/18/38 (1:6) & 12/9/38 (1:8).

1939

Wilson Wright (black, age 18). *Murder.* The crime was committed on 7/10/1937 in Chatham County. Executed for the killing of 66-year-old Morris Center (white), a storekeeper who was fatally pistol-whipped in his place of business. Motive: armed robbery. The Georgia electric chair cured Wilson Wright of his criminal tendencies on January 25, 1939. Source: *Times-Enterprise* (Thomasville, GA), 4/19/38 (5:4). See also: 1939 Tattnall Co. death cert. no. 1973. Also: 1930 U.S. Census (Savannah, GA), which notes the murdered man.

Harvey L. Nelson (white, age 35). *Murder.* The crime was committed on 5/26/1938 in Ware County. Filicide. Handgun slaying of 12-year-old J. C. Nelson (white, full name not recorded in any known source) as part of a foolhardy scheme to defraud an insurance company. Nelson had also fatally poisoned his wife in a prior incident. Ethel Nelson (white, age 32) had died in Coffee County on 12/10/1936. Her husband was sentenced to 20 years' imprisonment when a watered-down verdict was returned in that case. He was free pending appeal when he killed his own son for the sake of a $300 life insurance payout. He was executed on June 23, 1939. Source: *Augusta (GA) Chronicle*, 7/27/38 (1:6). *Waycross (GA) Journal-Herald*, 5/28/38 (8:3). Appeal: 187 GA 576–584. See also: 1939 Tattnall Co. death cert. no. 14882.

J. D. Vaughn (black, age 25). *Rape.* The crime was committed on 5/6/1939 in Walton County. Executed for indecently assaulting an adult white female (name withheld) in an incident that was described as "one of the worst in all the history of Walton county." The culprit also raped a black woman later that same day. He was caught when the latter's husband chased him down. Nothing could be found to say in Vaughn's defense, according to the hometown newspaper. Local blacks were too disgusted with him to even question the degree of his guilt. The electric chair closed this matter on July 7, 1939. It is doubtful that "J. D. Vaughn" was the actual name of this offender. His true identity is anyone's guess. Source: *Walton (GA) Tribune*, 5/26/39 (1:8) & 7/14/39 (1:3). See also: 1939 Tattnall Co. death cert. no. 17581.

Arthur E. Barker (white, age 34). *Murder.* The crime was committed on 10/31/1938 in Gwinnett County. Uxoricide. Executed for the murder of 33-year-old Millie Barker (white), who had her head forcibly pulled back by the hair and her throat cut by a razor with such intensity as to very nearly decapitate her. Motive: suspicion of infidelity. This wife-killer was put to death on July 26, 1939. Source: *Augusta (GA) Chronicle*, 7/27/39 (1:5). Appeal: 188 GA 332–336. See also:

1938 Gwinnett Co. death cert. no. 26112. Also: 1930 U.S. Census (Gwinnett Co., GA), which notes both parties.

Marion Hunter (black, age 24). *Murder.* The crime was committed on 12/21/1938 in Chatham County. Mass killer. Executed for the murders of 34-year-old James Sidney Tillman, 29-year-old Mary Eliza Tillman (whites, a married couple) and their two daughters: Clara Pearl Tillman (age 8) and Leola Tillman (age 6) as well as another white man named Thomas Chester (age 42), who was unrelated to them. The Tillmans were an impoverished family who lived in a roadside shack. They depended on what was then called "Public Relief" and any other pennies that they could scrounge. Their regular alms consisted of a gallon of milk, a loaf of bread and five silver dimes dispensed on a weekly basis. Marion Hunter stealthily crept into the bleak abode of the Tillmans late at night. He was armed with an iron pipe. It apparently had an elbow joint on one end because it worked like a mace to smash in the skulls of all four Tillmans, adults and little children alike, as they lay asleep on their pallets. The killer then stole an old shotgun that was there and went across the street (the former coastal highway) to a gas station where Thomas Chester, the night attendant, sat dozing in a chair. A single blast took his entire face off. Marion Hunter paused there just long enough to jimmy a coin-operated machine and steal all the nickels it contained. Motive: "Because I wanted to get me some money!" in Hunter's own words. His choice of targets belied this. The head of the Georgia NAACP even wrote off this case after an investigation by his organization confirmed that Hunter had absolutely nothing in his favor by way of mitigation or police misconduct. Even so, the condemned man was dragged to the electric chair proclaiming his innocence. The lethal current ended his babbling on August 4, 1939. Source: *Atlanta Constitution,* 12/22/38 (1:2). *Times-Enterprise* (Thomasville, GA), 8/4/39 (4:4). See also: 1938 Chatham Co. death cert. nos. 30230 thru 30234.

Clarence Sheffield (black, age 35). *Murder.* The crime was committed on 10/22/1938 in Ware County. Shotgun slaying of 31-year-old Bennie Ralls (black). Motive: the killer felt that Ralls had slighted him. This was no excuse for murder, at least in the eyes of the law. Clarence Sheffield learned so the hard way when he was seated in the Georgia electric chair on September 29, 1939. Source: 1939 Tattnall Co. death cert. no. 22359. Appeal: 188 GA 1–15. See also: 1910 U.S. Census (Bibb Co., GA), which notes Ralls as a minor.

Sheppard Bruno (black, age 44). *Murder.* The crime was committed on 9/18/1938 in Dougherty County. Shotgun slayings of 32-year-old Walter E. Moree and 33-year-old Willie Dorsey Aultman (whites), a separately married man and woman who were parked in a lonely lane unknown to their respective spouses. Motive: robbery. The woman was also shot once in the back of the head with a pistol and the man four times therewith. Theirs had been a fateful tryst indeed. The marauder who killed them was executed on November 17, 1939. Source: *Albany (GA) Herald,* 9/19/38 (1:4). *Augusta (GA) Chronicle,* 9/20/38 (1:3). Appeal: 189 GA 74–76. See also: 1938 Dougherty Co. death cert. nos. 22859 and 22860 plus 1939 Tattnall Co. death cert. no. 27414.

James W. Bivins (black, age 19). *Murder.* The crime was committed on 10/22/1939 in Schley County. Shotgun slayings of 23-year-old Thelmon Terry, 50-year-old Mollie Frazier and 35-year-old Coley Richardson (blacks). Motive: rampage. Bivins was on a manhunt for his brother-in-law because that man had shot and wounded his beloved sister. Unable to find him, Bivins then went on to terrorize the Ellaville "Colored District" by blasting away at anyone who dared to oppose him or say anything at all to him. Local blacks were furious with Bivins for shooting up their neighborhood and gunning down three innocent members of their community. The law, however, was allowed to take its course. Closure came on November 21, 1939, when this triple killer was executed at the Georgia State Prison. No appeals had been filed on his behalf. Source: *Ellaville (GA) Sun*, 10/27/39 (1:3) & 12/1/39 (1:3).

1940

James Johnson, alias "Fisher" (black, age 27) and **Joe Mathis** (black, age 27). *Murder.* Their crime was committed on 9/13/1939 in Newton County. Handgun slayings and severe pistol-whippings of 73-year-old John E. Trainer and 72-year-old Emma Trainer (whites), a married couple. Motive: robbery and home invasion. Both of these killers died in the Georgia electric chair on February 9, 1940. Source: *Augusta (GA) Chronicle*, 1/10/40 (4:7). *Master Detective*, 5/51. Also: 1940 Tattnall Co. death cert. nos. 5135 and 5136. Also see: 1930 U.S. Census (Newton Co., GA), which notes Mr. & Mrs. Trainer.

William L. Mims (black, age 37). *Murder.* The crime was committed on 10/4/1938 in Bibb County. Fatal stabbing of 57-year-old Dave F. Mitchell (white). Motive: obnoxious drunk. The homicide victim had reproached Mims for shouting profanities in public. That was all it took for this imbiber of cheap mash to redirect his malice at Mr. Mitchell. The subsequent sentence of death by electrocution was carried out in this case on March 22, 1940. Source: *Macon (GA) Evening News*, 10/6/38 (1:6). Appeal: 188 GA 702–706. See also: 1938 Bibb Co. death cert. no. 24831 and 1940 Tattnall Co. death cert. no. 8192.

Robert Brown (black, age 25). *Murder.* The crime was committed on 7/29/1939 in Jefferson County. Shotgun slaying of 37-year-old Keelon Eugene Thompson (white), a storekeeper. Motive: obnoxious drunk. Brown had been ejected from Thompson's place of business for disorderly conduct. Inebriates were not allowed there. Brown felt himself ill-used. So he went back to Thompson's store with a loaded shotgun and opened fire. He ended up in the Georgia electric chair on May 17, 1940. Source: *Augusta (GA) Chronicle*, 7/30/39 (1:3), 7/31/39 (2:4) & 8/30/39 (8:7). See also: 1939 Jefferson Co. death cert. no. 24161 and 1940 Tattnall Co. death cert. no. 13538.

Curtis Barkley (black, age 33) and **Oscar Fields** (black, age 24). *Rape.* The crime for which they were executed was committed on 10/1/1939 in Fulton County. Serial rapists. Specifically condemned for indecently assaulting 20-year-old Mary Frances Thomas (white), whom they carjacked for that purpose. This pair is confirmed to have also (on 10/28/39) carjacked two young couples who were double dating that night. The captives were brought to a remote spot and robbed of whatever intrinsic valuables they had on their persons. Then the two females of their party, Laverne Long (white, age 17) and Eva Krimes (white, age 16), were forcibly ravished by the culprits who took turns doing so while the other held off their boyfriends at gunpoint. The names of these three young ladies are here mentioned only because they have already been made a matter of public record in other published sources. Their attackers were legally put to death on August 16, 1940. Source: *Atlanta Journal*, 8/16/40 (2:3). Appeal: 190 GA 641–643. See also: 1940 Tattnall Co. death cert. nos. 21176 and 21177.

Eddie Brown (black, age 29). *Robbery with violence.* The crime was committed on 12/20/1939 in Lowndes County. Executed for shooting and severely wounding 20-year-old Elias Rykard (white), a filling station attendant, during the course of an armed stickup. A pistol was used during the commission of this felony. The gunman was declared a menace to society and ordered for execution. The sentence was carried out at the Georgia State Prison on August 23, 1940. Source: *Savannah Evening Press*, 8/23/40 (15:8). *Valdosta (GA) Daily Times*, 12/22/39 (5:2) & 8/23/40 (5:7). *Times-Enterprise* (Thomasville, GA), 12/22/39 (5:4). See also: 1940 Tattnall Co. death cert. no. 21179. Also see: 1940 U.S. Census (Lowndes Co., GA), which notes Elias Rykard.

Charlie Josey (black, age 21). *Murder.* The crime was committed on 7/10/1940 in Pike County. Shotgun slaying of 32-year-old Ollie Joe Cannafax, Jr. (white). Motive: disgruntled employee. The two men had had an argument. Josey then went to the homicide victim's house and told Mrs. Cannafax that her husband needed his shotgun. She handed this over unawares. The result became clear with Mr. Cannafax was slain with his own weapon. Charlie Josey atoned for this in the Georgia electric chair on August 23, 1940. Source: *Pike County Journal*, 7/12/40 (1:6) & 8/2/40 (1:6). See also: 1940 Tattnall Co. death cert. no. 21178 plus the gravestone of O. J. Cannafax in Zebulon Methodist Church Cemetery, Zebulon.

Fred Anderson (black, age 17). *Murder.* The crime was committed on 7/10/1937 in Laurens County. Handgun slaying of 20-year-old A. J. Page (white). Motive: big attitude. Anderson and some of his like-minded pals were running through the streets of Dublin on the above date. They took particular pleasure in jostling white people regardless of age or physical condition and dared them to do anything about it. They did this to young Mr. Page and when that man dared to say "Hey!" Anderson pulled out a pistol and shot him down. Three years of appeals followed, showing that this killer was not railroaded by a "racist justice system." He was executed at the Georgia State Prison on October 4, 1940. Source: *Augusta (GA) Chronicle*, 7/12/37 (3:4). Appeal: 190 GA 455–460. See also: 1940 Tattnall Co. death cert. no. 26159 and 1930 U.S. Census (Laurens Co., GA), which notes A. J. Page. The homicide victim's gravestone (in Blue Springs Baptist Church Cemetery, Rockledge, GA) doesn't identify him by anything more than his initials.

Henry William Hicks (black, age 18). *Rape.* The crime was committed on 9/14/1940 in Thomas County. Indecent assault on the person of a 16-year-old white female (name withheld). The details had to be censored to prevent mob violence. The trial was held in

Dougherty County because the selection of an impartial jury necessitated a change of venue. Hicks had his constitutional rights ensured by such measures, but this did not make him any less guilty. He made a voluntary confession that left nothing to the imagination. Prison guards escorted Hicks to the Georgia electric chair on October 18, 1940. Source: *Thomasville (GA) Press*, 9/27/40 (1:3). See also: 1940 Tattnall Co. death cert. no. 28730.

John William Sutton (black, age 22). *Murder.* The crime was committed on 9/12/1940 in Whitfield County. Fatal beating of 67-year-old Arthur L. Edwards (white), a storekeeper who was attacked in his place of business. Motive: robbery. The killer was executed on November 8, 1940. Source: *Dalton (GA) Citizen*, 9/19/40 (1:8) & 11/14/40 (14:2). See also: 1930 U.S. Census (Whitfield Co., GA), which notes Mr. Edwards. He had been known thereabouts as "Uncle Less."

Robert Lee Brannon, alias "Hardwick" (black, age 39). *Murder.* The crime was committed on 12/24/1930 in Floyd County. Uxoricide. Executed for the Christmas Eve killing of 32-year-old Bessie Brannon (black), who was deliberately chased down and fatally slashed with a knife. Motive: vindictiveness. This wife-killer had already been serving time in the Floyd County jail for spousal abuse. He was granted a holiday furlough and made use of it in the manner described above. The inadequate husband had found it easier to blame his harried wife for his shortcomings rather than himself. Robert Lee Brannon was executed at the Georgia State Prison on December 13, 1940. Source: 1940 Tattnall Co. death cert. no. 31508. Appeal: 188 GA 15–20. See also: 1930 U.S. Census (Rome, GA), which notes both parties.

Buddy Lawrence, known to some as "Andrew Lawrence" (black, age 28). *Murder.* The crime was committed on 8/24/1940 in Bacon County. Gunshot slaying of 56-year-old Alexander Steve Johnson (white), a filling station operator who was ambushed with malice aforethought. The killer lay in wait for Mr. Johnson after he had closed his place of business that night. It is unclear exactly what type of firearm was used. A widow and four children were left in dire straits by this gratuitous act of violence. The electric chair did service in the case of Buddy Lawrence on December 13, 1940. Source: *Waycross (GA) Journal-Herald*, 12/13/40 (1:3). See also: 1940 Bacon Co. death cert. no. 18931 and 1940 Tattnall Co. death cert. no. 31507. Also see: 1940 U.S. Census (Bacon Co., GA), which notes Mr. Johnson.

Jennings Waddell (black, age 35). *Murder.* The crime was committed on 7/20/1940 in Toombs County. Mass killer and child killer. Executed for the hatchet murders of 65-year-old Fannie Wright, 30-year-old Lillie Wright, 12-year-old Annie Wright and 3-year-old Otis Wright (blacks), who were all massacred in their beds. The Wrights were three generations of the same family. Motive: drunken rampage. Waddell trod the last few steps from his cell to his court-ordered death on December 27, 1940. Source: *Vidalia (GA) Advance*, 11/28/40 (1:1). See also: 1940 Tattnall Co. death cert. no. 31509.

1941

Eddie Bennie Hayes (black, age 18) and **Johnny Watson**, alias

"Shropshire" (black, age 31). *Murder.* Their crime was committed on 10/25/1939 in Coweta County. Shotgun slaying of 35-year-old Will Canady (black), whose house was then burned down in an attempt to destroy all traces of what had happened. Motive: robbery and home invasion. These killers were executed on January 3, 1941. Source: *Newnan (GA) Herald,* 3/14/40 (1:6). *Savannah Evening Press,* 1/3/41 (4:8). See also: 1941 Tattnall Co. death cert. nos. 2387 and 2388.

William Henry Bland (black, age 24). *Rape.* The crime was committed on 4/5/1941 in Henry County. All that is known of this case is that it involved an act of gross sexual indecency and necessitated the convening of a special session of Henry County Superior Court to adjudicate the matter. There was no post-conviction appeal. 1941 Tattnall County death certificate no. 12932 confirms that Bland was electrocuted at the Georgia State Prison on May 12, 1941. The superior court minutes book provides no details beyond the fact that a trial took place. Three separate requests for a copy of the indictment went unanswered.

Charlie Anderson (black, age 15) and **Willie Jenkins** (black, age 20). *Murder.* Their crime was committed on 1/7/1938 in Fulton County. Both executed for the shotgun slaying of 44-year-old Thomas Watson Adcock (white), a storekeeper who was blasted in the back when it was found that he had only four dollars in his cash drawer. A double event ended this case at the Georgia State Prison on May 23, 1941. Source: *Atlanta Journal,* 1/8/38 (1:4) & 1/11/38 (7:3). Appeal: 190 GA 556–562. See also: 1941 Tattnall Co. death cert. nos. 12933 and 12934, which note that the killers were respectively aged 18 and 23 at the time of their electrocution. See also Mr. Adcock's gravestone in Concord Baptist Church Cemetery (Rte. 101), Paulding Co.

Albert Alford (black, age 34). *Rape.* The crime was committed on 3/2/1941 in Hart County. Indecent assault on the person of a 72-year-old white female (name withheld) who was attacked in her own home on a "drizzling" Sunday afternoon while she was in the act of shucking corn. The aged woman tried to make a run for it but was pounced on by the assailant. He then forced her into a bedroom, tied her wrists, neck and ankles with strips torn from sheets to the four posts of her bed and then proceeded to do further unspeakable things to her. Six days later he attempted to do the same thing to another Hart County woman. It is significant to note that during this time Alford was a so-called trusty on the Hart County chain gang. This was how he upheld the honor system then reserved for "non violent offenders." It was incidents like these—more than anything else—that led to the discontinuance of the chain gangs in the 1950s. As for Albert Alford, he was executed at the Georgia State Prison on October 10, 1941. Source: *Hartwell (GA) Sun,* 3/14/41 (1:5). Appeal: 192 GA 650–651. See also: 1941 Tattnall Co. death cert. no. 25438.

1942

James Shivers (black, age 39). *Rape.* The crime was committed on an unknown date in Fayette County. The little information that has survived about this case consists of a State Prison Inmate File and a death certificate. The latter confirms that Shivers was electrocuted on January 30, 1942.

The original trial papers for *State vs. Shivers* could not be located despite a diligent search by Fayette County courthouse personnel. Nor is the prison inmate file publicly accessible. See: 1942 Tattnall Co. death cert. no. 1772.

Charlie Strickland (black, age 23). *Murder.* The crime was committed on 10/30/1941 in Terrell County. Shotgun slaying of 21-year-old Essie Mae Smith (black), who was blasted at point-blank range (as she sat at her sewing machine) by an assassin (Strickland) who stood outside her ground floor window. Motive: heterosexual jealousy. The killer was executed at the Georgia State Prison (Reidsville) on January 31, 1942. Source: *Dawson (GA) News*, 12/11/41 (5:1) & 2/5/42 (5:5). See also: 1941 Tattnall Co. death cert. no. 27978.

Edward Leroy Morton (black, age 25). *Murder.* The crime was committed on 10/7/1939 in Jefferson County. Police killer. Handgun slaying of 24-year-old Louis D. Hubbard (white), a Jefferson County deputy. Motive: resisting a raid on an illegal still. Morton paid with his own life for this at the Georgia State Prison (Reidsville) on February 6, 1942. Source: *Atlanta Daily World*, 2/7/42 (1:8). GA State Supreme Court case. no. 13287. See also: 1939 Jefferson Co. death cert. no. 24169 and 1942 Tattnall Co. death cert. no. 4001.

John Miller, alias "Henry Smith" (black, age 35). *Rape.* The crime was committed on 1/21/1942 in DeKalb County. Indecent assault on the person of an adult white female described only as "a farmer's wife." The attacker pled guilty and waived a jury trial in Stone Mountain Circuit Court. Less than three weeks later he was formally condemned at a special session of DeKalb County Superior Court. No appeals were filed. The sentence was carried out on March 6, 1942. Source: *Atlanta Daily World*, 2/5/42 (1:7). See also: 1942 Tattnall Co. death cert. no. 6687.

Howard P. Cone (white, age 23). *Murder.* The crime was committed on 6/22/1941 in Thomas County. Executed for the mutilation murder of 27-year-old Roy Marion Tucker (white), who was butchered in his own bed "Jack the Ripper" style. The decedent's head was cut off and placed elsewhere in the room. His body was "laid open from neck to crotch" with ribs pried apart and internal organs mangled. Motive: alcoholic frenzy, or so the killer said. On March 11, 1942, a post-execution autopsy probably saw Howard Cone laid out the same way. Source: *Times-Enterprise* (Thomasville, GA), 6/23/41 (1:3) & 3/11/42 (1:5).

Norman Williams (white, age 27). *Murder.* The crime was committed on 7/19/1937 in Elbert County. Handgun slaying of 58-year-old Lon Nathan Fortson (white). Motive: desperate fugitive. A convicted burglar, Williams had escaped from the Brooks County chain gang. He holed up in a shack on Mr. Fortson's farm. The latter unknowingly went to show the place to a prospective tenant on the above date. Williams saw him coming. His reaction was to shoot first and ask questions later. The prospective tenant and the farmer's son were also painfully wounded. Norman Williams ended up in the Georgia electric chair on May 15, 1942. Source: *Marietta (GA) Journal*, 7/20/37 (1:3). *Augusta (GA) Chronicle*, 9/15/37 (12:6) & 5/16/42 (10:7). Appeal: 192 GA 247–258. See also Mr. Fortson's gravestone in Elmhurst Cemetery, Elberton.

Dock Moore (black, age 24). *Murder.* The crime was committed on 4/3/1941 in Fulton County. Handgun slaying of 35-year-old Glenn A. Baxley (white), a parking lot attendant who was deliberately followed home from his place of employment. Motive: armed robbery. The culprit was put to death on July 2, 1942. Source: 1941 Fulton Co. death cert. no. 9156 and 1942 Tattnall Co. death cert. no. 16123. Appeal: 193 GA 877–882.

Son T. Mosley (black, age 19). *Murder.* The crime was committed on 10/16/1938 in Taylor County. Uxoricide. Ax murder of 22-year-old Minnie Pearl Hooten Mosley (black). Motive: adultery on her part. This angry young husband was executed at the Georgia State Prison on July 10, 1942. Source: *Butler (GA) Herald,* 4/13/39 (1:6), 6/25/42 (1:6) & 7/16/42 (1:5). GA Sup. Ct. case no. 12985. See also: 1938 Taylor Co. death cert. no. 26884 and 1942 Tattnall Co. death cert. no. 16120. Also: 1920 U.S. Census (Taylor Co., GA), which notes the homicide victim by her maiden name.

Charles E. Martin (white, age 24). *Murder.* The crime was committed on 2/3/1941 in DeKalb County. Uxoricide. Fatal stabbing of 24-year-old Dorothy A. Martin (white), who was knifed multiple times. Motive: marital estrangement. This particular wife-killer paid the full penalty of the law when he was made to sit in the Georgia electric chair on October 16, 1942. There was no watered-down verdict in his case. Source: *Marietta (GA) Journal,* 3/11/41 (1:6). See also: 1941 DeKalb Co. death cert. no. 3522 and 1942 Tattnall Co. death cert. no. 25147.

Buster Shaw (black, age 20). *Murder.* The crime was committed on 8/4/1942 in Brantley County. Mass killer. Executed for the handgun slayings of a white family consisting of 66-year-old George R. Strickland and 39-year-old Amanda Strickland (a married couple) and their two sons: Riley Strickland (age 13) and Harvey Strickland (age 9). Further details of the crime scene cannot be described with any adherence to decorum. Quadruple killer Buster Shaw died in the Georgia electric chair on October 16, 1942. Source: *Augusta (GA) Chronicle,* 8/15/42 (1:5). See also: 1942 Brantley Co. death cert. nos. 16678 thru 16681 and 1942 Tattnall Co. death cert. no. 22876.

W. Z. Willingham, alias "W. Z. Lewis" (black, age 26). *Murder.* The crime was committed on 8/7/1942 in Thomas County. Fatal stabbing of 43-year-old George McMath (black), a deaf-mute who was knifed multiple times. His body was tumbled into a railroad culvert. Motive: gambling dispute with the added element of robbery because the homicide victim's coin purse was stolen after he had been killed. The culprit was an Alabama drifter. His full name is not recorded in any known record. He was executed at the Georgia State Prison on November 26, 1942. Source: *Times-Enterprise* (Thomasville, GA), 8/11/42 (5:1), 8/19/42 (5:6) & 10/26/42 (1:7). See also: 1942 Thomas Co. death cert. no. 18461 and Tattnall Co. death cert. no. 25148.

1943

Raymond Dowdell (black, age 26). *Murder.* The crime was committed on 2/2/1938 in Muscogee County. Fatal stabbing of 21-year-old Minnie Pearl Thornton (black), who was knifed multiple times at the corner of 5th Avenue and 17th Street, Columbus. Motive: she had refused to give him money to squander. This black-on-black killer went to the electric chair on January 15, 1943. Source: *Columbus (GA) Ledger*, 2/4/38 (11:6). Appeal: 194 GA 578–582. See also: 1943 Tattnall Co. death cert. no. 1717. Also: 1930 U.S. Census (Columbus, GA), which notes the homicide victim.

Richard Smith (black, age 19). *Murder.* The crime was committed on 10/16/1938 in Fulton County. Executed for the killing of 67-year-old Thomas H. Herd (white), a night watchman who had a thick glass milk bottle smashed over his head. Motive: safe cracking gone awry. The culprit was eventually run down and sent to the Georgia electric chair on February 4, 1943. Source: *Atlanta Constitution*, 10/17/38 (1:8), 10/18/38 (1:6) & 2/5/43 (4:6).

Charles Coates (white, age 32). *Murder.* The crime was committed on 12/20/1940 in Catoosa County. Police killer. Handgun slaying of 29-year-old William F. Black Jr. (white), a Georgia state trooper who was shot three times. Motive: traffic-stop-turned-deadly. Coates was a Missouri fugitive. On 10/24/1940 he had been sentenced to a term of life imprisonment there under that state's habitual criminal statute. On 11/29/1940 he broke out of the Buchanan Co. (MO) jail along with two other thugs, they having somehow acquired the kitchen cutlery. Coates made it eastward to Chattanooga, where he reportedly married some female in an impromptu ceremony. She was with him when he tangled with the Georgia state trooper. She became a widow on March 12, 1943, when her husband died in the Georgia electric chair. Source: *Augusta (GA) Chronicle*, 12/22/40 (1:7) & 12/23/40 (1:3). See also: 1943 Tattnall Co. death cert. no. 6342.

Lewis Wilcoxon (black, age 17). *Rape.* The crime was committed on 9/22/1940 in Cobb County. Indecent assault on the person of a "young" white female (name withheld) who was attacked in her own house. The culprit was run down by dogs and then admitted his guilt. He died in the Georgia electric chair on March 26, 1943. It is significant to note that almost an entire month went by before the news of this execution was made public. This was because wartime censorship sometimes went to unnecessary lengths. Source: *Marietta (GA) Journal*, 9/23/40 (1:3), 11/11/40 (1:4) & 4/22/43 (1:6). See also: 1943 Tattnall Co. death cert. no. 6341.

Bernice Franklin (black male, age 17). *Murder.* The crime was committed on 3/30/1943 in Wayne County. Executed for the murder of 33-year-old Gladys O'Quinn Cameron (white), who was found face down in her water-filled bathtub with a towel knotted around her neck. Motive: sexual assault. The culprit had been paroled from the Colored Boys Reformatory at Milledgeville eight weeks earlier. He had originally been sent there for attempting to force himself on a white woman in Calhoun County. The Georgia electric chair saw to it that the criminal career of this youthful offender went no further on May 28, 1943. Source: *Jesup (GA) Sentinel*, 4/1/43 (1:4), 4/8/43 (1:2), 4/22/43 (1:7), 4/29/43 (1:7) & 6/3/43 (1:3). See also: 1943 Wayne Co. death cert. no. 8947 and Tattnall Co. death cert. no. 11181.

Joel Luther Palmer (white, age 30). *Murder.* The crime was committed on 7/18/1942 in Tift County. Police killer. Handgun slayings of 55-year-old Joseph Stephen Henderson and 26-year-old Mercer Leroy Denby (whites), they having respectively been the police chief of Tifton and one of his patrolmen. Motive: resisting arrest. Palmer paid the death penalty for this on May 28, 1943. Source: *Times-Enterprise* (Thomasville, GA), 7/20/42 (1:1), 8/29/42 (7:2) & 4/18/43 (5:3). See also: 1942 Tift Co. death cert. nos. 16197 and 20674 plus 1943 Tattnall Co. death cert. no. 11180.

Mose Sims (black, age 22). *Rape.* The crime was committed on 3/5/1942 in Fulton County. Indecent assault on the person of 45-year-old Delores C. Kuehnle (white), who was beaten and sexually violated after being lured from her parked car and chased down on a public sidewalk. The attack was brazen in the extreme. It cost the culprit his life in the manner prescribed by law on June 10, 1943. Source: *Atlanta Constitution*, 6/11/43 (20:1). Appeal: 195 GA 485–492. See also: 1943 Tattnall Co. death cert. no. 13707. Also: 1940 U.S. Census (Atlanta, GA), which notes the target of this atrocious assault.

Edmond Reed (black, age 25). *Murder.* The crime was committed on 8/20/1942 in Bibb County. Police killer. Handgun slaying of 41-year-old John Grady Favors (white). Motive: resisting arrest. No extenuating circumstances being found, the shooter was ordered for execution. The sentence was carried out on July 19, 1943. Source: 1942 Bibb Co. death cert. no. 16630 and 1943 Tattnall Co. death cert. no. 16088. Appeal: 195 GA 842–852.

Adel Johnson (black, age 21). *Rape.* The crime was committed on 1/4/1943 in Fulton County. Indecent assault on the person of a "middle aged" white female during the course of an armed home invasion. The woman's husband was confronted at gunpoint and forced to submit to being tied up. Then the man was made to watch helplessly as the culprit forced himself on his wife. Johnson was an escapee from the Fulton County chain gang. He stole clothing, money and an automobile from the aforesaid couple in a futile bid to outdistance the law. In addition, this same offender forcibly raped a 19-year-old girl of his own color on the same day that he had attacked the white man and woman. He was executed at the Georgia State Prison on August 10, 1943. Source: *Atlanta (GA) Journal*, 1/5/43 (4:3). Appeal: 196 GA 358–361. See also: 1943 Tattnall Co. death cert. no. 25572.

Marlin Hancock (white, age 43). *Murder.* The crime was committed on 1/17/1943 in Paulding County. Executed for the fatal beating and stomping of 38-year-old Hoke Mosely (white), who had bottles smashed over his head in addition to being battered with a lug wrench. Motive: an argument about who should be allowed to drive a car. Hothead Hancock was electrocuted at the Georgia State Prison on August 20, 1943. Source: 1943 Paulding Co. death cert. no. 1493 and Tattnall Co. death cert. no. 20722. Appeal: 196 GA 351–357.

Eugene Pittman (black, age 27). *Murder.* The crime was committed on 4/27/1942 in Polk County. Uxoricide, etc. Executed for the shotgun slayings of 21-year-old Ruby Pittman and 38-year-old Myrtis Goggins (blacks), two illicit lovers. Motive: irate cuckold. The homicide victims had been openly involved in a romantic relationship.

Eugene Pittman resorted to deadly force to exert his husbandly prerogative. Many observers believed that Pittman had been goaded into what he did, but there was no jury nullification in this case. The fault lay with Pittman himself (at least in the eyes of the law) for not having stopped to consider non-violent alternatives. He paid the death penalty at the Georgia State Prison on August 20, 1943. Source: 1942 Polk Co. death cert. nos. 8842 and 8844. Also: 1943 Tattnall Co. death cert. no. 20721. Appeal: 195 GA 598–600.

John Thomas Russell (black, age 27). *Murder.* The crime was committed on 11/23/1942 in Fulton County. Handgun slaying of 57-year-old George H. A. Thomas (white), the manager of the Black Rock Country Club, who was shot in the face with a Colt revolver. Motive: robbery and duplicity. Russell was described as "one of Atlanta's best known negro caddies" who "had worked for Mr. Thomas on and off for ten years." Lately released from the chain gang for some unspecified offense, Russell used Mr. Thomas' keys to clean out the safe in the country club office and abscond in that man's car. This caddie-turned-killer was put to death at the Georgia State Prison on August 20, 1943. Source: *Marietta (GA) Journal*, 11/26/42 (1:1). *Atlanta Constitution*, 8/21/43 (5:4).

Charlie Sexton (black, age 16). *Murder.* The crime was committed on 2/4/1943 in Paulding County. Shotgun slaying of 16-year-old Ernest J. Clonts (black), who was blasted from behind and also had his head mashed by the butt of that weapon. Motive: robbery and deceitfulness. The killer knew that Clonts had eight dollars in his pockets. This is what he did to gain possession of that money after having first put the intended victim off his guard with a phony show of comradeship. Sexton paid the death penalty on August 20, 1943. Source: 1943 Paulding Co. death cert. no. 8394 and Tattnall Co. death cert. no. 20724. Appeal: 196 GA 298–303.

Serena Hodo, alias "Trigg Hodo" (black male, age 22). *Murder.* The crime was committed on 8/12/1943 in Meriwether County. Ax murder of 58-year-old Thomas N. Mosely (white), a shopkeeper who was struck down in the bedroom of his home. Hodo and his accomplice (S. A. Ellison) then seized the keys to the homicide victim's place of business and robbed it for all they could carry. Both culprits were sentenced to death. Hodo was the first to go on September 24, 1943. Source: *Columbus (GA) Enquirer*, 8/18/43 (1:3). Also: 1943 Tattnall Co. death cert. no. 20731. Also: 1940 U.S. Census (Meriwether Co., GA), which notes both parties. See also: S.A. Ellison (executed 12/11/1943).

Tommie Lee Mathis (black, age 22). *Murder.* The crime was committed on 12/10/1942 in Spalding County. Shotgun slaying of 25-year-old Albert Nash (black). Motive: Mathis suspected Nash of petty theft. This did not justify murder in the eyes of the law. The killer was therefore assessed the full penalty of death by electrocution. That sentence was carried out on October 22, 1943. Source: 1942 Spalding Co. death cert. no. 27887 and 1943 Tattnall Co. death cert. no. 23164. Appeal: 196 GA 288–292.

Robert Williams (black, age 19). *Murder.* The crime was committed on

10/25/1942 in Laurens County. Uxoricide. Shotgun slaying of 18-year-old Zennie Lee Holland Williams (black), she having first been forced outdoors by a fire that was set beneath the house wherein she had taken refuge. Motive: marital estrangement. This wrathful young husband went to his own death in the execution chamber of the Georgia State Prison on October 23, 1943. Source: 1942 Laurens Co. death cert. no. 27274 and 1943 Tattnall Co. death cert. no. 25575. Appeal: 196 GA 503–505.

S. A. Ellison (black, age 17). *Murder.* The crime was committed on 8/12/1943 in Meriwether County. Accomplice in the ax murder of 58-year-old Thomas N. Mosely (white), a shopkeeper. Motive: burglary. Ellison's full name is not specified in any known record. He had his execution stayed while authorities dickered about his age, but the final decision went against him. The deciding factors were his full participation in the crime and his having done nothing to restrain the other guilty party (Serena Hodo), with whom he had acted in concert. The death sentence was carried out on December 11, 1943. Source: 1943 Tattnall Co. death cert. no. 28296. See also: 1930 U.S. Census (Meriwether Co., GA), which notes Ellison and his family. See also: Serena Hodo (executed 9/24/43).

H. T. Johnson (black, age 20). *Murder.* The crime was committed on 5/22/1942 in Henry County. Handgun slaying of 20-year-old Grady W. Solomon (black), who succumbed after 17 days in agony. Motive: rivalry for a female. Johnson (whose full name is not specified in any known record) went to the electric chair for this on December 31, 1943. Source: 1942 Henry Co. death cert. no. 12723 and 1943 Tattnall Co. death cert. no. 29688. Appeal: 196 GA 806–813.

1944

Willie Hubbard (black, age 29). *Rape.* The crime was committed on 3/28/1943 in Bleckley County. Indecent assault on the person of 64-year-old Pansy Deese (white), a maiden woman who was brutally manhandled by having an arm twisted behind her preparatory to being violated on her kitchen floor. The culprit had initially approached Miss Deese under the pretense of buying milk. He also stole her humble savings, which amounted to barely ten dollars. Venue changed from Bleckley County to Bibb County. The Georgia electric chair did the rest on January 5, 1944. Source: *Cochran (GA) Journal*, 6/10/43 (1:6). Appeal: 197 GA 77–82. See also: 1944 Tattnall Co. death cert. no. 4028.

Isaac Irwin (white, age 28). *Murder.* The crime was committed on 2/1/1942 in Bibb County. Handgun slayings of 57-year-old John N. Perdue and 60-year-old Lieu Williams Perdue (whites), a married couple. Motive: a dispute about farm work, the killer having been their hired man. He was executed on January 7, 1944. Source: *Official Detective*, 7/42. *Master Detective*, 8/47. See also: 1944 Tattnall Co. death cert. no. 4029. Further see the gravestone of Mr. & Mrs. Perdue in Scruggs Cemetery, Norwood.

Willie Hicks (black, age 18). *Rape.* The crime was committed on 1/30/1943 in Fulton County. Indecent assault on the person of 20-year-old Edna Strickland (white). The young woman and her beau were confronted by the culprit, who threatened them with a pistol. Hicks marched them into a patch of woods at gunpoint. Once there, the young man was held at bay with the aforesaid weapon while Miss Strickland was further mistreated. On February 3, 1944, it came the turn of Willie Hicks to get marched to a destination that was not of his choosing: the execution chamber at the Georgia State Prison. His body was wheeled out of that place feet first just a few minutes later. Source: 1943 Tattnall Co. death cert. no. 4030. Appeal: 196 GA 671–674. See also: 1930 U.S. Census (Fulton Co., GA), which notes the female assault victim as a minor.

Marvin Lewis Lee (black, age 22). *Rape.* The crime was committed on 6/6/1943 in Fulton County. Indecent assault on the person of 14-year-old Frances Gwin (white), who was attacked in her own bed by a gun-toting burglar (later identified as Lee), who also stole items of intrinsic value on the same occasion. This nocturnal marauder was executed on March 7, 1944. Source: 1944 Tattnall Co. death cert. no. 6324. Appeal: 197 GA 123–125.

Rock Reilly Hooten (black, age 26). *Murder.* The crime was committed on 5/12/1943 in Taylor County. Shotgun slaying of 67-year-old Vann Jackson (black), who was bushwhacked as he walked homeward and had the back of his head blown off. Motive: mugged for his wallet. The killer met his own demise in the Georgia electric chair on March 17, 1944. Source: *Butler (GA) Herald*, 5/20/43 (1:5) & 3/23/44 (1:4). See also: 1940 U.S. Census (Taylor Co., GA), which notes "Van" Jackson.

Herbert Rozier (black, age 71). *Murder.* The crime was committed on 4/15/1943 in Laurens County. Shotgun slaying of 45-year-old Wesley G. Davis (white). Motive: hooliganism. Rozier had terrorized a black woman and her child by breaking into their house and shooting up the place. He had also vandalized the woman's automobile by smashing its windows with an ax and ripping up its seats with a knife. Hearing the commotion, Mr. Davis went to investigate. He was met by Rozier, who gunned him down without even saying a word. Tight lipped or not, this cantankerous killer was adjudged a proper subject for capital punishment and was accordingly sentenced to death. He took his last seat in the Georgia electric chair on April 7, 1944. Source: 1944 Tattnall Co. death cert. no. 8595. Appeal: 197 GA 420–426. See also: 1930 U.S. Census (Laurens Co., GA), which notes Mr. Davis.

Oscar Reed (black, age 26). *Murder.* The crime was committed on 5/25/1943 in Dodge County. Executed for the mutilation murder of 30-year-old Lucille Brady Evans (white), who was beaten to death with a heavy work shoe that had metal cleats in its heel. Motive: sexual assault. Reed had "walked away" from the Dodge County convict camp. He had been a trusty there. The woman was attacked as she was in the act of carrying a hoe to her family's cotton field with no one else in sight. Venue changed from Dodge County to Bibb County. Oscar Reed went to his court-ordered death in the Georgia electric chair on April 28, 1944. Source: *Macon (GA) Telegraph*, 5/27/43 (1:6), 9/24/43 (7:4) & 4/29/44 (6:8). *Times-Journal* (Eastman, GA), 5/27/43 (1:1). Appeal: 197 GA 418–420. See also: 1943 Dodge Co. death cert. no. 14788.

Robert Walker (black, age 24). *Rape.* The crime was committed on 12/21/1941 in Jones County. Indecent assault on the person of 54-year-old Maud Hudson (white), a maiden woman who was described as a "cripple." She was all by herself in the house of her sister when the attack was perpetrated. The culprit (later identified as Walker) also stole a gun that he found there. Venue changed from Jones County to Bibb County. Walker walked to his execution at the Georgia State Prison on April 28, 1944. Source: 1944 Tattnall Co. death cert. no. 11217. Appeal: 194 GA 727–735.

Grady Ellison (black, age 35). *Murder.* The crime was committed on 3/28/1943 in Burke County. Executed for the fatal and prolonged beating of 31-year-old Nettie Mobley (black), a woman who had cohabitated with him and by whom he had an 11-year-old son. She was stomped, dragged through puddles and briar patches by her feet, beaten mercilessly with pecan limbs, stripped naked and had her teeth kicked out. Motive: she had dared to ask him for some grocery money. This brutal man was legally put down by electricity on May 25, 1944. Source: 1943 Burke Co. death cert. no. 6867 and 1944 Tattnall Co. death cert. no. 11222. Appeal: 197 GA 129–134.

William B. Stroup (white, age 40). *Rape.* The crime was committed on 4/3/1943 in Fulton County. Indecent assault on the person of a 12-year-old white female (name withheld), who was found wandering dazed 30 hours after she had been abducted while walking home from an errand. Stroup was executed on July 28, 1944. Source: *Atlanta Constitution,* 5/12/43 (5:1) & 7/29/44 (3:4).

1945

Henry Glass (black, age 20) and **Jimmie Lee Tye** (black, age 21). *Murder.* Their crime was committed on 12/11/1943 in Fulton County. Both executed for the fatal stabbing of 26-year-old Lonnie Johnson (black), a soldier then on leave. Motive: tavern brawl. The incident stemmed from the way in which Johnson (and perhaps military personnel in general) were cavorting with local girls. This was a wartime social irritant that cut across all ethnic lines. Henry Glass and Jimmie Lee Tye paid the price of their lethal jealousy on January 19, 1945, when they died in the Georgia electric chair. Source: 1943 Fulton Co. death cert. no. 29169. Also: 1945 Tattnall Co. death cert. nos. 1359 and 3648. Appeals: 198 GA 262–266 and 198 GA 491–493.

John J. O'Connor (white, age 19). *Murder.* The crime was committed on 3/25/1944 at Fort Benning. Executed under military authority for the shotgun slaying of 18-year-old Richard N. Campbell (white) during a breakout from the prisoner stockade of the aforesaid army base. The homicide victim was a U.S. Army private from Almont, MI. He was on guard duty when his tragic fate overtook him. The killer was a paratrooper during the rare intervals when he was not in trouble with the MPs. He reportedly came from Maspeth, Long Island. A U.S. Army hangman sent O'Connor to a dishonored grave on January 29, 1945. Source: U.S. Army Court-Martial Case File no. 257550 (National Archives). *Omaha (NB) World Herald*, 5/12/44 (8:5). *Times-Picayune* (New Orleans) 1/30/45 (2:1:4). Also see the executed man's burial record (Fort Benning Post Cemetery), which notes 10/4/1924 as his date of birth.

Emory Walter Fowler (white, age 21). *Murder.* The crime was committed on 2/22/1943 in Forsyth County. Executed for the fatal beating of 74-year-old Benjamin Perry Roper (white), a farmer and rural storekeeper who was attacked in his place of business. Motive: robbery. Fowler was a deserter from the Marine Corps. That fact almost certainly figured in the decision to deny him clemency. He was executed on March 2, 1945. A codefendant named Austin Watson was sent up for life. Source: *Forsyth County News*, 5/13/43 (1:1) & 3/8/45 (1:3). Appeal: 196 GA 748–755.

Willie Jackson (black, age 23). *Rape.* The crime was committed on 11/27/1943 in Fulton County. Indecent assault on the person of 60-year-old Myrtie F. Gantt (white), who was attacked in the kitchen of her own home while babysitting her 1-year-old grandchild. The rapist had posed as a deliveryman. He put a butcher knife to the woman's throat and used it to force himself on her while the terrified baby sat in its high chair screaming throughout. Willie Jackson died by high voltage at the Georgia State Prison on March 2, 1945. Source: *Atlanta Constitution*, 3/3/45 (3:4). Appeal: 198 GA 714–715. See also: 1945 Tattnall Co. death cert. no. 5922.

Lena Baker (black female, age 43). *Murder.* The crime was committed on 4/30/1944 in Randolph County. Handgun slaying of 67-year-old Ernest B. Knight (white), her employer. Motive: a sordid tale of alcoholism. A posthumous pardon was granted to this killer in the year 2005 based almost entirely on a revisionist theory that the murdered man had brought the situation upon himself. It reads like a typical "blame the victim" ploy. Ernest Knight is alleged to have been a heartless exploiter who played on luckless Lena's alcohol dependency to leverage her into a position of sexual servitude from which she finally rebelled. Maybe. This much is certain: Lena Baker had a prior conviction for prostitution. She was a notorious drunk and denizen of back-alley Cuthbert. She had three illegitimate children sired by unknown men and dumped them on her elderly mother. She is not known to have made any effort to reform herself. She had initially been hired to nurse Mr. Knight during a time of physical convalescence but grew increasingly reliant on him as a source of free liquor, thereby raising the question of just who was taking advantage of whom. This condemned murderess was executed at the Georgia State Prison on March 5, 1945. Source: 1945 Tattnall Co. death cert. no. 5921. See: *The Lena Baker Story* by Lela Bond Phillips (Atlanta: Wings, 2001). Also: "Missing Mama: The Lena Baker Story" by Seamus McGraw (containing original trial transcript) published on 8/25/2005 by the *Tennessee Tribune*. There is also a recently dedicated monument in the graveyard of Mount Vernon Baptist Church, Cuthbert GA, which marks the spot where Lena Baker lies.

Levonne C. Johnson (black, age 19). *Murder.* The crime was committed on 2/4/1945 in Newton County. Executed for the killing of 62-year-old Ezma Piper Berry (white), who was clubbed to death by a prowler in her home. The murder weapon was a hardwood stirring stick of the kind commonly used by rural folk when boiling their laundry. Motive: revenge. The homicide victim had said that Johnson was untrustworthy. He had therefore been dismissed from his job. This enraged him. He was executed at the Georgia State Prison on March 9, 1945. Source: *Marietta (GA) Daily Journal*, 2/5/45 (2:3) & 2/6/45 (1:6). *Official Detective*, 11/45. See also: 1945 Newton Co. death cert. no. 3363 and Tattnall Co. death cert. no. 5920. Also see: 1940 U.S. Census (Newton Co., GA), which notes both parties.

Edmond V. Smith (white, age 39). *Murder.* The crime was committed on 6/25/1944 in Pike County. Uxoricide. Executed for the fatal beating of 37-year-old Eloise Smith (white), she having suffered overt spousal abuse for an extended period of time to the peril of her life. The final incident in this regimen of mistreatment involved the smashing of her head against the stone sill of an outdoor well. The man who had sworn a sacred marriage vow to "cherish and protect her in sickness and in health" paid the death penalty at the Georgia State Prison on March 9, 1945. He was guilty of perjury as well as murder. Source: *Pike County Journal*, 6/29/44 (1:6). Appeal: 198 GA 849–858. See also: 1940 U.S. Census (Pike Co., GA), which notes both parties. 1945 Tattnall Co. death cert. no. 5919.

Curn L. Jones (black, age 23). *Murder.* The crime was committed on 8/30/1944 at Fort Benning. Executed under military authority for the fatal stabbing of 38-year-old Pvt. Dooley E. Parnell (white) in a racially charged tavern brawl. The homicide victim had blundered into a "colored only" canteen while on liberty that night. Jones resented this (perhaps emboldened by liquor) and went on the attack. His enlistment record says that Jones came from Dinwiddie Co., VA. He had been inducted into the army on 1/15/1942. His burial record (Fort Benning Post Cemetery) notes 9/15/1920 as his date of birth and also says that he was a private in Company A of the Infantry School Training Regiment. On April 18, 1945, a U.S. Army hangman carried out the sentence of a court-martial held at Fort Benning. Source: U.S. Army Court-Martial Case File no. 266723 (National Archives). See also: 1944 Muscogee Co. death cert. no. 19941 and 1945 Muscogee Co. death cert. no. 6650.

Ulysses Gilbert (black, age 22). *Murder.* The crime was committed on 11/23/1943 in Houston County. Fatal stabbing of 25-year-old Robert Horton (black), who had a knife plunged into his head with such force that the blade broke off and was left in his brain. Motive: rivalry for a female. The murdered man had caught Gilbert in the act of absconding with his estranged wife. What he did next, however, had no justification under Georgia law. Ulysses Gilbert went to the electric chair on April 27, 1945. Source: 1943 Houston Co. death cert. no. 27602 and 1945 Tattnall Co. death cert. no. 10363. Appeal: 198 GA 220–221.

David Watkins (black, age 16) and **Nathaniel Lamar** (black, age 20). *Murder.* Their crime was committed on 12/2/1943 in Bibb County. Both executed for the malicious killing of 67-year-old Ella Connell (white), who was beaten on the head with a metal-bladed electric fan and then dragged into her bedroom, where the culprits set her bed ablaze and opened the gas jets that were there in anticipation of blowing up the house. Motive: robbery and gross perfidy. The murdered woman had presented Lamar with a fruitcake that she had made for him. The Georgia electric chair did double duty in this case on May 11, 1945. Source: Appeals: 199 GA 1-11 & 81-97. Also: 1940 US Census (Bibb Co.) which notes all parties plus 1900 US Census which notes Mrs Connell. Also: 1945 Tattnall Co. death cert. nos. 10365 & 12589.

Edward Lee Green (black, age 23). *Rape.* The crime was committed on 2/24/1945 in Houston County. Indecent assault on the person of a married white female named Ella Mae Joyner (age uncertain), who he did "strike, beat and wound" in order to subdue her. This attacker was executed at the Georgia State Prison on June 1, 1945. Source: Original Case File (*State vs. Green*), Houston County Superior Court Archives, April Term 1945. See also: 1945 Tattnall Co. death cert. no. 12591.

Jack Roy Green, alias "Booty Green" (black, age 45). *Rape.* The crime was committed on 1/31/1945 in Sumter County. Indecent assault on the person of 65-year-old Rena Duckworth (white). The outrage began when Green attacked the woman's 73-year-old husband as he was plowing his field. The aging man was severely beaten and slashed with a knife. Then he was forcibly bound to a tree by means of his own plow line, which Green cut from the farmer's mule harness. The next thing this predator did was force his way into the Duckworth residence. He terrorized Mrs. Duckworth and threatened her with death if she did not give him some money. The lady yielded the small amount of cash that she had handy, but not being satisfied therewith, Green beat her up and raped her. The reward he reaped was execution by high voltage at the Georgia State Prison on June 29, 1945. Source: *Americus (GA) Times-Recorder*, 2/1/45 (1:7). *Times-Enterprise* (Thomasville, GA), 6/6/45 (2:3) & 6/29/45 (4:8). See also: 1945 Tattnall Co. death cert. no. 14810. Also: 1940 U.S. Census (Sumter Co., GA), which notes Mr. & Mrs. Duckworth.

Albert Smithwick (white, age 22). *Murder.* The crime was committed on 6/10/1944 in Chatham County. Executed for the killing of 37-year-old Julian Eli DeLoach (white), who was beaten to death with pine saplings and a blackjack. Motive: a female catalyst. Smithwick was a naive soldier boy from New Bern, NC. He was stationed at Liberty Field near Savannah when he fell in with a honky tonk woman named Viola Fields. She was the purported wife of a taxi driver named Julian DeLoach and reportedly used her feminine wiles to goad the young serviceman into doing what he did. She got off with a life sentence based on the old "Southern chivalry" dodge but died on 4/21/1951 at age 36. Her lover died in the Georgia electric chair on July 28, 1945. Source: *Times-Enterprise* (Thomasville, GA), 10/7/44 (2:6), 5/21/45 (4:7) & 6/29/45 (7:1). *Greensboro (NC) Daily News*, 7/29/45 (4:4:5). See also: 1944 Chatham Co. death cert. no. 12022. Also: 1945 Tattnall Co. death cert. no. 14811 and 1951 Tattnall Co. death cert. no. 9733.

Robert R. Gunnells (white, age 40). *Murder.* The crime was committed on 10/11/1944 in Baldwin County. Uxoricide. Handgun slaying of 23-year-old Bertha Logan Gunnells (white). Motive: she had refused to get into a car that he was driving on the grounds that he was drunk. This wife-killer was executed at the Georgia State Prison on August 24, 1945.

Source: *Union-Recorder* (Milledgeville, GA), 10/19/44 (1:4). Appeal: 199 GA 486. See also: 1944 Baldwin Co. death cert. no. 23016 and 1945 Tattnall Co. death cert. no. 16983.

Henry Hayes (black, age 27). *Robbery with violence.* The crime was committed on 9/7/1944 in Fulton County. Executed for assaulting, beating and robbing 35-year-old Lucy E. Wright (white) by taking cruel advantage of that woman's vulnerability after her car had broken down. Mrs. Wright was beaten unconscious and had to be hospitalized for 11 days with injuries that included a broken nose. The marauder stole her pocketbook, her ration cards (it then being wartime) and her money. There was also evidence of sexual assault. Henry Hayes was sent to the Georgia electric chair on August 24, 1945. It may or may not be significant to note that Mrs. Wright was a civic-minded lady who was then serving as president of the Fulton County P.T.A. Source: *Atlanta Constitution*, 9/8/44 (6:5). Appeal: 199 GA 251–254. See also: 1945 Tattnall Co. death cert. no. 16985.

Charlie Johnson (black, age 27). *Rape.* The crime was committed on 6/21/1945 in Early County. Indecent assault on the person of a 14-year-old white female (name withheld) who was jumped when she went to fetch a jug of water for her relatives, then at work in the fields. Johnson was a rover from Baker County. He was executed at the Georgia State Prison on September 21, 1945. Source: *Early County News*, 6/28/45 (2:3) & 7/26/45 (1:1). See also: 1945 Tattnall Co. death cert. no. 19161.

Noah Collins (black, age 30). *Murder.* The crime was committed on 4/13/1945 in Chatham County. Executed for the murder of 51-year-old Joe McKinney (black), a night watchman who was struck on the head with a club, stabbed and blasted with a shotgun. Motive: larceny. The crime scene was an all-black social club of which Collins was a member. He had a mind to steal some dues money that he knew was in the club's office. What he got instead was a seat in the Georgia electric chair on November 9, 1945. Source: 1945 Chatham Co. death cert. no. 6585 and Tattnall Co. death cert. no. 23539. Appeal: 199 GA 830–834.

Jesse Craiton (black, age 22). *Murder.* The crime was committed on 12/30/1944 in Fulton County. Handgun slaying of 59-year-old Peter D. Vergiotis, also known as "Pete Verge" (white), a storekeeper. Motive: armed robbery. Death in the electric chair was the fate of Jesse Craiton on November 9, 1945. Source: 1944 Fulton Co. death cert. no. 28864 and 1945 Tattnall Co. death cert. no. 23540. Appeal: 199 GA 829–830. See also: George McKay (executed 9/29/50).

Nathaniel Taylor (black, age 44). *Murder.* The crime was committed on 12/10/1944 in Laurens County. Fatal stabbing of 43-year-old Lutressa Brown (black). Motive: lovers' quarrel. There being no mitigating factors in this case, the killer was ordered for execution. Black-on-black killer Nathaniel Taylor paid the death penalty at the Georgia State Prison on November 30, 1945. Source: 1944 Laurens Co. death cert. no. 28965 and 1945 Tattnall Co. death cert. no. 23538. Appeal: 199 GA 512–513.

1946

Eddie Daniels (black, age 32). *Murder.* The crime was committed on

7/31/1943 in Grady County. Fatal stabbing of 36-year-old Juanita King (black), she having been knifed multiple times, "practically disemboweled" and even slashed on the soles of her feet. Motive: atavistic male jealousy. This retrograde killer paid the forfeit of his own life in the Georgia electric chair on February 8, 1946. Source: 1943 Grady Co. death cert. no. 15398 and 1946 Tattnall Co. death cert. no. 3842. Appeal: 199 GA 818–820.

Isaac Bonner (black, age 19). *Murder.* The crime was committed on 11/11/1945 in Bibb County. Shotgun slaying of 53-year-old Enrico DiVenuto (white), who was found lying face down in a puddle with the back of his head blown off. Motive: mugged for his wallet. Bonner was put to death for this felony on March 29, 1946. Source: *Macon (GA) Telegraph*, 11/13/45 (1:6), 11/14/45 (1:7) & 3/30/46 (6:1).

Leon Lewis (black, age 25). *Rape.* The crime was committed on 7/7/1945 in Fulton County. Indecent assault on the person of 27-year-old Frances Norman (white), a divorcee who had had a little too much to drink that night. Lewis was a taxi driver and Mrs. Norman was his passenger. Seeing a chance to "get me a white woman," this offender took advantage of Mrs. Norman's tipsy condition to force himself on her. He also beat her up when she tried to resist. The old "consensual sex" dodge was of no avail in this case because the victim's physical injuries bespoke the contrary. Try as he might, Leon Lewis was unable to talk his way out of bearing the responsibility for what he had done. He was executed on March 29, 1946. Source: *Atlanta Daily World*, 4/4/46 (1:5). Appeal: 200 GA 388–390. See also: 1946 Tattnall Co. death cert. no. 6354.

Willie Jones (black, age 28). *Murder.* The crime was committed on 2/27/1946 in Coffee County. Strangulation killing of 73-year-old Winnie Wilcox Kirkland (white). Motive: burglary and sexual assault. Venue changed from Coffee County to Ware County. Count another one for the Georgia electric chair on April 19, 1946. Source: *Times-Enterprise* (Thomasville, GA), 2/27/46 (5:6), 3/25/46 (2:3) & 9/7/46 (1:3). Also: 1946 Tattnall Co. death cert. no. 8546. Also see the murdered woman's gravestone in City Cemetery, Douglas GA, which notes that she was one day shy of her 74th birthday. See also: James C. Hill (executed 12/20/46).

Early Bryant (black, age 31). *Rape.* The crime was committed on 1/5/1946 in Fulton County. Indecent assault on the person of an adult white female (name withheld) who was attacked while walking along Roswell Road with a bag of groceries. Bryant admitted that he had grabbed the woman but insisted that he had run off when she started screaming. It was a lame defense. Bryant met his end in the execution chamber at the Georgia State Prison on May 31, 1946. Source: *Atlanta Daily World*, 3/6/46 (2:7). See also: 1946 Tattnall Co. death cert. no. 10745.

Anderson Burke (black, age 28). *Rape.* The crime was committed on 3/28/1946 in Oglethorpe County. Indecent assault on the person of 17-year-old Mavis Smith (white), she having been deliberately pounced on as she walked home from her job, the culprit having lain in wait for her. The girl was dragged into a field and there beaten into submission. Burke slyly left his shoes at the home of another black man so that person would be suspected instead of him. The ruse almost worked when investigators made plaster casts of shoeprints found at the scene and matched them with the aforesaid shoes. Here we have a case of one black man attempting to frame another. Anderson Burke—the true culprit—was executed at the Georgia State Prison on July 5, 1946. Source: *Oglethorpe (GA) Echo*, 4/4/46 (1:4). See also: 1946 Tattnall Co. death cert. no. 5020.

Aaron Nappier (black, age 40). *Murder.* The crime was committed on 9/12/1945 in Laurens County. Police killer. Handgun slaying of 74-year-old John J. Webb (white), who was shot four times at close range. Motive: resisting arrest for being drunk and disorderly. Nappier paid with his life for this at the Georgia State Prison on July 19, 1946. Source: 1945 Laurens Co. death cert. no. 27164 and 1946 Tattnall Co. death cert. no. 17137. Appeal: 200 GA 626–631.

James R. McKethan (white, age 21). *Murder.* The crime was committed on 10/8/1945 in Chatham County. Executed for the mutilation murder of 17-year-old George Luther Aids (white), who was struck with a hatchet, choked to death and then sawed into pieces. Next, the resultant body parts were further pared with a carving knife before being buried in several caches around town. Motive: the killer thought (perhaps wrongly) that the decedent had stolen his wallet. McKethan died by high voltage at the Georgia State Prison on August 2, 1946. Source: *Augusta (GA) Chronicle*, 10/19/45 (1:8) & 11/29/45 (3:2). See also: 1945 Chatham Co. death cert. no. 19868 and 1946 Tattnall Co. death cert. no. 17141.

Walter H. Yearwood (white, age 23). *Murder.* The crime was committed on 11/19/1945 in Clarke County. Handgun slaying of 40-year-old Harry W. Williamson (white), a publishing executive who was shot in the back of the head and later dumped into the Apalachee River. Motive: carjacking. Yearwood came from Bishop where his father was the town marshal. He had already disgraced his family by getting thrown out of the U.S. Navy in wartime. Drunk and aimless on the above date, young Yearwood was loitering about downtown Athens when Mr. Williamson gave him a ride in his car. Yearwood later said that Mr. Williamson had harangued him with "a temperance lecture" during the course of that ride, which irked him so much that he shot the man just to stop his preaching. Then the killer propped up Williamson's body in the passenger seat of the car and drove to his father's house so papa could see the handsome vehicle and "respectable company" that his ne'er-do-well son was keeping. This was too much for the elder Yearwood, who put out an all-points bulletin on his own boy. It was probably one of the most gut-wrenching things that this town marshal had to do in the entire course of his law enforcement career. The errant son was executed at the Georgia State Prison on October 22, 1946. Source: *Augusta (GA) Chronicle*, 12/12/45 (1:1). *Marietta (GA) Daily Journal*, 10/23/46 (6:3). See also: 1945 Fulton Co. death cert. no. 25738.

Alton Murray (white, age 28). *Murder.* The crime was committed on 11/7/1945 in Candler County. Police killer. Executed for the shotgun slayings of 52-year-old Tom Watson Brantley and 43-year-old Willie B. Jones (whites), the former being the sheriff of Candler County and the latter one of his deputies. Motive: resisting arrest. Murray died in the Georgia electric chair on November 8, 1946. Source: *Augusta (GA) Chronicle*, 2/8/46 (2:1) & 11/9/46 (2:7). See also: 1945 Candler Co. death cert. nos. 21983 and 21984.

Lee James Allen (black, age 15). *Rape*. The crime was committed on 10/17/1945 in Fulton County. Serial rapist. Specifically executed for an indecent assault on the person of a 41-year-old white female (name withheld) who was jumped as she walked along Memorial Drive in Atlanta. The woman was able to identify her self-confessed assailant when he was caught four months later. It was subsequently revealed that this offender had attacked ten other women throughout the preceding year, most of them at knifepoint. It being abundantly clear that Allen had no sense of restraint and would in all likelihood continue to be a menace to society, the sentence of death by electrocution was passed upon him. This was carried out at the Georgia State Prison on November 15, 1946. Source: *Augusta (GA) Chronicle*, 2/17/46 (2:2). Appeal: 201 GA 391–396. See also: 1946 Tattnall Co. death cert. no. 23744, which notes 12/30/29 as Allen's date of birth. See also: James Mangum (executed 3/5/48).

Johnnie Burns (black, age 21) and **Willie Stevenson** (black, age 16). *Murder*. Their crime was committed on 12/30/1945 in Lee County. Both executed for the ax murder of 47-year-old Lucius Thomas (black). Motive: so they could steal his purse containing $27.14. That purse became a very dear one to these offenders when they lost their lives for it at the Georgia State Prison on November 22, 1946. Source: 1946 Tattnall Co. death cert. nos. 23741 and 23742. Appeal: 201 GA 200–201. See also: 1940 U.S. Census (Lee Co., GA), which notes the murdered man.

James Rufus Williams (black, age 19). *Murder*. The crime was committed on 7/17/1946 in Irwin County. Prison-guard killer. Executed for the shotgun slayings of 60-year-old Joseph Bartow Morgan and 47-year-old Wilburn Tucker (whites) during a breakout from the Ocilla Work Camp. Motive: escape. Williams suffered death for this in the Georgia electric chair on November 29, 1946. Source: *Greensboro (NC) Daily News*, 7/19/46 (1:2). *Augusta (GA) Chronicle*, 11/29/46 (1:6). See also: 1946 Irwin Co. death cert. nos. 16603 and 16604 plus Tattnall Co. death cert. no. 23743.

Albert Parker (black, age 28). *Murder*. The crime was committed on 10/27/1946 in Berrien County. Executed for the murder of 71-year-old Marcus Lee (white), who was hacked to death with a sharp-edged hoe. Motive: mugging. Venue changed from Berrien County to Cook County. The killer was executed on December 13, 1946. Source: *Adel (GA) News*, 10/31/46 (12:3) & 11/14/46 (1:1). *Nashville (GA) Herald*, 12/12/46 (1:3) & 12/19/46 (1:7).

James C. Hill (black, age 19). *Murder*. The crime was committed on 2/27/1946 in Coffee County. Accomplice in the strangulation murder of 73-year-old Winnie Wilcox Kirkland (white). Motive: burglary and sexual assault. Venue changed from Coffee County to Ware County. This offender went to his own death in the Georgia electric chair on December 20, 1946. Source: 1946 Tattnall Co. death cert. no. 26413. Also: 1940 U.S. Census

(Coffee Co., GA), which notes Hill. See also: Willie Jones (executed 4/19/46).

1947

Arthur Brown Jr. (black, age 21) and **Morris Dorsey** (black, age 22). *Murder.* Their crime was committed on 6/19/1946 in Chatham County. Both executed for the murders of 71-year-old Abraham Aaron Barnwell and 78-year-old Mary Blidge Barnwell (blacks), a married couple who were beaten and hacked to death (apparently with machetes) for the sake of $22 that they had saved. Motive: home invasion. The killers probably thought that the Barnwells had much more. This pair perished in the execution chamber of the Georgia State Prison on February 8, 1947. Source: *Savannah Evening Press*, 6/19/46 (16:4) & 2/8/47 (10:5). Appeal: 201 GA 751–752. See also: 1940 U.S. Census (Chatham Co., GA), which notes the homicide victims.

Homer R. Knapp (white, age 38). *Murder.* The crime was committed on 11/18/1946 in Chatham County. Handgun slaying of 38-year-old Inez M. Lanier (white), who was shot six times including four times in the back. Motive: adultery turned deadly. Knapp was a former Savannah police officer who got involved with a married woman, lost everything, and then in typical male fashion chose to blame her for his downfall instead of his own stupidity. Knapp's career in law enforcement ended in the electric chair at the Georgia State Prison on April 18, 1947. Source: *Times-Enterprise* (Thomasville, GA), 11/19/46 (4:7). See also: 1946 Chatham Co. death cert. no. 22138 and 1947 Tattnall Co. death cert. no. 11184.

Willis Barnes (white, age 27). *Murder.* The crime was committed on 5/22/1945 in Ben Hill County. Handgun slayings of 49-year-old James H. Clark and 38-year-old Joseph Brown Peacock (whites), two cotton-mill bosses who were shot four and three times respectively. Motive: disgruntled employee. A third man named Garbert W. Mayes (white, age 39) was reported to have been critically wounded in this incident. He died on 12/23/1954, perhaps from the long-term effects of his injuries. The shooter was executed at the Georgia State Prison on April 25, 1947. Source: *Marietta (GA) Daily Journal*, 5/23/45 (1:7) & 7/19/45 (1:6). *Times-Enterprise* (Thomasville, GA), 5/23/45 (8:5). See also: 1945 Ben Hill Co. death cert. nos. 8312 and 8313. Also: 1947 Tattnall Co. death cert. no. 8882 and 1954 Ben Hill Co. death cert. no. 26881.

Lauren Porter (black, age 38). *Murder.* The crime was committed on 1/26/1947 in Oglethorpe County. Serial killer. Executed for the murder of 68-year-old William Roderic Cofer (white), who was shot in the back with a .22-caliber rifle and had his house burned down around him. The homicide victim was an aging farmer whose wife had died the previous year. He had attended a community barbecue the preceding day, at which some money had been given to him by well-meaning neighbors. Lauren Porter had been among this group. He resolved to filch those funds by whatever means necessary and did so the following day. Porter was subsequently confirmed to have been the perpetrator of the infamous "Goose Pond Murders" of 1939 and 1944, which had had Oglethorpe County on edge ever since. These began on 7/10/1939 when a storekeeper named Mary Agnes Tiller (white, age

30) was beaten almost beyond recognition with the sawed off barrel of a shotgun. The next was on 10/8/1939 when another rural storekeeper named Earl F. Poole (white, age 60) was shot in the back of the head execution-style (with a .38-caliber handgun) within his place of business. Cashboxes were stolen in each case. Another such homicide was barely avoided on 8/6/1943 when a third storekeeper named William A. Patrick (white, age 48) was severely wounded by a shotgun blast and then sniped at with a .41-caliber antique derringer that was fired through his bedroom window. This was followed on 8/26/1944 by the fatal wounding of a rural mail carrier named Lewis H. Brooks (white, age 33) by a shotgun blast fired from a concealed position along his route. The culprit's premeditation was clearly shown in this case by the fact that he had barricaded (with tree branches) the road on which the mailman was shot. A search of Porter's cabin soon after the fourth murder uncovered all of the aforesaid weapons. The Georgia electric chair ended this killer's reign of terror on April 25, 1947. Source: *Master Detective*, 11/49. Also see the gravestone of Mary Agnes Tiller in Wesley Chapel Cemetery, Lexington. Also: 1939 Oglethorpe Co. death cert. no. 24475 (Poole) and 1944 Oglethorpe Co. death cert. no. 19199 (Brooks). Also: 1947 Tattnall Co. death cert. no. 8885 (Porter). Also: 1930 and 1940 U.S. Census (Oglethorpe Co., GA), which note Cofer and Patrick.

Quiller Daniel (black, age 29). *Murder.* The crime was committed on 11/14/1946 in Franklin County. Shotgun slayings of 44-year-old Willie A. Carnes and 36-year-old Marilyn Webb (whites), who were found together in a parked automobile under scandalous circumstances. Motive: "Because I was intensely jealous of her," Daniel said. The killer was an ordinary farmhand. It is unclear whether he thought that he was being protective or perhaps had aspirations above his station. Whatever the case, this double killer was executed at the Georgia State Prison on May 2, 1947. Source: *Augusta (GA) Chronicle*, 11/20/46 (2:3) & 5/2/47 (15:2). See also: 1946 Franklin Co. death cert. nos. 26939 and 26940 plus 1947 Tattnall Co. death cert. no. 11189. Also: 1940 U.S. Census (Hart Co., GA), which notes both of the homicide victims as being separately married.

James Brown (black, age 22). *Rape.* The crime was committed on 5/6/1947 in Screven County. Executed for an indecent assault on the person of a 26-year-old white female (name withheld) who was deliberately abducted for that purpose. Brown had fled from the Bulloch County convict camp in a stolen truck. He used that vehicle to snatch the white woman and drive her to a "secluded spot" where he forced himself on her. Then he boldly drove that same vehicle "through the town of Sylvania with the woman huddled on its floor" before using it to run a private automobile off the road. This car was driven by a second white woman, whom he raped on her own front seat in the presence of her horrified 3-year-old child. The Georgia electric chair ensured that there would be no such further depredations by James Brown on June 17, 1947. Source: *Times-Enterprise* (Thomasville, GA), 5/22/47 (2:3). Also: 1947 Tattnall Co. death cert. no. 13504.

Hubert L. Reddick (black, age 17). *Murder.* The crime was committed on 6/17/1946 in Telfair County. Executed for the killing of 54-year-old Otis D.

Grooms (white), a roadside fruit stand vender who was abducted from his place of business in Lowndes County and found dead two days later in Telfair County with his throat cut. Motive: robbery. Venue changed from Telfair County to Bibb County. The callous disregard for human life that was shown by this young offender evinced an inauspicious propensity for going from bad to worse if ever given a chance to do so. He was therefore ordered for execution. The death sentence was carried out at the Georgia State Prison on June 30, 1947. Source: *Augusta (GA) Chronicle*, 6/24/46 (1:3). Also: 1947 Tattnall Co. death cert. no. 13505. Also see the gravestone of O. D. Grooms in Sunset Hill Cemetery, Valdosta.

Ebenezer Scott (black, age 27). *Murder.* The crime was committed on 9/15/1946 in Chatham County. Executed for the mutilation murder of 18-year-old Fannie Milton (black), she having been "extensively cut and stabbed in her home." Motive: brutish boyfriend. He was executed on August 1, 1947. Source: *Savannah Morning News*, 9/16/46 (7:2). *Savannah Evening Press*, 9/16/46 (5:2). See also: GA Supreme Court case no. 15737. Also: 1946 Chatham Co. death cert. no. 19936 and 1947 Tattnall Co. death cert. no. 17871.

Robert Lee Stanford (black, age 24). *Murder.* The crime was committed on 10/6/1945 in Richmond County. Handgun slaying of 41-year-old Harry Woo (Chinese), a grocer. Motive: armed robbery. This killer learned that Georgia law placed full value on Oriental lives when he heard himself sentenced to death in Richmond County Superior Court. That sentence was carried out on August 1, 1947. Source: *Augusta (GA) Chronicle*, 10/8/45 (1:3), 10/15/45 (1:3) & 8/2/47 (2:8).

Terrell Loughridge (white, age 26). *Murder.* The crime was committed on 8/20/1945 in Jefferson County. Handgun slaying of 23-year-old Calvin C. Rowland (white), a decorated European Theater of Operations veteran lately returned from abroad. Motive: carjacking. The killer was an escapee from the state prison complex near Reidsville. Straight back there he went as a condemned convict. He was executed on August 9, 1947. Source: *Augusta (GA) Chronicle*, 8/21/45 (1:2), 8/22/45 (2:1) & 5/18/46 (1:1). See also: 1945 Jefferson Co. death cert. no. 18658 and 1947 Tattnall Co. death cert. no. 22436.

Roosevelt Moore (black, age 26). *Murder.* The crime was committed on 7/28/1946 in Stewart County. Ax murder of 49-year-old Archie B. Brinson, known to some as "Pudding Brinson" (black), his father-in-law. Motive: Moore suspected that Brinson and his wife (Ethel) had snitched on him for being AWOL from the army. He was executed at the Georgia State Prison on August 15, 1947. Source: 1946 Stewart Co. death cert. no. 17101 and 1947 Tattnall Co. death cert. no. 17874. Appeal: 202 GA 357–360. See also: 1940 U.S. Census (Stewart Co., GA), which notes both parties as slightly older.

Jim Owen (black, age 42). *Murder.* The crime was committed on 3/18/1947 in Warren County. Shotgun slaying of 27-year-old Tommie Rogers (black), the killer having broken into the homicide victim's house for that purpose. Motive: rivalry for a female. The only thing that Owen gained from this futile misdeed was a seat in the

Georgia electric chair on October 6, 1947. Source: 1947 Warren Co. death cert. no. 6613 and Tattnall Co. death cert. no. 22443. Appeal: 202 GA 616–619.

Sweetie Bryant (black, age 28). *Murder.* The crime was committed on 8/6/1946 in Mitchell County. Shotgun slaying of 47-year-old Will Davis (black), his father-in-law. The murdered man was also battered so badly about the face and head with the butt of that weapon that it broke into pieces. Motive: child custody dispute. Sweetie Bryant died in the electric chair for this on October 10, 1947. Source: 1946 Mitchell Co. death cert. no. 16807 and 1947 Tattnall Co. death cert. no. 22441. Appeal: 202 GA 453–454.

Oscar L. Ford (black, age 20). *Murder.* The crime was committed on 10/19/1946 in Dougherty County. Shotgun slaying of 57-year-old Samuel A. Bailey (white), a grocer. Motive: armed robbery. This killer was executed on October 10, 1947. Source: Augusta (GA) Chronicle, 10/11/47 (8:2). Also: 1947 Tattnall Co. death cert. no. 22442. See also: 1940 U.S. Census (Albany, GA), which notes Mr. Bailey.

Nick Morakis (white, age 51). *Murder.* The crime was committed on 5/25/1945 in Morgan County. Police killer. Handgun slaying of 56-year-old Frederick H. Adams (white), the police chief of Madison. Motive: mutual antagonism. Morakis had several prior arrests and bond forfeitures for public intoxication. Chief Adams saw him walking "in the negro section of town" on the above date with something in a brown paper bag. Surmising this to be a bottle of illegal whiskey, the lawman accosted "the Greek," as Morakis was called. The latter was by that time fed up with what he regarded as police harassment. So he pulled out a pistol and opened fire, getting the drop on Adams. This cost Morakis his life. He was executed at the Georgia State Prison on November 18, 1947. Source: Vol. 40 *Southeastern Reporter* (2nd series), 121–128. See also: 1945 Madison Co. death cert. no. 9943 and 1947 Tattnall Co. death cert. no. 24804.

1948

Joe Porter (black, age 27) and **Leroy Scrutchens** (black, age 28). *Murder.* Their crime was committed on 10/31/1947 in Sumter County. Both executed for the killing of 64-year-old Perry R. Cannon (white), a night watchman at a lumber mill who was found there the next morning with his head caved in and his billfold missing. Motive: night-prowling. The killers met their fates in the Georgia electric chair on January 2, 1948. Source: *Tri-County News* (Americus, GA), 11/6/47 (1:5), 11/13/47 (1:8), 11/27/47 (1:8) & 1/1/48 (1:4). *Savannah Evening Press*, 1/2/48 (15:6).

Eddie Brown Jr. (black, age 23). *Murder.* The crime was committed on 6/27/1947 in Carroll County. Shotgun slaying of 28-year-old David Andrew Boyd (white), who was deliberately blasted in the back as he sat peacefully fishing in the Little Tallapoosa River. Motive: theft of his automobile. It was proven in court that Brown had fraudulently traded Boyd's vehicle to a used car dealer. He paid the death penalty for this at the Georgia State Prison on February 13, 1948. Source: *Times-Enterprise* (Thomasville, GA), 7/1/47 (4:4). Appeal: 203 GA 219–225. See also: 1948 Tattnall Co. death cert. no. 4239.

J. W. Torbert, also known as "Tolbert" (black, age 37). *Murder.* The crime was committed on 1/11/1947 in Randolph County. Shotgun slaying of 72-year-old Henry Peavy (white). Motive: big attitude. The killer had made a commotion that day by yelling at his wife while both were at work in Mr. Peavy's field. Peavy advised Torbert to tone it down or he would no longer be welcome there. Torbert responded to this by fetching his shotgun. He was subsequently executed at the Georgia State Prison on February 16, 1948. Source: 1947 Randolph Co. death cert. no. 1432 and 1948 Tattnall Co. death cert. no. 4240. Appeal: 203 GA 186–191. The full name of this killer is not specified in any known record.

James Mangum (black, age 16). *Rape.* The crime was committed on 9/18/1945 in Fulton County. Serial rapist. Specifically executed for an indecent assault on the person of 70-year-old Addie Reeves (white). Mangum was one member of a similarly-minded trio who had teamed up to go on "raping expeditions" throughout the Atlanta area. Their specialty was to pounce on frail or elderly white ladies, drag them into vacant lots and alternately take turns pinning them to the ground until all three had had their way with them. Then they would steal whatever personal valuables the victims had on their persons and flee. At least ten such attacks were confirmed to have taken place around this time. All were linked to the aforesaid trio. James Mangum was caught on 2/3/1946. The third attacker received a lesser sentence for testifying against Mangum and Allen. Mangum was electrocuted on March 5, 1948. His age was not enough to save him. Source: *Atlanta Constitution*, 3/6/48 (3:5). Appeal: 201 GA 519. Also: GA Supreme Court Case no. 15603. See also: James Lee Allen (executed 11/15/46).

L. P. Campbell (black, age 25). *Murder.* The crime was committed on 1/13/1947 in Floyd County. Handgun slaying of 68-year-old Joseph T. Chandler (white), who was carjacked during a breakout from the Floyd County convict camp. Motive: flight from custody. Campbell accrued a death sentence for this. He was executed at the Georgia State Prison on March 26, 1948. His full name is not specified in any known record. Source: *Rome (GA) News-Tribune*, 1/14/47 (1:5), 1/17/47 (1:1) & 3/25/48 (1:5). See also: 1948 Tattnall Co. death cert. no. 9088.

Red Lamar Nunn (black, age 33). *Murder.* The crime was committed on 7/4/1947 in Jefferson County. Uxoricide. Shotgun slaying of 35-year-old Plummer Nunn (black). Motive: she had "dodged" him, as he put it. The couple had attended a barbecue the previous evening. They had left that affair in each other's company. However sometime during the night "Miss Plummer" had returned to the cookout without her husband's knowledge, a circumstance that infuriated him. This wife-killer was executed on August 13, 1948. Source: 1947 Jefferson Co. death cert. no. 19562 and 1948 Tattnall Co. death cert. no. 18091. Appeal: 204 GA 73–76.

Sam Whitt Jr. (black, age 21). *Murder.* The crime was committed on 3/5/1947 in Fulton County. Uxoricide. Handgun slaying of 21-year-old Margrette Whitt (black), who was shot three times, their baby being only inches away. Motive: marital estrangement. This young wife-killer died in the Georgia electric chair on August 16, 1948. Source: 1947 Fulton Co. death cert. no. 985 and 1948 Tattnall Co. death cert. no. 18094. Appeal: 203 GA 538–540.

J. B. Beetles (black, age 31) and **William Cular Davis** (black, age 35). *Murder.* Their crime was committed on 1/16/1948 in Carroll County. Both executed for the killing of 75-year-old Charles B. Wike (white), a storekeeper who was bludgeoned with a heavy stick. His place of business was burnt. Motive: robbery. The law exacted life for life from this guilty pair on October 15, 1948. Source: *Carroll County Georgian*, 1/22/48 (1:2). *Times-Enterprise* (Thomasville, GA), 1/17/48 (7:5). Appeal: 203 GA 627–635. See also: 1948 Tattnall Co. death cert. nos. 25400 and 25401. No one bothered to record the identity of Beetles by anything more than his initials.

Charlie Garrett (white, age 25) and **Jewell Eller** (white, age 20). *Murder.* Their crime was committed on 8/25/1947 in Towns County. Both executed for the ax murder of 77-year-old Milton Melvin Maney (white), a rural storekeeper. Motive: robbery. The needless brutality of this misdeed resonated through the mountain counties to such an extent that few disapproved when the killers were sentenced to die. They paid the penalty at the Georgia State Prison on November 5, 1948. Source: *Augusta (GA) Chronicle*, 11/6/48 (1:4). See also: 1948 Tattnall Co. death cert. nos. 25410 and 25411. Also see the murdered man's gravestone in Boyd Chapel Cemetery, Hiawassee.

L. C. Brown (black, age 30). *Murder.* The crime was committed on 6/21/1948 in Greene County. Ax murder of 29-year-old William T. Jarrell (white), a convict guard on the Greene County chain gang. Brown stole the dead man's money and pistol before using "a giant earth moving machine" to cover up his body. Then he fled in a county work truck. A wide-ranging manhunt brought Brown to bay. He was executed at the Georgia State Prison on November 26, 1948. Still, no one thought to identify Brown by anything more than his initials. Source: *Herald-Journal* (Greensboro, GA), 6/25/48 (1:3), 7/9/48 (1:2) & 12/3/48 (1:4).

1949

Jesse C. Carroll (white, age 43). *Murder.* The crime was committed on 3/22/1948 in Muscogee County. Uxoricide. Handgun slaying of 36-year-old Daisy Carroll (white), who was shot six times. Motive: suspicion of infidelity. Wife-killer Carroll died in the Georgia electric chair on April 8, 1949. Source: *Times-Enterprise* (Thomasville, GA), 1/28/49 (6:4). See also: 1948 Muscogee Co. death cert. no. 8715 and 1949 Tattnall Co. death cert. no. 8697.

Junior Moore (black, age 24). *Murder.* The crime was committed on 6/11/1948 in Bibb County. Police killer. Rifle slaying of 61-year-old Walter L. O'Cain (white) when that lawman responded to a call about a prowler. Motive: resisting arrest. Exit Junior Moore at the Georgia State Prison on April 20, 1949. Source: *Macon (GA) Telegraph*, 6/12/48 (1:4). See also: 1948 Bibb Co. death cert. no. 11843 and 1949 Tattnall Co. death cert. no. 8698.

Morgan Persons (black, age 38). *Murder.* The crime was committed on 5/17/1948 in Worth County. Child killer. Executed for the murder of 15-year-old Eula Lee Grant (black, his stepdaughter), whose throat was cut with such force as to nearly decapitate her. Motive: because she had resisted his sexual advances. This was the last contact that Persons ever had with a female. He was carried dead from the execution chamber at the Georgia State Prison on May 20, 1949. Source: *Sylvester (GA) Local*, 5/20/48 (1:5). See also: 1948 Worth Co. death cert. no. 13804 and 1949 Tattnall Co. death cert. no. 11010.

A. C. Williams (black, age 32). *Murder.* The crime was committed on 4/3/1948 in Fulton County. Fatal stabbing of 23-year-old Jeriah Steed (black), who was chased down and knifed 17 times. Motive: the homicide victim had dared to ask the killer's girlfriend for a date. She too received a ferocious beating at his hands. He died in the Georgia electric chair on June 1, 1949. No one thought to record his entire name. Source: 1948 Fulton Co. death cert. no. 8074 and 1949 Tattnall Co. death cert. no. 13241. Appeal: 204 GA 837–846.

Andrew Dorsey (black, age 22). *Rape.* The crime was committed on 1/27/1947 in Fulton County. Incipient serial rapist. Executed for an indecent assault on the person of a black woman named Bertie Mae Kelley (age not recorded), who was snatched from a public sidewalk and dragged behind a house, where the culprit forced himself on her. Dorsey was also capitally convicted for the 9/8/1947 knifepoint rape of another black woman named Sara Crumley (age not recorded), who was grabbed while walking to her job that day. The Georgia electric chair put a permanent end to Dorsey's depredations on August 19, 1949. Source: 1949 Tattnall Co. death cert. no. 17944. Appeal: 204 GA 345–352.

John Albert Jones Jr. (black, age 16) and **Wilbur Gene Jones** (black, age 17). *Murder.* Their crime was committed on 12/31/1948 in Sumter County. Handgun slaying of 21-year-old Barney E. Devane (white), a gas station attendant who was shot twice in the head. Motive: armed robbery. Both of these teenagers died in the Georgia electric chair on September 12, 1949. Source: *Augusta (GA) Chronicle*, 1/9/49 (B:11:5). See also: 1948 Sumter Co. death cert. no. 28151 and 1949 Tattnall Co. death cert. nos. 20311 and 20312.

Lindsey Brown (black, age 26). *Murder.* The crime was committed on 10/2/1949 in Burke County. Hammer killing of 30-year-old Annie Bell Jackson Irvin (black). Motive: gambling dispute. Brown could not bear the embarrassment of losing to a woman, so he battered her to death in an effort to redeem his wounded machismo. He ended up losing his life in the same bargain. The Georgia electric chair saw to that on December 16, 1949. Source: *Augusta (GA) Chronicle*, 12/17/49 (2:2). See also: 1949 Burke Co. death cert. no. 20895 and Tattnall Co. death cert. no. 27908.

1950

Eddie Houser Jr. (black, age 21). *Armed robbery.* The crime was committed on 11/9/1949 in Peach County. Executed for the gunpoint stickup of 52-year-old Helen Marshall (white, a maiden woman), during which her pocketbook was stolen. The woman was described as the keeper of a small warehouse. The culprit was described as a multiple offender with numerous outstanding arrest warrants for similar crimes both in Georgia and beyond.

He came from Dooly County. The decision to execute him was almost certainly based on evidence of incorrigibility. Armed robbery was indeed a capital offense in Georgia at this time, but only nominally so. The statute had been kept on the books as a sentencing option for extreme cases and was very selectively enforced. Eddie Houser became one of those select few on January 27, 1950. Source: *Leader-Tribune* (Fort Valley, GA), 11/17/49 (1:5). See also: 1950 Tattnall Co. death cert. no. 1641. Also: 1940 U.S. Census (Peach Co., GA), which notes Miss Marshall.

Jesse Wyatt, alias "Jordan" (black, age 38). *Murder.* The crime was committed on 7/20/1949 in DeKalb County. Prison-guard killer. Executed for the murder of 66-year-old Jessie C. Haynes (white) at the Greater Atlanta Prison Farm. The homicide victim was beaten on the head with a shovel for no apparent reason. Wyatt's trial defense was based entirely on his mental capacity because there was absolutely no question of his guilt. He was executed on April 21, 1950. Source: 1949 DeKalb Co. death cert. no. 14219 and 1950 Tattnall Co. death cert. no. 9037. Appeal: 206 GA 613–618.

John Patrick Carrigan, alias "John Valor" (white, age 29). *Murder.* The crime was committed on 8/29/1949 in Fulton County. Handgun slaying of 26-year-old Beatrice Samples (white), who was shot in the head. Motive: to prevent the young woman from blabbing. Carrigan headed up a gang that had pulled a $24,000 payroll robbery earlier that year. Beatrice Samples knew about it. She was reported to have suddenly "found religion" and (perhaps foolishly) threatened to inform on the gang members if they did not first accompany her to church and then turn themselves in to the law. The gangsters did not share her piety. She might not have been a totally levelheaded person in the first place. Daft or not, she wound up in an early grave. So did the man who shot her. He was executed at the Georgia State Prison on April 28, 1950. Source: *Times-Enterprise* (Thomasville, GA), 9/15/49 (4:6) & 10/27/49 (7:6). See also: 1949 Fulton Co. death cert. no. 19508 and 1950 Tattnall Co. death cert. no. 9038.

Robert Frank Bryan (black, age 20). *Murder.* The crime was committed on 3/9/1949 in Chatham County. Handgun slaying of 71-year-old Nicholas A. Pahno (white), a storekeeper who was shot multiple times. Motive: armed robbery. The killer was executed pursuant to law on May 26, 1950. Source: 1949 Chatham Co. death cert. no. 4454 and 1950 Tattnall Co. death cert. no. 11511. Appeal: 206 GA 73–76.

Charlie Cade (black, age 20), **Lincoln Mays** (black, age 24) and **Curtis Wynn** (black, age 20). *Murder.* Their crime was committed on 12/19/1949 in Richmond County. All three executed for the torture killing of 50-year-old "M. K. Joe" (a Chinese grocer), who was attacked in his home. The culprits trussed up the Chinaman with leather belts. Then they slowly and purposefully carved bits of flesh from him (with butcher knives) until he could bear the agony no longer and divulged the combination to his safe. Motive: robbery. The Georgia electric chair was called into use for this trio on August 18, 1950. Source: *Augusta (GA) Chronicle*, 12/20/49 (1:6), 8/18/50 (1:8) & 8/19/50 (1:3).

George McKay (black, age 31). *Murder.* The crime was committed on 12/30/1944 in Fulton County. Accomplice in the handgun slaying of 59-year-old Peter D. Vergiotis (white), a storekeeper. Motive: armed robbery. The law finally caught up with George McKay in the execution chamber of the Georgia State Prison on September 29, 1950. Source: *Atlanta Constitution,* 9/30/50 (3:4). See also: Jesse Craiton (executed 11/9/45).

Jimmie Lee Gardner (black, age 26). *Aggravated burglary.* The crime was committed on 12/18/1949 in Clay County. Executed for forcibly entering the country store and residence of 58-year-old Winnie Mae Mills (white) late at night. He chased the woman from room to room with a butcher knife and then tortured her into revealing the hiding place of her money. More than two hours of surgery were needed to stitch up her wounds. Gardner was put to death on October 28, 1950. Source: *News Record* (Fort Gaines, GA), 12/22/49 (1:7), 7/27/50 (1:1), 9/21/50 (1:7) & 11/2/50 (1:5). See also: 1940 U.S. Census (Tift Co., GA), which notes Mrs. Mills.

Jimmie Richardson (black, age 51). *Murder.* The crime was committed on 4/14/1950 in Crisp County. Executed for the killing of 42-year-old Grace Burston (black) "by striking her on the head with a stick of wood and later with a smoothing iron. He then mutilated her body with his pocket knife, burned part of it in his fireplace but not being able to dispose of it completely that way, put the burned body in a burlap bag, hauled it by truck some 12 or 14 miles away and threw it in a river." Motive: estranged lover. Richardson paid for this in the Georgia electric chair on November 3, 1950. Source: 1950 Crisp Co. death cert. no. 7500 and Tattnall Co. death cert. no. 25792. Appeal: 207 GA 373–376.

John Wallace (white, age 52). *Murder.* The crime was committed on 4/29/1948 in Coweta County. Executed for the killing of 26-year-old Wilson Turner (white), who was severely beaten before being finished off by a shotgun blast. The younger man's body was then cremated in a char pit and its ashes scattered in a swamp. Motive: a conflicted one. Wallace was a large-scale dairyman in Meriwether County. He owned a 2,000-acre farm and was described as "wealthy." Turner was one of his tenants. One account said that Turner had rustled some of his landlord's cows. Another version alleged that the two had a falling-out about their involvement in the illegal liquor trade. All the money at this "wealthy" killer's disposal was not enough to save him from the fate that he had brought upon himself. He died (November 3, 1950) in the same electric chair that functioned for even the lowest rungs of Georgia society. Source: *Augusta (GA) Chronicle,* 5/6/48 (3:4) & 6/19/48 (1:5). *Marietta (GA) Journal,* 11/3/50 (1:5).

George A. Kersey (white, age 27) and **Thomas W. Lynch** (white, age 31). *Murder.* Their crime was committed on 3/8/1950 in Chatham County. Shotgun slaying of 37-year-old Edward Ernest Crosby (white), a trucker. Motive: attempted hijacking. These killers were executed at the Georgia State Prison on November 21, 1950. Source: *Augusta (GA) Chronicle,* 3/21/50 (3:1). Appeal: 207 GA 325–328. See also: 1950 Chatham Co. death cert. no. 4607 and Tattnall Co. death cert. nos. 25797 and 28801.

1951

Willie Harris, alias "Chess Williams" (black, age 45). *Murder.* The crime was committed on 7/10/1949 in Worth County. Shotgun slaying of 25-year-old Tiny Glenn (black female) by means of a blast fired through her kitchen window. Motive: rejected suitor. This black-on-black killer paid the death penalty at the Georgia State Prison on March 2, 1951. Source: *Sylvester (GA) Local*, 7/14/49 (1:3) & 7/21/49 (1:6). Appeal: 207 GA 287–291. See also: 1951 Tattnall Co. death cert. no. 7157.

Jimmie Cornelius Williams (black, age 27). *Rape.* The crime was committed on 9/9/1950 in Clinch County. Indecent assault on the person of a 19-year-old white female (name withheld), who was molested at knifepoint as she swept the porch of her rural home. The attacker had apparently waited until the victim's husband had left for work before making his move. It was a move that landed him in the Georgia electric chair on May 25, 1951. Source: *Times-Enterprise* (Thomasville, GA), 9/9/50 (4:3) & 10/5/50 (12:3). See also: 1951 Tattnall Co. death cert. no. 12280.

George Wilbur Bush, alias "Solesbee" (white, age 25). *Murder.* The crime was committed on 4/30/1947 in Clinch County. Executed for the handgun slaying of 52-year-old Buel L. Webster (white), a motor trailer dealer from Greenville, SC. Motive: carjacking. The homicide victim was purposefully marched into the woods and shot. His remains were found on 5/25/47 with a bullet in the head. Bush is confirmed to have also murdered a hitchhiker named Sam Mason (black, age 45) in Aiken, SC, four days earlier by the same means. Motive: robbery. The Georgia electric chair put an end to George Wilbur Bush on July 27, 1951. Source: *Augusta (GA) Chronicle*, 5/16/47 (1:2) & 5/27/47 (1:6). See also: 1947 Aiken Co. (SC) death cert. no. 5505. Also: 1947 Clinch Co. death cert. no. 11990 and 1951 Tattnall Co. death cert. no. 17181.

Eldred Byrd McLendon Jr. (white, age 37). *Murder.* The crime was committed on 6/13/1948 in Richmond County. Uxoricide. Handgun slaying of 34-year-old Dorothy Jones McLendon (white), who was shot three times in the back. Motive: pending divorce. This killer had previously been an Augusta policeman. He was executed on October 5, 1951. Source: *Augusta (GA) Chronicle*, 6/14/48 (1:3), 6/15/48 (1:2) & 10/6/51 (1:5). See also: 1930 U.S. Census (Augusta, GA), which is the only known source that identifies McLendon by more than just his initials.

Willie Ford Ballard (black, age 22). *Rape.* The crime was committed on 8/9/1951 in Gwinnett County. Indecent assault on the person of an adult white female (name withheld) who nearly died as a result. Ballard was a so-called trusty on a Gwinnett County road crew. He was engaged in mowing weeds that day when he espied "the young mother of two children at her home." Ballard parked his mowing machine and went on the attack. The object of his malice was later found "bleeding profusely and in critical condition" and even had to be carried into court on a stretcher in order to give testimony. No amount of prevarication was able to controvert the evidence in this case. The "consensual sex" dodge was disproven by the woman's injuries. The old "female enticement" angle was equally unavailing. Ballard had brought the entire situation on himself and he thus incurred the full penalty of the law. He paid that debt to society at the Georgia State Prison on November 2, 1951. Source: *News-Herald* (Lawrenceville, GA), 9/13/51 (1:5). See also: 1951 Tattnall Co. death cert. no. 26607.

Jim Parks (black, age 45). *Murder.* The crime was committed on 7/28/1951 in Pike County. Shotgun slaying of 37-year-old Dana Mae Green (black male). Motive: unintended victim. The killer thought that he was aiming at another black man with whom he had had an argument earlier that day. Malice aforethought being clearly proven, this in itself was enough to secure a capital conviction no matter whom Parks had gunned down. He died in the Georgia electric chair on December 14, 1951. Source: *Pike County Journal,* 8/9/51 (1:2). Appeal: 208 GA 508–510. See also: 1951 Pike Co. death cert. no. 17339 and Tattnall Co. death cert. no. 29390.

Vester McBurnett (white, age 41). *Murder.* The crime was committed on 12/24/1948 in Floyd County. Handgun slaying of 40-year-old George Horace Williamson (white), a "crippled storekeeper" who was shot three times on Christmas Eve as he sat helplessly in his wheelchair. Motive: none apparent. However, the sheer meanness of what was done put this case in a class by itself. A trial jury had no qualms about handing down a capital verdict. McBurnett met his own demise in a different kind of chair at the Georgia State Prison on December 17, 1951. Source: *Rome (GA) News-Tribune,* 12/24/48 (1:3) & 1/20/49 (1:2). *Times-Enterprise* (Thomasville, GA), 12/14/51 (6:7) & 12/17/51 (4:5). Appeal: 206 GA 59.

1952

Henry L. Brock (white, age 36). *Murder.* The crime was committed on 12/28/1948 in Floyd County. Uxoricide. Shotgun slaying of 30-year-old Mary L. Brock (white), the killer having stalked her on a bicycle. Motive: marital estrangement. Wrathful husband Henry Brock was executed at the Georgia State Prison on February 21, 1952. Source: *Marietta (GA) Journal,* 1/20/49 (1:6). See also: 1948 Floyd Co. death cert. no. 26766 and 1952 Tattnall Co. death cert. no. 6758.

Homer Almond (black, age 47). *Murder.* The crime was committed on 8/20/1951 in DeKalb County. Strangulation killing of 55-year-old Winifred Garnett Gabriel (white), whose nude body was discovered hidden behind a coal pile in the basement of her home. A man's necktie had been used as a noose in this case. Motive: sexual assault. The perpetrator was executed at the Georgia State Prison on March 1, 1952. Source: *Augusta (GA) Herald,* 3/1/52 (1:4). See also: 1951 DeKalb Co. death cert. no. 18240.

Clifton Williams (black, age 29). *Murder.* The crime was committed on 4/6/1951 in Richmond County. Uxoricide. Executed for the fatal stabbing and illegal burial of 26-year-old Dorothy Williams (black). Motive: bigamy on his part. The body was found on 5/16/1951. It is also noteworthy that on 3/13/1951 another attempt had been made upon the life of Dorothy Williams when her husband tried to force-feed her a poisonous substance called creoline. The man was executed at the Georgia State Prison on March 14, 1952. Source: *Augusta (GA) Chronicle,* 3/15/52

(14:4). *Augusta (GA) Herald,* 3/14/52 (1:3). Appeal: 208 GA 704–705. See also: 1951 Richmond Co. death cert. no. 12164.

Pat Reece (white, age 32). *Murder.* The crime was committed on 8/31/1950 in White County. Shotgun slaying of 38-year-old Monroe Wilson Fields (white). Motive: a quarrel over the sale of an automobile. Reece wound up seated in the Georgia electric chair for this on April 4, 1952. He was flat on his back when they wheeled him into the morgue. Source: *Times-Enterprise* (Thomasville, GA), 9/1/50 (7:4). See also: 1950 White Co. death cert. no. 21296 and 1952 Tattnall Co. death cert. no. 14337. See also the gravestone of the executed man ("A. Pat Reece") in Friendship Baptist Church Cemetery, Cleveland, GA, which gives 4/24/18 as his date of birth.

Eli Griffin (black, age 41). *Murder.* The crime was committed on 8/21/1951 in Putnam County. Fatal stabbing of 38-year-old William D. Elder (white) while both were engaged in loading lumber onto a truck. Motive: the killer resented being spoken to in a condescending manner, or so he said. Eli Griffin found himself in the Georgia electric chair on April 17, 1952. Source: 1951 Putnam Co. death cert. no. 21487 and 1952 Tattnall Co. death cert. no. 9293. Appeal: 208 GA 746–750.

Arthur Darden (black, age 20). *Murder.* The crime was committed on 3/1/1951 in Grady County. Executed for the killing of 26-year-old Eugene Butler (black), who was fatally slashed (his jugular vein being severed) with the jagged stump of a broken whiskey bottle. Motive: an argument about a spilled drink. Darden wound up paying a lot more than the cost of a drink when the State of Georgia added the price of murder to his tab. He paid that reckoning in the electric chair on April 25, 1952. Source: *Times-Enterprise* (Thomasville, GA), 3/13/51 (4:8). Appeal: 208 GA 599–600. See also: 1951 Grady Co. death cert. no. 6351 and 1952 Tattnall Co. death cert. no. 11745.

Napoleon Wise (black, age 19). *Murder.* The crime was committed on 6/18/1951 in Emanuel County. Rifle slaying of 47-year-old Alonzo Thomas Horton, Jr. (white), a tavern owner. Motive: resentment for having been ejected from the aforesaid premises. Napoleon Wise (who was apparently wise in nothing but his name) wound up being sent to the Georgia State Prison under sentence of death. He was executed on June 6, 1952. Source: *Times-Democrat* (Thomasville, GA), 6/20/51 (7:7). See also: 1951 Fulton Co. death cert. no. 13889 and 1952 Tattnall Co. death cert. no. 14340.

John Henry Thornton (black, age 23). *Murder.* The crime was committed on 5/30/1951 in Fulton County. Handgun slaying of 25-year-old Evalena Teamer (black). Motive: an argument over who should eat some roast meat. Thornton also attempted to kill the young woman's husband by firing three shots at him as he lay in his bed. Thornton was executed at the Georgia State Prison on July 11, 1952. Source: *Savannah Morning News,* 7/12/52 (8:1). Appeal: 209 GA 51–52. See also: 1951 Fulton Co. death cert. no. 13673.

James Blackstone, also called "Blackston" (black, age 29). *Murder.* The crime was committed on 6/22/1951 in Coffee County. Uxoricide. Ax murder of 20-year-old Lucille Blackston (black). Motive: she had disobeyed his orders to go visit her mother that night. He had wanted her temporarily out of the way so he could romp with another woman, but Lucille was not deceived. Their 2-year-old child was later found standing next to the butchered body of its mother. James Blackstone or "Blackston" wound up forfeiting his own life for this. The Georgia electric chair saw to it on July 25, 1952. Source: *Douglas (GA) Enterprise*, 6/28/51 (1:1) & 7/31/52 (1:5). Appeal: 209 GA 160–161.

Horace Johnson (black, age 31). *Murder.* The crime was committed on 12/25/1951 in Jones County. Executed for the Christmas Day killing of 40-year-old Leila Inez Mims Varnom (white), a married woman who reportedly consorted with black men unbeknownst to her husband. She turned up dead (with her throat cut) in an abandoned farmhouse where Johnson had taken her after the pair had emerged from an unsavory dancehall. She had even explained her presence at that otherwise all-black venue (to others who were wary of her being there) by saying that she was Johnson's war bride. The exact reason why Johnson killed this female was probably "date rape," but news reports sidestepped the question, preferring to leave it to their readers' imaginations. Apparently the interracial aspects of this case were deemed sufficiently salacious in their own right. Horace Johnson was executed at the Georgia State Prison on October 7, 1952. Source: *Macon (GA) News*, 1/2/52 (1:1), 1/3/52 (1:6), 1/5/52 (1:1) & 10/8/52 (1:5). Appeal: 209 GA 333–335.

Henry Savage (black, age 34). *Murder.* The crime was committed on 1/31/1952 in Chatham County. Shotgun slaying of 26-year-old Laysie Millan, alias "Miller" (black male). Motive: the homicide victim had interfered in an argument between Savage and his common-law wife. Millan was that woman's brother. Shotgun Henry Savage paid the price of murder when he was executed at the Georgia State Prison on November 21, 1952. Source: *Savannah Morning News*, 2/1/52 (2:1). Appeal: 209 GA 374. See also: 1952 Chatham Co. death cert. no. 433, which notes the slain man as "Lacy Millen." Also: 1952 Tattnall Co. death cert. no. 29159.

1953

Abraham Pinckney (black, age 66). *Murder.* The crime was committed on 9/28/1952 in Berrien County. Executed for the handgun slaying of 57-year-old Walter Reppard Henderson (white) in the aftermath of a homicidal domestic dispute. Pinckney had already killed his common-law wife named Mary Clements (black, age 52) and that woman's daughter named Rosa Lee Spikes (black, age 32) that same day because he thought that they had lured him away from his house and contrived a story to enable them to get stud service from a younger man. Pinckney's employer (Mr. Henderson) ran to the scene of the commotion and demanded that the shooter surrender his weapon. Pinckney's response was to gun down Henderson as well. He was tried solely on an indictment involving Mr. Henderson. Two other charges concerning the murdered women were held in abeyance. This triple killer was executed at the Georgia State Prison on February 27, 1953. Source: *Nashville (GA) Herald*, 10/2/52 (1:1), 1/22/53 (1:1) & 3/5/53 (4:5). See also: 1952 Berrien Co. death cert. nos. 24505 and 24507.

Jesse Starr (black, age 23). *Rape.* The crime was committed on 8/21/1951 in Floyd County. Indecent assault on the person of 18-year-old Barbara Ann Jones (white), who was attacked while in the company of her boyfriend. The couple was parked in a reputed lovers' lane. The boy was forced to lie on the floor of his vehicle while a knife was held to his throat throughout. The girl was molested on the front seat next to him. Both were also robbed of their money and other valuables. The marauder was eventually executed at the Georgia State Prison on April 16, 1953. Source: 1953 Tattnall Co. death cert. no. 9886. Appeal: 209 GA 259–261. See also: 1940 U.S. Census (Floyd Co., GA), which notes Starr as a youngster.

Amos Patrick (black, age 33). *Murder.* The crime was committed on 7/24/1952 in Clarke County. Fatal stabbing of 26-year-old Dora Mae Dupree Lewis (black), who was knifed 52 times by post-mortem count. Motive: lovers' quarrel. Lethal lover Amos Patrick paid with his own life for this at the Georgia State Prison on May 8, 1953. Source: *Times-Enterprise* (Thomasville, GA), 3/20/53 (3:1). See also: 1952 Clarke Co. death cert. no. 15173 and 1953 Tattnall Co. death cert. no. 12217.

Robert Remer Strickland (white, age 20). *Murder.* The crime was committed on 7/14/1951 in Chatham County. Shotgun slaying of 21-year-old James L. Lewis (white), a cab driver. Motive: robbery and carjacking. There were no extenuating circumstances. Strickland accordingly wound up in the Georgia electric chair on August 24, 1953. Source: *Augusta (GA) Chronicle,* 8/25/53 (1:1). See also: 1951 Chatham Co. death cert. no. 15486.

Samuel Bowens, alias "Sammie Adkins" (black, age 22). *Murder.* The crime was committed on 1/26/1952 in Screven County. Fatal beating of 22-year-old Janie Lee Dunbar (black, his purported wife) who was battered in her bed "with a slab of wood." Motive: an ongoing argument of several days' duration. Bowens won the argument with his lover but lost the court battle that ensued. He was executed at the Georgia State Prison on August 28, 1953. Source: 1952 Screven Co. death cert. no. 3987 and 1953 Tattnall Co. death cert. no. 21832. Appeal: 209 GA 524–525.

Willie Burgess (black, age 53). *Murder.* The crime was committed on 2/15/1953 in Chatham County. Shotgun slaying of 27-year-old Louise Bush (black), his purported wife, because he thought that she had put a hex on him, or so he said. The Georgia electric chair was the fate of Willie Burgess on November 14, 1953. Source: *Savannah Morning News,* 2/16/53 (18:2) & 11/13/53 (44:2). See also: 1953 Tattnall Co. death cert. no. 26549.

Robert E. Calhoun (black, age 29). *Murder.* The crime was committed on 11/3/1952 in Coweta County. Handgun slaying of 32-year-old James McGinty (black). Motive: an escalating argument that had begun earlier that day between their respective wives, both men having been drawn into it. Robert Calhoun lost his power of self control and ended up dead for it. He was executed at the Georgia State Prison on December 18, 1953. Source: *Augusta (GA) Chronicle,* 12/19/53 (2:3). See also: 1952 Coweta Co. death cert. no. 24983 and 1953 Tattnall Co. death cert. no. 29284.

Isaiah Harris (black, age 34). *Rape.* The crime was committed on

11/15/1953 in Ware County. Indecent assault on the person of a "young" white female (name withheld) who was attacked in her home while tending her small child. Harris was a so-called trusty at the Ware County convict camp. He simply "wandered away" from that place on the above date and went on a crime spree. Three homes and businesses were burglarized by this offender on that same eventful day. In the rape case, Harris threatened to kill the young woman's baby if she did not submit to him. She was later found in a battered condition with teeth marks all over her face. The fallout from this scandal had far-reaching consequences. It marked the end of both the chain-gang system and county work camps. There had been too many problems with escaped prisoners and wayward trustys to a point where the public had had enough. The Ware County work camp was the first one to fall. Its superintendent was fired for negligence. The camp was shut down and all of its inmates transferred to Reidsville. As for Isaiah Harris, the trusty-turned-terrorist, he too was sent to the Georgia State Prison. He died in the electric chair there on December 23, 1953, without the benefit of appeal. Source: *Waycross (GA) Journal-Herald,* 11/16/53 (14:4). *Augusta (GA) Chronicle,* 12/3/53 (7:8) & 12/24/53 (16:8).

1954

Paul Wright (black, age 18). *Murder.* The crime was committed on 4/20/1953 in Walton County. Fatal stabbing of 43-year-old Sarah Belle Daniel (white). Motive: residential burglary. Wright posed no future danger to society after he was executed at the Georgia State Prison on January 22, 1954. Source: *Augusta (GA) Chronicle,* 1/25/54 (14:5). *Walton (GA) Tribune,* 4/29/53 (1:6) & 1/27/54 (7:5). See also: 1953 Walton Co. death cert. no. 12360 and 1954 Tattnall Co. death cert. no. 1869.

Doyle Scott (white, age 30). *Murder.* The crime was committed on 3/14/1953 in Glynn County. Shotgun slaying of 29-year-old Ruby May Daniels (white). Motive: adultery turned deadly. Either one or both of these people had previously sworn a sacred oath that had included the words "and forsaking all others." The price they paid for not honoring that pledge is now a matter of public record. Doyle Scott was carried dead from the execution chamber at the Georgia State Prison on February 5, 1954. Source: 1953 Glynn Co. death cert. no. 6519 and 1954 Tattnall Co. death cert. no. 4195. Appeal: 210 GA 137–139.

Lindsey Heard (black, age 20). *Rape.* The crime was committed on 9/7/1953 in Cherokee County. Indecent assault on the person of a white female named Laura Hancock (age uncertain), who was attacked in her home by a knife-wielding assailant later identified as Lindsey Heard. The culprit had been a so-called trusty at the Cherokee County Work Camp. He had been there since the summer of 1947 for a robbery perpetrated in Muscogee County. He simply walked over to a farmer's house on the aforesaid date and helped himself to a watermelon. He even had the effrontery to knock on the farmhouse door and demand a carving knife with which to cut it. The farmer's wife (Mrs. Hancock) being alone at the time, handed that utensil to the visitor rather than reprove him. It soon became apparent to Lindsey Heard that nobody else was there. So he pounced on the hapless woman and used the carving knife to force himself on her. He was executed in the Georgia electric chair on May 25, 1954. Source: *North Georgia Tribune* (Canton, GA), 9/10/53 (1:1), 10/1/53 (1:5) & 5/27/54 (1:6). Appeal: 210 GA 523–527.

Ozzie Jones (black, age 31). *Rape.* The crime was committed on 7/11/1952 in Chatham County. Indecent assault on the person of a 20-year-old white female (name withheld). The victim was a waitress who occupied a tourist cabin behind her place of employment. The offender's wife was a cook in the same establishment. Ozzie Jones got drunk on the aforesaid evening and burst into the humble abode of the waitress, knowing that she was there. He forced himself on the young woman and then topped all by stealing the few coins that she had. Death in the electric chair was the fate of Ozzie Jones on June 11, 1954. Source: *Savannah Morning News*, 7/14/52 (16:1). Appeal: 209 GA 685. See also: 1954 Tattnall Co. death cert. no. 13999.

Herman Lee Miller (black, age 17) and **Willie Jackson Jr.** (black, age 16). *Rape.* Their crime was committed on 6/28/1953 in Baldwin County. Both executed for perpetrating an indecent assault on the person of an 18-year-old white female (name withheld) under circumstances that proved them to be anything but trustworthy. These teenage offenders were so-called trustys at the Negro Juvenile Delinquents Home near Milledgeville. Both had been assigned to assist in a search of the surrounding area for escapees. They resolved instead to tag-team the first white girl who crossed their path. This much they accomplished at the cost of their lives. The Georgia electric chair ended their days on June 15, 1954. Source: *Panama City (FL) News*, 6/16/54 (10:5). Appeals: 210 GA 412 and 80 SE (2nd) 319. See also: 1954 Tattnall Co. death cert. nos. 13998 and 14000.

Sylvester Seymour (black, age 32). *Murder.* The crime was committed on 12/23/1952 in Richmond County. Rifle slaying of 61-year-old Thomas G. Broome (white), who was shot twice in the head. Motive: robbery and ingratitude. The killer's girlfriend needed some money with which to get a coat off of layaway. Thomas Broome had lent small sums to Seymour in the past. It is not known whether Seymour asked Broome for another loan or just shot him in cold blood before rifling his pockets. It was in this way that Seymour's girl got her coat in time for Christmas. Thomas Broome spent his holiday on ice in the Augusta morgue. The man who murdered him got 2,000 volts of electricity shot through his body courtesy of the State of Georgia on August 6, 1954. He did not survive the experience. Source: *Augusta (GA) Chronicle*, 5/26/54 (16:3). See also: 1952 Richmond Co. death cert. no. 30170 and 1954 Tattnall Co. death cert. no. 19082.

Howard Leroy Booker (black, age 32). *Robbery with violence.* The crime was committed on 1/9/1952 in Fulton County. Executed for feloniously assaulting and stealing from the person of 28-year-old Sarah Babbitt (white). She was beaten, kicked, dragged into a thicket, pawed in a sexual manner and slashed across her breasts. Motive: purse snatching. The assailant made off with two trolley tokens and $1.50 in money. Booker was also sentenced to 20 years' imprisonment for an unrelated rape committed in Clayton County. He was ordered for execution based on what was deemed his ongoing and future propensity for antisocial behavior. This perceived menace (Booker) was permanently removed from that status when he died in the Georgia electric chair on September 17, 1954. Source: *Augusta (GA) Chronicle*, 3/23/54 (1:3). *Marietta (GA) Journal*, 4/7/54 (1:1). *Atlanta Journal*, 3/12/53 (23:2) & 9/17/54 (39:5). Appeal: 210 GA 34–35. See also: 1954 Tattnall Co. death cert. no. 21462.

Elliot Simon, alias "Eddie Lee Simons" (black, age 55). *Murder.* The crime was committed on 3/7/1954 in Colquitt County. Rifle slaying of 32-year-old Mallie Coates (black male). Motive: adultery with the homicide victim's wife. This case was marked closed when Elliot Simon died in the Georgia electric chair on November 5, 1954. Source: *Moultrie (GA) Observer*, 3/8/54 (1:4), 10/13/54 (1:1) & 11/5/54 (1:5).

Calvin Eugene Davis (black, age 18). *Murder.* The crime was committed on 2/21/1954 in Schley County. Rifle slaying of 70-year-old Nora Jones (black), who was shot down in her own home as she sat unsuspectingly by her hearth. Motive: theft of the old woman's money. It is not known exactly how much cash the killer stole through this means but it certainly did not do him much good. He would up dead in the Georgia electric chair on November 12, 1954. Source: 1954 Schley Co. death cert. no. 4084 and Tattnall Co. death cert. no. 26395. Appeal: 211 GA 76.

Charles Lewis King (black, age 17) and **Joe Lee Jones** (black, age 16). *Murder.* Their crime was committed on 3/20/1953 in Upson County. Both executed for the deliberate killing of 65-year-old Daniel Edgar Henderson (white), who was hacked with an ax and beaten on the head with an iron pipe respectively wielded by each culprit. He was also buried in a shallow grave. Motive: robbery. These youthful killers paid their reckoning on November 19, 1954, in the execution chamber at the Georgia State Prison. Source: *The Free Press* (Thomaston, GA), 3/24/53 (1:2) & 11/23/54 (1:4). Appeal: 210 GA 94–96.

1955

James Willie Morgan (white, age 17). *Murder.* The crime was committed on 12/20/1953 in Richmond County. Handgun slaying of 20-year-old Eugene Talmadge Bryant (white), a taxi driver who was shot four times in the back. Motive: carjacking. This case elicited a lot of comment about the tragic waste of two young lives. Photographs of Morgan show him to have been a well made, good-looking type who might have otherwise gone on to better things. Such was his veneer. However, he was also described as ill-bred and the product of a dysfunctional environment. The trial jury became convinced that Morgan's future path was unalterably set by a near-total lack of morality. His age was therefore not accepted as a mitigating factor, and no recommendation for mercy was forthcoming. The Georgia electric chair did the rest on January 7, 1955. Source: *Augusta (GA) Chronicle*, 12/21/53 (1:3), 12/22/53 (1:4), 3/9/54 (1:7) & 1/8/55 (1:8). *Headquarters Detective*, 5/55.

Howard Jackson (black, age 42). *Murder.* The crime was committed on 11/21/1953 in Coweta County. Uxoricide. Shotgun slaying of 32-year-old

Carrie Willie Jackson (black). Motive: impending divorce. This wife-killer had been placed under a "peace bond" four days earlier. Such slips of paper are nowadays called "restraining orders," and they remain as ineffective as ever. Jackson fled in the aftermath of what he had done. He was nabbed nine months later. The Georgia electric chair ended his days on April 15, 1955. Source: *Newnan (GA) Times-Herald*, 11/26/53 (1:1). Appeal: 211 GA 490. See also: 1953 Coweta Co. death cert. no. 27562 and 1955 Tattnall Co. death cert. no. 9469.

Tom Williams (black, age 52). *Murder.* The crime was committed on 5/15/1954 in Colquitt County. Specifically executed for the killings of 68-year-old Walter C. Rowland and 42-year-old Gladys H. Rowland (whites), a married couple. The man was struck down from behind with a shovel and then slashed to death with a finely honed knife. The woman was chased through her house (room to room) by the knife-wielding assailant before being fatally shredded by numerous wounds from that weapon. Recidivist killer. Williams came from Miller County. He had been sentenced to a term of life imprisonment there in 1940 for fatally shooting another black man in the back while arguing with him about the ownership of a pistol. Williams spent seven grueling years on the Miller County chain gang. Then he was transferred to its Colquitt County counterpart. Walter Rowland was the superintendent there. Williams somehow ingratiated himself to both Captain and Mrs. Rowland—indeed to such an extent that the Rowlands used their influence to get him paroled. They even gave him a job and a cabin on their farm. However, the Rowlands paid a terrible price for thinking that they could change the nature of the beast. Williams repaid their kindness in the manner described above. Furthermore, Williams was the prime suspect in another double murder that happened in Colquitt County one day prior to that of the Rowlands. Someone—very probably Williams—burst into an all-night diner and fatally gunned down two white men named Edward T. Norman (age 41) and Jefferson Davis Croft (age 42), they having respectively been the proprietor and a customer of that place. Mr. Norman was shot in the face with a .22-caliber rifle. Both men were also battered almost beyond recognition with blunt objects and slashed in the same rending manner as Mrs. Rowland. Williams admitted his guilt concerning the Rowlands but stubbornly denied the diner slaughter even when the rifle that had killed Mr. Norman was found in his closet. Tom Williams died in the Georgia electric chair on April 15, 1955. Source: *Augusta (GA) Chronicle*, 5/18/54 (1:2). *Master Detective*, 9/54. See also: 1954 Colquitt Co. death cert. nos. 10067, 10073, 10079 and 10080, plus 1955 Tattnall Co. death cert. no. 9468.

Sylvester Fuller (black, age 22). *Robbery with violence*. The crime was committed on 11/25/1954 in Calhoun County. Executed for a felonious attack on the person of 72-year-old Allen W. Eubanks (white), a watchman at the Calhoun County public works camp. The homicide victim was beaten about the head and body with a piece of timber so that he was left traumatically injured. The aging man's skull was fractured, his nose was broken, and one of his eyes was gouged out. Fuller further admitted stealing $21 from Mr. Eubanks' pockets. He was put to death for all of this at the Georgia State

Prison on June 17, 1955. Source: *Albany (GA) Herald*, 12/2/54 (9:2), 12/12/54 (8:4) & 6/13/55 (2:4). See also: 1955 Tattnall Co. death cert. no. 16647. Also see: 1940 U.S. Census (Calhoun Co., GA), which notes Fuller.

1956

Walter Philpot (black, age 37). *Murder.* The crime was committed on 12/24/1954 in Muscogee County. Executed for the ax murder of 48-year-old Lloyd Lockhart (black), his stepfather. Motive: family problems. This Christmas Eve ax killer was put to death on January 27, 1956. Source: 1954 Muscogee Co. death cert. no. 30287 and 1956 Tattnall Co. death cert. no. 4459. Appeal: 212 GA 79.

Aubrey Lee Williams (black, age 27). *Murder.* The crime was committed on 10/4/1952 in Fulton County. Handgun slaying of 65-year-old Harry H. Furst (white), a liquor store owner. Motive: armed robbery. This killer was executed on March 30, 1956. Source: *Atlanta Constitution*, 10/6/52 (20:2). *Augusta (GA) Chronicle*, 3/31/56 (1:5). See also: 1952 Fulton Co. death cert. no. 23114 and 1956 Tattnall Co. death cert. no. 7211.

Willie Grady Cochran (white, age 36). *Murder.* The crime was committed on 6/20/1955 in Calhoun County. Child killer. Handgun slaying of 14-year-old Patricia Ann Cook (white), who was abducted from her home and shot in the back. Motive: sexual assault. The girl's body was found in the Etowah River. It was wrapped in a quilt, bound with chains and weighted down with "a huge wrench." Recidivist offender. Cochran had previously been imprisoned for the crimes of rape and felonious assault with intent to commit rape. He was on parole from a 20-year sentence when he attacked Miss Cook. He was executed on April 13, 1956. Source: *Augusta (GA) Chronicle*, 6/26/55 (1:4) & 4/14/56 (1:2).

James L. Turner, alias "Glover" (black, age 26). *Murder.* The crime was committed on 3/8/1955 in Calhoun County. Executed for the deliberate killing of 80-year-old Joe Richardson (black), who was battered to death with a hammer. Motive: theft of the old man's money. This black-on-black killer was put to death on June 8, 1956. Source: 1955 Calhoun Co. death cert. no. 29112 and 1956 Tattnall Co. death cert. no. 14876. Appeal: 212 GA 199.

Frederick Mosley (black, age 23). *Rape.* The crime was committed on 12/15/1953 in Fulton County. Incipient serial rapist. Specifically executed for an indecent assault on the person of an adult white female named Thelma Irene Knott. This sex offender was dubbed "the Laundromat Rapist" because he had attacked two concierges of such places during a 4-month period and was suspected of additional offenses of a like nature that had gone unreported. The culprit held a loaded pistol to the heads of each victim and threatened them with death if they dared to make any resistance. The second known attack happened on 5/4/1954, the target being an adult white female named Christine Smith. The State of Georgia divested itself of this public menace by means of capital punishment on June 29, 1956. Source: *Atlanta Constitution*, 10/8/54 (28:5). Appeals: 211 GA 611 and 212 GA 356. See also: 1956 Tattnall Co. death cert. no. 14869.

Paul Cooper (black, age 47). *Murder.* The crime was committed on 4/9/1955 in Worth County. Uxoricide. Shotgun slaying of 34-year-old Mary Cooper (black). Motive: marital breakdown. Recidivist killer. Cooper had reportedly been paroled several years earlier after serving time for killing another black man near Red Rock. He was executed on September 21, 1956. Source: *Sylvester (GA) Local*, 4/14/55 (1:7) & 4/21/55 (1:3). See also: 1955 Worth Co. death cert. no. 12184 and 1956 Tattnall Co. death cert. no. 22232.

1957

Amos Reese (black, age 28). *Rape.* The crime was committed on 10/20/1953 in Cobb County. Indecent assault on the person of a married white female (name withheld) who was alone with her 4-month-old baby at the time. Reese was a so-called trusty at the Cobb County convict camp. He was also a known sex offender who had been sent up in 1945 for acts of gross indecency. These included at least two attempts to force himself on white women. Later in 1950 (while serving his sentence) Reese was found to be infected with a sexually transmitted disease. Returned to the work camp after treatment, he somehow euchred his way into a trusty position despite a ban on that privilege for prisoners convicted of sex crimes. Reese was driving a work truck on the above date when his route took him past the white woman's house. He was already fueled up on moonshine whiskey by then. He parked the truck and walked up to the woman's door. He pushed his way in when she answered the doorbell and raped her. The Georgia electric chair was called into service for Amos Reese on January 4, 1957. Source: *Marietta (GA) Journal*, 10/21/53 (1:6), 10/22/53 (1:6), 10/23/53 (1:7) & 11/1/53 (1:1). See also: 1957 Tattnall Co. death cert. no. 1997.

John F. Corbin (white, age 29). *Murder.* The crime was committed on 1/19/1954 in Fulton County. Handgun slaying of 20-year-old Oscar Marion Roebuck (white), a gas station attendant. Motive: armed robbery. No mitigating factors being found in this killer's favor, he was ordered for execution. The sentence was carried out at the Georgia State Prison on February 8, 1957. Source: *Augusta (GA) Chronicle*, 1/20/54 (9:1). *Atlanta Constitution*, 2/9/57 (5:1). Appeals: 211 GA 400 and 212 GA 231.

Jennings E. Fields (white, age 29). *Murder.* The crime was committed on 2/6/1954 in DeKalb County. Police killer. Handgun slaying of 48-year-old James Lonnie Mize (white), who was shot with his own service weapon, which had been deceitfully wrested from him. Motive: resisting arrest. Fields paid the death penalty for this at the Georgia State Prison on March 5, 1957. Source: *Greensboro (NC) Daily News*, 2/8/54 (2:1:1). See also: 1954 DeKalb Co. death cert. no. 2863 and 1957 Tattnall Co. death cert. no. 7142.

John D. Newberry (white, age 48). *Murder.* The crime was committed on 9/6/1956 in Miller County. Uxoricide. Executed for the brutal killing of 44-year-old Willie Mae Welch Newberry (white), who was beaten with a wrecking bar and also had her throat cut. Motive: possibly deranged. The condemned man was described as "an illiterate farm worker" and "a one handed former mental patient." He was executed on March 8, 1957. Source: *Miller*

County Liberal, 9/14/56 (1:5) & 3/15/57 (1:6).

Leon I. Domingo (black, age 21). *Murder.* The crime was committed on 10/2/1954 in Muscogee County. Police killer. Handgun slaying of 26-year-old Harold O. Stewart (white). Motive: obnoxious drunk. This assassin was a New Jersey soldier stationed at Fort Benning. He died in the Georgia electric chair on March 15, 1957. Source: *Columbus (GA) Ledger,* 10/2/54 (1:4) & 10/3/54 (1:3). *Trenton (NJ) Sunday Times-Advertiser,* 10/14/56 (2:1:2). See also: 1954 Muscogee Co. death cert. no. 23540 and 1957 Tattnall Co. death cert. no. 7148.

Isaiah Styles, known to some as "Isaac" Styles (black, age 33). *Murder.* The crime was committed on 2/18/1956 in Burke County. Handgun slaying of 25-year-old Annie Smith (black), who was shot nine times with a .22-caliber pistol. Motive: wrathful lover. Styles had the nerve to say that the homicide victim had cheated on him and that he shot her as many times as he did "to make sure that she was dead." The fact that he was himself a married man then cheating on a lawful spouse of his own did not bother him. He was put to death in the Georgia electric chair on March 15, 1957. Source: *Augusta (GA) Chronicle,* 2/20/56 (3:2), 5/8/56 (15:1) & 12/8/56 (8:5). See also: 1956 Burke Co. death cert. no. 28053 and 1957 Tattnall Co. death cert. no. 7141.

Don Mitchell Coleman (black, age 38) and **James Toler** (black, age 18). *Murder.* Their crime was committed on 6/1/1956 in Fulton County. Both executed for the murder of 30-year-old Mary Inez Johnson (white), an office secretary who was battered to death with a hammer. Motive: payroll robbery. No extenuating circumstances were accredited for either defendant. Death by electrocution was the sentence imposed. A double event of that kind was carried into effect at the Georgia State Prison on March 19, 1957. Source: *Greensboro (NC) Record,* 6/5/56 (16:4). *Atlanta Journal,* 3/19/57 (1:4). See also: 1956 Fulton Co. death cert. no. 14064.

Robert Lee Elder (black, age 37). *Murder.* The crime was committed on 11/4/1956 in Fulton County. Executed for the killings of about 40-year-old Mary Jordan (his purported wife) and 23-year-old Catherine Jordan (that woman's daughter), black females, who were both stabbed multiple times with an ice pick and then buried in his flower garden. Motive: disillusionment with his domestic arrangements. This offender was executed at the Georgia State Prison on March 19, 1957. Source: *Augusta (GA) Chronicle,* 11/15/56 (2:1:3). *Atlanta Journal,* 3/19/57 (1:4). *Panama City (FL) News,* 3/20/57 (1:5). See also: 1956 Fulton Co. death cert. no. 27362.

Harold E. Hill (white, age 24). *Murder.* The crime was committed on 10/9/1954 in Richmond County. Executed for the excessively violent slaying of 66-year-old Frederick W. Noegel (white), a grocer who was blackjacked in his place of business and then stabbed numerous times with a butcher knife. Motive: robbery. A disgusted trial jury refused to recommend mercy. Hill's day of earthly reckoning came on March 25, 1957, when he was jolted dead in the Georgia electric chair. Source: *Augusta (GA) Chronicle,* 10/10/54 (1:5), 10/17/54 (1:1) & 3/26/57 (1:1).

Grady Justice (black, age 28). *Rape.* The crime was committed on 9/28/1956 in Fulton County. Indecent assault on the person of a 48-year-old white female (name withheld) who was also beaten and choked during a residential burglary. Justice was executed at the Georgia State Prison on July 26, 1957. Source: *Atlanta Constitution*, 11/9/56 (12:3). *Atlanta Journal*, 7/26/57 (3:1). Appeal: 213 GA 166.

George Krull (white, age 34) and **Michael Krull** (white, age 32). *Kidnapping with bodily harm.* The crime was committed on 4/14/1955 in Walker County. Both executed under federal authority for the forced abduction of 53-year-old Sunie Jones (white), a maiden woman. She was snatched from a sidewalk in Chattanooga, TN, and brought across the Georgia state line to the Chickamauga Battlefield National Historic Site, where the culprits not only beat her to within an inch of her life but also forced themselves on her. The woman survived through sheer tenacity. Her attackers were executed at the Georgia State Prison on August 21, 1957. Source: *Augusta (GA) Chronicle*, 8/22/57 (3:4:1). *Official Detective*, 12/74.

Fred Gordon Mullins (black, age 40). *Murder.* The crime was committed on 7/20/1956 in Harris County. Uxoricide. Executed for the ax murder of 39-year-old Marie Mullins (black). Motive: alcoholic brutality. Nothing could be found in this man's favor. He was put to death at the Georgia State Prison on September 6, 1957. Source: *Augusta (GA) Chronicle*, 8/13/57 (3:7). Appeal: 213 GA 331. See also: 1957 Tattnall Co. death cert. no. 22772. Also: 1940 U.S. Census (Harris Co., GA), which notes this ill-fated couple.

Lem Dupree (black, age 58). *Murder.* The crime was committed on 10/11/1956 in Laurens County. Shotgun slaying of 47-year-old Annie Smith (black). Motive: temper tantrum. The homicide victim was among a party consisting of five women and children cowering in a shack. Dupree was terrorizing them by firing shotgun blasts through the windows of that structure. One of the children was permanently blinded by buckshot during this incident. Annie Smith was fatally wounded. Shotgun Lem Dupree was much more quiescent when he trudged into the execution chamber at the Georgia State Prison on September 16, 1957. Source: 1956 Laurens Co. death cert. no. 24316 and 1957 Tattnall Co. death cert. no. 22769. Appeal: 213 GA 348.

John Henry White (black, age 26). *Rape.* The crime was committed on 8/20/1957 in Berrien County. Indecent assault on the person of an 18-year-old white female (name withheld) who was attacked in her own home. The culprit had escaped from the Bibb County prisoner stockade. He was a convicted forger. He drove a stolen work-crew truck to a point in Berrien County where the young mother was tending her baby in a farmhouse. The fugitive surprised the object of his malice, raped her, and then absconded with a set of her husband's clothes. He did not get far enough to escape the consequences of his actions. The Georgia electric chair proved that to everyone on October 4, 1957. Source: *Augusta (GA) Chronicle*, 10/5/57 (7:1).

1958

Edward Samuel Smith (black, age 21). *Rape.* The crime was committed on 9/15/1956 in Richmond County. Incipient serial rapist. Executed for an indecent assault on the person of a 15-year-old white female (name withheld) who was terrorized in a motel room that she shared with her husband. The girl was beaten, choked and hit on the head with a rock. The culprit also threatened to kill her 3-week-old baby. In addition, Smith faced one other count for forcible rape and three more for felonious assault with intent to commit rape in unrelated cases. He was executed on January 17, 1958. Source: *Augusta (GA) Chronicle*, 6/18/57 (1:6), 8/10/57 (1:2), 1/17/58 (4:3) & 1/19/58 (3:4).

William Golden (black, age 19). *Murder.* The crime was committed on 10/18/1955 in Chatham County. Handgun slaying of 38-year-old William E. Fonvielle (black), a pharmacy clerk who was gunned down in his place of employment. Motive: attempted robbery. This black-on-black killer was executed at the Georgia State Prison on April 18, 1958. Source: *Savannah Morning News*, 10/19/55 (28:4), 10/20/55 (2:7) & 4/19/58 (2:7:3). Appeal: 213 GA 481. See also: 1920, 1930 and 1940 U.S. Census (Savannah, GA), which note Fonvielle and his family.

Albert Curry (black, age 27). *Murder.* The crime was committed on 7/13/1958 in Harris County. Executed for the fatal beating of 67-year-old John C. Grant (white), who was then robbed of his wallet. Motive: mugging. A predator by any description, Curry was sent straight to the electric chair without the benefit of appeal. He met his end at the Georgia State Prison on September 19, 1958. Source: *Marietta (GA) Journal*, 7/20/58 (2:1). See also: 1958 Muscogee Co. death cert. no. 18434 and Tattnall Co. death cert. no. 26191.

Leroy Dobbs (black, age 35). *Rape.* The crime was committed on 10/28/1957 in Cobb County. Indecent assault on the person of a 23-year-old white female (name withheld) during the course of an armed burglary. Dobbs had broken into the young woman's home. He was toting a .22-caliber rifle. The female occupant initially got the drop on him with a shotgun, firing a blast that singed the intruder's face. Dobbs then shot the crime victim with his own weapon and raped her. He did not escape the consequences of his actions. The Georgia electric chair saw to that on November 7, 1958. Source: *Marietta Daily Journal*, 11/3/57 (1:6). See also: 1958 Tattnall Co. death cert. no. 28661.

Otha Adams (white, age 53). *Murder.* The crime was committed on 11/15/1957 in Colquitt County. Sororicide, child killer, and baby killer. Specifically executed for the hammer slaying of 3-year-old Harris Hagin, Jr. (white) during an incident in which he likewise killed that child's sibling Brenda Diane Hagin (white, aged 11 months) by the same means. Also murdered on that occasion was the killer's sister, Mary Adams Hagin (white, age 45), by means of a shotgun blast. Motive: none discernible; possibly deranged. Otha Adams died in the Georgia electric chair on November 14, 1958. Source: *Augusta (GA) Chronicle*, 11/16/57 (1:2) & 5/8/58 (21:1). See also: 1957 Colquitt Co. death cert. nos. 26688, 26689 and 26690. Also: 1958 Tattnall Co. death cert. no. 28662.

Henry R. Woods (black, age 19). *Murder.* The crime was committed on 7/19/1957 in Fulton County. Fatal stabbing of 25-year-old Joy Lee McCord (white), a secretary at a loan company. Motive: robbery with violence. This transgressor was executed at the Georgia State Prison on December 19, 1958. Source: *Marietta (GA) Daily Journal,* 7/21/57 (1:3) & 12/11/58 (3:3). See also: 1957 Fulton Co. death cert. no. 18900 and 1958 Tattnall Co. death cert. no. 31639.

1959

James C. Murray (black, age 53). *Murder.* The crime was committed on 2/16/1958 in Bryan County. Shotgun slaying of 59-year-old Melvin Dewey Abbott (white), who had employed him as a handyman. The homicide victim was both a physician and a retired navy captain. Motive: alleged murder for hire. Shotgun Jim Murray suffered death by electrocution for this at the Georgia State Prison on February 6, 1959. Source: *Pembroke (GA) Journal,* 2/20/58 (1:3) & 2/12/59 (1:6). *Marietta (GA) Daily Journal,* 2/18/58 (8:1). Appeal: 214 GA 350. See also: 1959 Tattnall Co. death cert. no. 4822. Also see Dr. Abbott's gravestone in North Side Cemetery, Pembroke.

Frank Junior Hill (black, age 35). *Murder.* The crime was committed on 7/20/1958 in Dougherty County. Executed for the killing of 43-year-old Gussie M. Porter (black female), who was beaten to death with an oaken pick handle. Motive: heated argument. Hill was killed via the Georgia electric chair on June 5, 1959. Source: *Marietta (GA) Daily Journal,* 4/12/59 (2:1). Appeal: 214 GA 794. See also: 1958 Dougherty Co. death cert. no. 17396 and 1959 Tattnall Co. death cert. no. 15466.

William Charlton (black, age 22). *Murder.* The crime was committed on 4/18/1958 in Chatham County. Executed for the fatal stabbing and slashing of 38-year-old Pearlie Tatum (white male), an airman who was then moonlighting as a gas station attendant. Motive: attempted robbery. The killer was put to death on August 7, 1959. Source: *Marietta (GA) Daily Journal,* 8/7/59 (2:1). Appeal: 214 GA 778. See also: 1958 Chatham Co. death cert. no. 8914.

Eddie Wilson (black, age 36). *Murder.* The crime was committed on 1/6/1959 in Atkinson County. Uxoricide. Fatal stabbing of 27-year-old Mary L. Wilson (black). Motive: she had refused to be reconciled with him after an abusive relationship of ten years' duration. Eddie Wilson suffered death in the electric chair for this on December 18, 1959. Source: 1959 Atkinson Co. death cert. no. 10 and Tattnall Co. death cert. no. 31954. Appeal: 215 GA 446.

1960

Homer Bunckley (black, age 25). *Robbery with violence.* The crime was committed on 2/7/1959 in Talbot County. Executed for the severe beating of 64-year-old Ruby Anderson (white), who sustained a fractured skull (among other painful injuries) when three thugs invaded the little grocery store of which she was the proprietress. Bunckley was the leader as well as the one who actually battered the woman. His two accomplices drew sentences of life imprisonment instead of the death penalty even though they had made no effort to restrain Bunckley's physical aggression. The Georgia electric chair removed whatever future threats Bunckley posed on January 15, 1960. Source: *Marietta (GA) Daily Journal*, 3/12/59 (2:1), 11/20/59 (2:1) & 12/8/59 (2:1). See also: 1960 Tattnall Co. death cert. no. 2213.

Ernest Albert (white, age 33). *Murder.* The crime was committed on 2/13/1959 in Columbia County. Executed for the killing of 56-year-old Cullen E. Purvis (white), a cab driver who was beaten to death with an iron pipe. Motive: robbery. The miscreant was pronounced dead in the execution chamber of the Georgia State Prison on March 4, 1960. Source: *Augusta (GA) Chronicle*, 2/18/59 (1:7). See also: 1959 Columbia Co. death cert. no. 3050 and 1960 Tattnall Co. death cert. no. 8697.

Frank Wilson (black, age 53). *Murder.* The crime was committed on 8/24/1959 in Warren County. Shotgun slaying of 51-year-old Leroy Toulson (white), a cotton farmer. Motive: bickering over a sharecrop arrangement. The killer was executed on June 10, 1960. Source: *Augusta (GA) Chronicle*, 8/27/59 (4:4:4). See also: 1959 Richmond Co. death cert. no. 23432 and 1960 Tattnall Co. death cert. no. 16098.

Herring Davis (black, age 39). *Murder.* The crime was committed on 7/23/1959 in Meriwether County. Rifle slaying of 81-year-old George Frank Hall (white), a grist mill operator. Motive: robbery. The loot consisted of eight dollars and eighty cents. The killer had probably surmised that the elderly homicide victim had a much higher sum. The Georgia electric chair made it all the same to Herring Davis on June 24, 1960. Source: *Times-Enterprise* (Thomasville, GA), 8/27/59 (5:2). *Augusta (GA) Chronicle*, 6/25/60 (2:5). See also: 1959 Meriwether Co. death cert. no. 17899.

Nathaniel Johnson (black, age 24). *Rape.* The crime was committed on 1/27/1960 in Richmond County. Indecent assault on the person of a 33-year-old white female (name withheld) who was forcibly abducted from a hospital parking lot and driven to a remote location where the graver felony took place. This sex offender was executed at the Georgia State Prison on July 1, 1960. Source: Augusta (GA) Chronicle, 1/29/59 (2:2:3) & 7/2/60 (1:1).

Oscar James Wimis (black, age 44). *Murder.* The crime was committed on 4/8/1960 in Fulton County. Executed for the killing of 59-year-old Lovette Pierce Blackmon (white), the manager of a small grocery store, who was beaten to death in his place of business with a wooden 2' × 4'. Motive: robbery. Two thousand volts of electricity evened the score with this transgressor on November 21, 1960. Source: *Marietta (GA) Journal*, 4/11/60 (10:1). See also: 1960 Fulton Co. death cert. no. 10478 and Tattnall Co. death cert. no. 31714.

1961

Roy Lee Mullins (white, age 23). *Murder.* The crime was committed on 12/22/1959 in Fannin County. Police killer. Executed for the sawed-off-shotgun slaying of 39-year-old Hobert Luther Brown (white). Motive: resisting arrest. Mullins was a notorious desperado in the mountain counties of north Georgia and southeast Tennessee. His specialties consisted of burglaries, armed robberies and forced abductions, perhaps to the number of 100 all told. He had lately broken out of the Cherokee County jail and was on the run with two kidnapped gas station attendants when Officer Brown barred his way. Roy Lee Mullins paid his debt to society in the Georgia electric chair on January 20, 1961. Source: *Augusta (GA) Chronicle*, 12/24/59 (1:5). *Marietta (GA) Daily Journal*, 12/23/59 (2:1) & 1/22/61 (2:1).

Thurmond Johnson (black, age 26). *Murder.* The crime was committed on 6/26/1960 in Richmond County. Executed for the mutilation killing of 70-year-old Ella Louise Cummings (black), a highly respectable church woman. She was abducted from her home, beaten in a maniacal manner and repeatedly hacked about the head and face with a hatchet. Johnson also slashed the woman dozens of times with a well-honed knife before dumping what remained of her in a roadside ditch. Motive: possibly deranged. The State of Georgia exacted the death penalty on March 24, 1961. Source: *Augusta (GA) Chronicle*, 6/29/60 (11:2), 6/30/60 (2:1:6) & 3/25/61 (2:1).

George Watts (black, age 20). *Rape.* The crime was committed on 12/5/1960 in Muscogee County. Incipient serial rapist. Specifically executed for an indecent assault on the person of a 9-months' pregnant 23-year-old white female (name withheld) who was attacked after the culprit had forced his way into her home at gunpoint. Further details of this incident are far too sickening for repetition. Watts also faced prosecution for felonious assaults on two other women with intent to commit rape. He was executed at the Georgia State Prison on August 11, 1961. Source: *Marietta (GA) Daily Journal*, 2/21/61 (2:1) & 2/22/61 (2:4). Appeal: 217 GA 83. See also: 1961 Tattnall Co. death cert. no. 22367.

1962

Sammie Lee Smith (black, age 25). *Murder.* The crime was committed on 7/10/1960 in Houston County. Executed for the killing of 33-year-old Jerry Cooper (black), who was found on his bedroom floor with his throat cut. Motive: sore loser. The homicide victim had won Smith's money in a card game the previous day. Smith burglarized Cooper's residence that ensuing night by cutting his way through a screen door. Then he attacked his rival, determined to get back the money that he had lost. Smith ended up in the Georgia electric chair on November 14, 1962. Source: 1962 Tattnall Co. death cert. no. 32711. Appeal: 218 GA 216. See also: 1940 U.S. Census (Houston Co., GA), which notes Cooper was a youngster.

1963

Orelander Jones, alias "Goolsby" (black, age 20). *Murder.* The crime was committed on 12/24/1962 in Jasper County. Handgun slaying of 54-year-old Anastasia Tyler Smith (white), a rural storekeeper. She had tried to defend herself with the aforesaid weapon, it being her own. The culprit somehow wrested it from her. Then after shooting her therewith, Jones severely beat the dying woman and garroted her with a "binding cord." Motive: robbery. Death in the electric chair was meted out to him at the Georgia State Prison on October 4, 1963. Source: *Monticello (GA) News*, 12/27/62 (1:6), 1/3/63 (1:6), 2/14/63 (1:3) & 10/10/63 (1:5). Appeal: 219 GA 245. See also the burial record for Mrs. Smith at Westview Cemetery, Monticello.

Ollie Chandler (black, age 18). *Murder.* The crime was committed on 5/22/1962 in Lowndes County. Shotgun slaying of 49-year-old Hugh Lane (white), who was ambushed inside his own house. Motive: disgruntled employee. Chandler (a farmhand) had demanded $7.50 that he thought to be in arrears. Mr. Lane disputed this. So Chandler murdered him in the aforesaid manner, stole money in excess of the disputed amount, and beat it over the state line into Florida. He ended up in the Georgia electric chair on October 18, 1963. Source: *Marietta (GA) Daily Journal*, 10/18/63 (1:7). *Official Detective*, 9/62.

1964

J. W. Pugh (white, age 35). *Murder.* The crime was committed on 5/4/1962 in DeKalb County. Executed for the rifle slaying and illegal cremation of 38-year-old Gottlob Pistor (white), a German immigrant less than one year in America. The homicide victim was shot inside of his own home with his own weapon. Then his body was put inside of his own car, which was driven to a remote place and torched. Motive: adultery with the dead man's wife. Pugh (whose full name is not specified in any known source) had previously tried to do away with Pistor by placing dynamite in the muffler of his car. He was executed at the Georgia State Prison on January 14, 1964. Source: *Times-Enterprise* (Thomasville, GA), 6/26/62 (1:2) & 9/13/62 (9:1). *Marietta (GA) Daily Journal*, 1/15/64 (3:1). *Official Detective*, 10/62. *Headquarters Detective*, 10/64. *Master Detective*, 7/75. Also see Pugh's grave marker in Cross Plains Baptist Church Cemetery, Forsyth Co.

Bernard Dye (white, age 31). *Murder.* The crime was committed on 1/17/1961 in McDuffie County. Executed for the rifle slaying of 28-year-old Otis Durham Rabun (white), whom he suspected of undue familiarity with his wife. It is not known whether this killer's worries were imagined or real. That point became immaterial when he died in the Georgia electric chair on October 16, 1964. Source: *Times-Enterprise* (Thomasville, GA), 1/18/61 (5:3) & 10/16/64 (2:4).

Index

www.ingramcontent.com/pod-product-compliance
Ingram Content Group UK Ltd.
Pitfield, Milton Keynes, MK11 3LW, UK
UKHW041835100926
8556IPUK00018B/970

9 780786 498697